COMMUNICATION FOR DEVELOPMENT IN THE THIRD WORLD

THEORY AND PRACTICE
FOR EMPOWERMENT

2nd Edition

Srinivas R. Melkote
H. Leslie Steeves

Sage Publications
New Delhi • Thousand Oaks • London

Copyright © Srinivas R. Melkote and H. Leslie Steeves, 2001

First published in 2001 by

Sage Publications India Pvt Ltd
M-32 Market, Greater Kailash, Part 1
New Delhi 110 048

Sage Publications Inc
2455 Teller Road
Thousand Oaks, California 91320

Sage Publications Ltd
6 Bonhill Street
London EC2A 4PU

Published by Tejeshwar Singh for Sage Publications India Pvt Ltd, typeset by Asian Telelinks, New Delhi in 10/12 pt. Times and printed at Chaman Enterprises, Delhi.

Library of Congress Cataloging-in-Publication Data

Melkote, Srinivas R., 1952–
    Communication for development in the Third World: theory and practice for empowerment/Srinivas R. Melkote, H. Leslie Steeves.—2nd ed.
      p.cm. (cloth) (pbk.)
    Includes bibliographical references and index.
    1. Communication in economic development—Developing countries. 2. Developing Countries—Economic Policy. I. Steeves, H. Leslie. II. Title.
    HD76. M45338.9'009172'4—dc21   2001   00-065808

ISBN: 0–7619–9475–0 (US–Hb)   81–7036–950–9 (India–Hb)
          0–7619–9476–9 (US–Pb)   81–7036–951–7 (India–Pb)

Sage Production Team: Parul Nayyar, O.P. Bhasin and Santosh Rawat

CONTENTS

The challenge for communication research in developing countries is the design of strategies that bear in mind our colonial past and our semi-feudal semi-capitalist present to focus on how to transcend the negative aspects of these realities. Those committed to Third World development need to go beyond critiques of Western theories to design proactive recommendations and models. Srinivas Melkote's first edition of this book, published in 1991, was a major contribution by a son of India: it described the rise and fall of the media-for-modernization paradigm that dominated the 1960s and 1970s, and hinted at the emergence of another kind of development and an alternative kind of communication strategy to match. Ten years later, he and Africa specialist Leslie Steeves have collaborated on a new edition that tells us what has taken the place of the inaugural older paradigms and how well these new perspectives have fared in light of the old critiques.

The retrospective strength of the first edition, which questioned the old materialist development vision, is complemented in the new edition by new conceptualizations of liberation that come from theology and yet focus on the distribution of material power in the here-and-now. The new edition also presents research literature that goes behind development messages designed by the state and non-governmental organizations to analyze reasons for this discourse in the media, (both historical and contemporary) as well as the economic, environmental, religious, and gender-based literature. The focus in the field has been on the media *yantra* (instrument) rather than on the message: this analytical focus on the nature of discourse is very welcome.

I met Srinivas in the mid-1970s when I worked in India's space agency on the Satellite Instructional TV Experiment in Ahmedabad. Srinivas was an M.A. student who had decided that the bottom line was how residents of a village had interpreted satellite television programs. This then was the focus of his thesis. I remember Srinivas as a gentle, soft-spoken young man who was asking difficult ungentle questions then, questions like: Did it work? Who benefited most? He went on to ask similar questions in the doctoral program at Iowa. Srinivas worked with Joseph Ascroft, the first African communication researcher sent by the United Nations Educational, Scientific and Cultural Organization (UNESCO) to the US to learn how to use media to diffuse Western innovations to develop Third World societies. Joseph Ascroft's doctoral dissertation fieldwork in his native Malawi raised doubts about the modernization impacts of media pipelines in highly stratified developing societies. Joseph Ascroft has continued to have a major influence on this scholar, professor and academic administrator.

H. Leslie Steeves was an assistant professor at Iowa when Srinivas attended. There, she became increasingly interested in Africa, served on the committees of several graduate students studying development support communication, and also chaired Iowa's interdisciplinary Women in Development program. Fifteen years later, they found themselves together, both professor now, at a conference at the University of Texas organized by Karin Wilkins on redeveloping communication for social change from its modernization era origins. Professor Steeves is well known in the field for her work on gender in communication and development, and her attention to Africa. She chairs the African Studies Committee at the University of Oregon where she directs the master's and doctoral programs in Communication. As Srinivas talked about revising the first edition, it became clear that Professor Steeves would be an excellent collaborator: the evidence is in this new edition.

Michigan State University   **Bella Mody**

Communication for Development
in the Third World

The second edition of this book builds on the framework provided by the earlier edition. In this edition, we will continue to trace the history of development communication, present diverse approaches and their proponents, critique these approaches as appropriate, and provide ideas and models for development communication in the 21st century. However, in contrast to the first edition, which is organized historically, the organization of the second edition is primarily conceptual. Following two introductory chapters, the body of the book is divided into three parts, representing modernization, critical, and liberation perspectives. We end with a chapter that argues for communication strategies for empowerment, defined beyond the level of the individual as collective social action.

The second edition is also updated to include the literature on development and communication from the 1990s, and integrated with the theory and practice of development communication. The newer literature includes contributions from postmodernism, feminist studies, environmental studies, and postcolonial studies. We critically examine the discourse on modernization and development that has guided much of development theory and practice in the Third World since World War II. Two overlapping areas that we explore in some detail are liberation theology and empowerment, themes that resonate in the literature and practice of development in the 1990s. Underlying goals throughout the book include: critiquing the power of dominant knowledge systems, challenging the truth claims of modernism, and sensitizing the reader to the relationship between dominant knowledge and the exercise of social power.

Our interest in examining the discourse on modernization and development is not just to indulge in a textual analysis, but to identify and critique interventions and practices that have been promoted by the discourse, and analyze their political, economic and cultural origins and consequences. We examine the local and "other" contexts and assert the heuristic value of alternative, non-Western, local experiences and knowledge systems to the tasks of social change.

There are several individuals who we wish to acknowledge. We thank Professors Bella Mody and Arvind Singhal for reading the manuscript and providing us with their comments. We are especially thankful to Professor Joseph Ascroft for his input in Chapter 2 and the historical overviews of development/development communication theories. Colleagues who provided insights and ideas include Rebecca Arbobast, Professor Archie Smith, Jr., Professor Karin Wilkins, and Dr. Sundeep Muppidi. Our students, Sanjanthi Velu, Prahalad Sooknanan, Fay Patel, Ashley Overbeck, and Kumi Siiva helped us on innumerable occasions during the writing of this book. We are indebted to them.

We hope that the readers will like the new edition and find it useful. That will give us the ultimate satisfaction.

Bowling Green, Ohio   **Srinivas R. Melkote**
Eugene, Oregon   **H. Leslie Steeves**

I

INTRODUCTION AND OVERVIEW

CHAPTER 1

INTRODUCTION TO COMMUNICATION, DEVELOPMENT, AND EMPOWERMENT IN THE THIRD WORLD

> There is no universal path to development.
> Each society must find its own strategy.
> Friberg and Hettne (1985: 220)

The second half of the 20th century brought a tradition of communication research and practice geared toward Third World development needs, an area that has come to be known as *development communication*. Research and projects addressing development communication flourished during the First Development Decade in the 1960s. The works of Daniel Lerner (1958), Wilbur Schramm (1964), Everett Rogers (1962, 1969), and many others such as Fredrick Frey, Lucien Pye, and Lakshmana Rao, attested to this lively interest.

Since the 1970s, Western development aid and all facets of the process, including communication, have been challenged. Many large and expensive projects promoting social change have failed to help their intended recipients, or have resulted in even worsened conditions for them. Development's primary focus on economic growth has ignored other crucial, yet non-material aspects of human need. Further, economic development aid has contributed to much corruption and large gaps between the wealthy elite and the masses in Third World countries. Charges of gender bias, ethnocentrism and even racism abound in the literature of development studies and development communication as well. Increasingly, scholars have debated the value, purpose, and meaning of communication for development, debates which certainly parallel those on development itself.

This book explores the scholarship and practice of communication for development and empowerment in the Third World. However, the exploration cannot begin without first clarifying our understandings of key concepts, and how these meanings compare and contrast with how others use and define them. The most obvious are the four concepts in the title of the book and this chapter: *communication, development, empowerment,* and *Third World*. Combinations of these four yield additional concepts and accompanying controversies as well. Definitions of development communication vary not only with definitions of the terms that comprise it, but are also complicated by assumptions about related areas of study and practice. These include *development education, development journalism, international communication, transnational communication, international journalism, cross-cultural,* and *intercultural communication.* Most readily agree that development communication is concerned with the role of communication in social change, but so are all of these other fields. Of course there are substantial differences in focus, emphasis and scope, but these need to be explicated in each instance.

Terminology is a problem *within* the rubric of development communication and related areas, and varies enormously from text to text. The distinctions made between *development communication* (DC) and *development support communication* (DSC) constitute one example.[1] Other areas of continued contradiction and confusion include the distinction between *development communication* and *communication development,* and the meaning of *participatory communication.*[2]

The definition and boundaries of all these overlapping interdisciplinary areas have become even more fluid and nebulous in the past decade. The end of the Cold War, alongside greater polarization along ethnic, religious, and nationalistic lines, increased transnationalization, greatly increased information flow and influence, and a growing consciousness of marginalized groups and diminishing resources have challenged and changed the issues and questions.

Throughout this volume, beginning here, we attempt to untangle the contested and overlapping meanings of these terms and the areas of study and practice they signify. At the same time, we argue for the integrity and value of development communication. We agree that old views of the field are no longer appropriate. Yet, as long as development projects are carried out, development communication will take place. Planned yet self-reflexive communication, accounting for mistakes of the past, will remain crucial to the relative success—and ongoing transformation—of development.

THIRD WORLD

We retain the term "Third World" in the title of the book's second edition quite deliberately, recognizing that the term is controversial and many would not make this choice. Hence, we take some space to explain our decision and our assumptions about the Third World, including its location and its characteristics.

What is the Third World?[3] Annual surveys of undergraduate students in the authors' classes show that while classifications of alignment/non-alignment no longer contribute to popular conceptions of the term, connotations of poverty, unemployment, famine, overpopulation, and economic underdevelopment remain strong. These connotations are contrasted to those of First World, which is the opposite.

John Isbister (1991) traces the Third World notion to 18th-century France, where the three social classes were described as the first, second, and third estates. The first and second estates had the political power. The term third estate, or *tiers état*, became a revolutionary slogan during the French Revolution, which began in 1789 and sought to win and transfer political power from an elite few to the third estate.

Most scholars credit the French demographer Alfred Sauvy with first using the term Third World in a global sense (Isbister 1991; Pletsch 1981). However, they disagree somewhat on what Sauvy meant by the term. According to Isbister, in observing the state of the world following World War II, Sauvy saw that the majority were dispossessed and excluded, as had been the third estate in 18th-century France. Isbister (1991: 15) further notes that revolutionary theorists such as Jean-Paul Sartre used the term as "the banner of the hungry and oppressed." Pletsch (1981), however, illustrates how Sauvy used the term in the context of the Cold War, to describe the "neutral" contested part of the world, the part that both the First and Second Worlds wished to conquer.

Regardless of Sauvy's original intent, the term quickly converted to a political category implying neutralism in the context of the Cold War. In this sense, many politicians, journalists, social scientists, and others suddenly found the term useful in the early 1950s. The idea was also taken up by the Non-Aligned Movement, which included countries that did not wish to be officially aligned with either the West or the East. This group included many ex-colonies that gained political independence in the 1950s and 1960s.

Today, the major connotation of Third World is "underdeveloped," or simply "poor." So, in the popular imagination, the world now is divided into modern versus traditional (or poor) parts and the modern part was subdivided until 1989 into communist (or socialist) and free parts (Pletsch 1981). Now it tends to be simply a division between modern and poor. This picture is somewhat complicated by the emergence of so-called newly industrializing countries (e.g., Taiwan, South Korea, Mexico, Brazil, Singapore, Hong Kong, and the Philippines), yet the global geographic distinctions remain primary. Most of our students in the US think of Third World as economically poor, and as places in Africa, most of Latin America, Asia, and the Pacific.

This geographic picture is reinforced by the most common Mercator map projections of the world on a flat surface (see Figures 1.1 to 1.3). The Mercator projection was developed in the 16th century as an aid to navigation, but eventually it became a reference base on which to put any kind of geographical information. The projection maintains directional accuracy[4] and reproduces shapes quite well. However, the price paid is that distances and areas are magnified toward the Poles, so that Greenland, for instance, looks enormous compared to what it really is relative to Southern landmasses such as Africa and South America. Many say that Mercator's projection promotes a Eurocentric view of the world. The North Pole is at the top. Europe is in the center and is disproportionately large. Also, only the top two-thirds of the globe are usually shown and the equator is down toward the bottom of the map, which further emphasizes countries in the North. Therefore, it may be argued that this popular visual reinforces the geographic conception of the Third World, i.e., of Third World as other, smaller, and apart.

Figure 1.1
World Map: Mercator Projection Comparing the North and South

Note: The Mercator map distorts the world to the advantage of European colonial powers. "The North" is half as large as "The South," though it appears to be much larger on the Mercator map.

Source: Arno Peters. *Map of the World: Peters Projection.* © Akademische Verlagsanstalt. Distributed in North America by Friendship Press. Used by permission.

Figure 1.2
World Map: Mercator Projection Comparing Europe and South America

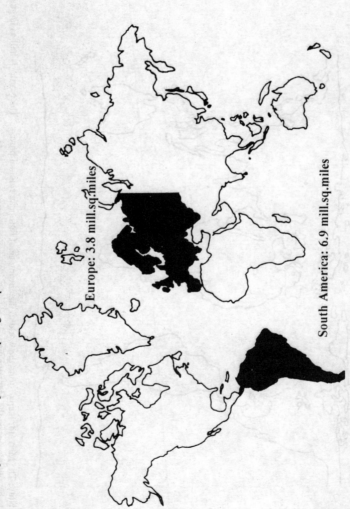

Europe: 3.8 mill.sq.miles

South America: 6.9 mill.sq.miles

Note: The Mercator map shows Europe larger than South America, which is almost double the size of Europe.
Source: Arno Peters. *Map of the World: Peters Projection.* © Akademische Verlagsanstalt. Distributed in North America by Friendship Press. Used by permission.

Figure 1.3
World Map: Mercator Projection Comparing North America and Africa

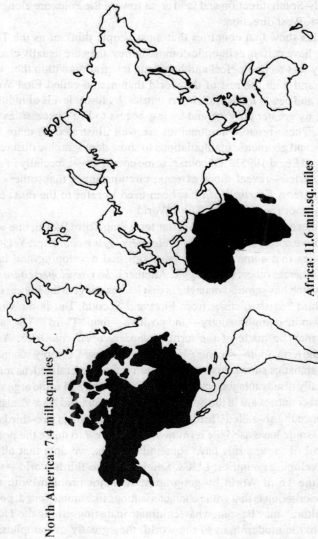

North America: 7.4 mill.sq.miles

Africa: 11.6 mill.sq.miles

Note: In the Mercator map North America appears to be larger than Africa, which in fact is much larger.
Source: Arno Peters. *Map of the World: Peters Projection.* © Akademische Verlagsanstalt. Distributed in North America by Friendship Press. Used by permission.

Newer map projections, such as the Peters projection (Figure 1.4) attempt to correct some of these problems. The Peters projection is an "equal areas" projection, meaning that all quadrants on the map represent equal land or sea areas. Also the equator is in the center. However, here, shapes are distorted, so that land areas toward the equator are elongated in a North–South direction and land areas toward the Poles are elongated in an East–West direction.

Statistics show that countries that most people think of as the Third World do have certain economic commonalties: they are usually characterized by less technological and linguistic integration within their own societies and with the rest of the world than are so-called First World countries and newly industrializing countries, by lower levels of industrialization, by greater poverty, and by less access to life's necessities and comforts. These broad commonalties are well illustrated on maps that use colors and geometric manipulations to show demographic difference (Kidron and Segal 1995).[5] Of course, some countries—especially in sub-Saharan Africa—reveal more extreme circumstances than others do. Hence, the term *Fourth World* has been used to refer to the most economically poor regions of the Third World.

Given these realities, is there a better term than Third World, one with more positive connotations? Many prefer *developing countries*. Yet, that term implies that some countries have finished developing and have "arrived," whereas others still struggle. Another is *less developed countries* (*LDCs*), which has some advantages in that it does not give the impression that a "Third" exists distinct from First and Second. But is the world "less" any more complimentary—and positive—than "Third?" The same criticism may be made of the term *underdeveloped countries*. Additionally, the term *South*—versus *North*—has been used. Simply scanning maps and statistics shows this categorization is overgeneralized, as many economically disadvantaged countries are in the North and some arguably First World countries are in the South, such as Australia and New Zealand. Finally, since the so-called Third World in fact constitutes two-thirds of the world, some have used the term *two-thirds world* to make the point.

While all of these terms have some advantages, we note that all of them—developing countries, LDCs, South, and two-thirds world—still delineate the Third World by geography. A major problem with the geographic criterion is that while characterizations like unintegrated, poor, and agricultural, may be somewhat legitimate in distinguishing the Third World from the modern part of the world, they greatly overemphasize

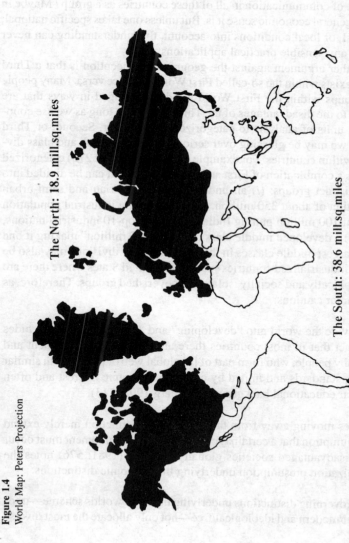

Figure 1.4
World Map: Peters Projection

The North: 18.9 mill.sq.miles

The South: 38.6 mill.sq.miles

Source: Arno Peters. "World Map: Peters Projection." In Ward L. Kaiser, *A New View of the World: Handbook to the World Map: Peters Projection.*
© 1987 by Friendship Press. Used by permission.

the importance of these characterizations in comparison to others (Pletsch 1981). That is, in lumping together all Third World countries based on these characterizations, we ignore gigantic differences between them in other areas—historical backgrounds, cultural traditions, geographical conditions, and language situations. Take, for example, Honduras, the Philippines, and Nigeria. Is it really meaningful to describe and analyze the role of communication in all of these countries as a group? Maybe in a very general economic sense it is. But unless one takes specific national, regional, or local conditions into account, this understanding can never lead to any sensible practical applications.

Another argument against the geographic conception is that a Third World exists within the so-called First World and vice versa. Many people and groups within the First World are disadvantaged in ways that are similar to the disadvantages of the Third World. As long as we use countries as units of analysis to categorize them as First, Second, or Third World, we may be glossing over serious ethnic, regional, and class divisions within countries. For example, Tehranian (1994: 275) categorized India as a combination of First and Third Worlds. "It can be divided into three distinct groups: (*i*) an underdeveloped agrarian and semi-urban population of about 350 million, (*ii*) a developing industrial population of about 100 million putting India among the top-10 industrial nations, and (*iii*) a developed middle class of nearly 400 million" making it one of the largest middle classes in the world. Similar divisions may also be seen in industrialized countries such as the United States where there are geographically and socially isolated impoverished groups. Therefore, as one scholar cautions:

> To divide the world into "developing" and "developed" nations hides the fact that in most countries there are also groups of affluent and wealthy people, who form part of [a] global web of people with similar living standards and united by common economic interest and often similar educational background (Ernberg 1998: 113).

Yet, does moving away from the geographic distinction merely extend the presumption that a certain type of economic development must occur in all disadvantaged societies globally? Pletsch (1981: 576) notes the modernization presumption underlying the economic distinctions:

> The governing distinctions underlying the three worlds scheme—traditional/modern and ideological/free—not only allocate the most diverse

societies and cultures to the same categories, they also imply a pseudo-chronological or historical relationship among the categories themselves. The traditional societies are all destined to become modern ones, according to this scheme, somehow and to some degree.

To address all of these problems, some prefer to define Third World in terms of oppression by some combination of race, class, gender, and nation, which then becomes inclusive of groups living within industrialized countries. The recognition of oppression does not necessarily imply a particular type of development as the solution. It merely affirms the struggle for empowerment (Isbister 1991; Mohanty 1991a). We concur with this view of Third World, which is consistent with its revolutionary origins, connoting opposition to systematic disadvantage by class, race, ethnicity, language, and/or national origin. Therefore, we assume that *development* and *development communication*, the central concepts of this book, are not processes that occur a long way away, but occur everywhere, in virtually any community on the planet.

At the same time, we recognize that the most extreme and widespread situations of poverty, unemployment, illiteracy, hunger, disease, sanitation, and refugee displacement are located in geographic areas conventionally labeled the Third World. Therefore, much of what we say—and most of our examples—have geographic specificity consistent with the conventional conceptions of Third World. We will use the terms developing countries, South, and Third World interchangeably when used in this sense. At the same time, we emphasize that the ideas and processes we describe are not geographically specific, and that development, communication, empowerment, and development communication can occur everywhere.

COMMUNICATION

Issues of words and language are certainly issues of communication. As the media of mass communication spread in the early 20th century, the potential for terms like Third World to be transmitted and legitimized greatly increased. Scholars in fields such as sociology, psychology, and political science increasingly questioned mass media's influence and potential to effect change—both in individuals and in society. These questions led to a plethora of communication models and accompanying assumptions and theories about the components of the process, the process itself, and the context in which communication takes place, as different communication contexts have yielded their own sub-fields of communication studies. As we shall see, scholars of communication and development have created models consistent with development contexts and goals.

The earliest models of communication describes or assumes a relatively linear process whereby someone sends a message to someone else via a channel and gets a response, called feedback. Interference in the process—whether psychological or environmental—is often called noise. This exchange process may occur on more or less equal basis. But when the initiative and ability lie overwhelmingly with the sender, the result is an impersonal, one-way flow of messages. Of course, this is the case with mass communication, where the media create and send messages, with few opportunities for feedback from audience members and seldom via the same channels. Given the sheer volume of messages transmitted by the mass media and broad media access, especially in societies with market economies, early theories assumed that mass media had considerable power to inform and influence.

Much has happened since the 1950s and 1960s when the early models and theories of communication were being devised. Empirical research revealed flaws in these ideas, pointing to the need for considerable refinement to account for differences in context and audience demographics. Additionally, enormous advances have been made in communication technologies, resulting in rapid increases in information flows globally. Radio and television stations have multiplied exponentially. The Internet is revolutionizing our home and work environments, as is the cellular phone and fax machine. All this has largely been a result of the convergence of three technological inventions: computers, which provide information-storage and data-transfer capacities previously unknown; satellites, which relay information over vast distances quickly; and digitization, which converts any kind of communication data—pictures, sound, text—to a binary code that can be readily transmitted, decoded and delivered to the intended individual or audience.

Social scientists interested in questions of message transfer and effects have developed increasingly sophisticated hypotheses to address problems with the early theories and also to account for the increased complexity of the communication environment. Studies based on these new theories have supported the role and power of mass media in, for example: setting an agenda for public discourse; influencing public opinion; persuading or educating in the context of planned campaigns; providing role models for children and others to imitate; providing varied gratifications that may meet audience needs; and cultivating audiences' perceptions of society, in a manner more consistent with media content than statistical reality (McQuail 1994). New information technologies have inspired new and more elaborate arguments about the power of these technologies to deliver information, set agendas, persuade, socialize, educate, satisfy myriad audience needs, and democratize societies.

At the same time that social scientists have been analyzing mass media's effects on society, critical scholars have challenged the relatively linear nature of the models and their isolation from economic and political processes in society. These scholars assumed links between culture and communication in the idea of communication as shared meaning, versus information transmission or persuasion (Carey 1989). Communication is the maintenance, modification, and creation of culture. In this sense, the processes and institutions of communication, of culture, and of development are all woven together. It becomes impossible to think of communication as predominantly a process of information transmission.

Because of the assumed inseparability of culture and communication, many critical scholars argue that communication reinforces hegemonic values and priorities in society. The hegemonic process is assumed to be subtle and seductive, such that most audience members do not resist the values embedded in messages; and, in fact, they actively accept them. The fact that hegemony allows the mainstream transmission of some alternative perspectives gives an illusion of balance, even though only selected non-mainstream messages are allowed, messages that can be most easily co-opted by the dominant system. Hence, a major focus of much critical work is to carry out textual analyses that expose the dominant values embedded in media content, based on the assumption that exposure alone provides an important consciousness-raising function that may challenge hegemony. There are many textual conventions that powerful groups use to reinforce dominant messages, conventions supported by standard traditions and values of media practice. These include, for instance, making light of non-mainstream views, undercounting those with alternative views, overemphasizing support for mainstream views, and an over-reliance on government and corporate sources. Media traditions that reinforce these conventions include focusing on events versus on context, on conflict versus on consensus, and on individuals versus on groups. Additionally, economic motives, deadlines, and competition between journalists contribute to what gets in the media and how it is represented.[6]

One key tool on which we will briefly elaborate is language and the selection of labels that support hegemonic agendas. Several prominent critical theorists and philosophers have developed arguments about the power of the dominant discourse to shape society and in fact create reality. There are numerous historic examples of this. For instance, in missionary and colonial times all African people were classified into "tribes" headed by "chiefs" regardless of the hierarchical or egalitarian nature of the group (Staudt 1991: 12). This was a way to establish linguistic relationships of superiority and inferiority consistent with the values and style of Europeans. In contemporary society, it is frequently evident in the news that the policy or public relations implications of word choices outweigh accuracy in selections, as the United States' initial refusal to use the word *genocide* for the 1994 Rwandan slaughter of Tutsis by Hutus.

A careful examination of the language and imagery of development certainly provides insights into values and agendas of those communicating. Earlier we discussed the term Third World and alternatives to that term. One alternative is *underdeveloped*. Suppose instead that the term *overexploited* is used. The meaning changes immediately in a way that may challenge our usual ways of thinking. Further, many nouns and adjectives have been used to describe people in developing countries— including here in this volume. In recent articles and texts, it appears that *peasant* is no longer acceptable for general use.[7] However, many other terms appear to be used nearly interchangeably. These include: *poor, oppressed, marginalized, disadvantaged, peripheral, exploited, neglected, excluded, disempowered, dispossessed, disenfranchised, devalued, vulnerable*, and *underprivileged*. Even the term *development starved* has been used (Moemeka 1994). This set of labels suggests substantial variation in intended meaning and appropriate context of use. Some labels appear ethnocentric, depending on the context. Others appear more politically correct. Staudt (1991: 14) points out that in the context of development projects, the individuals to whom technologies or services are directed are commonly referred to as *targets*, suggesting military imagery, or as *beneficiaries*, suggesting welfare imagery and also assuming a positive outcome. While most scholars and practitioners of development communication want to avoid offence, it is clear that subtle—and sometimes blatant—forms of racism, sexism, and ethnocentrism do remain evident, and must be continuously examined and exposed.

In addition to theorizing relationships between communication and culture and examining the power of the dominant discourse, critical scholars have focused much attention on the role of large institutions in controlling global communications. They point out that the organizations that are most influential in disseminating information are the largest ones, including private corporations, foundations, governments and their branches, and major political parties. These large political and economic institutions have power and influence over the manufacture and distribution of hardware, provision of training, decisions about message channels, the creation of messages, and export of cultural products (e.g., television programs) in a manner consistent with their values. Some of the largest organizations today are the transnational corporations. "Most governments do not have an economic power matching that of large transnational companies and are unable to control the global flow of capital, which often affects the development of nations more than political decisions" (Ernberg 1998: 113–14).

The inventions of the information age have strengthened critical scholars' concerns and arguments about large political and corporate institutions, and their roles in influencing global cultural change supportive of Western economic, political, and ideological values. Critical scholars concede that hegemony is never complete, and that resistance is possible. The Internet, in particular, allows greatly expanded possibilities for information access, information sharing, and coalition-building by marginalized groups. Yet possibilities translate into realities for very few, and most of the world's people have still not talked on the telephone. Illiteracy and other barriers and biases make Internet access still inconceivable for the vast majority.

In sum, many scholars and practitioners continue to think of communication as a relatively linear process of information transmission, causing or contributing to change in knowledge, attitudes and/or behaviors. Others view communication as a much more complex process, inseparable from culture, which is sustained and challenged by global and local economic, political, and ideological structures and processes.

Like communication, development means different things to different scholars and practitioners. Therefore, the theory and practice of development communication cannot be meaningfully discussed without defining development as well as communication. Although the importance of defining development should be obvious, relatively few studies of development communication bother to do so, leaving it to the reader to figure out the authors' assumptions. Jo Ellen Fair and Hemant Shah (1997) looked at 140 recent studies of communication and development and found that only about a third conceptualized development.

Where definitions are provided, understandings about development do vary greatly. Though most would agree that development means improving the living conditions of society, there has been much debate on just what constitutes improved living conditions and how they should be achieved. In later chapters we will detail three perspectives or ways of thinking about and practicing development in considerable detail. Here we introduce them briefly.

The first is *modernization*, based on neo-classical economic theory, and promoting and supporting capitalist economic development. This perspective assumes that the Western model of economic growth is applicable elsewhere, and that the introduction of modern technologies is important in development. Evidence of modernization can be readily observed in local-level projects that aim to persuade people to adopt technologies, and also in the macro-level policies of governments and aid organizations that pressure Third World countries to sacrifice education and human services for economic growth.

Critical perspectives constitute a second way of thinking about development. These perspectives challenge the economic and cultural expansionism and imperialism of modernization; and they argue for political and economic restructuring to produce a more even distribution of rewards in society. These perspectives do a good job of exposing and critiquing the flaws of modernization, yet they have been less successful so far in proposing concrete alternatives, and they seldom form the primary basis of funded development projects.

Liberation or *monastic* perspectives constitute the third area of scholarship and practice on development that we highlight in this volume. The Brazilian educator Paolo Freire (1973) is among the most well-known proponents of development as liberation. These perspectives derive largely from liberation theology, which prioritizes personal and communal liberation from oppression, as the key to empowerment and self-reliance, which is the goal of development. Liberation theology assumes that all people want to become fully human, which means free and self-reliant, and that they have the internal capacity to develop themselves on their own terms. However, internal and external forms of oppression restrict their ability to do so. Therefore, the purpose of development is liberation from oppression, with a focus on both individuals and communities. Large Western governments and corporations constitute one major source of oppression because they are motivated by a desire to make a profit, which usually means that workers, consumers, and others are exploited in the process. However, liberation theology argues that the oppressors are oppressed too, because they don't realize that their oppression is dehumanizing. The human potential of all is therefore best reached by working toward universal human liberation. As long as oppressors and oppressed exist, neither can be free.

This mode of thought differs from the other two (i.e., modernization and critical perspectives) in that the basic premises and goals are primarily spiritual, not economic; however, material realities are not ignored as in other theologies. Liberation theology recognizes links between material and non-material needs and the impact of unmet material needs and economic exploitation on spiritual growth. Proponents of liberation perspectives do not necessarily side with critics of modernization. The basic premise is that individuals must be free to choose, and that their choice is not inevitably against the values of modernization.

It is important to emphasize that the three perspectives highlighted here and elsewhere in this book are neither mutually exclusive nor exhaustive. They certainly overlap, and in fact we will argue that all three offer valuable insights and arguments. Further, there are other themes in the scholarship and practice of development that intersect with these three that have challenged their assumptions and methodologies. These include the *basic needs, sustainable development*, and *women and development* perspectives or themes, all introduced in the early 1970s. The *basic needs* perspective argues for prioritizing the survival needs of the world's poor—versus assuming that the benefits of infrastructure development will "trickle down." Another significant theme has been the *sustainable development* or *sustainable environment* perspective. This perspective assumes that maintaining the biological diversity of the plant is essential to the survival of humanity. Hence development that does not prioritize environmental sustainability is doomed to fail. A third major theme or perspective is *women in development* (WID) or, more recently, *gender and development* (GAD). Proponents of this perspective demonstrate that most development aid has ignored or marginalized women's views and interests. As women's roles are central to most development goals, failing to consider women seriously jeopardizes project success.

EMPOWERMENT

Another key—and controversial—concept that we explore in this book is *empowerment*. The construct of empowerment is mentioned frequently in the communication and development literature, but terms, exemplars, levels of analysis, and outcomes have not been fully explicated. Empowerment cannot be understood without first defining *power*. As scholars and practitioners, it is important that we consider power and control in development theory and practice. From Foucault (1980), we assume that power is meaningful only in social relations. It is constituted in a network of social relationships. There are several kinds of relational power (Rowlands 1998: 13). These include: power over (controlling power); power to (generate new possibilities without domination); power with (collective power, power created by group process); and power from within (spiritual strength that inspires and energizes others). "Power over" is especially relevant here, as it refers to those who have access to formal decision-making process. *Real* change may not be possible unless we address power inequities between marginalized individuals and groups at the grassroots and those who make policy and aid decisions. The other kinds of power—power to, power with, and power from within—may be instrumental in attaining greater power over.

Like power and the other concepts explored in this chapter, empowerment means different things to different people. In recent years, much has been written about alternative, highly participatory, empowerment-oriented approaches to development. These are varied, and they are not mutually exclusive.[8] Jo Rowlands (1998) reviews the literature of empowerment, dividing it into three overlapping dimensions: personal empowerment (developing individual consciousness and confidence to confront oppression), relational empowerment (an increased ability to negotiate and influence relational decisions), and collective empowerment (collective action at the local or higher level to change oppressive social structures). Santi Rozario (1997) traces the history of the empowerment concept, which she argues has been overused. She divides empowerment into two primary models: One model "is based on empowering the individual, not on encouraging collective social action by the oppressed" (p. 46).[9] The other model is consistent with Paolo Freire's approach, which emphasized "conscientization and radical social action" (p. 47).

Our interest is in Rozario's latter model, consistent with Rowlands' third model, collective empowerment. Given the nature of this book, which can be described as the study and practice of directed social change, and given the power inequities in societies between and among individuals, groups, and organizations, our definitions of empowerment are connected to the building and exercise of power for social change. In this book, empowerment is defined as the process by which individuals, organizations, and communities gain control and mastery over social and economic conditions (Rappaport 1981); over democratic participation in their communities (Zimmerman and Rappaport 1988); and over their stories. In our approach, there is an increased interest "in local autonomy, culture and knowledge; and the defense of localized, pluralistic grassroots movements" (Escobar 1995a: 215). These and other themes and perspectives pervade the scholarly and professional literature of development studies and development communication, alongside an underlying approach reflecting one or a combination of primary approaches highlighted in this book.

DEVELOPMENT COMMUNICATION

The theory and practice of development communication as described in this book, either explicity or implicity, reflect varied underlying views about communication, development, and empowerment. These views usually are linked by shared assumptions that yield consistency with development communication as well. Development communication scholars and practitioners still tend to be split between those who view communication as an organizational delivery system versus those who view communication more broadly, as inseparable from culture and from all facets of social change. This orientation rests on certain assumptions consistent with certain divisions in views on development, empowerment, and development communication.

The links are perhaps most evident in the case of the information transmission view of communication and the modernization perspective on development. For those who view communication as a process of message delivery, it is easy to view development as a process of modernization via the delivery and insertion of technologies, and/or inculcating certain values, attitudes, and behaviors in the population. Communication and information are persuasive tools that can assist in the modernization process. Communication in the form of market research can assist in decisions about development goals and communication strategies. Persuasive or marketing communications subsequently "sell" development ideas and associated technologies to target audiences. In this sense, development communication under the modernization framework is often viewed as a process of persuasive marketing.

In contrast, critical frameworks reject marketing models that aim to spread and support Western technologies and economic and political values. Critical perspectives also view persuasive campaigns as manipulative and potentially harmful, with inadequate attention to the larger cultural context in which people live. Additionally, proponents of these perspectives observe that large development projects involve multiple economic interests that may benefit others more than the population supposedly served. North American and European expatriates live lavishly in developing countries at the expense of taxpayers at home, and often doing jobs for which local expertise is available. Additionally, corrupt leaders and government officials in developing countries find ways to enhance their wealth with foreign aid, hence increasing gaps between the haves and the have-nots. For those with critical perspectives, therefore, development communication is a process of consensus building and resistance. It is not a linear process, but must be historically grounded, culturally sensitive, and multi-faceted, with attention to all the political, economic, and ideological structures and processes that comprise society.

A focus on empowerment has a direct consequence on the objectives of development communication. In the future, just the delivery of new information and technological innovations will be inadequate. Empowerment requires more than just information delivery and diffusion of innovations. An important focus of development communicators will be to help in the process of empowerment of marginalized individuals, groups, and organizations. This calls for grassroots organizing and communicative social action on the part of women, the poor, minorities, and others who have been consistently and increasingly marginalized in the process of social change. The implication for development communication, then, is a reconceptualization of its role. Greater importance will need to be given to the organizational value of communication (than the transmission function) and the role of participative social action communication in empowering citizens. This will also imply a multidisciplinary focus. Development communication will need to borrow and adapt concepts and practices from social work, community psychology, community organization and other areas engaged in empowering people, communities, and organizations.

Liberation perspectives suggest yet a different way of defining and operationalizing development communication. As the purpose of development is assumed to be freedom from oppression, and personal and communal empowerment, the development communication process must support these goals. Therefore, development communication is not message exchange but rather "emancipatory communication" that will free people to determine their own futures. That should include everyone participating in the process, not just the so-called target groups. The assumption is that once people get in touch with their sources of oppression as well as their sources of power, they will then be able to find solutions. The nature of emancipatory communication may vary. Many projects grounded in liberation perspectives include spiritual practice, consistent with the religion of the group involved. Additionally, Paolo Freire and others advocate particular forms of *dialogue* (interpersonal and small group strategies) that will lead to expanded consciousness and power— and therefore liberation. These dialogic processes enable participants to identify and explore issues that have meaning for them.

Aside from differences in underlying assumptions about communication and about development, the scholarship and practice of development communication vary greatly in strategic scope, i.e., the range of methods and approaches included as part of development communication. Given the convergence of mass communication and information technologies, it makes sense that all of these technologies would be relevant. Also significant are small group, interpersonal and pedagogic strategies of communication, as are traditional forms of communication and folk media. Some authors include religious and spiritual practice as crucial elements of development communication. In most texts, however, authors emphasize particular strategies of communication, with less attention to the others.

Finally, development communication involves issues at all levels of consideration. What is possible at the micro (individual and grassroots) level often depends on constraints at the macro (global or national) and meso (large community or regional) levels. Yet, at the same time, action at the grassroots may influence higher-level policy and practice. We believe that no useful theory can ignore any level of analysis and practice. Yet most development communication texts focus attention at one level, therefore, neglecting major issues (and populations) relevant to the process.[10]

Obviously, we cannot ignore serious problems of individual and local deprivation while waiting for modernization to be revised. Yet, development projects may not be able to empower certain classes of people until larger structures of global capitalism are first addressed. This is clearly illustrated in a recent book titled *Disposable People: New Slavery in the Global Economy* (Bales 1999). The book reports research estimating 27 million economic slaves globally. These are not people exploited in sweatshops, but children and adults forced to work by violence and threats of violence. The violence and force do not come exclusively from the economic motives of business owners, but additionally from families who want consumer goods and are willing to sacrifice family members to get them. For instance, the title of Bales' (1999) chapter on forced prostitution in Thailand is "One Daughter Equals One Television." Clearly, these are problems requiring interventions at multiple levels. They cannot be alleviated by grassroots projects alone.

ORGANIZATION OF THE BOOK

Though the perspectives of the role of communication in development as held in the 1950s and 1960s have changed, the need for development communication remains important. This book will trace the history of development communication, present diverse approaches and their proponents, critique these approaches as appropriate, and provide ideas and models for development communication in the next century. We will critically examine the dominant development paradigm that has guided much of the development theory and practice in the Third World since World War II. Our interest in examining the perspectives on development is to identify and critique interventions and practices that have emerged from those perspectives and analyze their political, economic and cultural consequences. An underlying theme throughout the book, is to critique the power of dominant systems of knowledge, question the truth claims of modernism, and sensitize the reader to the relationship between dominant knowledge and exercise of social power. In this approach, we are informed by the work of postmodern, feminist, and postcolonial scholars. We examine the local and "other" contexts and assert the heuristic value of alternative, non-Western, local experiences, and knowledge systems to the tasks of social change (Crush 1995). With more scholarship in this area, it should, hopefully, puncture the notion that all expertise in development and change can only come from the North or from local experts trained abroad. Local knowledge and experiences used to solve local problems are not only practical but they will resuscitate these subjugated knowledge systems and boost the self-confidence of the local people, the women, and the other marginalized groups and individuals. It is critical to the success of self-reliant and autonomous self-development activities (Parpart 1995).

Our approach is interdisciplinary. We recognize that the scholarship and practice of development communication has many disciplinary origins besides communication studies: political science, economics, sociology, social psychology, social work, education, women's studies, community psychology, community organization, and more. We aim to synthesize this material and present it in a conceptually organized manner, eliminating disciplinary jargon.

The book is divided into five parts. In Part I, this introductory chapter is followed by a brief overview of the evolution of the theory and practice of development communication (Chapter 2). As the remainder of the book is divided conceptually versus historically, Chapter 2 aims to provide historical context for the volume as a whole.

Part II focuses on modernization theory, including the dominant discourse of modernization, and development communication under modernization. We begin, in Chapter 3, with an introduction to modernization theory and discourse, and its evolution from the early years of development to the present. Chapter 4 details strategies of communication under modernization, especially strategies based on models of diffusion and social marketing. Examples from historic and contemporary projects are provided.

Part III discusses critical perspectives on communication and development. Chapter 5 critiques the dominant development discourse looking specifically at the inherent biases in the discourse. This chapter describes many of the consequences of this discourse, often negative, that flow directly from its biases. Challenges to modernization, including dependency and world systems theories (from Marxism), women and development, and sustainable development, are then reviewed. Alternative approaches also are suggested. In Chapter 6, we take a critical look at the communication strategies used to guide social change in Third World countries. We then describe the newer, alternative roles for communication in development, including the renewed interest in local cultures and the use of indigenous communication media for development and change. We conclude this chapter by describing and critiquing the present interest in using information and communication technologies (e.g., the Internet) for rural development in the Third World.

In Part IV, we return to liberation perspectives on development. This is a departure from most development communication texts, which seldom extend their consideration beyond Freire's basic ideas and methodologies on dialogic communication. We begin, in Chapter 7, with an introduction to liberation theology and its role in development and in freedom struggle globally. Although liberation theology is often associated with Roman Catholicism in Latin America, there have been liberation theologies associated with Protestantism (as in African–American liberation theology), and with every major religion, including Buddhism, Hinduism, Islam, and Judaism. Areas of overlap between critical and liberation perspectives are also considered. Chapter 8 discusses the ways in which liberation theology has been operationalized in development projects. This necessitates attention to meditation and prayer as communication—forms of communication seldom considered in communication studies, yet crucially important to the daily lives and well-being of most of the world's people.

In Part V, the final section of the book, we focus on communication and empowerment. We summarize our own views, synthesizing insights from previous chapters and arguing for new directions in theory and practice. We recognize the failures and harmful outcomes of much development aid, yet we support the crucial importance of development interventions under many circumstances in improving people's lives. Likewise, we agree with most critiques of development communication, yet we believe in its necessity and value, to the extent that legitimate critiques are addressed. We agree with those who argue—usually from critical, liberation, or feminist perspectives—that development should prioritize the needs of groups most oppressed. Additionally development must be culturally and historically sensitive, recognizing the nature and relative salience of key social divisions, such as gender, class, race, ethnicity, age, religion, and nation.

The key goal of development must be empowerment, whether at the individual, community, or national level. Empowerment is multi-faceted, in that, creative survival requires both material and non-material resources, resources that vary by context. In Chapter 9, we attempt to reconceptualize the role of development communication in facilitating empowerment outcomes. However, there is no single recipe for facilitating empowerment. All models and experiences of communication for development offer useful lessons and insights. Careful case studies documenting approaches and outcomes from multiple perspectives are needed as we move forward in rethinking development communication.

SUMMARY

This chapter discusses key terms used repeatedly in this text. The meaning of *Third World* has evolved historically. It has been used to refer to the oppressed and revolutionary groups within a country (Isbister 1991) and it has referred to the block of countries with neutral status in the context of the Cold War (Pletsch 1981). Today, the term is most commonly used to refer to those countries (in Asia, Africa, and Latin America) considered less technologically advanced and poorer than so-called First World countries. Other labels often used interchangeably with Third World are developing countries, less developed countries (LDCs), under-developed countries, and South. We occasionally use all of these terms. We critique, however, the geographic connotations of Third World (and the other terms) in that there are oppressed groups within every First World country and elite groups within every Third World country. Additionally, the geographic grouping foregrounds economic status and disregards enormous variation on other dimensions.

Communication has often been used to refer to a linear process of information exchange, resulting in knowledge acquisition or persuasion. However, we prefer a definition that emphasizes a process of shared meaning that takes place in a cultural and political-economic context and is inseparable from that context. Hence, the processes and institutions of communication, culture, politics, economics, and development are all interwoven. The role of communication in society cannot be understood apart from other processes and structures of society, and their unique histories and circumstances.

Development is usually understood to mean the process by which societal conditions are improved. However, there is much disagreement on what constitutes improvement. For instance, a modernization perspective, based on neo-classical economic theories, assumes that a Western model of economic growth is universally desirable. Critical perspectives, grounded in Marxist thought, challenge the economic and cultural expansionism and imperialism of modernization, arguing for new economic arrangements to create more even distribution of rewards in society. Liberation perspectives derive largely from liberation theology, which prioritizes personal and communal liberation from oppression as the key to empowerment and self-reliance, which should be the goal of development. These perspectives overlap each other, and with additional themes and perspectives included in this text, e.g., in the areas of basic needs, women and development, and sustainable development.

Empowerment, the goal of development from liberation and other perspectives, is defined as the process by which individuals, organizations, and communities gain control and mastery over social and economic conditions, over democratic participation within their communities, and over their stories (Freire 1970; Zimmerman and Rappaport 1988). While some use this term to refer exclusively as empowerment within the individual, we are concerned with collective empowerment.

The meaning of *development communication*, the focus of this text, varies depending on how one views and defines the component concepts of development and communication. Our understanding of development communication emerges from our understanding of development as empowerment and communication as shared meaning. It involves issues at all levels of consideration: the grassroots, large community, regional, national, and global levels.

NOTES

1. Moemeka (1994: viii) sees DSC as a historic phase that has passed, i.e., as the second of three stages in the place assigned to communication in development. The

third stage is DC. In contrast, others such as James (1994: 331–32), Jayaweera and Amunugama (1987: xix) and Melkote (1991: 263), distinguish DC and DSC by level, scope and nature of strategy, with DC associated with macro-level hierarchical entities, and DSC with grassroots participatory entities.

2. Brenda Dervin and Robert Huesca (1997) do an excellent job of sorting out meanings of participatory communication, distinguishing participation-as-end vs. participation-as-means assumptions in research and practice.

3. For a comprehensive analysis of the term 'Third World', see Melkote and Merriam (1998).

4. The advantage of Mercator's projection for navigational purposes is that it maintains the true direction of any one point relative to another. So that, for instance, if you draw a line diagonally anywhere at 45 degrees to the equator it always points northeast or northwest.

5. See also comparative statistics contained in annual reports of organizations such as the United Nations Development Programme (1998) and the World Bank (1999).

6. For an analysis of textual conventions and reinforcing media values and traditions, see Gitlin (1980) and Steeves (1997).

7. We do occasionally use the term peasant in this text, but only in reports of research by others who use the term.

8. In addition to other lines of argument to be discussed, they include communitarian theory (Tehranian 1994), and environmentally-oriented perspectives, including ecofeminism.

9. She traces this model to Solomon (1976), who blamed internalized oppression for African Americans' marginalization and powerlessness in the larger society.

10. Some texts, for instance, focus primarily on *macro-level* issues of information flow (Reeves 1993; Stevenson 1994) and/or of communication and information technologies and policies (Sussman and Lent 1991; Woods 1993), though from varying ideological perspectives. Moemeka's (1994) collection also is directed at the macro-level, emphasizing the role of world trade in development communication. Most other recent texts emphasize theory and strategy at more local levels, with little attention to global power structures. Several of these—Mody (1991), Nair and White (1993), White et al. (1994), Riano (1994), Jacobson and Servaes (1999)—tend (with some internal inconsistencies) to align themselves with Freire's dialogic pedagogy and criticize diffusion and marketing approaches that reinforce top-down participation. Others (Hornik 1988; Singhal and Rogers 1999) see value in diffusion and marketing models but attribute failures to poor planning.

CHAPTER 2

EVOLUTION OF THE THEORY AND PRACTICE
OF DEVELOPMENT COMMUNICATION[1]

Development is fundamentally about mapping and making, about
the spatial reach of power and the control and management of
other peoples, territories, environments, and places.
Jonathan Crush (1995: 6–7)

Throughout history, no nation or people have been the sole repository of knowledge. Instead, all cultures and nations have generated
ideas, this knowledge has accumulated over time, and diffused
from area-to-area and people-to-people (Hamelink 1983; Linton 1936).
Of course, some nations developed the ability to acquire and apply technological knowledge faster than others and they used it to place themselves
above others in wealth and power, and to control the wealth and overall
development of other nations (see Appendix A).

A review of ancient history shows that Europe, which was to dominate
the world technologically and culturally from the 16th to the 19th centuries, did not lead before then. Between approximately 3500 BC and
1500 BC, the river valley civilizations of Mesopotamia (in West Asia),

Egypt (in North Africa), Indus Valley (Indian subcontinent), and also China were dominant in technology, architecture, and the arts. The Roman civilization (500 BC), which followed the Greek age in Europe, laid the groundwork for the advancement of European peoples who in recent history have wielded hegemonic power.

Spurred by the rise of European merchant classes and the merchant marines, technological knowledge and power emerged most decisively in Western Europe around AD 1500. The period from the 16th to early 20th century was one of expansionism and exploitation which saw the subjugation and reduction to serfdom of vast numbers of human beings across the southern two-thirds of the globe known as the Third World (Brookfield 1975). The first period of European expansion ended in the early 19th century, leading to the decolonization of the Americas and the suppression of the transatlantic slave trade (Goldthorpe 1975). However, expansion continued unabated into the interior parts of Africa and Asia. The voices of colonial dissatisfaction gathered in volume in the early 20th century as some European colonial leaders, such as the Dutch in the East Indies and the British in Africa, initiated an *era of ethical concern* by raising questions about the motives and consequences of intervention. These leaders conceded some responsibility for the exploitation of colonized peoples and their territories (Brookfield 1975). The struggles for complete freedom from colonial rule were realized in the decades following World War II. First, the Asian colonies and then the African colonies won their independence by the 1960s.

DEVELOPMENT AID SINCE WORLD WAR II

It is obvious that development interventions are not new and have occurred throughout history. However, development in its modern form dates back to World War II, and to international concern in preventing future wars. The more than 50 years since World War II have witnessed the political emancipation of most of the Third World from colonization and the birth of the United Nations and its various executing or multilateral agencies, marking the formal beginning of development aid to Third World countries. Shortly thereafter, numerous bilateral aid agencies were established within Western industrialized countries, such as the United

States Agency for International Development (USAID). International and grassroots non-governmental organizations multiplied and grew during these years as well (see Appendix B).

In 1941, Winston Churchill and Franklin Roosevelt signed the Atlantic Charter in which they outlined some common principles that should lead to a better world, including economic collaboration leading to equal access to trade, improved labor conditions, and world peace. Twenty-six nations signed this charter. Later, in 1943, 47 nations signed an agreement to collaborate on aid to war refugees. They called their multilateral organization the United Nations Relief and Rehabilitation Administration (UNRRA). The United Nations (UN) was formed on October 24, 1945, largely as a result of world consensus that aid was important in the prevention of future wars. The UN replaced the old League of Nations, which had been formed after World War I. The wording on one part of the UN charter pledged international economic and social co-operation and aid. This made the UN different from the League of Nations, which was connected more by military and diplomatic agreements than a commitment to economic aid. The original UN members were the 50 allied nations. By 1965, the UN membership had doubled, and by 1985, it had tripled. The current total is 185. More than half are former colonies that achieved independence following World War II.[2]

The UN consists of a General Assembly, for which each member country supplies five representatives. These representatives plus outside experts function on committees that are concerned with financial, social, cultural, and humanitarian questions. The most important group with regard to development aid policy is the Economic and Social Council, with members elected by the General Assembly. The Economic and Social Council has an important impact on UN policy with regard to the many multilateral organizations that make up what is known as the UN family, for instance, the International Bank for Reconstruction and Development (IBRD, also known as the World Bank), the Food and Agriculture Organization (FAO), the United Nations Development Programme (UNDP), the United Nations High Commissioner for Refugees (UNHCR), the World Health Organization (WHO), and the United Nations Educational, Scientific and Cultural Organization (UNESCO). Each of these organizations have their own sets of goals and official affiliations with dues-paying countries. Revenue also comes from donations, e.g., UNICEF (United Nations Children's Fund)[3] drives. They are linked to the UN via specific agreements, and it is these that give and administer aid and loans, conduct research, and make policy recommendations in their own areas of specialization. These organizations sponsor many projects related to development communication in their areas of interest.

Food and Agriculture Organization (FAO). This specialized UN-agency has as its aims to raise levels of nutrition and living standards; to improve the production, processing, and marketing of food and agricultural products; to promote rural development and to eliminate hunger. Development support communication (DSC) forms an important component in many of FAO's activities such as agriculture, forestry, fisheries, nutrition, population, and environment (Mayo and Servaes 1994).

International Labor Organization (ILO). This was the first specialized agency of the UN. The ILO is an organization for workers, employers, and governments. Its main sphere of activity is to promote social justice. In the last few decades, the ILO has been broadening its goals in the areas of civil liberties and employment policy (Mayo and Servaes 1994).

United Nations Development Programme (UNDP). The UNDP performs a service function and primarily acts as a funding agency for technical co-operation. It also coordinates external co-operation at the request of national governments. Importantly, the UNDP mandate is to promote human development with the objective of helping developing countries attain self-reliance through the building and strengthening of national capacity (Mayo and Servaes 1994). The concept of development support communication (DSC) was first articulated within the UNDP in the 1960s by Erskine Childers. It ascribed a management function to DSC: "Communications were not confined to information or broadcasting organizations and ministries, but extended to all sectors; and their success in influencing and sustaining development depended to a large extent on the adequacy of mechanisms for integrated and coordinated multi-sectoral project planning" (Mayo and Servaes 1994: 4).

United Nations Educational, Scientific and Cultural Organization (UNESCO). Among all the agencies of the UN, UNESCO is recognized as the lead player in the field of social communication. The UNESCO considers communication as a major program in its own right, not just as a support to, or as a vector of the development process. Its communication policy is operationalized within three broad areas: the free flow of ideas by word and image, communication for development, and the development of·socio-cultural impact of new communication technologies. The United Nations Educational, Scientific and Cultural Organization is committed to programs within these three broad areas (Mayo and Servaes 1994).

United Nations Population Fund (UNFPA). This agency's chief objective is the challenges posed by population growth. It helps developing countries find solutions to their population problems and to achieve a balance between population and resources. The UNFPA has assisted population programs and activities in most developing countries and toward these ends, it has employed information, education, and communication strategies (Mayo and Servaes 1994).

United Nations Children's Fund (UNICEF). This agency's chief concern has been to address the needs of children living in the developing countries. It has played a very important role (in association with the World Health Organization) in providing help to countries to tackle debilitating diseases such as malaria, tuberculosis, trachoma, leprosy, and infant malnutrition. It has also worked with national governments in strengthening their health care infrastructures as well as expanding primary education. The United Nations Children's Fund has actively relied on communication activities to garner public interest and support for its programs. In partnership with the UNDP, UNICEF set up a DSC unit in the 1960s to stimulate and improve participation in all its projects (Mayo and Servaes 1994).

World Health Organization (WHO). The WHO has as its goal the ensuring of health for all people, i.e., not just the absence of disease but a state of complete physical, mental, and social wellness. In the last 50 years, it has implemented an aggressive immunization program to help control or eradicate many of the deadly diseases around the world. This has resulted in the eradication of diseases such as yaws and smallpox and control of many others. More recently, the WHO has started to combat the Acquired Immuno Deficiency Syndrome (AIDS) virus by launching the Global Program on AIDS (Mayo and Servaes 1994). Communication strategies used by WHO in support of its programs have included the mass media, interpersonal communication, and community organization.

In general, in the early post-World War II years, the attention of the UN, its multilateral agencies—especially the World Bank—and their most influential member, the United States (US), was consumed by relief and rehabilitation work in war-ravaged Europe. To this end, the US launched the European Recovery Program, also known as the Marshall Plan, the first and largest government-sponsored foreign assistance project. The US President Truman's administration contributed 2.5 percent of its GNP, a proportion which has yet to be matched (Hoy 1998: 16–17). Goals of the Marshall Plan included humanitarian assistance, rebuilding European markets for US goods, and enabling Europe to resist Soviet influence in Eastern Europe. The success of the Marshall Plan inspired similar projects in Third World countries. Starting in the 1950s and on into the 1960s, the attention of the United Nations turned increasingly to the Third World where two-thirds of the world's population resided. This population enjoyed, in 1955, only 15 percent of the world's income, and was made up predominantly of subsistence farmers.

Particularly significant among multilateral agencies has been the IBRD or the World Bank. The World Bank was established in 1944 when economists from Europe and the US met in Bretton Woods, New Hampshire to consider Europe's need for reconstruction following World War II. The International Monetary Fund (IMF) and the General Agreement on Tariffs and Trade (GATT) were created at the same time. The World Bank, a lending agency, would provide credit, the IMF would regulate global monetary exchange,[4] and GATT would liberalize trade. Initially, the World Bank's goal was to facilitate private capital transfers to help rebuild Europe, consistent with the global climate at the time.

Concern for the plight of the people in the Third World countries moved US President Truman to propose the 1949 Point Four program, which was to be the Third World version of the Marshall Plan. He observed that:

More than half the people of the world are living in conditions approaching misery. Their food is inadequate. They are victims of disease. Their economic life is primitive and stagnant. Their poverty is a threat both to them and to more prosperous areas. For the first time in history, humanity possesses the knowledge and skill to relieve the suffering of these people (Daniels 1951: 10–11).

The four points of the Point Four program were simple. First, the US would support the UN and help strengthen its ability to enforce its decisions. Second, the US would continue its work in revitalizing the world economy. Third, the US would "strengthen freedom-loving peoples around the world against the evils of aggression." Fourth, the US would "embark on a new program of modernization and capital investment" (Truman 1949).

The philosophical consistencies between the Marshall Plan and the Point Four program were very clear. Both aimed to alleviate suffering, and both aimed to do so via capital investment. Countries considered non-communist or "freedom-loving" qualified as beneficiaries of aid. Clearly, therefore, alleviating Third World suffering consisted of inserting the Western cornucopia of advances in agriculture, commerce, industry, and health. The key to prosperity and peace, said Truman in his 1949 inaugural address, was "greater production" through "a wider and more vigorous application of modern scientific and technical knowledge" (Daniels 1951: 11). The outcome of this proposal increasingly was equated with *development*.

In 1950, Truman created the United States' first bilateral aid organization, the Technical Co-operation Administration (TCA). Its replacement, the Mutual Security Administration (MSA) provided primarily military aid, and only secondarily economic support and food aid. Economic support went to those countries considered strategically aligned with the US.

The 1961 Foreign Assistance Act established the USAID and the Peace Corps, a people-to-people overseas volunteer program. In the Foreign Assistance Act, US President Kennedy sought to shift the balance of international aid from strategic goals toward development goals, including the alleviation and prevention of social injustice and economic chaos. Of course, the two types of goals always have been closely linked by the assumption that US foreign assistance ultimately supports its national security and political-economic interests.

As has been evident in this overview, there has been much historical consistency between the development goals and priorities of the United Nations family of organizations, the World Bank, and the US; this is in part because the US has played such a powerful role in the UN. Additionally, the Development Assistance Committee (DAC) coordinates all development assistance supplied by bilateral aid agencies of the Organization for Economic Co-operation and Development (OECD). The OECD is made up of 27 industrialized nations, and aims to coordinate and encourage global economic growth. The DAC was established in 1961, at the start of the First Development Decade, and has 22 members, with the World Bank, IMF, and UNDP as permanent observers. It monitors and assesses the Official Development Assistance (ODA) provided by member countries.[5] It also provides policy guidance in members' aid programs, carries out critical reviews, maintains statistics, and establishes a context for dialogue and consensus-building (Hoy 1998: 28).

As we have seen, in the post-World War II years most aid attention was directed to Europe. In the 1950s and 1960s, economic development assistance focused on Third World countries and primarily took the form of infrastructure planning and development. In the 1970s, under World Bank President Robert McNamara's influence, the priorities were integrated rural development and basic needs; in the 1980s, the focus was "structural adjustment," or loan conditions including maintaining competitive exchange rates, reducing government spending, and privatizing government agencies; in the 1990s, human development has become a major theme, including concerns of human rights, gender issues, and environment (Hoy 1998). Additionally, globalization and enormous increases in private capital flows to developing countries are forcing the World Bank, other United Nations agencies and bilateral agencies to adapt. Changes proposed include writing off debts of the world's poorest countries, providing small loans (via local banks) to the poor to start their own businesses, and increased collaboration with NGOs (Hoy 1998; see also Appendix B).

All of the above changes have shaped development as it takes place today. In later chapters, we will provide examples of projects—and project communication—reflecting these themes. Nonetheless, the goals and underlying values that shaped the Marshall Plan and the First Development Decade of the 1960s are still with us and have influenced the theory and practice of development communication, as well as development in general. Next, we examine some of these values, or *biases*, more closely, as they constitute themes that reappear frequently through the book. They include pro-innovation, pro-persuasion, pro-top-down, pro-mass media, and pro-literacy biases.

EARLY PRO-TRANSFER OF INNOVATIONS PERIOD

The United Nations named the 1960s, the First Development Decade and set goals of economic growth in developing countries. These goals represented key UN donor agencies, primarily the World Bank, and were largely consistent with the goals of newly forming bilateral aid organizations.

In the 1960s, the emphasis was on technological transfer from the North to the South. Although the traditional practices of the people of developing countries had enabled them to survive for millennia, the prevailing wisdom of the times dismissed them without any evaluation. It was after all *known* that Western agriculture, medicines, tools, and techniques outstripped corresponding traditional practices. Therefore, it made unquestionable sense that the Third World people discard unconditionally their *primitive* ways and embrace the technologies that had wrought such extraordinary progress in the *advanced* countries of the North. This orientation eventually came to be known as a *pro-innovation bias* (Rogers 1976a). It has held fast to this day, though the innovations obviously have changed over time and new themes and biases have emerged as well.

Initially, the pro-innovation transfer paradigm appeared alluringly simple and straightforward. It had been largely derived from the highly successful program under the Marshall Plan to resuscitate war-ravaged Europe. The essence of the plan consisted of making finance and material resources available for pre-existing European expertise to apply to reconstruction (Arkes 1972). It was soon clear, however, that the post-colonial Third World problem was quite different. There was no adequate pre-existing base of expertise except within the erstwhile colonialists themselves. More significantly, masses of people had to have their traditional lifestyles changed radically. Development, therefore, involved not simply the transfer of capital and technology, but also the communication of ideas, knowledge, and skills to make possible the successful adoption of innovations.

What was then needed was an expanded base of expertise to, *inter alia*, persuade and motivate the people of the Third World to cast aside their traditional ways in favor of the new. To the pro-innovation bias, consequently was added a *pro-persuasion bias*, and with it, the implicit acknowledgement that Third World people were not inclined to submit meekly to radical change. So, a burgeoning stream of Third World students traveled to the developed countries for training and education, reciprocated by a corresponding stream of *experts* representing multilateral (World Bank, UNESCO, FAO), bilateral (USAID), and voluntary (Catholic Relief Services, International Red Cross) aid agencies gradually flooding the Third World.

PRO-PERSUASION AND PRO-TOP-DOWN BIASES

In the early days of development, before transistorization made possible the ubiquity of radio sets, the task of convincing people through persuasive communication to change their life ways, fell to the *extension services*. Extension had long been and continues to be regarded as a logical and systematic method for disseminating productive and useful knowledge and skills to receivers.

To elaborate briefly, in most developing countries the various government departments or ministries (health, education, agriculture, labor, transportation, etc.) include an extension or outreach function. The ministry of agriculture usually operates the largest extension system. Agricultural extension services globally have been modeled substantially after those in the US, as a result of post-World War II aid. For instance, Obibuaku (1983) notes that extension in the modern sense was not known in many African countries until the early 1960s, when USAID sent extension experts to work with the ministries of agriculture. Prior to this time, agents were given only technical training, and extension work consisted primarily of the provision of supplies, not education. The extension division in the ministry of agriculture was "charged with the function of teaching the farmers such techniques and practices of modern agriculture as will transform the country's agriculture from a predominantly subsistence type to a modern one" (Obibuaku 1983: 37).

Many observers have noted that, despite attempts, the US model of extension has not been fully replicated in developing countries. Compton (1989) points out that the extension leg of the college/research/extension triad has remained weak and that there is often little or no communication between extension workers and agricultural research universities.[6] Field agents who work directly with farmers typically have one or two years of post-secondary school training. Also, the main emphasis in their training is on agricultural practices—versus communication theory and method. These agents are sometimes assisted by fieldworkers who have no formal training.[7]

Despite the many criticisms raised in recent years by development communication theorists, as we will discuss later, most extension programs have been based on Everett Rogers' (1962, 1983) diffusion of innovations model. In the 1940s and 1950s, the diffusion of innovations research tradition gained momentum in the US. Starting with Bruce Ryan and Neil Gross' studies of the diffusion of hybrid seed corn in the 1940s, and Paul Lazarsfeld and colleagues' studies of voting behaviors, much research data were gathered showing that information about decision options was communicated by the mass media to key opinion leaders, and from them to others throughout the social system (Rogers 1962).

The diffusion model assumes that a proper combination of mass-mediated and interpersonal communication strategies can move individuals from a process of awareness (usually of a new technology) through interest, evaluation, trial, and finally the adoption of that technology. Criticisms of the model include its "pro-innovation," "pro-persuasion" and "top-down" nature—that is, its strong emphasis on adoption and underemphasis on recipient input into development decisions and processes (Colle 1989).

Not only did extension operating methodology embrace the pro-innovation bias but also took it upon itself to decide what innovations were best for its clients, followed by campaigns to convince them of the wisdom of its choice. The original extension responsibility to collect, collate, and convey *all* relevant research-generated information to potential clients was no longer adequate. The information disseminating extension agent was now expected to evolve into a *change agent*: "a professional person who attempts to influence adoption decisions in a direction that he feels is desirable" (Rogers 1962: 283). And so was set in motion a one-way flow of influence-oriented messages from change agencies at the top to the rural peasantry at the bottom, a process of communication which eventually earned itself the derisive sobriquet, *top-down communication*. This approach held that peasants were rational enough to see the value of adopting innovations selected for them but incapable of making rational choices from among an array of alternatives put before them. Thus, the early pro-innovation transfer model became expanded as shown in Figure 2.1.

Figure 2.1
Pro-persuasion Model of Development

Additionally, extension programs based on diffusion have relied extensively on agent-to-client face-to-face communication, augmented here and there by certain demonstration multiplier effects involving "master farmers," called the "training and visit" (T&V) system.[8] Colle (1989) points out that hundreds of diffusion studies around the world have questioned farmers about their information sources at different stages of adoption and appear to indicate that, while mass media are useful in increasing awareness, it is face-to-face communication that is most important for trial and ultimate adoption. As mass media were not widely available in developing countries in the early years of development, it became a precedent to allocate most extension resources to field staff at the expense of exploring other kinds of methods. Additionally, Colle (1989) notes that most research and extension programs relying on diffusion assumptions often overlook the "quality and fit" of communications materials:

> For example, if radio were used specifically to create "awareness" and the material was boring and broadcast at inappropriate times . . . , diffusion researchers would be unlikely to discover much radio influence at the "adoption" stage (Colle 1989: 64).

Simple numerical and logistic obstacles have exacerbated the overemphasis on interpersonal communication. The available pool of extension personnel, grossly outnumbered by the thousands of people spread over huge geographic areas difficult to navigate, was woefully unequal to the task. Besides, extension agents were primarily subject-matter specialists (agriculture, health, etc.) to which was added a patina of communication skills that may have been useful in the interpersonal or the small-group interaction situation. This certainly came nowhere near addressing the main problem, which was one of mass communication.

So, extension tended to focus its attention mainly on the closest and most accessible, most receptive, and thus, easiest to convince farmers who, as diffusion studies were to show later, as a class had more education and income than the rest (Rogers 1969). They were also disproportionately male, even in places such as sub-Saharan Africa where women constitute the vast majority of subsistence farmers (Boserup 1970; Staudt 1985b).

Aside from these biases, the individuals reached by extension workers were very few. What was needed was a great multiplier. Diffusion and two-step flow studies in the US highlighted the power of the radio, especially in early stages of the diffusion-adoption process. The advent of transistorized radio in the late 1950s, cheap, portable, and independent or electrification, accompanied by the publication of Daniel Lerner's premature pronouncement, "The Passing of Traditional Society" in 1958, offered great promise of satisfying this need.

PRO-MASS MEDIA AND PRO-LITERACY BIASES

Lerner (1958) examined the correlations between the expansion of economic activity being equated with *development* and a set of *modernizing* variables, chief among which were urbanization, literacy, mass media use, and democratic participation. His findings suggested that the spread of literacy in an urban milieu and the emergence of a *mobile personality* highly *empathetic* to modernizing influences provided the means to create within Third World societies a *climate of acceptance* of change. Implicit in his formulations, and in those of Wilbur Schramm (1964) who followed him, was the belief that the interaction of literacy and mass media was the means by which the masses would eventually break free of their stupefying bonds of traditionalism, heralding, as it were, the *passing of traditional society*.

Figure 2.2
Change Agency Communication and Mass Media Model of Development

Thus were born two new biases: the *pro-mass media bias* and its concomitant, the *pro-literacy bias* to help multiply the effects of change-agency interpersonal communication (see Figure 2.2). In this model, the mass media would be responsible for creating widespread awareness of, and interest in the innovations espoused by aid agencies. Contained in their messages would be the persuasive components which, by some alchemy of the *bullet theory* of communication, would produce a *climate of acceptance*. Change agents would then furnish targeted segments of adopters with the details of information and the skills necessary to make adoption of the innovations feasible. Early adopters would then presumably constitute role models for others in their social system to emulate. By these *demonstration effects*, the innovations would *trickle down* to the rest of the community. Over time, therefore, the innovations would diffuse across whole social systems.

There were strong precedents for this expectation in diffusion research in the US, as previously noted. However, even with the addition of mass media and literacy, the expected diffusion of innovations in the Third World did not eventuate as it had done in Western countries. In the industrialized West, when the rate with which an innovation diffused throughout a social system from the earliest adopter to the last *laggard* was cumulatively plotted over time, an S-shaped curve resulted. But when these studies were replicated in the Third World, the curves which resulted were considerably less than the total "S," signifying adoption by very few people (Ascroft and Gleason 1981; Whyte 1991b). In the few instances where completed S-shaped curves were indeed struck, they occurred only in those Third World social systems which somehow had already developed a "climate of acceptance" (Rogers 1969).

How were these findings to be explained? Was there something wrong, something intrinsically unattractive about the innovations selected for diffusion? Were the channel linkages between source and receiver sufficient to the task of reaching all potential adopters adequately? Or was there something perversely recalcitrant about the Third World farmers? Of these questions, communication researchers of the 1960s apparently chose to focus mainly on the last.

IN-THE-HEAD PSYCHOLOGICAL CONSTRAINTS TO DEVELOPMENT

In the Western world, hard-headed non-adopters of innovations were labeled *laggards* and described as *localite*, i.e., whose attention was "fixed on the rear-view mirror" rather than "on the road to change ahead" (Rogers 1962: 171). Non-adopters in the Third World were regarded in the same vein. The problem was that whereas non-adopters in Western nations constituted a small minority of holdouts, the Third World non-adopters were usually the vast majority. Curiously, this discrepancy alarmed nobody. The attitude seemed to be that most peasants were non-adopters, therefore, laggard, and so recalcitrant. They were thus to blame for failing to adopt perfectly good innovations.

The research based on these suspicions "confirmed" them. In 1969, Rogers drew upon the works of such development scholars as Hagen(1962), Hoselitz (1960), Inkeles (1969), Lerner (1958), and McClelland (1967) to abstract 10 in-the-head socio-psychological factors that were believed to constrain peasant adoption of innovations. He synthesized them into what he termed the *subculture of peasantry* (Rogers 1969). Thus, a new bias: the in-the-head psychological constraint bias was now added to the rest, suggesting a major modification to the formerly, fairly simple model of development.

The model implied that development of peasants would not ensue unless the psychological maladies afflicting them were first overcome. The burden that this orientation placed upon the powers of persuasion of change agents was onerous indeed. Changing peasants no longer consisted of simply convincing them of the superiority of Western innovations over their traditional ideas and practices; it now required the radical modification of a traditional mindset as a precondition of conversion.

Publication of the socio-psychological constraints had a chilling effect on development communication research. If the notion of a subculture of peasantry was true, then the prospect of producing change in such peasants was bleak indeed. To those concerned with designing strategies for bringing about peasant development, the variables in question: familism, fatalism, religiosity, and lack of deferred gratification, to mention a few of the in-the-head constraints, seemed essentially "non-manipulable" (Roling 1973).

EXTERNAL SOCIO-ECONOMIC CONSTRAINTS ON DEVELOPMENT

By the 1970s, US-trained Third World communication scholars began to assert themselves. They challenged the style and manner of US-dominated development communication research (Ascroft et al. 1973; Beltran 1976; Diaz-Bordenave 1976; Rahim 1976). Some were skeptical of the in-the-head variable bias which seemed to have led researchers into a *cul de sac*. They argued that the findings yielding the 10 factors of the subculture of peasantry were an artifact of the measurement instruments used. The factors seemed to be more in the eye of the beholders than in the reality of the peasants. This view led to an attempt to rethink diffusion research and implications for professional practice.

Field studies in Kenya supported this hypothesis. There, researchers found at least six non-psychologically based factors, which they termed "bottlenecks," and which together made it difficult, even impossible, for farmers to adopt recommended innovations (Ascroft 1973):

1. Lack of knowledge and skills about innovations to be adopted;
2. Lack of people involvement in the development planning process;
3. Lack of financial and material inputs necessary for adoption;
4. Inadequate market development for sale/purchase of produce;
5. Lack of infrastructure to facilitate distribution of information and material; and
6. Lack of off-season employment opportunities in rural areas.

Of the six factors, the lack of knowledge and skills was arguably an in-the-head rather than an external variable. However, removal of this lack depended upon receiving external inputs, not upon the individual changing long-held attitudes and beliefs.

The Kenya-based researchers showed that the removal of the above constraint plus the other lacks resulted in an accelerated adoption of innovations (Ascroft et al. 1973). To brand peasants as recalcitrant change-resisters without the prior removal of these bottlenecks constraining adoption, therefore, seemed tantamount to indicting them for a crime they had yet to have an opportunity to commit. So was created an alternative bias: the *external constraints on adoption bias*.

Similar conclusions about the prevalence of external constraints were being reached by development aid agencies. In 1973, Robert McNamara, then president of the World Bank, delivered his now famous "New Directions in Development" speech in which he called for a reassessment of existing development strategies (World Bank 1973). His contention was that, taken as a whole, development strategies had so far failed to produce the desired advancement of Third World countries. Indeed the plight of their people seemed to have deteriorated during the 1960s, which ironically had been proclaimed the First Development Decade at a time of optimism and faith in mainstream values and strategies.

A major shortcoming of existing strategies, McNamara believed, was the piecemeal approach to removing constraints. Needed, he argued, was a multidisciplinary broad-fronted *integrated rural development* approach which would seek, in one fell swoop, to remove all identifiable bottlenecks constraining adoption among peasants. McNamara additionally observed that the benefits of infrastructure development had not trickled down to the poor. Hence, he called for prioritizing basic needs, including food, shelter, education, and employment.

The findings about the external constraints on adoption, while perhaps not negating the possibility of internal psychological factors militating against adoption, at least provided a way out of the research *cul de sac*. For example, one of the major external constraints on development was the paucity of adequate, reliable, relevant, and timely information to overcome a lack of knowledge and skills about recommended innovations among potential peasant adopters. If peasants were not receiving information at all, or if they were receiving it in a form which they were unable to translate into useful knowledge and skills, researchers should subject the information sources and the messages constructed to greater scrutiny. Specifically, were the mass and interpersonal communications somehow at fault—encoded, structured, and treated in ways not useful to consumers? How and when were faulty communication strategies used? Did faulty communications at the outset fail to identify problems with the innovation(s) to be diffused? Were the channel linkages between sources and receivers too distant to encompass all receivers?

Some students of development communication began to focus their attention on searching for factors that could presumably make development projects more relevant to the needs of disadvantaged groups. They realized that many of the earlier projects had not given enough attention to the communication constraint. Their efforts, therefore, resulted in the conceptualization of communication as a dynamic support to development projects and activities, termed *development support communication* (DSC). The DSC specialist has the job of *bridging the communication gap* between the technical specialists with expertise in specific areas of knowledge (such as health, agriculture, and literacy) and potential users who may need such knowledge and its specific applications to improve their performance, increase their productivity, or improve their health. The DSC expert is expected to translate technical language and ideas into messages that would be comprehensible to users. It is in this context that the first edition of this book was grounded.

Box 2.1
Diversity in the New Millennium

If an attempt was made to reduce the earth's population to a hypothetical village of 100 people keeping all the existing ratios intact, we would have:

- 52 Asians, 21 Europeans, 14 from the Western hemisphere and 8 Africans
- 52 females and 48 males
- 70 would be non-white and 30 would be white
- 70 would be non-Christian, 30 would be Christian
- 89 would be heterosexual and 11 would be homosexual
- 6 people would possess 59 percent of the entire wealth and they would all be Americans
- 80 would live in sub-standard housing
- 70 would be functionally illiterate
- 50 would suffer from malnutrition
- 1 person would have college education
- 1 person would own a computer

Source: *Diversity in Action*, Fall 1999, Marathon-Ashland Petroleum Company.

CHALLENGES FOR THE 21ST CENTURY

Much has changed since 1991 when the first edition of this book was published, making it no longer possible to endorse one primary remedy for the problems of development communication. The end of the Cold War has brought ethnic and religious conflicts, highlighting the relevance of these social divisions in the development process. Feminist and environmental movements have altered traditional ways of thinking in every discipline, including development studies and communication studies. Questions of ethics in interventions across lines of class and culture increasingly challenge development choices and methodologies. The trend toward globalization has made links between processes of communication for development and processes of politics, economics, and ideology in society much more evident and problematic. New technologies are exponentially increasing global information flows and suggesting new dilemmas, as well as new strategies for communication in development. Also, while early critical communication scholarship (to be discussed in Chapters 4 and 6) focused on the economic expansionist goals of the nation-state, in the 1990s, a growing recognition of globalization led increasingly to the framing of these goals within the context of transnational corporations and the global network society (Castells 1996, 1997, 1998; Nordenstreng and Schiller 1993).

Castells' (1996, 1997, 1998) recent three-volume series on the network logic of the information age describe a new global paradigm in which power,

> is no longer concentrated in institutions (the state), organizations (capitalist firms), or symbolic controllers (corporate media, churches). It is diffused in global networks of wealth, power, information and images, which circulate and transmute in a system of variable geometry and dematerialized geography. Yet it does not disappear (Castells 1997: 359).

Certainly Castells is right in observing power shifts that accompany the increased transcendence of time and space by information networks. However, to the extent that networks generate profits, these power shifts will not produce much change in the basic reward structure of the market, which assumes interrelated divisions of labor, power, knowledge, and wealth. In this global network/market system, the financial benefits will continue to go to those already at or capable of reaching the top, most of whom live in so-called industrialized nations. Additionally, Castells concludes that the network society will continue to widen the gap between the haves and the have nots, increasingly divided into those with access to cyberspace and other forms of mobility and those without access. While the increased globalization of the planet is rendering national boundaries less relevant, Castells (1998) concedes that a "Fourth World" that consists of large parts of Africa, South America and Asia will be almost completely excluded as irrelevant to the global network economy. Many scholars and other observers are now referring to a *digital divide* that separates peoples and countries in terms of their access and use of the new electronic networks of information.

We do not reject the value of the DSC specialist as an aid in many development contexts, but neither do we endorse it—or endorse it in the same manner—in every instance. Each intervention varies by historical, cultural, political, and economic context. To the extent that interventions are desirable, there are many ways of assessing goals and proper approaches. This text attempts to untangle this postmodern complexity, providing an introduction to mainstream approaches, critiques of these approaches, and new possibilities for the 21st century.

SUMMARY

Development in its modern form dates back to World War II. The years since World War II have witnessed the political emancipation of most of the Third World from colonization and the birth of the UN, marking the formal beginning of development aid to Third World countries. Concern for the plight of the people in the Third World countries moved US President Truman to propose the 1949 Point Four program, which was to be the Third World version of the Marshall Plan. The philosophical consistencies between the Marshall Plan and the Point Four program were very clear. Both aimed to alleviate suffering and both aimed to do so via capital investment. Countries considered non-communist or "freedom-loving" qualified as beneficiaries of aid.

In the 1960s, the emphasis was on technological transfer from the North to the South. Initially, the pro-innovation transfer paradigm appeared alluringly simple and straightforward. It had been largely derived from the Marshall Plan to resuscitate war-ravaged Europe and aimed to make funds available for pre-existing European expertise to apply to reconstruction. It was soon clear, however, that the postcolonial Third World problem was quite different, as there was no adequate pre-existing base of expertise or infrastructure. More significantly people's lives had to radically change. Development, therefore, involved not simply the transfer of technology but also the communication of ideas and skills to make possible the successful adoption of innovations. To the pro-innovation bias, consequently was added a *pro-persuasion bias*. The extension system decided what innovations were best for its clients, followed by campaigns to convince them of the wisdom of its choice. And so was set in motion a one-way flow of influence-oriented messages from change agencies at the top to the rural peasantry at the bottom, a process of *top-down communication*.

Two new biases: the *pro-mass media bias* and its concomitant, the *pro-literacy bias* were introduced to help multiply the effects of change-agency interpersonal communication. The mass media would create widespread awareness of, and interest in the innovations espoused by aid agencies. Contained in their messages would be the persuasive components which, by some alchemy of the *bullet theory* of communication, would produce a *climate of acceptance*. However, even with the addition of mass media and literacy, the expected diffusion of innovations in the Third World did not eventuate as it had done in Western countries. In the industrialized West, when the rate with which an innovation diffused throughout a social system from the earliest adopter to the last *laggard* was cumulatively plotted over time, an S-shaped curve resulted. But when these studies were replicated in the Third World, the curves which resulted were considerably less than the total "S," signifying adoption by very few people. Thus, a new bias: the in-the-head psychological constraint bias was now added to the rest, suggesting a major modification to the formerly fairly simple model of development. The model implied that development would not ensue unless the psychological maladies afflicting peasants were first overcome. Changing them no longer consisted of simply persuasion; it now required the radical modification of a traditional mindset as a precondition of conversion.

By the 1970s, US-trained Third World communication scholars began to challenge the style and manner of US-dominated development communication research. So was created an alternative bias: the *external constraints on adoption bias*. The findings regarding external constraints on adoption, while perhaps not negating the possibility of internal psychological factors working against adoption, at least provided a way out of the research *cul de sac*. For example, one of the major external constraints was the paucity of information to overcome a lack of knowledge and skills about innovations among potential adopters. Students of development communication began to focus on searching for factors that could make projects more relevant to the needs of disadvantaged groups. They realised that many of the earlier projects had not given enough attention to the communication constraint. Their efforts, therefore, resulted in the conceptualization of communication as a dynamic support to projects and activities, termed *development support communication* (DSC). The

DSC specialist has the job of *bridging the communication gap* between the technical specialists with expertise in specific areas of knowledge and potential users.

While the addition of the DSC specialist may be helpful in many instances, it is crucial to recognize that every development situation is unique and complex, and that the local level of the development project is ultimately inseparable from global and national political-economic structures and processes. Additionally, the exponential spread of new technologies in the 21st century, increased globalization and the decreased supremacy of the nation-state bring new complexities and challenges to development communication. The advisability of and nature of intervention, including communication intervention, varies by historical, cultural, political, and economic context. Analyses of context should consider relevant social divisions (such as gender, class, race, and religion), issues of environment, and other ethical issues involved.

NOTES

1. Portions of this chapter have been revised from a conference paper prepared with the help of Dr. Joseph Ascroft, Iowa City, USA.
2. For details, see UN Internet web sites, e.g., http://www.un.org/members.
3. UNICEF originally stood for the United Nations International Children's Emergency Fund.
4. The World Bank and the IMF are often confused, yet their goals are distinct. The World Bank is a development institution that provides loans to encourage development. The IMF does have a fund from which countries can borrow, although its main mission is to monitor monetary and exchange rate policies. In addition, the IMF serves all member nations, whereas the World Bank only lends to developing nations (see Hoy 1998: 76–79 for a discussion of areas of difference and overlap).
5. Financial assistance is classified as ODA only if private capital is unavailable and if there is a grant element of at least 25 percent, making the terms clearly more favorable than available in commercial markets. Additionally, it should not include military and security assistance. However, as Hoy notes, military assistance is usually included in countries' internal aid statistics, which confuses reports of aid (Hoy 1998).
6. The USAID model, introduced to many countries in the two decades after World War II, was based on the US Department of Agriculture's Federal Extension Service and land grant colleges. According to Adams (1982: 53), "In its pure form it has rarely taken root because few countries in the Third World had universities with sufficient status and funds to link research with a dynamic extension service in the surrounding countryside."

7. See, e.g., Blum (1986). Both the authors of this book are familiar with agricultural extension systems in developing countries through their travels and research.

8. Under this system, introduced by the World Bank and still in use, master farmers embarked on a regular schedule of travel to fixed sites where they gave demonstrations. See Benor and Harrison (1977).

DEVELOPMENT DISCOURSE, MODERNIZATION THEORY, AND COMMUNICATION

CHAPTER 3

THE ENTERPRISE OF MODERNIZATION AND
THE DOMINANT DISCOURSE OF DEVELOPMENT

> Knowledge is power, but power is also knowledge. Power decides
> what is knowledge and what is not knowledge.
>
> Claude Alvares (1992: 230)

Among the most powerful paradigms to originate after World War II, with enormous social, cultural, and economic consequences, was that of modernization. Modernization is based on liberal political theory and is therefore grounded in the grand project of "Enlightenment," namely reasoning, rationality, objectivity, and other philosophical principles of Western science. Modernization approaches, including more recent neo-classical economic theories, extol scientific rationality and individualism. Economic growth via the Western model of adopting a capitalist economic system, building up formal infrastructure, and acquiring technologies is prioritized. Implicit in the discourse of modernization is a certain philosophy of what development in the Third World should be, and how it should be brought about.

Thus, a *dominant paradigm* of development guided intellectual thinking and practice from the 1940s through the 1960s, and was influential in development communication theory and practice as well. Everett Rogers (1976b: 121) noted, "this concept of development grew out of certain historical events, such as the Industrial Revolution in Europe and the United States, the colonial experience in Latin America, Africa, and Asia, the quantitative empiricism of North American social science, and capitalistic economic/political philosophy." Rogers distilled four overlapping elements in this conception of development (Rogers, 1976c: 49):

1. Economic growth through industrialization and accompanying urbanization was the key to development. It was approximately equal to passing through the Industrial Revolution. It was also assumed that development performance could be measured quantitatively in economic terms.
2. The choice of the scientific method was to be the Western quantitative empirical research while the technology was to be capital-intensive and labour-extensive,[1] imported predominantly from the West.
3. In order to guide and speed up the process of development, planning should be centralized and controlled by economists and bankers.
4. Underdevelopment was mainly due to problems within developing nations rather than in their external relationships with other countries.

Certainly economic growth and scientific values constitute key themes in "development" as the solution to "underdevelopment." Most problems plaguing Third World nations were diagnosed as economic in nature. As Rogers noted (1976c), economists were ultimately in charge of development plans. Five-year plans were launched in several countries to dovetail development activities and help bring about orderly economic progress. Bilateral and multilateral aid organizations were involved in these plans. This approach was at the macro level. Problems were identified and solutions offered at the higher levels of government. Information and other inputs were then channeled down to local communities. Participatory or autonomous development by local communities was considered slow, inefficient, and more often than not, unlikely (Rogers 1976c).

In the dominant paradigm, *industrialization* was considered the main route to successful economic growth. At least, that was the means by which North America and West Europe had developed in the late 19th century. So, Third World countries were encouraged to invest in a program of industrialization such as hydroelectric projects, steel industries and a diversity of manufacturing units. Development performance was measured by *quantitative indicators* such as: gross national product (GNP) and per capita income. These indicators were considered objective and straightforward to measure, especially when compared with alternative concepts such as freedom, justice, and human rights. They also related to the quantitative and empirical bias of North American social sciences (Nordenstreng 1968; Rogers 1976c).

As a corollary to prioritizing economic growth, quantitative empirical science, a product of Enlightenment in Europe, was uncritically accepted as the dominant scientific methodology. The aim of this science was to produce knowledge, and to understand, categorize, explain, and predict aspects of the external reality (Singleton et al. 1993). Some of the important characteristics that distinguish this method from other ways of knowing are:

Science is positivist. Derived from the writings of Comte and Mill, positivism is the dominant feature of the Western scientific method. This involves other concepts such as quantification, hypothesis testing, and objective measurement (Wimmer and Dominick 2000). A major assumption of positivistic science is that: (*a*) reality is objective and exists apart from the observer; and (*b*) it can be seen and experienced by all in essentially the same way. In this type of research, the measurement instruments exist independently of the researcher.

Science is empirical. The scientist is concerned with an external world that is knowable and potentially measurable. Thus, non-empirical or metaphysical explanations are ruled out.

Science is objective. Clear rules and procedures are constructed to distance the researcher from the objects or phenomena being studied. This is to control the subjectivity of the researcher and maximize the trustworthiness of the results.

Science had played a major role in the articulation of the colonial discourse (Adams 1995) and was then recommended for the development of the ex-colonies in the Third World. President Kennedy of the US made the following recommendation to the US Congress extolling the benefits of modern science:

> Throughout Latin America millions of people are struggling to free themselves from bonds of poverty and hunger and ignorance. To the North and East they see the abundance which modern science can bring. They know the tools of progress are within their reach (Kennedy 1961).

This quote demonstrates the 1960s faith in Western science to solve problems of underdevelopment. Science was the backbone of technology that was ushered in after the Industrial Revolution. In the developing countries of the South, the science-based technology was to increase manifold the per capita production of material goods (Ullrich 1992). It constituted the core of the industrialization that was prescribed for developing countries. More often than not, the capital and machine-intensive technology substituted for labor that was abundantly available in the Third World nations. The badly needed capital for the new technology was provided by national governments, and often, supplemented by loans from bilateral and multilateral agencies, and transnational corporations.

It is abundantly clear that the dominant paradigm of modernization supports a Western political-economic agenda and also is consistent with the values of Western science, grounded in Enlightenment thought. However, in this chapter we show that the origins and implications of modernization go well beyond economic theory and motives. Modernization also is a social and psychological theory, in that it suggests a social evolutionary path and has implications for individual values and priorities as well. Additionally, and very significant in our discussion, modernization is an ideology and a discourse. In fact, the discourse of modernization has invented a new way of thinking for people of many countries in the South (Melkote and Kandath 2001). Thus, modernization is not just one type of process, but a package of mutually reinforcing processes that suggest particular goals for change. Tipps (1973: 204) describes the modernization process as:

> a transition, or rather a series of transitions from primitive, subsistence economies to technology-intensive, industrialized economies; from subject to participant political cultures; from closed, ascriptive status systems to open, achievement-oriented systems; from extended to nuclear kinship units; from religious to secular ideologies; and so on. Thus conceived, modernization is not simply a process of change, but one which is defined in terms of the goals toward which it is moving.

These interwoven changes are motivated by a combination of altruistic, ideological and political-economic motives, and all enable the West to manage, produce, and organize the Third World politically, economically, sociologically, psychologically, scientifically, militarily, and perhaps above all, imaginatively (Crush 1995). In this chapter we discuss three major facets of modernization: modernization as an economic model, as social evolutionary theory, and as discourse.

MODERNIZATION AS AN ECONOMIC MODEL

The dominant paradigm of development that ruled the social sciences prescribed a particular economic path to modernization: the neo-classical approach that had served as an important model for Western economists. Adam Smith in *The Wealth of Nations* (1776) originally proposed this approach, which was later supported and enriched by other Western economists such as Ricardo, Schumpeter, Keynes, Hirschman, and Nurske.

The dominant paradigm encouraged macro-economic planning and promoted a high degree of state intervention in the economy. The model was mainly concerned with rapid economic growth as measured by the rate of growth of output (i.e., the GNP). Thus, an important goal of economists was to accelerate and maintain high rates of growth. The theory of development in this orthodox economic approach was simple. There were two main factors that were important: (1) *productive resources* a society had, and (2) *economic institutions* to use and to guide the use of the resources (Weaver and Jameson 1978: 9).

Productive Resources

The quantity of output of goods and services of a system was a function of several factor inputs: capital, labor, land and other natural resources, technology, infrastructure, and entrepreneurship. A brief discussion of the salient features of each input is useful.

Labor. The emphasis was on increasing the quality and quantity of output by specialization and division of labor. The quality of labor could be enhanced and adapted to the needs of modern industry by improving its physical and mental capacities (Weaver and Jameson 1978). Developing nations were persuaded to invest in the improvement of human resources mainly through the upgrading of skills and attitudes. These were to be brought about through institutional programs and other training sessions (Schultz 1963). Also, the model promoted the migration of labor from the traditional rural sectors into the urban, manufacturing areas.

Capital. Capital formation occupied a very important place. Individuals and entire societies were required to defer consumption and save capital so that it may be invested to build such physical capital as heavy industries, steel factories, mills, and dams (Weaver and Jameson 1978). Development of heavy industry was significant since it was used to produce other goods and machinery. Thus, industrialization, particularly the capital-intensive variety, was given utmost importance (Hirschman 1958; Nurske 1953). In fact, industrialization was synonymous with development. One important means of generating sufficient capital for industrialization was through redistribution of income and resources to capitalists and entrepreneurs. The assumption was that these groups would reinvest the capital in productive ways to generate more capital. Weaver and Jameson summarize this approach very well:

> Theorists who take this starting point suggest that development will come about if profits can be increased, for that increases capitalists' income, which will lead to increased savings, which will lead to increased investment in capital goods, which will lead to industrialization—which equals development (Weaver and Jameson 1978: 12).

The approach of creating inequality initially by redistribution of income and resources to capitalists with the hope of a *trickle-down* of benefits later to others in the population was a fond notion of several post-war economists such as Arthur Lewis, Ragnar Nurske, and Harvey Leibenstein. It was articulated very well in the Harod-Domar and Mahal-anobis planning models in India (Weaver and Jameson 1978).

Land. Industrialization was dependent on the efficient use of land. Many economists believed that industrial development had to be preceded by agricultural development (Eicher and Witt 1964; Johnston and Mellor 1961; Myrdal 1968; Schultz 1964). At least, that is the way it had happened in the Western countries. Agriculture made several important contributions for an orderly and effective development of industry. It produced surplus food and labor that directly benefited the industrial sector. Also, the export of agricultural output provided resources for the import of physical capital such as machinery needed for local industry. Importantly, a developed agricultural sector provided an effective and efficient internal market for industrial output.

The key to greater productivity in the agricultural sector was to shift from human/animal labor-intensive techniques to a machine-intensive approach. Weaver and Jameson noted:

> This means more and more capital-intensive agriculture, and generally it means larger and larger farms with more and more output per worker. United States agriculture has carried this furthest: four percent of the labor force produces enough food for the whole population, plus a considerable amount for export. This is the pattern suggested for agriculture, and a similar pattern of capitalization is suggested for natural resource industries (Weaver and Jameson 1978: 14).

Technical- and management-intensive schemes such as the Green Revolution were vigorously pursued in many countries in Southeast Asia. Farmers were encouraged to adopt high-yielding strains of staple crops such as rice, wheat, and maize along with a host of other production techniques. At least initially, this helped some of these countries to increase grain production for domestic (mainly urban) consumption and export to the international market.

Technology and Entrepreneurship. Technology was viewed as central to the growth of productive agricultural and industrial sectors (Abramovitz 1956; Denison 1962; Schumpeter 1934; Veblen 1966; Weaver and Jameson 1978). Therefore, the hiring of foreign experts and transfer of technical know-how from the developed Western nations was considered extremely crucial for development in Third World nations.

Finally, the entrepreneur was the catalyst in the process of economic development. Like Lerner's (1958) grocer in Balgat, Turkey, the entrepreneur was a risk-taker. He/she wanted to discard the traditional way of doing things and imitate or supplant new techniques, especially those practiced in the West. Rogers (1962) and Schramm (1964) describe the entrepreneur as an innovator who "destroys the old way and initiates a process which will replace the old way with an innovation which is organizationally more successful" (Weaver and Jameson 1978: 15).

Economic Institutions

In addition to productive resources, the orthodox economic model relies on a set of institutions to guide the use of resources. These include the Bretton Woods institutions, the UN agencies, the IMF, the World Bank, private corporations, government ministries, and research universities. Following the requirements and assumptions of the capitalist paradigm, these were characterized by and/or otherwise promoted (Weaver and Jameson 1978):

1. The private ownership of all factors of production;
2. An interrelated market system for means of production (labor, land, and capital) and for output;
3. A private capitalist firm for production of output (a private organization with no direct control from any other authority except itself, functioning rationally to produce the optimum profit in an orderly market); and
4. Free trade at the international, national, and local levels.

The development strategy that was emphasized was the principle of *laissez-faire*. In French, this would mean—complete independence. Thus, in the orthodox paradigm, the capitalists and entrepreneurs were to be left alone by the government and other authorities. To the extent possible, the role of the government was to be confined to maintaining law and order, and providing the right climate for capitalists to engage in profitable production.

In sum, this was the economic model that had worked successfully in England and later in the United States, and it was precisely the model that was prescribed for the development of the Third World nations. As we will show later, the system did not always transfer readily to developing nations. Additionally, it was frequently insensitive to the needs of certain demographic and minority groups, and it resulted in much environmental degradation.

Nonetheless, the model remains dominant today, adapting to rapid political-economic and technological changes. It is abundantly evident in development policies and projects emphasizing private sector development and entrepreneurship, and technological advancement. It is also evident in international agreements, such as the North American Free Trade Agreement (NAFTA) of 1994 and GATT. As the goals of economic development have increasingly been framed globally, within transnational structures and networks (e.g., the World Trade Organization) that transcend space, time, or nation-states, modernization has taken new forms (Appadurai 1996; Castells 1996, 1997, 1998). Yet the basic assumptive framework emphasizing profit, privatization, and technological growth remains intact.

MODERNIZATION AS SOCIAL EVOLUTION

Cowen and Shenton (1995) posit that the idea of development was quite old even before "Truman's invocation" (p. 29). In Europe, more than a century earlier, the idea of development was used to create order out of the social anarchy of poverty, unemployment, and rapid urbanization. The notion of development was used to craft managerial strategies and interventions to cope with the social disorder in 19th-century Europe and later in the colonies (Cowen and Shenton 1995). However, with the creation of the Third World in the post-Bretton Woods period, theories and concepts that recapitulated the unique West European and North American transition from a traditional to a modern society were used to prescribe models of development for the Third World. An important concern among industrialized nations was how to develop the societies just emancipated from centuries of colonial rule.

The main trend in sociological theory was extrapolation of concepts generated from the West European and North American analysis to the study of development in the Third World nations. As Fejes comments, "it was generally assumed that a nation became truly modern and developed when it arrived at that point where it closely resembled Western industrial nations in terms of political and economic behavior and institutions, attitudes toward technology and innovation, and social and psychic mobility" (Fjes 1976: 4). The dominant paradigm vis-a-vis Third World development was based on an application of the evolutionary concept of Darwin to social change:

> Not only was change in one social sphere able to stimulate change in others, but social modernization was able to generate continuing change, and also to absorb the stress of change and adapt itself to

changing demands. In other words, the process seemed relatively irreversible. Once the necessary conditions were established for take-off, a country took off, became modern, and stayed modern (Schramm 1976: 46).

Theories in Sociology of Development

The transition of European societies from a traditional and feudal structure toward more advanced social stages, has been an important concern of social theorists from the classical to the modern age. Considerable litera-ture is available on the forces and set of relationships that propelled Europe from the largely agricultural-feudal order to the complex, highly differ-entiated, capitalist-industrial society. In fact, "the issue of European trans-formation has given rise to what is, without doubt, the core of classic and of most modern sociological theory" (Portes 1976: 56). Social theor-ists during this time were concerned with the upheaval of the existing societies and the new social forms arising from industrialization, urban-ization, and modernization. These scholarly efforts resulted in various theories on social evolution. Portes (1976: 61) noted that Morgan, Comte, Spencer, Kidd, and Ward were the proponents of the evolutionary per-spective in human societies. In their theories of development, the trans-formation of cultures was compared to the evolution of organisms as articulated in the biological sciences. In other words, these theorists saw very little difference in the phylogeny of biological species and the transformation of human societies. The growth of cultures was inextric-ably tied, as in the growth of organisms, to a series of inevitable and irreversible stages. In these theories of social evolution, the development of societies followed a unilinear path and the major stages of growth were universal. However, it was quite transparent that these social theorists were preoccupied with the historical transformation of the Western countries. In their models, the highest stage of development or evolution was represented by advanced European nations of the 19th and early 20th centuries.

Charles Darwin's classic *On the Origin of Species* (1859) was the inspiration for the evolutionary view of social change. Yet Darwin's thesis was intended to explain the phylogeny of species, not social systems. Darwin argued that all organisms had evolved from simpler forms and that the general direction of biological evolution was unilinear, i.e., toward more complex forms. The early social theorists of the *evolutionist school* applied Darwin's ideas to the process of modernization of human societies. The more prominent of these theorists were Herbert Spencer and William Sumner. Spencer even applied Darwin's famous principle of *the survival of the fittest* to human cultures. He claimed that Western societies were superior to all other races and had excelled because they were better adapted to face the changing conditions in the process of modernization of societies. This school of thought, termed *Social Darwinism*, won acceptance even among intellectuals in the latter half of the 19th century (Berger 1974; Robertson, 1977; Ryan 1976).

The theories of social evolution influenced and gave rise to significant concepts and hypotheses in the sociology of development. However, while the earlier theories were explanatory of the historical transformation of the West, the newer theories in the 20th century were used to compare the development of Third World nations with those in Europe and North America, often in overly simplistic bipolar fashion. These newer ideas emerged not just from social evolutionary theory, but also from the larger context of Enlightenment thought, which encouraged dualistic thinking and concepts.

Tradition versus Modernity

The earlier models were based on a dichotomous conception of tradition versus modernity (Eisenstadt 1976). These theories were essentially bipolar, where the universal stages in the earlier theories of social evolution were reduced to ideal-typical end points. These ideal-typical extremes, however, were descriptive of the assumed beginning and end points of the process of social transformation of the nations in Europe and North America. Portes (1976: 62) noted that "theorists in this tradition were less concerned with encompassing the entire history of mankind than with apprehending that moment of European transition from a feudal-agricultural to a capitalist-industrial order." This is not surprising, as it clearly reflected Enlightenment thought, including assumptions about dualistic values, one-half of which was considered important for scientific progress in society and the other half unimportant to progress.[2] Several of these bipolar theories of modernization are given in Table 3.1.

In these theories, the earlier state was the traditional society, which was conceptualized as a small, mostly rural community where everybody knew each other, where interpersonal relations were close with strong group solidarity and kinship ties. The end stage, on the other hand, was a large, mostly urban society where interpersonal relations were

Table 3.1
Bipolar Theories of Modernization

Maine (1907)	Status versus Contract
Durkheim (1933)	Mechanic versus Organic Solidarity
Toennies (1957)	*Gemeinschaft* versus *Gesellschaft*
Lerner (1958)	Traditional versus Modern Society
Cooley (1962)	Primary versus Secondary Social Attachments
Redfield (1965)	Folk versus Urban Societies
Castells (1996, 1997, 1998)	Fourth World versus Network Society

impersonal, where there was hardly any group solidarity and close kinship ties. This society was conceptualized as a loose association of people in which tradition and shared norms and values no longer had a dominant influence. Also, in these theories, as articulated cogently in Durkheim's analysis, the two ideal types differed based on the social bond—"organic" in the traditional set-up and "mechanistic" in the modern society. The transformation from the traditional to the modern society required greater functional specialization and structural differentiation. These structural changes brought about value shifts in the direction of individualization, secularism, universalism and rationalization.

Bipolar theories and models continue to the present, as indicated in Table 3.1. Castells (1997: 359) predicts a new global paradigm based on the network logic of the information age in which power "is diffused in global networks of wealth, power, information and images . . . . Yet it does not disappear." The new network society of those with access to cyberspace will contrast sharply with a Fourth World, that is almost completely excluded as irrelevant to the global network economy.

Pattern Variables Scheme

The pattern variables scheme was a contribution of Talcott Parsons (1964a) to general social theory. However, this scheme served as an extension of the classic bipolar theories and was used by the theorists of the functionalist perspective as a tool for diagnosing social change in different societies, particularly the contrast between the Western societies and those in the Third World (Portes 1976: 62). Hoselitz (1960) used the pattern variables schemes as a model of the sociological aspects of economic growth. In this scheme, traditional societies have certain common characteristics: ascribed roles that are functionally unintegrated and oriented toward narrow particularistic goals. Modern societies, on the other hand, had roles assigned or acquired through achievement rather than birth; they were oriented toward broad, secular, and universal norms (Levy 1996; Portes 1976). When attempts were made to transform the pattern variables scheme as a theory of societal development, the consequence was a set of generalizations extrapolating concepts from the European and North American historical experience to describe and prescribe modernization in Third World countries (Hoselitz 1960).

Development as Social Differentiation

This notion of development was a direct extension of the social evolutionary theories of the 19th century. According to this theory of development, societies modernize through greater and greater differentiation in their institutions. In simpler societies, there is hardly any differentiation in social institutions. A single institution may perform several functions. For example, the family may not only serve the function of reproduction but also take care of socialization, education, and even economic production. However, human societies, like organisms in biological theory, pass through evolutionary stages to reach higher levels of complexity as exhibited through greater specialization of functions. A process of differentiation takes place where several institutions take over the functions that were hitherto undifferentiated and performed by one or a couple of institutions. The process of differentiation was then followed by the concomitant process of integration. As Portes commented:

> the theory of society based on this notion is one in which pressures faced at a given point are eliminated through increasing specialization and differentiation, which, in turn, give rise to problems of integration, which are solved through emerging networks of interdependence. The whole process results in an ever-growing societal "complexity" or "systemness" (Portes 1976: 63).

Again, this theory of social differentiation was employed for the comparative diagnosis of development in developed and underdeveloped societies (Smelser 1973).

Evolutionary Universals

This was another contribution of Parsons (1964b) to general social theory. He identified and described structural features of the systems in the West that helped them to survive in their environment in the process of societal development: bureaucratic organization, money, markets, democratic association, and common legal system. These universals were prescribed as essential for modernization of the underdeveloped societies.

As Schramm noted, perhaps the best overall summary of this structural-functionalistic approach was Karl Deutsch's (1961) concept of *social mobilization* defined as "the process in which old social, economic, and psychological commitments are eroded and broken down and people become available for new patterns of socialization and behavior" (Schramm 1976: 46). An index of this process included not only higher social differentiation and integration of roles and institutions, but also the development of evolutionary universals described earlier.

In sum, the Western countries were treated as models of political, economic, social, and cultural modernization that the Third World nations would do well to emulate. The advanced Western nations had a wide range of systemic autonomy, i.e., their capacity to cope with a range of social, cultural, technological, and economic issues in the process of social change (Eisenstadt 1976: 31). The Third World nations, on the other hand, lacking the higher differentiation of roles and institutions, the evolutionary universals, and other qualitative characteristics of industrial societies, were limited in their capacity to cope with problems or crises or even master their environment.

Unilinear Model of Development

Among the proponents of the unilinear model of development, Walt Rostow and Daniel Lerner deserve special mention. They stated explicitly that once key institutions and certain behavior patterns were established, development was more or less sustained. The changes were irreversible and the process of development moved in a common universal direction.

Rostow expounded his economic growth theory in *The Stages of Economic Growth: A Non-Communist Manifesto* (1960). Essentially, he constructed a five-stage model of transition ranging from a traditional economy to a modern industrial complex: the traditional society, preconditions for take-off, take-off, drive to maturity, and the age of high mass consumption. He believed that every society would pass through these five stages of economic growth leading finally to the last phase: the age of high mass consumption. In Rostow's model, the traditional society was "hampered by limited production facilities, based on pre-Newtonian notions of science and technology, and constrained by rigid social structure and irrational psychological attitudes" (Rostow 1960: 4–5).

The preconditions for take-off were developed when insights of modern science were applied to new production functions in agriculture and industry. People increasingly believed that economic progress was necessary for a better life and also were willing to save and take risks in pursuit of private profit. Institutions such as banks appeared to mobilize savings, infrastructure developed, notably in transportation and communications. It was during the take-off stage that a nation transformed from a traditional into a modern state:

> The take-off is the interval when the old blocks and resistances to steady growth are finally overcome. The forces making for economic progress, which yielded limited bursts and enclaves of modern activity, expand and come to dominate the society. Growth becomes its normal condition. Compound interest becomes built, as it were, into its habits and institutional structure (Rostow 1960: 7).

During this period, the rate of investment and savings increased from 5 percent to 10 percent of the national income, new industries expanded yielding huge profits, which were reinvested in new physical capital. In turn, the new factories stimulated the factors of capital and labor. Finally, there were revolutionary improvements in the agricultural sector.

After the take-off, a steady rate of growth in the economy could be regularly sustained. Output was ahead of population increases, there was an improvement in technology giving rise to new and more efficient industries, and the economy found its place in profitable international trade. Finally, the society entered the stage of high mass consumption. Large numbers of people gained a command over consumption that went beyond basic necessities to include luxury goods and services. The United States, Canada, Japan, and countries of Western Europe constitute examples of nations that have reached the final stage of mass consumption.

Lerner saw the dynamic of social development as: a nucleus of mobile, change-accepting personalities, a growing mass media system to spread the ideas and attitudes of social mobility and change, the interaction of urbanization, literacy and industrialization, higher per capita income and political participation (Lerner 1958). Lerner believed that these institutional developments (which had already occurred in Western nations) would lead to a take-off toward modernization. Lerner also suggested a psychological prerequisite among individuals called *empathy*. More will be said about this in the next section. Like other social theorists, Lerner saw systemic interconnections between the various institutional developments. As Schramm noted: "the essential point was that growth in one of these spheres stimulates growth in others, and all spheres of society moved forward together toward modernization" (Schramm 1976: 45–46).

MODERNIZATION AS INDIVIDUAL CHANGE

All modernization theories emphasizing evolutionary change were not necessarily at the macro level. While social and institutional evolution is considered necessary for modernization, some have argued that this cannot occur unless individuals change first (Weiner 1966). Weiner believed that attitudinal and value changes were prerequisites to creating a modern, socio-economic polity. However, the cause–effect relationship was hard to establish, and there was no categorical answer to whether attitudes or institutions change first. Nevertheless, all scholars in this disciplinary area believed that neither modern science and technology nor modern institutions could be successfully grafted on a society whose people were basically traditional, uneducated, self-centered, or unscientific in their thinking and attitudes (Weiner 1966).

McClelland, Inkeles, Hagen, Lerner, and Rogers were among those who emphasized individual values and attitudes. The intellectual source for this school of thought was Weber's (1958) thesis on the *Protestant Ethic* and the general trend in American sociology on value-normative complexes. However, Portes (1976) comments that while these scholars borrowed Weber's conceptualization, they did not necessarily use it within a proper historical-structural context. Weber's thesis on the *Protestant Ethic* was firmly anchored within the power relationships, structural constraints, and political-economic interests of Catholic Europe. Such was not the case with these writings regarding the value-normative complexes of individuals in Third World countries.

Let us summarize the hypotheses of scholars in this area:

David McClelland (1966) was interested in identifying and measuring the variable that might be the impulse to modernization. There were several questions which interested him. Why did some nations "take-off" into rapid economic growth while others stood still or declined? Why were the Greeks of 6th century BC very enterprising? Why did North

America, which was inhabited by the English, develop faster than South America, occupied by Spaniards at about the same time? In other words, McClelland was interested in what impulse produced economic growth and modernization. What was this impulse and where did it originate?

McClelland (1966) hypothesized a *mental virus* that made people behave in a particularly energetic way. This virus received the name "n.Ach" or need for achievement. It was identified in a sample of a person's thoughts, by examining whether the thoughts were about *doing things better* than they had been done before, doing things more efficiently and faster with less labor. When the popular literature of a country was coded for the presence of n.Ach over long periods of time, it was found that there was a direct relation between the virus and economic growth. For example, the literature of the Greeks in 6th century BC had higher content of n.Ach than in later Greek literature. Similarly, the English literature of the 16th century had more n.Ach content than the Spanish literature of the same period. Could it be that the n.Ach virus might be a part of the impulse to economic growth? McClelland (1966) found that this became more apparent when a nation's *infection level* with the virus was estimated by coding the imaginative stories the country used to teach its very young children. It was found that this led to a spurt in economic activity a few years later. McClelland conducted an experiment in the city of Hyderabad in India where a group of businessmen were *injected* with the virus via a 10-day self-development course (McClelland 1966). Later, these men took their work more seriously, became innovative, and overall had a genuine desire to excel.

McClelland cautioned that n.Ach by itself was not enough. The other input which was equally important was the social consciousness, i.e., working for the common good. Therefore, in summary, the impulse to modernization, according to McClelland, consisted in part of a personal variable—n.Ach—and in part of a social virtue—interest in the welfare of others (McClelland 1966).

Everett Hagen (1962) attempted to empirically determine measures that influenced entrepreneurial activity. He introduced the concept of *withdrawal of status respect*, a complex psychoanalytic variable. Portes summarized this concept thus:

Humiliations resulting from status withdrawal among parents have certain psychic consequences for their sons who, in turn, transmit them to their own children. After a complicated evolution of complexes and stages, the "virus" finally matures and is ready to do its work in society (Portes 1976: 70).

Thus, according to Hagen, certain creative individuals rejected traditional values, took on new roles, and became innovative. He provided examples of Soviet Russia, Japan, and Germany where economic development was sustained by creative individuals whose ancestors had suffered *withdrawal of status respect*. Clearly, according to Hagen, the impetus for socio-economic development was provided by a psychological characteristic present in certain groups of people.

Daniel Lerner (1958) based a substantial part of his elaborate theory of modernization on social-psychological variables. At the heart of his model was a nucleus of mobile, change-accepting individuals. These individuals could be distinguished by their high capacity for identification with new aspects of their environment. Lerner called this attribute *empathy* which signified the capacity of a person to put himself/herself in another person's shoes. For example, a Turkish goatherd would exhibit empathy if he could imagine himself as the president of his country or the editor of a newspaper. Lerner believed that a high empathic capacity was the predominant personal style in Western countries that were also industrial, urban, literate, and participant. Lerner suggested the development of empathy as an indispensable skill for people moving out of traditional settings.

Alex Inkeles (1966) developed his conceptual model of individual modernity based on research in six developing countries. He argued that the transformation of individuals was both a means to an end and an end in itself of the development process. Inkeles used nine attitude items to construct standard scales of modernity, which he later used to identify the character of the modern person: (*i*) readiness for new experiences and openness to innovation, (*ii*) disposition to form and hold opinions, (*iii*) democratic orientation, (*iv*) planning habits, (*v*) belief in human and personal efficacy, (*vi*) belief that the world is calculable, (*vii*) stress on personal and human dignity, (*viii*) faith in science and technology, and (*ix*) belief in distributive justice (Inkeles 1969). The psychological characteristics outlined above, delineated Inkeles' concept of the spirit of modernity which he considered an essential prerequisite for economic growth.

Other scholars concerned with the role of value-normative complexes in modernization prepared exhaustive lists of the social-psychological attributes of modernity. Some of these were: mobility, high participation in organization and electoral process, interest articulation, interest aggregation, high ambitions for self and children, institutionalized political competition, secularism, appetite for national and international information, achievement motivation, desire for consumption of new goods and technology, preference for urban areas, new attitudes about wealth, work, savings and possibility of change, desire for geographical mobility, socio-economic and political discipline, and deferral of gratifications (Horowitz 1970; Kahl 1968; Portes 1974; Schnaiberg 1970).

Everett Rogers (1969) studied peasants and subsistence farmers in India, Nigeria, and Colombia, as they constituted a majority of the population in these and most other Third World countries. He assumed that modernization could not occur unless peasants were individually and collectively persuaded to change their traditional ways of life. Rogers' research indicated a *subculture of peasantry* that was characterized by 10 elements:

1. *Mutual distrust in interpersonal relations:* In general, peasants were suspicious, evasive, and distrustful of others in the community and non-co-operative in interpersonal relations with peers.

2. *Perceived limited good:* Peasants believed that all good things in life are available in limited quantities. Thus, one could improve one's position only at somebody else's expense.

3. *Dependence and hostility toward government authority:* Peasants had an ambivalent attitude toward government officials, though they depended upon them for solving many of their problems. However, there was a general distrust of government leaders.

4. *Familism:* The family played an important role in the life of the peasant. Peasants were prepared to subordinate their personal goals to those of the family.

5. *Lack of innovativeness:* Peasants were reluctant to adopt modern innovations, had a negative attitude toward change, and their behavior was not fully oriented toward rational economic considerations.

6. *Fatalism:* Peasants believed that their well-being was controlled by a supernatural fate. This had a dysfunctional consequence on directed social change.

7. *Limited aspirations:* Peasants exhibited low aspirations for advancement. Also, they had low levels of achievement motivation and suffered from inconspicuous consumption.

8. *Lack of deferred gratifications:* Peasants lacked the ability to post-pone satisfaction of immediate needs in anticipation of better rewards in the future.
9. *Limited view of the world:* First, they were not time conscious. Second, they were localites.[3] They were oriented within their communities and had no orientation to the world beyond their narrow group. Consequently, they had very limited geographic mobility.
10. *Low empathy:* Peasants exhibited mental inertness. They could not imagine themselves in new situations or places.

Hence, like the others—Lerner, McClelland, Inkeles and Hagen—Rogers' work argued that individuals must change before development could truly "take off." The work also revealed an *individual blame* bias. This stereotypical view of traditional individuals, as unresponsive to calls for modernization, hence in need of fundamental change, was the overwhelming perspective of the dominant paradigm, as espoused by these earlier theorists.

While few—if any—scholars today would promote individualistic, psychological theories of underdevelopment (see Chapter 5 for critiques), more subtle forms of individual blame or related stereotypes are evident in much of the literature. For instance, in a review of Western scholarship on women in development, Chandra Mohanty (1991b) argues that Western feminists "discursively colonize" the lives of women in developing countries and assume a "composite, singular 'third world woman'" (p. 53). This monolithic woman is victimized by a "monolithic notion of patriarchy" as well (pp. 53–54). Mohanty discusses several areas of victim status commonly assumed by feminist scholars: of male violence, of the colonial process, of religion, of family systems, and of the development process. Women also are assumed to be universal dependents. In general, Third World feminists have increasingly critiqued the assumptions and conclusions of much Western scholarship as ethnocentric, even racist, and irrelevant to their concerns (Minh-ha 1986–87; Mohanty 1991a, 1991b, Spivak 1988). Hence, while explicit theories of individual inferiority are no longer promoted, the discourse of development often reveals ethnocentric and patriarchal beliefs about the disempowered status of people in general or subgroups in developing countries. As we will discuss next, this discourse has also helped create or reinforce internalized forms of oppression, which has further functioned to sustain underdevelopment.

MODERNIZATION AS DISCOURSE

Beyond models of economics and of social evolution, modernization is culture, ideology, and discourse. These concepts are difficult to define and they are closely entwined. Also, all involve non-material symbols and representations, as well as the institutions that produce and influence these symbols and representations. *Culture* is arguably the broadest of the three terms, encompassing the other two. Raymond Williams (1976) calls culture "one of the two or three most complicated words in the English language" (p. 76).[4] The anthropologist Edward Hall (1976) describes three major characteristics of culture: that culture is shared by members of groups, and helps define them; that culture is learned, not innate; and that this learning is interrelated (p. 16).[5] Additionally, as discussed in Chapter 1, culture is inseparable from communication, to the extent that communication is defined as shared meaning (see Carey 1989). *Ideology*, a theoretical concept from Marxist thought, usually refers to the social relations of signification or representation, in that these relations are connected to social location and economic class. In his well-known essay, "Ideology and Ideological State Apparatuses," Louis Althusser (1971) assumes an important role for ideological expression (e.g., in popular culture and in everyday language) in shaping and reinforcing human experience. To the extent that culture is class-based, ideology plays a major role in creating and sustaining culture. Finally, the concept of *discourse*, as used in this book, has emerged largely from post-structuralism. While discourse may be defined simply as "verbal utterances of greater magnitude than the sentence" (O'Sullivan et al. 1994: 92), post-structuralist thought assumes a key role for discourse in actively constructing meaning. In contrast to ideology theory, which usually assumes that economic and social structures are crucial in shaping meaning, post-structuralism (e.g., from Foucault, Saussure, and Derrida) assumes that material structures are meaningless except to the extent that they are given meaning by discourse. We do not take sides in this book on the relative importance of "things" versus "words," nor is this the place for a detailed conceptual argument.[6] Rather we assume that discourse does contribute to ideology, to culture, and to all facets of society, and that modernization is importantly reflected in—and reflective of—discourse, ideology, and culture.

Role of Discourse in Modernization

An examination of modernization discourse from the beginning reveals the goal of replacing non-Western ideological, cultural, and even language systems, with Western systems; in essence, reshaping the reality of people in the Third World. In the three decades that followed World War II, the knowledge systems and the existential reality of the people in the Third World were gradually replaced by the concepts of progress and development imported from the West. Scholars consider US President Harry Truman's 1949 inaugural address as the symbolic watershed separating the earlier era of fascism and colonialism from the neocolonialism of the post-World War II period. While the earlier eras were painted discursively with a negative brush, the post-World War II era was associated with the mantra of *development* and a *fair deal* to the underdeveloped areas of the world (Truman 1949).

Truman's policy provided the official framework to channel Western ideas of modernization and development to the newly constituted Third World nations. As previously discussed, this included Western concepts of science, technical knowledge, industrial production, and capitalist-democratic form of government. It was widely believed that such transfers of knowledge, practice, and expertise would benefit the underdeveloped countries and help them become more like the West.

Third World countries thus became the target of new mechanisms of power embodied in endless programmes and "strategies." Their economies, societies and cultures were offered up as new objects of knowledge that, in turn, created new possibilities for [acquiring] power. The creation of an enormous institutional network (from international organizations and universities to local development agencies) ensured the efficient functioning of the modernization apparatus. Once consolidated, it determined what could be said, thought, imagined; in short, it defined a perceptual domain, the space of development (Escobar 1995a: 214).

The modern and "developed" First World, the socialist Second World, and the "underdeveloped" Third World were conceived, in part, in this discourse, as discussed in Chapter 1. The diverse societies in the South, with different cultures, geographies, and histories were lumped into the overarching concept of the Third World; what held this group together was the imagined concept of "underdevelopment." Thus, putting a twist on Edward Said's (1978) definition of the Orient, the development discourse enabled the West to manage the Third World, not just economically, politically, and socially, but also discursively and imaginatively (Crush 1995).

Spatial Reach of Discursive Power

The new developmentalism facilitated institutional interventions in Third World countries giving rise to greater mechanisms of control. In exchange for developing these countries and their economies, the everyday realities of the people were transacted and translated into objects of scientific pursuit. Escobar (1984–85: 387–90) has identified the strategies that extended the power of centralized agencies and government departments to penetrate, organize, manage, and control the peoples of the Third World:

- The progressive incorporation of more and more issues into the framework of development problems consequently led to the emergence of new fields of intervention for development experts.
- The professionalization of development into new fields of knowledge, disciplines, and careers resulted in establishing the nature of the Third World, to classify it, and to formulate policies for a future designed within the logic of Western economic rationality.
- The institutionalization of development on global, national, regional, and local levels with the respective development institutions as implementers of centrally devised development policies had the effect of creating a tight network and system of regulatory controls down to village level in the South.

The discursive practice of development articulated knowledge and power through the construction of social problems (Wilkins 1999). "Birth rates and infant mortality were identified as too high, literacy rates as too low and so on, with the effect that the objects of the development discourse came to see themselves along the lines set out for them by Western development experts" (Braidotti et al. 1994: 23).

Soon, individuals in the so-called underdeveloped countries started imagining their "underdevelopment." Their physical and social realities were produced and reproduced in the dialectic of development and underdevelopment, "marginalizing or precluding other ways of seeing and doing" (Escobar 1992: 22). Apparently, a space was created and constantly produced and reproduced through the representative knowledge derived from the scientific control or neocolonization of these countries and their people (Escobar 1992). Thus, development was reduced to "mapping and making, (it was) about the spatial reach of power and the control and management of other peoples, territories, environments and places" (Crush 1995: 7). The discursive and spatial reality of development was present in all countries of the South: governments and institutions devising five-year plans for development, foreign and domestic experts defining and analyzing development problems in cities and rural areas, and generous international loans to facilitate development projects. In short, one could not escape "development" in the Third World.

Through every possible mechanism—economic, political, social, discursive, and spatial—modernization aimed to replace nearly everything indigenous with imports from the West, both material and non-material (see Eisenstadt 1976: 33). This meant a dismantling of most things non-Western including traditional culture. Traditional culture included religion, which often seemed the greatest impediment to progress. It also included indigenous gender roles, to be replaced by Western norms on these roles. And it included indigenous views on the environment, to be replaced by Western values. Hence, we conclude this chapter with a very brief discussion of the modernization discourse in three areas: religion, gender, and environment. These three will be discussed in further detail in our critique of modernization in Chapter 5.

Religious Bias in Modernization

"Oriental" values and religions were seen as a bulwark of traditionalism and a repository of ideas that were incompatible with modernity (Weber 1964). Islam was criticized for its tradition-bound rigidity, Hinduism for its asceticism, and Buddhism for its otherwordly emphasis. Following Max Weber's thesis in *Protestant Ethic and the Spirit of Capitalism*, several generations of sociologists sought to identify a set of cultural values in Third World nations that inhibited modernization. In general, Asian—and other non-Christian (especially non-Protestant)—religions were seen as obstacles to progress (Bellah 1965; Rose 1970). Commenting on Weber's interpretation of Asian religions, Singer noted:

> In his studies of India, China, and Asia generally, where he did not see anything resembling the development of European industrial

capitalism, Weber reasoned that the religions of those countries must lack the counterparts of a *Protestant Ethic* that would provide the characterological foundation for the economic motivation required, as one among several factors, to spark and foster a development of industrial capitalism (Singer 1972: 275–76).

For example, Weber identified the theological ideas of *samsara* (rebirth) and *karma* (fate) as the dogmatic foundation of Hinduism. When combined with caste ritualism, they made it impossible to rationalize the economy and inhibited the capacity for progress or modernization. The encouragement of asceticism was also perceived as a major problem. Shankara's philosophy of *advaita*, which called for renunciation of this world for an otherworldly asceticism, was considered as synonymous with Hindu theology. Shankara's concept of Hinduism was, therefore, criticized as life-negating and pessimistic by evangelizing Christians who sought to prove the superiority of Christianity over Hinduism (Srinivas 1973).

Weber's ideas were extended to provide a recipe for the modernization of India. This called for the jettisoning of the caste system, the joint family, ritualism, and almost all other cultural arrangements, practices, institutions, and beliefs characteristic of Hinduism (Singer 1972). In fact, Rose contends that it is these practices and institutions that have kept India economically backward. The joint family system, according to Rose, fostered dependency and submissiveness, whereas casteism hampered occupational mobility. Beliefs in superstitions and magic were rampant even among educated Indians. It was not uncommon for a top government official to consult astrologers for proper timing before any action. Related to these irrational behaviors were others that were just as uneconomical. It was common in Asia to spend extravagant amounts of money over occasions such as marriage celebrations and religious festivals (Rose 1970). Most of these did not contribute to a rationalized economy.

In general, the materialist assumptions of modernization have been incompatible with religious and spiritual dimensions of society and culture. As we will discuss later (in Chapters 5, 7, and 8), religion and spirituality have generally been overlooked as positive resources for development, but rather have been viewed as areas of resistance that need to be overcome through creative strategizing. Western stereotypes of Third World women as victims of religion meant that the combination of gender and religion further marginalized women in the development process.

Patriarchal Bias in Development Discourse

Dominant views in sociology pertaining to sex-roles in relation to the public–private sphere distinction certainly have influenced discursive practices in development. Modernization exported a Western patriarchal model in which the male breadwinner headed the family unit while the woman raised children and managed the household. These assumptions helped guide institutional practices and interventions pertaining to development. Young (1993: 19) posits:

> When women were explicitly considered, it was virtually always as mothers and childbearers. It was further assumed that everyone's interest would be best served by helping women improve the way in which they cared for their children and catered for the family's needs. As a result, family welfare programmes were devised which gave women instruction in home economics, in improved nutrition, health, and hygiene.

The restricted role for women in development influenced initiatives that rendered them virtually invisible in most development projects. Males were assumed to be engaged in income-generating economic initiatives. The modernization bias toward production for the market thus ignored women's economic roles and female-dominated ventures in agriculture, industry, marketing, and the service sectors (Boserup 1970). Since women were perceived as playing an insignificant role in the marketplace, their position in development discourse was reduced to that of a welfare recipient (Kabeer 1994). This notion was directly influenced by the 19th-century European Poor Laws (Moser 1989). Under the Poor Laws, anyone who did not perform a productive role in the marketplace was viewed as a failure and his/her basic needs then became the responsibility of welfare/charity organizations. Thus, in the discourse of development, women were relegated to the social welfare sector that was of marginal utility to development. As Kabeer puts it:

> As long as economic growth was seen as the overriding objective of development, these welfare programmes were very much of a residual nature, offered only when the requirements of mainstream planning had been met and dispensed with in times of economic austerity. Women entered them passively, rather than actively, as recipients rather

than contributors, clients rather than agents, reproductive rather than productive (Kabeer 1994: 6).

Development discourse, then, created an imaginary Third World woman who was passive, dependent, and ignorant, i.e., a victim of under-developed societies (de Groot 1991; Mohanty 1991b). This discourse was accepted uncritically by most government officials and development workers in the Third World. In short, women were seen as an impediment to the modernization of societies in the South.

Consequently, development theory and practice in the first two post-colonial decades (the 1950s and 1960s) ignored women on the assumption that they would eventually be forced to adopt a more "progressive" stance towards development once the modernization process had been set in motion and Third World men had learned how to organize their societies along modern lines (Parpart 1995: 257).

Beginning in the 1970s, however, women globally began organizing for change, incorporating their agendas into global conferences and treaties and new WID and GAD branches of aid agencies. These critiques and areas of activism are discussed further in Chapter 5.

Androcentric View of Nature in Development Discourse

The early views about nature may be described as androcentric. Western scientific method, with its roots in the experiments of Bacon in the early 17th century, regarded nature as an object that was to be subjugated and exploited for instrumental purposes. "The discipline of scientific know-ledge, and the mechanical inventions it leads to, do not merely exert a gentle guidance over nature's course; they have the power to conquer and subdue her, to shake her to her foundations" (Fox-Keller 1985: 38–39).

The logic of scientific rationality in development discourse vis-à-vis environment and nature has been to regard it as a dead and brute matter waiting for man to shape and exploit it for his own needs. Shiva reveals the anthropomorphic nature of society's relationship with nature vis-à-vis development:

Science-dominated society has evolved very much in the pattern of Bacon's Bensalem, with nature being transformed and mutilated in modern Solomon's Houses—the corporate labs of today and university research programmes they sponsor. With the new biotechnologies, Bacon's vision of controlling reproduction for the sake of production is also being realized, while the Green Revolution and the Bio-Revolution have already created what in New Atlantis was only a utopia (Shiva 1992: 209).

With the ushering in of industrialization and its concomitant processes of commodity production, nature evolved from being a brute matter to a natural resource: any material or conditions existing in nature which may be capable of economic exploitation (Meeker 1987). Thus, the value of nature was its singular capacity to feed the voracious appetite of the development machine. Devoid of logic or intelligence of its own, it was the "knowing" scientist who possessed the rationality, competence, and power to understand the opaque structure of nature and exploit it for instrumental ends. In this way, the scientific method in the development discourse revealed its colonizing mentality over nature (Braidotti et al. 1994; Fox-Keller 1985).

In the latter part of the 20th century, the degradation of nature and re-source depletion due to its rapacious exploitation for development became quite obvious. Nature was, after all, more than just brute matter; it was a complex ecological system capable of breakdown with disastrous consequences to humankind. The institutional discourse then moved from mere exploitation to management of natural resources. Today, "sustainable development" or "sustainable environment" is the key phrase to describe the relationship of the development machine with environment. The discourse of sustainable development adopted by mainstream organizations is couched in the technical language of systems theory and is defined, analyzed, managed, and controlled by development experts, who claim an epistemologically superior position in the debate on scarcity of natural resources and sustainability of the natural environment.

The vulnerability of nature has thrown open a new area for institutions of development to intervene, manage, regulate, and govern.

To carry out these formidable objectives, the state has to install the necessary institutions like monitoring systems, regulatory mechanisms and executive agencies. A new class of professionals is required to perform these tasks, while ecoscience is supposed to provide the episte-mology of intervention. In short, the experts who used to look after economic growth now claim to be presiding over survival itself (Sachs 1992: 33).

A good example is the discourse of population control and management, also an area where the discourse of gender and the discourse of environment merge. Neo-Malthusians such as Paul Ehrlich (1968) and the Club of Rome's *Limits to Growth* (Meadows 1972), explained the problem of underdevelopment and endemic poverty in the countries of the South on the reckless growth in population, especially among the poor. Malthus (1766–1834) wrote about the limits to population growth in Europe imposed by agriculture. He postulated that while the agricultural output increased in arithmetic progression, population would increase in geometric progression thus leading to a vicious cycle of underdevelopment. In the discourse on modernization during the decades following World War II, economists using the Malthusian hypothesis blamed the sluggish development in the Third World on the explosion in population growth which encouraged a spate of anti-natalist programs in the South (Braidotti et al. 1994). The development establishment then took over the task of managing the "population crisis." The Food and Agriculture Organization and the Economic and Social Council intervened to monitor and arrange for adequate food supplies to the Third World, while the UNFPA and state governments were assigned the role of monitoring and managing population growth (Braidotti et al. 1994).

Thus, the articulation of high fertility rates in the South was defined as a problem of crisis proportions in the countries of the South and the prime reason for the overexploitation and degradation of the environment. As it is women who bear children, women's fertility was discursively blamed for overpopulation and all problems presumed to be a consequence of overpopulation (e.g., environmental degradation and unemployment). Women became the "targets" of innumerable projects to technologically control their fertility (Jaquette and Staudt 1985).

In general, the new aggressive role of the state, development institutions, and private industry to carefully husband natural resources for development reveals the beginning of an era of neo-developmentalism. "Today, survival of the planet is well on its way to becoming the wholesale justification for a new wave of state intervention in people's lives all over the world" (Sachs 1992: 33). These interventions and their accompanying discourses must be continuously examined and challenged. The dominant paradigm remains dominant in part by appropriating, transforming, minimizing, or otherwise manipulating and neutralizing its critics. This is an issue that is discussed further in Chapter 5.

SUMMARY

One of the most powerful paradigms to originate after World War II, with enormous social, cultural, and economic consequences, was that of modernization. Theories and concepts that recapitulated the development of West European and North American nations were used to generate models of development for the Third World. In the modernization theories, the definition of a modern nation resembled Western industrialized nations in all areas of society, including political and economic behavior and institutions, attitudes toward technology and science, and cultural mores. The economic model that grounded modernization theories was the *neo-classical* approach that had served as the basis for Western economies. The dominant paradigm was mainly concerned with economic growth as measured by GNP rates and encouragement of all factors and institutions that accelerated and maintained high growth in areas such as capital-intensive industrialization, high technology, private ownership of factors of production, free trade, and the principle of *laissez-faire*.

The modernization paradigm has emerged not only from economic theory, but also from social evolutionary theory. At the macro level, theories applied Darwin's ideas to the process of modernization of human societies. The theories of social evolution influenced and gave rise to important concepts in the sociology of development such as, the various bipolar theories of modernization. In these theories, the universal stages in the earlier theories of social evolution were reduced to ideal-typical extremes: *Gemeinschaft versus Gesellschaft*, traditional versus modern societies, etc. The Third World nations were usually described as traditional while the industrialized nations of the West signified the modern counterpart. The advanced Western nations had a wide range of systemic autonomy, i.e., their capacity to cope with a range of social, cultural, technological, and economic issues in the process of social change (Eisenstadt 1976: 31). The Third World nations, on the other hand, lacking the higher differentiation of roles and institutions, the evolutionary universals, and other qualitative characteristics of industrial societies, were limited in their capacity to cope with problems or crises or even master their environment. As globalization is quickly altering the role of the nation-state in the global economy, bipolar theories are likely to change accordingly. For instance, Castells (1996, 1997, 1998) predicts a growing economic distinction between those who have access to information technologies and a "Fourth World" that is left behind. Those in the "Fourth World" will be disproportionately from Africa, Asia, and Latin America, the present "Third World."

At the micro level, theories on individual psychological attributes stressed that attitudinal and value changes among individuals were prerequisites to the creation of a modern society. Scholars such as David McClelland, Daniel Lerner, Alex Inkeles, and Everett Rogers described certain value-normative complexes that were responsible for the modernization of individuals in the West and which the Third World was lacking. These scholars posited that modernization of the Third World was dependent on changing the character of individuals living there to resemble more closely the attitudinal and value characteristics of people in Western Europe and North America.

Finally, this chapter discussed modernization as a discourse, that is, a set of words and symbols that have dialectically supported all other structures and processes of modernization. The Third World, as conceived today, was invented in this discourse and "underdeveloped" countries were identified with this signifier. In the three decades that followed World War II, the knowledge systems and the existential reality of the people in the Third World were gradually replaced by the concepts of progress and development imported from the West. The new developmentalism facilitated institutional interventions in the Third World countries giving rise to greater and greater mechanisms of control. In exchange for developing these countries and their economies, the everyday realities of the people were transacted and translated into objects of scientific pursuit. Soon, individuals in the so-called underdeveloped countries started imagining their "underdevelopment." Their physical and social realities were produced and reproduced in the dialectic of development and underdevelopment, marginalizing local narratives and knowledge structures. Mainstream development discourse had a secular orientation that viewed religious values and obstacles to progress. It also had a patriarchal bias that was institutionalized through development institutions. As for the environment, there was a strong anthropomorphic bias in which nature was considered as dead and manipulable matter to be exploited rapaciously for economic growth.

NOTES

1. This is defined as a strategy where little importance is paid to the use of human labor in development.
2. Dualisms of Enlightenment thought include: objectivity versus subjectivity; reason versus emotion; public sphere versus private sphere; technology versus nature; activity versus passivity. In each case the first half is considered superior. The first half is also associated with the world of science and with men and masculinity. The second half is associated with the world of nature and with femininity.
3. These are individuals who are oriented within their communities and not the outside world.
4. Williams assumes a web of significance among many facets of non-material and material culture, including lifestyles, modes, and processes of intellectual, spiritual, and artistic work, and the concrete products of all this work.
5. We thank Christine Kellow (1998: 26) for suggesting this synopsis in Hall.
6. For an excellent conceptual discussion of these issues, see Michèle Barrett's chapter "Words and Things," in Barrett (1999).

CHAPTER 4

COMMUNICATION APPROACH IN THE MODERNIZATION OF THE THIRD WORLD

> [In the Third World] Villages are drowsing in their traditional patterns of life . . . the urge to develop economically usually comes from seeing how the well-developed countries or the more fortunate people live.
>
> Wilbur Schramm (1964: 41–42)

Most communication practice and scholarship in the Third World development literature are consistent with modernization theory that was discussed in Chapter 3. At both the macro and micro levels, communication is viewed as a product and reinforcer of economic growth and development. At the macro level, communication scholars aligned with this perspective support global and national policies that facilitate "free flows" of media and information technology, content (news, advertising, entertainment, messages, and data) and hardware, as they view these products as crucial for Third World development and participation in the global economy. At the micro level, they support persuasive marketing campaigns (in areas such as agriculture, population, and health) as the most efficient means to transform traditional individuals and societies.

This chapter is devoted to studying the various communication approaches used for development since the end of World War II. Four interrelated conceptual as well as operational areas that have contributed greatly to an understanding of the social-scientific foundations of mass communication in general and development communication in particular, and their role in social change theory and practice, may be described as: (*i*) communication effects approach, (*ii*) mass media and modernization approach, (*iii*) the diffusion of innovations approach, and (*iv*) social marketing approach. All four areas or approaches are grounded in Enlightenment philosophy, discussed in Chapter 3. The scholarship of communication effects helped lay the groundwork for uses of mass media in support of modernization. The diffusion of innovations research provided a model for communication interventions in local-level projects. As the diffusion model proved increasingly inadequate, project planners have turned to social marketing to guide project communications. Social marketing remains the predominant model used for large and complex projects funded by bilateral and multilateral aid agencies. Infotainment, or enter-education, is also used and follows a consistent model. Often social marketing and enter-education campaigns are used together in a complementary fashion.

COMMUNICATION EFFECTS APPROACH

World War I can be considered a watershed in mass communication theory and research. The Libertarian theory of public communication, which assumed that individuals were by nature rational, proved to be increasingly unworkable with the advent of the War. In the West, people were bombarded with War-inspired propaganda, and leaders began to get concerned over its apparent power to mobilize people to fight and maintain their morale in adverse conditions. Harold Lasswell conceptualized mass media effects during this period. His model, which was strongly influenced by Freudian theory, was in direct contradiction to Libertarian philosophy (Davis and Baran 1981). His verbal model (see Figure 4.1) suggested the following question: WHO says WHAT in which CHANNEL to WHOM and with what EFFECT? (Lasswell 1948).

Figure 4.1
Graphic Presentation of Lasswell's Formula

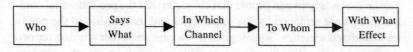

While the Libertarian school emphasized the latent rationality of men and women, Lasswell drew on Freudian theory to assume that human behavior is essentially irrational. Based on this conceptualization, a framework emerged that has been called the *hypodermic needle* (Berlo 1960) of mass communication effects. This theory is also known by several other names: *bullet theory* (Schramm 1971); and *stimulus-response theory* (DeFleur and Ball-RoKeach 1975).

Concept of Mass Society

There were several assumptions behind the *stimulus-response* theory of mass media effects. Lowery and DeFleur (1988, 1995) noted that a starting point for understanding the development of the earliest theoretical models used to study mass communication effects was the concept of *mass society*: a description of modern Western societies in the early 19th century. These authors contended that there was a close tie between the concept of Western countries as mass societies and the earlier theories of mass communication effects.

Since the mid-18th century, three trends occurred that transformed Western societies from feudal, agricultural, and pre-industrial communities to military-industrial complexes. These trends—identified broadly as industrialization, urbanization, and modernization—transformed social relationships, norms, values, and material culture quite drastically. For example, the Industrial Revolution, which changed the workplace, work ethics, and relationships, led to a factory system, migration into urban areas, the introduction of large-scale bureaucracy, and more. Urbanization led to a profound change in social order, new institutions, norms, values, and beliefs, while modernization led to further stratification of people via adoption of innovations and greater consumption of material goods (Lowery and DeFleur 1988, 1995).

Thus, through these trends, traditional loyalties, norms and values were eroded. There was widespread *anomie* among the inhabitants of the big cities, greater differentiation, distrust and stratification. The strong inter-personal bonds between people that characterized the pre-industrial com-munities were replaced by the impersonal and tedious life in the newly industrialized societies. Sociologists, historians, and other scholars termed the new communities *mass society*. This was, "an image of a modern society as consisting of an aggregate of relatively 'atomized' individuals acting according to their personal interests and little constrained by social ties and constraints" (McQuail and Windahl 1981: 42). In this kind of society, the new mass media were perceived to have immense power because their impact would not be constrained by other competing social and psychological influences on individuals. In other words, people in *mass society* were more susceptible to the powerful influences of the mass media.

Thus, the earliest theoretical models on media effects conceptualized the impact of mass media on individuals as direct, powerful, and uniform (see Figure 4.2). The apparent success of propaganda during World War I and during the Spanish–American War at the turn of the 19th century (which historians point out was a consequence of exaggerated reports from the newspapers owned by Pulitzer and Hearst) simply reinforced the view of powerful media effects. The *bullet theory* and *hypodermic needle* theory, noted above, were colorful terms used to describe the concept of powerful mass media. The *stimulus-response* model also explained the same kind of effect. Every stimulus **S** (or message) was thought to produce a definite response **R** in the receiver **O** (McQuail and Windahl 1981: 42).

Figure 4.2
Models Denoting Powerful Effects of Mass Media

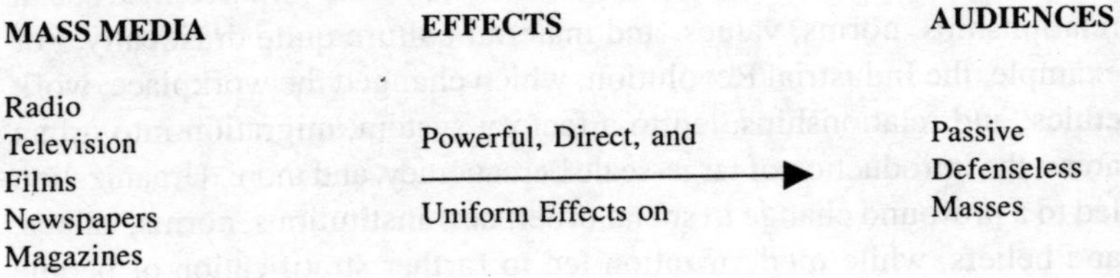

MASS MEDIA	EFFECTS	AUDIENCES
Radio		
Television	Powerful, Direct, and	Passive
Films	—————————————→	Defenseless
Newspapers	Uniform Effects on	Masses
Magazines		

With the addition of new media of mass communication, i.e., film and the radio in the 1920s, and the growth of advertising in the United States, the study of strong and uniform effects gained additional momentum. During the period between the two World Wars, the mass media were viewed as powerful instruments that could be successfully used to manipulate people's opinions and attitudes, and thereby their behaviors, in a relatively short period of time. Katz (1963: 80) notes that, "the model in the minds of the early researchers seems to have consisted of: (*i*) the all-powerful media, able to impress ideas on defenseless minds; and (*ii*) the atomized mass audience, connected to the mass media but not to each other."

The predominance of interest in effects of media and effectiveness of channels led to other formulations. Communication became the object of scientific study. An influential model called the *telephone model* was developed by Shannon and Weaver (1949). Diaz-Bordenave (1977) has noted that several concepts such as: signal, code, message, channel, source, destination, encoding, and decoding were first described in the Shannon and Weaver model (see Figure 4.3). While this model was developed in the area of information theory, it was used analogically by behavioral and communication scientists.

Figure 4.3
Shannon and Weaver's Model of Communication

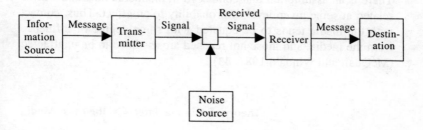

Source: Shannon and Weaver, 1949: 5. *The Mathematical Theory of Communication.* © 1949 by the Board of Trustees of the University of Illinois. Used with the permission of the University of Illinois Press.

The other early models in communication developed by Schramm, Berlo, and others conceptualized communication as a linear and one-way process always flowing from the source of communication to a passive receiver (see Figure 4.4). The earlier models of Schramm and the SMCR model of Berlo conceptualized the communication flow as a simple, mechanistic process of message transmission (Diaz-Bordenave 1977) (see Figure 4.5). In the post-World War II period, the Source-Message-Channel-Receiver (SMCR) model became popular with *communication for development* professionals.

Figure 4.4
One-way, Linear Model of Communication

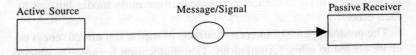

Figure 4.5
Berlo's Formula for the Process of Communication

All the models described above reinforced the *omnipotent source* and the *passive receiver* assumption:

> There is an assumption that contact from the media message will be related at some given level of probability to an effect. Thus, contact with the media tends to be equated with some degree of influence from the media, and those not reached are assumed to be unaffected (McQuail and Windahl 1981: 43).

Theory of Minimal Effects of the Mass Media

The study of propaganda and the powerful effects of mass media engaged some of the best minds in sociology, psychology, and political science. New areas of inquiry began to open up. Some of the newer questions were: What specific effects do mass media have on individuals and the general community? What is the process by which these effects occur? (Severin and Tankard 1987 [1979]). Lazarsfeld, Berelson and Gaudet's work (1948) on political decision-making in the 1940 US presidential election campaign reconceptualized the process and effects of mass media from dominant effects to limited effects. Also called the *voter study*, this was an example of administrative research applied to critical questions.[1] This study questioned the powerful nature of mass communication in society, people's exposure to media messages, and the impact of media on their political decisions. The researchers discovered that individuals were more influenced in their political decisions by members of their primary and peer groups than the combined mass media. The mass media seemed to have relatively little impact in influencing people's political decisions. Even overall exposure to mass media was quite low. Toward the election day, the majority were somewhat exposed. But, on the whole, exposure was not high. These findings, therefore, rejected the bullet theory of uniform and powerful media effects.

The researchers did identify one segment of people more exposed to the mass media than other individuals, called influentials or opinion leaders. These opinion leaders then influenced others in the community. Thus, the effects of mass media were indirect. This notion was described in the two-step flow theory (see Figure 4.6). The two-step flow theory suggested that the first step of influence was from the mass media to opinion leaders, while the second step was from these leaders to others in the community (Katz and Lazarsfeld 1955). The two-step flow theory was tested and confirmed in Decatur, Illinois, in the United States. Using the snowball sample, the researchers discovered that opinion leadership was not confined to the elite but found at all levels of society (Katz and Lazarsfeld 1955). Essentially, these studies suggested the relative weakness of mass media in directly influencing individual personal decisions.

Figure 4.6
Two-step Flow Model of Communication Effects

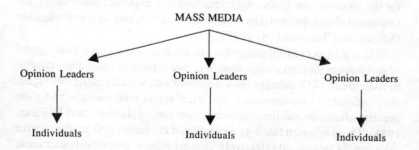

MASS MEDIA

Opinion Leaders   Opinion Leaders   Opinion Leaders

Individuals   Individuals   Individuals

The work of other social scientists (Hovland et al. 1949, 1953; Klapper 1960), further undermined the great power of the mass media in bringing about direct and lasting effects on the audience. For example, Carl Hovland and colleagues did pioneering work in the area of communication and persuasion (Hovland et al. 1949). Their research on war propaganda films examined how and why individuals responded to persuasive messages, showing that the mass media were ineffective in improving the attitudes of soldiers toward their allies and increasing their motivation to fight. Rather the social categories (for example, educational level) to which people belonged and individual differences were more predictive of certain effects than mass media exposure. People defended themselves against persuasive messages in three ways: *selective exposure, selective perception*, and *selective retention*.

Klapper (1960) suggested that people *expose* themselves to messages selectively. There was a tendency for individuals to expose themselves relatively more to those items of communication that were consonant with their beliefs, ideas, and values. Further, regardless of exposure to communication, an individual's *perception* of a certain event, issue, person, or place could be influenced by his/her latent beliefs, attitudes, wants, needs, or other factors. Thus, two individuals exposed to the same message could go away with diametrically different perceptions about it. Additionally, research showed that even *recall* of information was influenced by factors such as an individual's needs, wants, moods, and perceptions (Allport and Postman 1947; Jones and Kohler 1958; Levine and Murphy 1958).

Thus, what we learn from these selective processes is that the individual is not a defenseless target for persuasive communication. He/she is very active in receiving, processing, and interpreting information. The three selective processes outlined above could function as rings of defenses for the receiver (see Figure 4.7) with selective exposure constituting the outermost shield, followed by selective perception and selective retention (Severin and Tankard 1987 [1979]).

In fact, Klapper (1960) suggested that the mass media were more agents of reinforcement than causal agents of behavioral or attitudinal change in individuals. The demographic categories to which people belonged, their individual characteristics, and their social relationships had a far greater influence than the combined mass media (Lowery and DeFleur, 1988). These research findings contradicted the earlier notion of powerful mass media that could effectively convert nearly anybody. Under most

Figure 4.7
Rings of Defense of Receivers

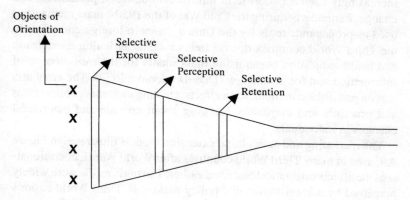

conditions, people were not passive or defenseless against the onslaught of persuasive messages.

The theory of minimal mass media effects contributed to the refinement of theories and methods in communication studies.[2] The survey sampling designs of Lazarsfeld and colleagues at Columbia University, the experimental designs of Hovland and colleagues at Yale, the functionalistic and middle-range theories of Merton, Klapper, and others have made significant contributions to our conceptualizations of communication effects. With greater refinement in theoretical concepts and methodological designs, the "minimal-effects" researchers were able to move away from the simplistic "bullet theory" and "hypodermic needle" concepts of mass media effects. They were able to discover and explain more adequately the role of interpersonal influences and other social-psychological variables on media diffusion and impact.

While the research after World War II clearly showed the rather limited capacity of the mass media to affect important behavioral and attitudinal changes, this did not mean that they were discarded as agents of social change. For example, Davis and Baran (1981: 37) noted that even in the United States, Hovland's study (which indicated that the mass media were not very effective in changing people's attitudes and morale) was "accepted for its *administrative* rather than *critical* research value. It was concerned with making communication more effective for immediate, short-term persuasion."

The findings of the minimal effects research aside, mass media were increasingly used for short-term information delivery, persuasion, and change. Particularly during the Cold War of the 1950s, mass media were used as propaganda tools for the United States in foreign countries. In the Third World countries diverse fields such as agricultural extension and health education began using mass media for the *transmission* of information and for *persuasion* (Diaz-Bordenave 1977). The emphasis was on particular communication effects: creating awareness of new ideas and practices and eventually bringing about attitude and behavioral changes in individuals.

The marketing and agricultural extension models illustrated in Figure 4.8, used in many Third World countries after World War II, operational-ized the effects orientation described earlier. The mass media were widely perceived by administrators and policy-makers in Third World nations as important vehicles for bringing about speedy behavioral change among their peoples, particularly in favor of the modernizing objectives of the state. Diaz-Bordenave pointed out that (1977: 13–14).

The pressures of economic development goals, the size and dispersion of target audiences in developing areas, the availability of modern com-munication technology, and an interest in selling expensive communi-cation equipment all worked to make media an important element in rural development programs. Development personnel strived to use the latest gadgets in carrying out aggressive multimedia campaigns.

The preoccupation with effects suggests that the mechanistic stimulus-response model has not entirely vanished. It still underlines much thinking about the nature and role of mass communication in development. For some, the process of persuasion has remained synonymous with the pro-cess of mass communication (McQuail and Windahl 1981). This is evident in all the approaches guiding communication to support modernization, approaches followed at both the macro and micro levels.

Figure 4.8
Marketing and Agricultural Extension Models

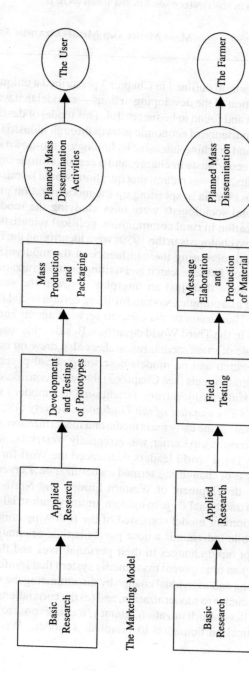

The Marketing Model

The Agricultural Extension Model

Source: Diaz-Bordenave. 1977: 13. *Communication and Rural Development.* © Unesco 1977. Used with permission.

MASS MEDIA AND MODERNIZATION APPROACH

The dominant paradigm outlined in Chapter 3 prescribed a unique model for the modernization of the developing nations—a model that was tested in Western nations and found to be successful. This model of development underlined the importance of economic growth through industrialization, capital-intensive and machine-intensive technology, a top-down structure of authority with economists in charge, and a certain attitude and mindset among individuals. It was natural that questions would be raised about the role of the mass media in speeding up the modernization process.

Thus, while rural sociologists were busy studying the modernizing role of communication in rural communities, political scientists, economists, and social psychologists in the 1950s were identifying the functions of mass media and measuring their influence in the modernization of developing countries. In the research and writing on modernization, communication was more than just an interplay between the source and receiver. It served as a complex system fulfilling certain social functions (Hellman 1980). Thus, mass media came to serve as agents and indices of modernization in the Third World countries. Besides this macro-level analysis of the role of mass media, researchers also drew on communication effects research and on models describing social-psychological characteristics of individuals (see Chapter 3) that were considered necessary for a successful transition from a traditional to a modern society.

Daniel Lerner's *The Passing of the Traditional Society* (1958), illustrates the major ideas of the early mass media and modernization approach. Modernization, according to Lerner, was essentially Westernization. However, since many Third World leaders denounced the West for political reasons, the process of change was termed modernization. Lerner's model recapitulated the development of Western Europe and North America from a feudal and traditional stage to modern, military-industrial societies. His social development model consisted of the following components: (*a*) a core of mobile individuals whose psychological orientation made it easier to accept rapid changes in their personal lives and the overall social system, (*b*) an omnipotent mass media system that reinforced and accelerated societal and individual change by disseminating the new ideas and attitudes conducive to modernization, and (*c*) the correlations between the important indices of urbanization, literacy, media exposure, and economic and political participation to establish a modern Western-type society.

According to Lerner, traditional society was non-participant. People were deployed by kinship into communities, isolated from one another and from the center, without an urban–rural division of labor. Thus people developed few needs that required economic interdependence. Their worldviews were limited to their physical horizons, and their decisions involved other known people in familiar situations. On the other hand, modern society was participant and functioned by consensus. Here, people went through formal schooling, read newspapers, were paid in cash for jobs, used cash to consume goods in a free and open market, and were free to vote in elections and express opinions on matters external to their personal lives. Lerner identified and explained a psychological pattern in individuals that was both required and reinforced by modern society: a mobile personality. This person was equipped with a high capacity for identification with new aspects of his/her environment and internalized the new demands made by the larger society. In other words, this person had a high degree of empathy, the capacity to see oneself in the other fellow's situation (also discussed in Chapter 3). Lerner stated that empathy fulfilled two important tasks. First, it enabled the person to operate efficiently in modern society, which was constantly changing. Second, it was an indispensable skill for individuals wanting to move out of their traditional settings. As Fjes noted, "empathy allows the individual to internalize the process of modernization by not only being able to cope with change, but expecting and demanding it . . . it is the psychic nexus of all the attitudes and behavior necessary in a modern society" (Fjes 1976).

The second element in Lerner's model were the mass media. They performed a special function: by exposing individuals to new people, ideas, and attitudes, they accelerated the process of modernization. Lerner posited that in the West, particularly in the United States, psychic mobility began with the expansion of physical travel. The expansion of physical or geographical mobility meant that more people commanded greater skill in managing themselves as new persons, living in new situations than did people in any previous historical period. The development of mass media accelerated this process even more. According to Lerner, the earlier increase of psychic experience through transportation was multiplied by the exposure to mediated experience. Thus, the mass media were important agents of modernization. People in the Third World could expand their empathy by exposure to mass media, which showed them new places, behavior, and cultures. In short, mass media had the potential of blowing the winds of modernization into isolated traditional communities and replacing the structure of life, values, and behavior there with ones seen in the modern Western society.

In Lerner's model, mass media were both an index and agent of modernization. The social change occurred in three phases. First and most crucial was urbanization. After about 10 percent urbanization was reached, the take-off occurred. In the second phase, literacy rates began to rise dramatically. With increasing rates of urbanization, literacy, and industrial development in the third phase, there was a great spurt in the growth of the modern mass media. Lerner said that mass media systems flourished only in societies that were modern by other standards. Thus, the mass media functioned as important indices of modernization. In Lerner's model, there was a close reciprocal relationship between literacy and mass media exposure. The literate developed the media, which in turn accelerated the spread of literacy. All of these developments triggered a rise in political participation (such as voting) found in all advanced Western societies. While all of these generalizations came out of the data collected in the Middle East, Lerner suggested that the historical sequence of these changes was natural, as exemplified in the development of the Western societies.

Lakshmana Rao (1963) also suggested that communication was a prime mover in the development process. He selected two villages in India for his study: *Kothooru*, a village on the verge of modernization, and *Pathooru*, a village isolated and steeped in traditional customs and beliefs. Rao suggested that the laying of a new road to *Kothooru* from a nearby city started the process of modernization. Among other things, this road brought new people, ideas, and the mass media, while at the same time allowing the villagers to visit urban centers. All of this new information opened up people's minds. They were not only ready for change but demanding and expecting it. The new ideas and innovations were first available to the elite and then trickled down to others.

It was the quantity and quality of information that triggered change in *Kothooru*, while *Pathooru* remained unchanged. The new road and the mass media brought in modern ideas and values from outside. Traditional ideas and modes of behavior were gradually dislodged. There was a great spur to education. Importantly, the new developments led to new jobs and higher productivity. As Schramm commented, "More productivity leads to improved income, to widening consuming habits, to increased economic activity within the village (such as shops and restaurants), to new appetites for consumer goods, to a seeking after new opportunities, and so on in a chain of related development" (Schramm, 1964: 49).

While Lerner observed the role of communication as the harbinger of new ideas from outside, Rao concluded that new communication helped to smooth out the transition from a traditional to a modern community. The availability of new information to the people at the top and its eventual and autonomous trickle down to others in the lower reaches of the hierarchy increased empathy, opened up new opportunities, and led to a general breakdown of the traditional society.

Role of Mass Media in Modernization: Optimism of the 1950s and the 1960s

The role of the mass media in development was accorded a central position in the modernization paradigm. For example, Wilbur Schramm (1964) reiterated that the modernization of industrial or agricultural sectors in developing nations required the mobilization of human resources. Education and mass media, then, were vested with crucial responsibility in the process of mobilization of human resources. He noted:

> the task of the mass media of information and the "new media" of education is to speed and ease the long, slow social transformation required for economic development, and, in particular, to speed and smooth the task of mobilizing human resources behind the national effort (Schramm 1964: 27).

Some scholars went further to state that the major problem in developing countries was not a shortage of natural resources but the underdevelopment of human resources. Thus, education and mass media had the enormous task of building human capital. The powerful role of the mass media in modernization was clearly implied in Lerner's and Rao's research and many other studies in the 1950s and 1960s. These studies complemented the postulates of the dominant paradigm of development. Mass media were the vehicles for transferring new ideas and models from the West to the Third World and from urban areas to the rural countryside. Schramm echoed the dominant thinking during this historical period in his influential book *Mass Media and National Development* (1964). He noted that in the Third World, "villages are drowsing in their traditional patterns of life . . . the urge to develop economically and socially usually comes from seeing how the well-developed countries or the more fortunate people live" (Schramm 1964: 41–42). The mass media thus functioned as a "bridge to a wider world" (Schramm 1964). Importantly, they were entrusted with the task of preparing individuals in developing nations for a rapid social change by establishing a "climate of modernization" (Rogers 1976c). Lerner posited that the process of modernization began when something "stimulates the peasant to want to be a freeholding farmer, the farmer's son to want to learn reading so he can work in the town, the farmer's wife to stop bearing children, the farmer's daughter to want to wear a dress and do her hair" (Lerner 1963: 348). On a macro level, the modern mass media were used in one-way and top-down communication models by leaders to disseminate modern innovations to the public. Schramm recommended that, "the task of the mass media of information and the 'new media' of education is to speed and ease the long, slow social transformation required for economic development, and, in particular, to speed and smooth the task of mobilizing human resources behind the national effort" (Schramm 1964: 27).

The mass media were thought to have a powerful and direct influence on individuals. Thus, the bullet model of mass media effects seemed to hold in Third World countries in the 1950s and 1960s, even though this model had been discarded earlier in North America. The strength of the mass media lay in their one-way, top-down and simultaneous and wide dissemination. Further, since the elites in every nation were required to modernize others in the population, their control of the prestigious mass media also served their economic and political interests. Influential research at this time such as Lerner's (1958) Middle East study and Lakshmana Rao's (1963) Indian study, generated high expectations from the mass media. They were considered as *magic multipliers* of development benefits in Third World nations. Administrators, researchers, and fieldworkers sincerely believed in the great power of the mass media as harbingers of modernizing influences. This period in development history was characterized by a spirit of optimism. There were other contributory factors:

Certainly, the media were expanding during the 1950s and 1960s. Literacy was becoming more widespread in most developing nations, leading to greater print media exposure. Transistor radios were penetrating every village. A predominantly one-way flow of communication from government development agencies to the people was implied by the dominant paradigm. And, the mass media seemed ideally suited to this role (Rogers 1976b: 134).

This period was also characterized by a spate of research activity to demonstrate the correlation between exposure to the mass media and modernity. Surveys conducted by Frey (1966) in Turkey, Rogers (1965, 1969) in Colombia, Inkeles and Smith (1974) in six developing nations, and Paul Neurath's (1962) field experiments in India on the effectiveness of radio forums, provided impressive evidence for the impact of mass media on modernization. Also, Rogers' (1969) survey of peasants in Colombia, India, Kenya, and Brazil showed the role of mass media as an intervening variable between functional literacy and various measures of modernization such as: empathy, agricultural innovativeness, political knowledge, and educational aspirations for children.

Therefore, the connection between the availability of mass media and national development was crucial. Both Lerner (1958) and Schramm (1964) showed a high correlation between the indices of modernity and availability of mass media: the more developed the nation, the higher the availability of mass media outlets. The converse was also true. As Schramm notes, "the less-developed countries have less-developed mass communication systems also, and less development in the services that support the growth of mass communication" (Schramm 1964: 112). In an attempt to reduce the gap between nations labeled as mass media *haves* and *have-nots*, UNESCO even suggested a minimum standard for mass media availability in the Third World (Schramm 1964; see also Chapter 6). Researchers had demonstrated a strong and statistically significant positive correlation between the development of the mass media and important indices in the economic, social, and political spheres. The establishment of a critical minimum of mass media outlets was strongly encouraged if the developing nations were to achieve overall national development.

Therefore, information was considered the missing link in the development chain. The quality of information available and its wide disseminiation was a key factor in the speed and smoothness of development. Adequate mass media outlets and information would act as a spur to education, commerce, and a chain of other related development activities.

"Free Flow" of Media Arguments

All of the above beliefs and projects were supported by "free flow" policies initiated by the US the (including the US government, private business, and media) following World War II and quickly embraced by the newly formed United Nations. The free flow ideology is highly individualistic, and consistent with Enlightenment thought. It assumes that the individual's right to information is greater than what might be in the best interests of the larger group. It also assumes that individual information access is a fundamental human right. The free flow ideology was institutionalized in two UN declarations. The first, the UN Declaration on Freedom of Information (1946), assumed that the free flow of information between countries was "of greater importance than the right of nations to bar this movement of media products across their borders" (Schement et al. 1984: 165). The second, the UN Universal Declaration of Human Rights, included freedom of information as a fundamental human right, and as a part of the right to freedom of speech. It declared (in Article 19) the right of everyone to "hold opinions without interference and to seek, receive and impart information and ideas through any media regardless of frontiers" (United Nations 1996: 127).

Proponents of free flow ideology have argued, consistent with modernization, that existing world distribution patterns are due to self-regulating market forces. They note that the distribution of information content and hardware has never been equal, therefore not all individuals or demographic groups should be expected to have equal ability at all times to send and receive messages. The key issue is individual freedom to work toward this ability and opportunity. As the US and other Western industrialized nations have greater economic capacity to relay information and develop new markets for their products and associated values, the idea of free flow (and the related idea of free trade) has always been appealing. It also certainly influenced USAID policy with regard to the development of communications and assumed links between communications and markets.[3]

DIFFUSION OF INNOVATIONS RESEARCH

While scholars and policy-makers were making macro-level arguments and funding experiments on the role of media in supporting modernization, diffusion of innovations theory gradually evolved as the local-level framework to guide communications planning for modernization. Diffusion of innovations also has important theoretical links with communication effects research. As pointed out earlier, the emphasis was on particular communication effects: the ability of media messages and opinion leaders to create knowledge of new practices and ideas and persuade the target to adopt the exogenously introduced innovations.

History of Diffusion Studies

Until the early 1900s, scholars disagreed on the question whether ideas were independently developed in different cultures, or whether an idea was invented in one culture and borrowed or diffused into another. The dominant position initially was that of cultural evolutionists who hypothesized that each major culture develops naturally (Frey 1973). These ideas culminated in the 19th century into the *evolutionist school* of anthropology.

Around 1890, there was reaction in Europe and North America against the inconsistencies of evolutionist thought (Heine-Geldern 1968). Evidence indicated that most cultures had a predominance of borrowed or diffused elements over those that developed from within a particular culture (Herskovits 1969; Kroeber 1944; Linton 1936). Three principal figures, Franz Boas in the United States, Gabriel Tarde in France, and Friedrich Ratzel in Germany, were the proponents of *diffusionist theory* (Heine-Geldern 1968).

Gabriel Tarde (1903), a French sociologist, was one of the first to propose the S-shaped curve of diffusion and also to write about the important role of opinion leaders or change agents in the diffusion or "imitation" process. However, it was the new awareness of the nature and role of mass communication effects (i.e., minimal effects of mass media) in the 1940s that led to a renewed interest and need for theoretical and methodological reformulations in the field of communications. An important development was the increased overlap between mass communication and small group research, as both were recognizing the validity and complexity of the two-step flow idea, discussed earlier. Katz (1963) noted that this effected a convergence of interest among mass communication researchers and rural sociologists who were studying the diffusion and acceptance of new farm practices. Mass communication researchers too gradually shifted their focus from interpersonal influence on individual decision-making to a broader understanding of interpersonal networks of communication through which influence and innovations disseminated through society. A couple of the earliest studies in the US that helped conceptualize the process of diffusion of innovations were the Ryan and Gross hybrid corn study in Iowa (1943) and the sociometric studies on physicians (Coleman et al. 1957).

The diffusion of innovations approach was rooted in the postulates and implicit assumptions of exogenous change theory. This approach, as Golding (1974: 43) pointed out:

> suggests that static societies are brought to life by outside influences, technical aid, knowledge, resources and financial assistance and (in a slightly different form) by the diffusion of ideas. The stranglehold of apathy, stoicism, fatalism, and simple idleness is held to have gripped the peasantry of the Third World until advanced countries produced both the tools and the know-how to coax them into action.

The notion of exogenously induced change permeated assumptions of fundamental concepts in diffusion research. The earliest definition of development was "a type of social change in which new ideas are introduced into a social system in order to produce higher per capita incomes and levels of living through more modern production methods and improved social organization" (Rogers 1969: 18). Modernization, or the "development" of the individual, was seen as "the process by which individuals change from a traditional way of life to a more complex, technologically advanced, and rapidly changing style of life" (Rogers 1969: 48). The necessary route for this change from a traditional to a modern person was understood as the communication and acceptance of new ideas from sources external to the social system (Fjes 1976).

Everett Rogers, whose work has been central in this area, identified the following main elements in any analysis of diffusion of an idea or innovation: (a) the *innovation*, which is any idea considered new by the recipient, (b) its *communication* through certain *channels*, (c) among members of a *social system*, and (d) over *time* (Rogers with Shoemaker 1971). Katz provided a similar definition of diffusion: "the process of spread of a given new idea or practice, over time, via specifiable channels, through a social structure such as neighborhood, a factory, or a tribe" (Katz 1963: 77).

The year 1960 may be considered a watershed in the export of diffusion studies from the West to the developing nations. This period saw a sharp increase in the number of diffusion studies globally. Rogers noted that by the mid-1970s nearly half of all diffusion studies were being conducted in Third World nations. The number of studies increased from a mere 54 in 1960 to more than 800 by 1975 (Rogers 1976a: 208). An apparent reason for this sharp rise may have been the technological determinism that reigned supreme during this period in developing nations. Technology and the concomitant process of industrialization were thought to be the key to modernization. As Rogers aptly commented:

> So, micro level investigations of the diffusion of technological in- novations (e.g., in agriculture, health, family planning, etc.) among villagers were of direct relevance to development planners and other government officials in developing countries. These research results, and the general framework of diffusion, provided both a kind of theor- etical approach and an evaluation procedure for development agencies (Rogers and Adhikarya 1979: 70).

Model of Diffusion

Diffusion studies conceptualized, confirmed, and elaborated five stages in the adoption process of the individual decision-maker (Frey 1973; Lionberger 1960; Rogers 1962). Adoption was defined as the process through which the individual arrived at the decision to adopt or reject the innovation from the time he/she first became aware of it. The five stages were: awareness, interest, evaluation, trial, and adoption.[4] At the awareness stage, the individual recipient was exposed to the innovation but lacked complete information on it. At the interest stage, the recipient sought more information on the innovation. At the evaluation stage, the individual mentally decided whether the innovation was compatible with present and future needs. At the trial stage, the individual made the decision to try it on a limited scale. At the adoption stage, the individual decided to continue full use of the innovation. The early diffusion studies also indicated that at the awareness stage the mass media and cosmopolite information sources were reported as influential while at the evaluation and adoption stages, interpersonal and localite[5] sources of information seemed to be the dominant modes of influence (Rogers 1962).

The starting point for the numerous studies of diffusion by rural soci- ologists was the collection of reports depicting the relative speed with which an innovation was adopted by members of a social system, such as farmers living in small, well-defined communities (Frey 1973). These data exhibited a consistent pattern across different communities for different kinds of innovations. When the cumulative percentages of adoptions were graphically plotted against time, they formed the classic S-shaped curve. Thus, the adoption rate of innovations had a rather slow start, then as the early adopters started to influence the rate, there was a fairly rapid rise slackening again at the top asymptotically forming the S-shape (see Figure 4.9).

Figure 4.9
Cumulative S-shaped Curve of Diffusion

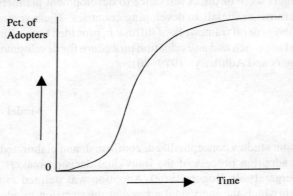

When the absolute number of adoptions were plotted for a distinct time period, a bell-shaped, normal frequency curve was obtained as shown in Figure 4.10.

Figure 4.10
Standard Normal Diffusion Curve

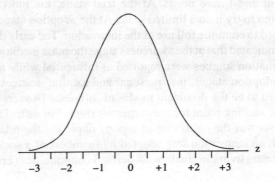

In this curve, the majority of adoptions were found to occur near the mean. The adopters were classified into five different categories on the basis of the two measures of the normal curve, the mean and the standard deviation. The categories were: innovators, early adopters, early majority, late majority, and laggards. The *innovators*, or the individuals who were the earliest in adopting innovations, constituted 2.5 percent and lay at a distance of two units of standard deviation to the left of the mean. The next 13.5 percent of adopters lay between one and two standard deviations from the mean on the left and were called the *early adopters*. The *early majority* who comprised 34 percent of adopters lay between the mean and one standard deviation to the left. The next group of adopters (34 percent) were labeled *late majority* and they were located between the mean and one standard deviation to the right, while the last 16 percent of adopters were called *laggards* and were placed at a distance of one standard deviation to the right of the mean (Rogers 1969).

The diffusion studies indicated a great difference among the adopter groups in terms of their personal characteristics, media behavior and position in the social structure. The relatively early adopters were usually younger, had a higher social status, had more favorable financial status, engaged in more specialized operations, and were equipped with greater mental abilities than later adopters. In terms of communication behavior, earlier adopters used more mass media and cosmopolite information sources. Also, the social relations of earlier adopters were more cosmopolite than for later categories, and the earlier adopters had more opinion leadership characteristics (Frey 1973).

An important ingredient of the diffusion and adoption process was the innovation itself. The characteristics of an innovation, as perceived by the individuals in a social system, affected its rate of adoption. Five attributes were enumerated that would affect its rate of adoption: (*i*) relative advantage, or the degree to which an innovation was superior to the ideas it superseded; (*ii*) compatibility, or the degree to which an innovation was consistent with existing values and past experiences; (*iii*) complexity, or the degree to which an innovation was relatively difficult to understand and use; (*iv*) divisibility, or the degree to which an innovation could be tried on a limited basis; and (*v*) communicability, or the degree to which the results could be disseminated to others (Rogers 1962).

Diffusion research revealed findings on the underlying power-influence structure in the peasant communities. In a study of modern and traditional villages in Colombia, Rogers discovered that innovators were opinion leaders in the more modern villages, whereas in the traditional villages, since their distance from fellow villagers was very great, they were accorded little opinion leadership (Rogers, 1969). Frey (1973: 396) noted:

> In general, many diffusion studies suggest a picture of the underlying power-communication process that shows the innovator as an individual with comparatively strong communication links to more modern sectors outside his community. He may or may not have a conspicuously large opinion leadership domain himself, but in the more progressive community the innovators are either powerful themselves or at least linked to early adopters who are disproportionately influential in the community.

In sum, the diffusion of innovations research established the importance of communication in the modernization process at the local level. In the dominant paradigm, communication was visualized as the link through which exogenous ideas entered the local communities. Diffusion of innovations then emphasized the nature and role of communication in facilitating further dissemination within local communities:

> since invention within a closed system like a peasant village is a rare event, until there is communication of ideas from sources external to the village, little change can occur in peasant knowledge, attitudes, and behavior. Communication is, therefore, central to modernization in such circumstances (Rogers 1969: 48).

Modernization was defined as the process by which "individuals change from a traditional way of life to a more complex, technologically advanced, and rapidly changing style of life" (Rogers 1969: 48). Thus, diffusion of innovations studies documented the impact of communication (interpersonal and mass media) on the change from a traditional to a modern way of life.

SOCIAL MARKETING OF FAMILY PLANNING, HEALTH, AND PRO-SOCIAL INNOVATIONS

Over time, diffusion theory alone proved inadequate as a guide to communications planning in development campaigns. The diffusion concepts are imprecise, and the diffusion model does not sufficiently account for recipient feedback, which is crucial to campaign success. Communication efforts both in First World and Third World contexts have increasingly turned to science-based commercial marketing strategies to disseminate ideas to promote social causes, a process called *social marketing*. Examples in the First World include campaigns to discourage tobacco smoking, encourage use of auto seat belts, stop drinking and driving, promote healthful diets, discourage teen sex (or encourage safe sex), and prevent HIV/AIDS and other sexually transmitted diseases. In the Third World context, the major themes have included family planning, equal status for women, responsible sexual relationships, adult literacy, responsible parenthood, and HIV prevention and control.

Social Marketing

Until the early 1970s, communication models in family planning or other health-related areas reinforced the active source and passive receiver stereotype. Communication campaigns used one-way, top-down, source to receiver transmission models with the belief that effects would occur autonomously once the target received the message (Rogers 1973). Opinion leaders, change agents, and mass media outlets such as the radio were used to transmit persuasive messages. The assumption in these strategies was that knowledge was the missing link in the adoption and use of the service or product.

The incorporation of social marketing techniques in the 1970s emphasized the challenges of changing the values and knowledge as well as behavior pattern of the receivers. The concept of social marketing was first introduced in 1971 and was defined as "the design, implementation, and control of programs calculated to influence the acceptability of social ideas and involving considerations of product, planning, pricing, communication, distribution, and marketing research" (Kotler and Zaltman 1971: 5). Today, the definition of social marketing has broadened and is described as "the application of commercial marketing technologies to the analysis, planning, execution, and evaluation of programs designed to influence the voluntary behavior of target audiences in order to improve their personal welfare and that of their society" (Andreason 1995: 7). Social marketing has introduced several new concepts in the dissemination of ideas and services: *audience segmentation, market research, product development, incentives,* and *facilitation* to maximize the target group's response (Kotler 1984).

Market research is a detailed investigation of the market for the specific product, idea, or service; the segments within the broad audience group; behavioral and knowledge characteristics of the audience segments; and the cost-benefit analysis of reaching and influencing the different groups via communication campaigns. *Product development* involves the development of not just one product, but a host of other products that will appeal to the different market segments in terms of their varied needs. "In other words, whenever possible, the social marketer does not stay with the existing product and try to sell it—a sales approach—but rather, searches for the best product to meet the need—a marketing approach" (Kotler 1984: 26). The use of *incentives* offers the target audience monetary or psychological incentives to increase the level of motivation in the adoption and use of the product or service. Finally, *facilitation* makes it relatively easier for the target to adopt the innovation by reducing the effort or time required on the part of the user.

Social marketers take a holistic view of the process by emphasizing the four Ps in the marketing chain: Product, Pricing, Placement, and Promotion:

> Their job is to promote the organization's objectives and products, using communication media . . . they advise what products will be acceptable to the target public, what incentives will work best, what distribution systems will be optimal, and what communication program will be effective. They think in exchange terms rather than solely in persuasion terms (Kotler 1984: 27).

Family Planning Communication

Communication efforts in family planning relied on the "clinic approach" until the end of the 1960s. In this approach, contraceptive services and products were advertised through the mass media and made available in family planning clinics (Rogers 1973). The positive social and health value of these services and products were considered adequate for their successful distribution and use by the intended beneficiaries. This passive communication approach was gradually replaced by an active strategy in the 1970s. Trained health extension agents took the message of family planning to the homes of prospective clients and their communities. A supporting cadre of agents such as medical doctors, midwives, and even barbers brought the message of family planning to a greater and greater number of people. To a large extent, this approach in the "field era" was influenced by similar work in agricultural extension. Extension agents were supplemented by social advertising: radio shows, posters, folk media performances, mobile film vans, etc., to bridge the knowledge gap and also to publicize the availability of contraceptive products and services (Rogers 1973).

The field approach to family planning in the 1970s was quite successful. The knowledge levels of and favorable attitudes toward family planning services and contraceptives reached high levels. However, there was relatively little adoption of these services or products (Rogers 1973). Two major reviews of communication efforts in family planning (Rogers 1973; Schramm 1971) published in the mid-1970s, painted a bleak picture. They revealed that communication efforts lacked a coherent and systematic strategy (Piotrow et al. 1997). They showed:

1. A limited evidence of coherent communication planning and strategic design.
2. A lack of multimedia communication campaigns and poor service delivery.
3. A lack of attention to the different communication needs of varied audience segments.
4. A naïve assumption that knowledge and awareness will automatically lead to behavior change.
5. A lack of systematic pretesting of messages.
6. A lack of a clear understanding of the relationship between communication strategies and behavior change.
7. A lack of formative and summative evaluations of communication campaigns.

Since the 1990s, the Population Communication Services (PCS) aided by USAID, has adopted a strategic communication framework to overcome past weaknesses in family planning communication. Strategic communication describes an operational framework that incorporates the concepts of social marketing and behavior change models in the design, execution, and evaluation of communication strategies intended to influence behavior change.

The concepts of audience research, market segmentation, product development, incentives, and promotion are contributions from social marketing research applied to strategic family planning communication. In addition, the communication process itself has evolved into a convergence model where participants create and share information in order to reach a mutual understanding (Rogers and Kincaid 1981). This orientation, then, pulls in formative research procedures such as focus groups, audience surveys, and pretesting of messages into communication research in family planning (Piotrow et al. 1997).

Behavior Change Models. Stage models in several disciplines such as social psychology, marketing, rural sociology, and psychotherapy, identified a series of steps that an individual would pass through from first awareness to adoption. This hierarchy of effects in behavior change indicated a similar step process in family planning communication. Some of the most frequently used stage models of behavior change used in family planning are listed in Table 4.1.

Table 4.1
Stage Theories in Behavior Change

Stage Models	Hierarchy of Effects	Source
Social Psychology	Cognition–Attitude–Behavior change	Hovland, Lumsdaine, and Sheffield (1949)
Diffusion of Innovations	Awareness–Interest–Evaluation–Trial–Adoption	Rogers (1962)
	Knowledge–Persuasion–Decision–Implementation–Confirmation	Rogers (1983, 1995)
Marketing and Advertising	Attention–Interest–Comprehension–Impact–Attitude–Sales	Palda (1966)
Social Marketing	Cognition–Action–Behavior–Values	Kotler (1984)
Psychotherapy	Precontemplation–Contemplation–Preparation–Action–Maintenance	Prochaska, DiClemente, and Norcross (1992)
Family Planning and Reproductive Health	Knowledge–Approval–Intention–Practice–Advocacy	Piotrow, Kincaid, Rimon II, and Rinehart (1997)

The stage theories represent behavior change as a sequence of steps with intermediate goals. These dictate that the communication process should also be a stage process needing different messages and approaches at each step of the behavior change process.

Communications in HIV/AIDS Prevention

In the absence of pharmacological, immunological, and medical interventions for the prevention and cure for HIV/AIDS, changing behavior has been recognized as the only possible way to contain the spread of this disease (Edgar et al. 1992; Freimuth et al. 1990; Maibach et al. 1993; WHO 1988). Although the human immunodeficiency virus (HIV) has been identified as the etiological agent causing AIDS, transmission of this virus depends largely on human behavior related to sexuality and drug use. Communication plays an important role in this process because it disseminates information that may prevent risk behavior and spread awareness leading to a reduction of social stigma (Melkote and Muppidi 1999). AIDS-prevention programs, disseminated through mass media or community awareness campaigns, are directed towards changing sexual practices and use of intravenous needles. However, not all of these programs are successful and sometimes fail to bring about appropriate behavior change. In order to minimize the chances of failure an array of psychosocial theories have been developed to drive communication campaigns and to predict the consequences of interventions (Maibach et al. 1993).

Theories and Models of Individual Behavior Change

As the transmission of HIV is affected significantly by individual behavior, individual behavior change theories have remained the theoretical anchor for most preventive efforts (UNAIDS 1999). Health communication scholars have tried to understand how individuals process information and have identified the factors that contribute to appropriate behavior change. Some of these theorists have, implicitly or explicitly, assumed that if individuals were provided with the "right" information they would adopt the recommended behavior. Some others have endorsed the need to provide behavioral skills along with information so that individuals are able to carry out the desired behavior.

Psychosocial models of high-risk behaviors may be divided into three streams: those that focus on predicting risky behavior, those that deal with behavior change, and models that predict maintenance of safe behavior (UNAIDS 1999). The psychosocial models described here do not consider the interaction of social, cultural, and environmental factors as occurring independently of individual behavioral variables (Auerbach et al. 1994). Psychological theories and models that have been frequently used in HIV/AIDS prevention campaigns are briefly reviewed below. As in the case of family planning behavioral change models described earlier, these theories focus on the stages that individuals are assumed to pass through in the process of behavior change. Of the theories discussed below, only the *AIDS Risk Reduction and Management Model* was developed exclusively for AIDS.

Health Belief Model. Since the 1950s, the health belief model (HBM) has been extensively employed in social science research to explain health-related behavior. The HBM grew out of research by social scientists in the US Public Health Services to explain the reluctance of people to participate in disease risk-reduction programs. The HBM is based on value-expectancy theory. Behavior is seen as a function of the subjective value (desire to avoid illness) and as an outcome of the subjective probability or expectation (remedial or preventive action to ward off the illness). These basic components are expanded to form the framework for the model. The model assumes that individuals will take preventive actions (risk-reduction behaviors) when: they believe they are susceptible to a disease (self-perception of risk) and that the consequences will be severe; they believe that taking preventive actions will be beneficial in reducing the threat of contracting the disease (e.g., condoms are effective against HIV infection), and that this perceived benefit will be sufficient to overcome perceived barriers such as costs or the inconvenience of undertaking the actions (e.g., using condoms); and they perceive a stimulus, either internal, such as pain, or external, such as mass media campaigns, newspaper articles, or personal involvement that serve as cues for action (Rosenstock et al. 1994; UNAIDS 1999).

Theory of Reasoned Action. The theory of reasoned action (Ajzen and Fishbein 1980; Fishbein and Ajzen 1975) is an extension of the HBM (Kashima and Gallois 1993). The theory of reasoned action is based on the idea that the most immediate determinant of a person's behavior is the person's behavioral intention—what the person intends to do. Influencing behavior, then, is to be accomplished through influencing a person's intentions. Intention in turn is a joint function of one's positive or negative feeling toward performing the behavior, and one's perception of social pressure to perform or not to perform that behavior. This theory guides interventions by focusing on attitudes toward risk reduction, response to social norms, and behavioral intentions vis-à-vis risky behavior (UNAIDS 1999).

Social Cognitive Theory. The HBM as well as the theory of reasoned action assume that cognitive determinants bring about behavior change, i.e., perception of susceptibility, severity of effects, benefits of action, and intention to perform behavior. But, Bandura cautions that "to achieve self-directed change, people need to be given not only reason to alter risky habits but also the behavioral means, resources, and social supports to do so. It will require certain skills in self-motivation and self-guidance" (Bandura 1994: 25).

Self-efficacy and social modeling are two elements of Bandura's theory that have been widely used in HIV/AIDS campaigns (Freimuth 1992). Self-efficacy refers to a person's belief in his/her personal ability to effect change, which determines what course of action that person will choose, how long it will be sustained in the face of resistance, and his/her resiliency to bounce back following setbacks. Social modeling is based on the principle that people learn vicariously by observing the actions of others. And further, people are more likely to judge their own capabilities, in part, by how well those whom they regard as similar to themselves exercise control over situations. If people see models similar to them solving problems successfully, they will develop a stronger belief in their abilities. This ties in with self-efficacy, since only if actors are confident of their ability to act, can they act effectively. Social modeling has been used extensively in television campaigns (including enter-education campaigns, to be discussed) in order to provide knowledge about HIV/AIDS, as well as strategies to cope with stressful situations in interpersonal sexual encounters. Research additionally shows that the most successful role models are demographically and attitudinally related to the audience (Michal-Johnson and Bowen 1993: 156). The dual variables, self-efficacy and modeling have been used widely in campaigns on HIV/AIDS because of their holistic approach that provides the knowledge, the skill, and the confidence to undertake preventive measures against AIDS.

AIDS Risk Reduction and Management (ARRM). The AIDS risk reduction and management model (ARRM) (Catania et al. 1990) combines elements from the HBM and social cognitive theory to describe the process through which individuals change their behavior. It tries to understand why individuals fail to make the behavioral transition. The ARRM has been specifically designed to understand and predict AIDS-related behaviors. Hence, the analytical framework that it offers can be considered most relevant in studying high-risk sexual practices and how and why individuals adopt preventive behaviors. The ARRM is ideally suited for longitudinal studies in order to understand why people fail to progress through the various stages. This understanding would allow for effective intervention since it would be possible to identify the position of the person in the change process and address the particular needs for that stage. The ARRM identifies three stages:

Stage One is labeling high-risk behavior as problematic, which incorporates the notion of susceptibility from the health belief model. This involves knowing which sexual activities are associated with HIV transmission, believing that one is personally susceptible to contracting HIV, and believing that having AIDS is undesirable. Stage Two is making a commitment to changing high-risk behaviors, which includes weighing costs and benefits, and evaluating response efficacy, incorporating the efficacy concept from social cognitive learning theory. Stage Three is seeking and enacting solutions, that is taking steps to actually perform the new behavior and then performing it. This enactment is influenced by social norms and problem-solving options, and it may include seeking help (Auerbach et al. 1994: 85).

According to Auerbach, Wypijewska, and Brodie (1994), stage models, such as ARRM, are useful diagnostic tools to determine at which stage a target group is situated, and, therefore, the most appropriate interventions. They contrast gay men in the United States as a group highly aware of the risks of unprotected sex to Hispanic/Latino women as a group which does not recognize this risk. Obviously campaigns directed at providing AIDS information to a community that is already knowledgeable leads to wasted expenditure (Catania et al. 1990). Unlike other models and theories that concentrate on changing "high-risk" behavior, the ARRM approach takes cognizance of the fact that change is a process and may not be achieved by a one-shot campaign.

Table 4.2 presents an overview of the most frequently used theories of human behavior at the individual, social, and community levels. The theories listed in Table 4.2 offer pointers to communication campaigns and public health programs that attempt to effect health behavior changes as well to individuals and societies experiencing a shift in behavior patterns (Piotrow et al. 1997).

Table 4.2

Overview of Most Frequently Used Theories of Human Behavior

Level	Theory or Model	Behavioral Determinants	Examples of Program Application
Individual Level	Health Belief Model	Perceived susceptibility	Increase level of risk perception
		Perceived severity	Influence beliefs of severity
		Perceived benefits and barriers	Assess and influence beliefs about benefits/barriers of changing behavior
		Cues to action	
	Theory of Reasoned Action	Attitudes	Assess and influence attitudes
		Subjective norms	Assess and influence norms in the social group
		Behavioral intentions	Assess and influence behavioral intentions
	Social Cognitive Theory	Outcome expectancies	Sexual communication, need for social support to reinforce behavior change
	Social Learning Theory	Self-efficacy	Modeling of safer behaviors
	Stages of Change	Precontemplative	Assess and influence outcome expectations and norms, perceived risk
		Contemplative	Assess and influence self-efficacy, intention
		Preparation	Assess and influence self-efficacy, intentions and outcome expectations
		Action	Assess and influence outcome expectations and norms
		Maintenance	Assess and influence norms, self-efficacy
	AIDS Risk Reduction Model	Labeling	Assess and influence risk perception, aversive emotions and knowledge
		Commitment	Assess and influence perceptions of enjoyment, self-efficacy and risk reduction
		Enactment and maintenance	Assess and influence communication, informal networking, formal help-seeking

(Table 4.2 contd.)

(Table 4.2 contd.)

Level	Theory or Model	Behavioral Determinants	Examples of Program Application
Social and Community Level	Diffusion of Innovation	Change agent	Who are the influential people in the community
		Communication channels	Most effective means to spread information including community leaders
	Social Influences	Context	Assess type of social networks in community
		Context of social interactions	Equip young people with social skills including peer pressure resistance skills
		Social norms	Assess and influence social norms
		Social rewards and punishments	
	Social Network Theory	Social networks	Assess composition of social network
		Social support	Assess, build up social support
	Theory of Gender and Power	Social sexual norms and power dynamics	Address social structure of gender relations
	Empowerment	Community organization	Assess community priorities
		Community building	Assess key activities of the community and facilitate alliance-building
	Social Ecological Model for Health Promotion	Intra-personal (knowledge, attitudes, perception of risk)	Increase in knowledge, skills development, influence risk perception
		Social, organizational, cultural (social networks)	Community organizing, mass media
		Political factors (regulation)	Advocacy
		Policy	Advocacy; community organizing
	Socio-economic and Environmental Factors	Resources; living conditions	Social services
		Access to prevention	Increasing access to prevention (condoms)

Source: UNAIDS 1999: 47.

Communication/Education Interventions in HIV Risk Reduction

Communication and education campaigns have been chiefly used to increase awareness of AIDS, decrease behaviors associated with HIV/AIDS infection, promote safe sex behavior, and prevent discrimination against people with AIDS by reducing the social stigma attached to the disease. Social marketing techniques have been used to address these goals and also to increase the sales of products and services to prevent sexually transmitted diseases. The channels used for mass education have included targeted media, electronic and print media, peer education, use of social networks, peer counseling, and school-based interventions (UNAIDS 1999).

Social marketing techniques have especially been used among at-risk populations globally to promote the distribution, sales, and use of condoms. The four Ps of social marketing—Product, Price, Place, and Promotion—have been researched in relation to the characteristics of specific populations. Commercial advertising and packaging of condoms, appropriate price and convenient locations (truck stops, bars, hotels) for sale/distribution have resulted in dramatic increases in condom sales in countries such as the Ivory Coast, Uganda, and Malaysia where condoms were practically unavailable prior to social marketing campaigns (UNAIDS 1999, World Bank 1997). Other countries where there has been some success in increasing condom use include India, Zambia, and Pakistan (UNAIDS 1999).

India. We use India as a case study to examine how the AIDS organizations have incorporated strategic communication strategies to combat the spread of HIV/AIDS. In India, about one-half of the nearly one billion population is in the sexually active age group of 15–49 years. During the 1990s, the occurrence and spread of HIV/AIDS in India showed the following trends (NACO 1997–98): HIV is prevalent in almost all parts of the country; HIV/AIDS is spreading from urban to rural areas; HIV/AIDS is also spreading from high-risk behavior groups to the general population since the early 1990s; one in every four cases reported is a female; and about 89 percent of the reported cases are from the sexually active and economically productive age group of 15–49 years.

The Indian Government constituted a national AIDS committee at the highest policy-making level in 1986 and launched a national AIDS control program in 1987. A strategic plan for the prevention and control of AIDS was prepared for the five-year period 1992–97. The objectives of this plan were to establish a comprehensive, multisectoral program for the prevention and control of HIV/AIDS that would: prevent HIV transmission; decrease the morbidity and mortality associated with HIV infection; and minimize the socio-economic impact resulting from HIV infection (NACO 1997–98). Some of the immediate objectives were to: ensure a high level of awareness of HIV/AIDS and its prevention in the population; promote the use of condoms; and target behavior change interventions at groups identified as high risk.

The information and communication campaigns included both the provision of information as well as changing behaviors of vulnerable groups. The communication campaigns adopted a multimedia strategy using a wide range of media as well as social marketing techniques. The strategy also included the development of specialized packages for groups practicing risky behavior, counseling training, as well as the provision of counseling services.

The National AIDS Control Organization (NACO) in India is giving the highest priority to an effective sustained strategy to bring about changes in behavior (e.g., avoid multipartner sex, sterilization of needles/syringes, use of condoms, etc.) to prevent further infection (NACO 1997–98). One strategy to combat the problem has been to involve all sectors of society. The NACO has adopted a policy of networking and advocacy to involve the participation of non-governmental organizations, business, industry, policy-makers, youth groups, educational establishments, and others. This has been driven by the realization that AIDS is not just a health problem but a social problem of huge proportion that has the potential to inflict serious socio-economic consequences on society.

Entertainment–Education

In the 1970s, the idea of using television as an instructional/development medium appealed to both administrators and development experts because of its immense potential in propagating useful ideas and practices. The Satellite Instructional Television Experiment (SITE) launched in India in the mid-1970s, broadcast instructional television programs to remote villages. However, research studies later showed that most viewers prefer television entertainment shows to educational programs. Two examples illustrate the trend toward increasing the entertainment content of television programs (Rogers 1987):

1. In American Samoa, an educational television system introduced in 1967 now serves as a channel for broadcasting American entertainment shows.
2. The transmitter in Kheda district in Gujarat, India that produced local development programs was closed down in the mid-1980s when the audience switched to viewing the Ahmedabad television station when it started to broadcast national programs (mostly entertainment) into Kheda district.

Meanwhile, in mass communication theory, the *minimal effects hypothesis* was gradually losing its appeal by the early 1970s (Lowery and DeFleur 1995). Since the early 1940s, research testing this hypothesis had shown that mass media were not particularly effective in changing opinions and attitudes of the audience members. However, new research in the area of agenda-setting showed that the mass media were very effective in increasing the cognition levels of audiences of salient events and thus serving as important agents of surveillance (Shaw and McCombs 1974). Another area of research labeled as the uses and gratifications perspective (Blumer and Katz 1974) put the focus on an active audience member as opposed to the passive receiver stereotype depicted in the minimal effects theories. In the uses and gratifications model, audience members actively selected media products to satisfy a range of needs: new information, entertainment, news, relaxation, and more. This research showed that audiences were actively selecting radio and television programs to gratify their perceived needs. Another dramatic change has been the rapid increase in radio and television receivers in the Third World since the early 1970s. "Between 1965 and 1995 the number of radios in developing countries grew more than tenfold, from 82 million to 997 million. The number of television sets grew from only 13 million to 707 million" (Piotrow et al. 1997: 11). A parallel development in the Third World has been the trend toward increasing commercialization and privatization of television and radio channels.

These concomitant developments have provided a fertile ground for the growth and popularity of entertainment–education programs (also known as enter-education programs). In this approach, educational content is embedded in entertainment programs in media such as radio, television, records, videos, and folk theater:

Entertainment–education is the process of purposely designing and implementing a media message to both entertain and educate, in order to increase audience knowledge about an educational issue, create favorable attitudes, and change overt behavior. This strategy uses the universal appeal of entertainment to show individuals how they can live safer, healthier, and happier lives (Singhal and Rogers 1999: xii).

Singhal and Rogers (1999) point out that entertainment–education programs either directly or indirectly facilitate social change:

1. At the individual level by influencing awareness, attention, and behavior toward a socially desirable objective; and
2. At the larger community level of the individual audience member by serving as an agenda setter, or influencing public and policy initiatives in a socially desirable direction.

Combining entertainment with education is not a new phenomenon in most cultures around the world. However, the concept of deliberately using an entertainment–education theme to further social objectives set by a country or a community is relatively new. The idea of a *telenovela* with a pro-social theme originated in Peru in 1969 with the show *Simplemente Maria* which told the rags-to-riches story of a single mother who achieved financial success through her proficiency and hard work on her Singer sewing machine (Singhal and Rogers 1988, 1999). Inspired by the success of the Peruvian soap opera, the Mexican commercial television network Televisa produced four programs on Mexican cultural history and pride between 1967 and 1970, under the leadership of Miguel Sabido, a writer–producer at the Televisa (Singhal et al. 1993). Sabido then made several more with other themes, some of which ran over a year on Televisa. One of the shows, called *Ven Conmigo*, dealt with adult literacy while another, called *Accompaname*, stressed family planning (Singhal and Rogers 1988). Sabido's basic methodology was as follows (Singhal et al. 1993: 3–4):

1. Decide on the main message or central value to relay. Also identify related values (e.g., family harmony, family communication, and child development) that are important to the main message and may be significant in message reception. Make sure that all the values to be promoted are consistent with the views of key opinion leaders, including political leaders, TV executives, and religious leaders.

2. Develop positive and other role models, consistent with social learning theory.
3. Write the script and produce the program within a well-defined and high quality telenovela system.

A central idea underlying the enter-education strategy is that people learn from positive role models with whom they can identify (from social learning theory). Therefore, it is important to make sure that positive role models support all of the values important to the message. Other kinds of role models may also be included, for instance, negative roles that reject the values promoted. There may be yet others (doubters) who are in-between and eventually see the light and become believers. The script is written and characters developed so that the audience hopefully will want to identify with and imitate positive role models, and avoid behaviors associated with the negative role models.

According to Singhal and Rogers (1988: 111), "Pro development soap operas in Mexico promoted knowledge and values to the viewing audience so that these individuals could better understand the reality of their social problems, and seek possible solutions." Following the example of Mexico and spurred by the efforts of Population Communications International (PCI), the Indian television authority experimented with *Hum Log* (1984–85), a soap opera dealing with social problems in contemporary Indian society. This show too became very popular with Indian viewers, leading to sentimental protests when it was finally pulled off the air in 1985 after running 156 episodes (Singhal and Rogers 1988).

The success of both Mexico and India with their pro-development soap operas prompted other developing countries (such as Kenya, Nigeria, Egypt, Brazil, Jamaica, Bangladesh, Turkey, Thailand, Indonesia, Tanzania, and Zaire) to adopt this entertainment strategy to their specific needs (Singhal and Rogers 1988, 1999). Examples of popular programs include: *Thinka Thinka Sukh* (India), *Tushauriane* (Kenya), *Ushikwapo Shikimana* (Kenya), and *Twende Na Wakati* (Tanzania). Table 4.3 lists some of the most popular and researched entertainment–education programs from different parts of the Third World along with their themes and effects.

Entertainment–education programs represent a unique kind of social marketing where pro-social ideas are marketed within media products. Most evaluation research uses surveys or focus groups. Some evaluations rely on data collected at infrastructure access points, such as family planning clinics and adult education centers. Evaluations usually aim to find

Table 4.3

Popular Entertainment–Education Programs in the Third World

Country	Enter-educate Program	Themes	Effects
Peru	*Simplemente Maria* (TV)	Adult literacy; Self-employment	Established *telenovela* as a dominant genre of TV broadcasting
Mexico	*Ven Conmigo* (TV)	Adult education	Facilitated increased enrollment in adult education programs
Mexico	*Acompaname* (TV)	Family planning; Family harmony; Gender equality	Increased awareness and adoption of family planning products and services
India	*Hum Log* (TV)	Family planning; Family harmony; Gender equality; National integration	Improved awareness, attitude, and behavior toward the projected themes
Mexico and Latin America	*Cuando Estemos Juntos Détente* (Rock Music videos)	Teenage sexual responsibility	Disseminated information on contraceptives and encouraged sexual restraint among teenagers
Philippines	That Situation; I Still Believe (Popular music albums)	Sexual responsibility	Influenced knowledge, attitude, and behavior related to sexual responsibility
Nigeria	Choices; Wait for Me (Music videos)	Sexual responsibility; Family planning	Increased awareness and adoption of family planning products and services
Jamaica	Naseberry Street (Radio)	Family planning	Increased awareness and adoption of family planning products and services
Kenya	*Ushikwapo Shikimana* (Radio)	Family planning	Increased awareness of family planning and importance of spousal relationship
Tanzania	*Twende Na Wakati* (Radio)	HIV prevention	Increased adoption of condom use; Decreased sharing of razors and needles; Encouraged monogamous relationships
India	*Thinka Thinka Sukh* (Radio)	Women's empowerment; Family harmony; Gender equality; HIV prevention	Improved awareness, attitudes and behaviors toward the projected themes

Source: Compiled from Singhal and Rogers 1999.

out whether people are exposed to programs, whether they recalled the messages, whether they liked the characters, and whether they acted (or intended to act) on the messages. Results show primarily cognitive changes though some changes have been recorded that require behavior and value shifts. Modeling theory, self-efficacy, and para-social interaction models have been used to predict and explain the hierarchy of effects produced by these media programs.

Much evaluation data are vulnerable to several criticisms. First, it is often difficult to validate self-reports of effects. Second, as entertainment–education usually takes place within the context of a larger campaign and myriad other external messages and stimuli, it is often difficult or impossible to sort out the effects of these programs from other influences. Finally, critics have rightly noted that mass media audiences, for example, those who have access to television, frequently constitute only small segments of the target population. The most at-risk populations may not be reached by entertainment–education, populations that may disproportionately include women (e.g., Lurtha 1991; Worthington 1992). Hence, these programs may be preaching to more elite economic groups or the already converted.

Despite the above, inherent challenges in successfully operationalizing enter-education programs, their popularity in many contexts and their effectiveness in creating awareness and spreading information are quite well established. They are most effective when used as a part of larger campaigns that involve systematic research and varieties of message and media strategies (including interpersonal and group communication) alongside the enter-education programs.

Summary

Four overlapping conceptual as well as operational areas that have contributed greatly to an understanding of the social-scientific foundations of communication and mass communication in general, and their role in social change theory and practice in particular, have been: (*i*) the Communication Effects Approach, (*ii*) the Mass Media and Modernization Approach, (*iii*) the Diffusion of Innovations Approach, and (*iv*) the Social Marketing Approach.

Communication Effects Approach: The earliest models of media effects conceptualized the impact of mass media as direct, powerful, and uniform on individuals living in modern, industrial societies termed *mass societies* by sociologists. The *bullet theory* and *hypodermic needle* theories were colorful terms used to describe the concept of powerful effects. The early models developed by Lasswell, Shannon and Weaver, Berlo, Schramm, etc., conceptualized communication as a linear and one-way process flowing from a powerful source to a passive receiver. However, there was a shift in opinion among scholars after the Second World War. New research showed the rather weak impact of mass media in affecting important behavioral and attitudinal changes. Communication scholars suggested that mass media were more agents of reinforcement than direct change. This shift in emphasis made little difference to formulations advocating the use of mass media for development in the Third World countries. Here, uses of media for *transmission* of information and for *persuasion* were transferred to fields such as agricultural extension, health, and education. The mass media were perceived by administrators and policy-makers as important tools to bring about quick behavioral change, particularly in favor of the *modernizing* objectives of the state. The powerful effects idea pervades much discourse regarding the nature and role of mass media in developing nations even today.

In the *Mass Media and Modernization Approach* the mass media served as agents and indices of modernization in developing nations. At the micro level, research in this tradition focused on social-psychological characteristics of individuals, which were considered necessary for a successful transition from a traditional to a modern society. Daniel Lerner's *The Passing of the Traditional Society* illustrates the major ideas under the mass media and modernization approach. He posited that people in traditional societies could expand their empathy by exposure to the mass media which showed them new places, behaviors, and cultures. In short, the mass media had the potential to blow the winds of modernization into isolated traditional communities and replace the structures of life, values, and behaviors there with ones seen in modern Western societies.

In this approach, mass media were considered as ideal vehicles for transferring new ideas and models from the developed nations to the Third World and from urban areas to the rural countryside. The mass media were entrusted with the task of preparing individuals in developing nations for rapid social change by establishing a *climate of modernization*. They were thought to have powerful, uniform, and direct effects on individuals in the Third World, even though this premise was discarded in North America in the 1940s.

Research in this tradition generated high expectations from the mass media. They were considered *magic multipliers* of development benefits in Third World nations. Information, therefore, was considered the missing link in the development chain. The quality of information available and its wide dissemination was a key factor in the speed of development (Schramm 1964). Adequate mass media outlets and information would act as a spur to education, commerce, and a chain of other related development activities.

Diffusion of Innovations theory has important theoretical links with both communication effects research and research on the role of media in modernizing traditional societies. The emphasis was again on communication effects, i.e., the ability of media messages and opinion leaders to create knowledge of new practices and ideas among the target audience and to persuade them to adopt the exogenously conceived and introduced innovations. Researchers firmly believed that the necessary route to the *development* of an individual from a traditional to a modern person was the acceptance of new ideas from sources external to the social system.

Everett Rogers, whose work has been central in this area, identified the following elements in the diffusion of an idea or an innovation: the *innovation*, its *communication, the channels of communication*, and the *social system* within which and for which the process occurs. Adoption was defined as the process through which the individual arrived at the decision to adopt or reject an innovation from the time of first awareness. The five stages were: awareness, interest, evaluation, trial, and adoption. Diffusion studies indicated differences among adopter groups in terms of their personal characteristics, media behavior, and position in society. Early adopters were usually younger, had higher social and financial status and were equipped with greater mental ability than later adopters.

The diffusion of innovations research established the importance of communication in the modernization process at the local level. In the dominant paradigm, communication was visualized as the important link through which exogenous ideas entered the local communities. Diffusion of innovations then emphasized the nature and role of communication in facilitating further dissemination within the local communities.

Over time, diffusion theory proved to be inadequate as a guide for communications. Hence, it has been largely replaced by *Social Marketing*, which provides a model for the strategic, scientific determination of message and media strategies to disseminate ideas to promote social causes. In the Third World context, major themes have included family planning, equal status for women, responsible sexual relationships, adult literacy, responsible parenthood, and HIV/AIDS prevention and control. Until the early 1970s, communication models in family planning or other health-related areas reinforced the active source and passive receiver stereotype. Communication campaigns guided by diffusion theory used one-way, top-down, source to receiver transmission models with the belief that effects would occur autonomously once the target received the message. The incorporation of social marketing techniques in the 1970s emphasized the challenges of changing the knowledge and values, as well as the behavior patterns, of the receivers. Social marketing introduced several strategic concepts in the dissemination of ideas and services: *audience segmentation, market research, product development, incentives,* and *facilitation* to maximize the target group's response. Since the 1990s, for instance, Population Communication Services (PCS) aided by the USAID, has adopted a strategic communication framework to overcome past weaknesses in family planning communication. Strategic communication describes an operational framework that incorporates the concepts of social marketing and behavior change models in the design, execution, and evaluation of communication strategies intended to influence behavior change.

Another major theme in social marketing has been HIV/AIDS prevention. Communication plays an important role in this process because it disseminates information that may prevent risk behavior and spread awareness leading to the reduction of social stigma. Communication and education campaigns have been chiefly used to increase awareness of AIDS, to decrease behaviors associated with HIV infection, promote safe sexual behavior, and prevent discrimination against people with AIDS by reducing the social stigma attached to the disease. Social marketing techniques have also been used to increase the sales and use of condoms and other products and services to prevent sexually transmitted diseases.

Entertainment–education programs have become increasingly popular in the last two decades, often as a part of social marketing campaigns. In this approach, educational content is embedded in entertainment programs in media such as radio, television, records, videos, and folk theater. Singhal and Rogers (1999) point out that entertainment–education programs either directly or indirectly facilitate social change. These programs present a unique kind of social marketing where pro-social ideas are marketed as media products. Effects tend to be mostly cognitive changes, though some changes have been recorded that require behavior and value shifts.

1. Lazarsfeld's important work lies in the areas of administrative and critical research. Administrative research deals with structuring and operation of mass media industries to serve optimally the interests of the investors, media professionals, and the public. Critical research, on the other hand, examines broader questions involving human existence and the role of mass media in a society. For more information, see Lazarsfeld (1941).

2. For a detailed analysis and description of research pertaining to powerful and minimal effects of mass media, see Lowery and DeFleur (1988, 1995).

3. The United States Agency for International Development's objectives have included "encouraging the development of communication systems in all countries which respect the principles of free flow of information and maintaining US access to valuable global communications resources such as frequencies and orbital slots" (USAID 1984: 3). Also, USAID's "specific objectives" make a direct link between "amounts of information available to individuals" and the "efficient functioning of competitive markets" (USAID 1984: 4).

4. In his later writings, Rogers introduced new terms to describe the stages in the innovation-decision process: knowledge, persuasion, decision, implementation, and confirmation. See Rogers (1983, 1995). However, the earlier terms described in the text have remained popular with extension professionals in developing countries.

5. Localite communication channels are those from within the social system of the adopter (or rejector) such as close friends, neighbors, peers, and other significant members of the community. See Rogers (1962, 1983).

III

CRITICAL PERSPECTIVES ON COMMUNICATION AND DEVELOPMENT

CHAPTER 5

DECONSTRUCTING THE DOMINANT PARADIGM OF DEVELOPMENT

> For two-thirds of the people on earth, this positive meaning of the word "development" is a reminder of *what they are not*. It is a reminder of an undesirable, undignified condition. To escape from it, they need to be enslaved to others' experiences and dreams.
>
> Gustavo Esteva (1992: 10)

In this chapter, we take a critical look at the dominant development paradigm that we introduced in Chapters 3 and 4. We begin with an overview of biases and consequences of the modernization paradigm, and its scientific underpinnings. Then we critique multiple facets of this paradigm, beginning with economic models, including critiques made by proponents of basic needs approaches, dependency theory, and world-system theory. Critiques of social evolutionary modernization models and related psychological theories are reviewed next. We note that most critiques foreground the economic *class* bias of modernization; however, they neglect other important social divisions and development variables, including religion, gender, and environment. Therefore, we also discuss critiques of the role accorded to religion, to women, and the environment in the dominant discourse of development. Additionally, several key definitions related to development are posed and alternative approaches are suggested. In Chapter 6, we will extend our critique to communication approaches under modernization.

BIASES OF THE DOMINANT PARADIGM OF DEVELOPMENT

The assumptive basis for modernization has been around for at least 400 years. The historical, political, and cultural conditions that shaped the ideas of "development" as an antidote to social anarchy and chaos, and as a stimulus to "progress" were first constructed in Europe. During this long sojourn through European history, it is possible to identify several factors that provided the groundswell support for idea of continuous and unrelenting material progress: humanistic ideas of the Renaissance, the Protestant work ethic, modern science, and the rise of European states (Friberg and Hettne 1985). The capitalist elite, state bureaucrat, and the scientist were the more dominant factors.

The scientific method was an important outcome of the Renaissance period. It replaced religion and scriptures as a tool to gain knowledge or help guide human actions. However, within a short period it became *the* method to guide and analyze social change. The determinism of positivistic science made its tenets non-negotiable:

> For the first time in human history, human beings had succeeded in unraveling a method of gaining knowledge as certain as the knowledge that earlier had only been available via revealed scripture. This technique of knowledge acquisition was so reliable that the knowledge acquired thereby was for all practical purposes non-negotiable. It was this claim which would soon conflict with the natural rights of man (Alvares 1992: 228).

Over time, modern science derived many of its propositions and laws from its application in industry, therefore, limiting the appropriate use of these propositions to one context.[1] Nonetheless, the assumptions of science quickly pervaded other institutions as well. A powerful coalition between the state, the elite capitalist, and the scientific-technical expert must be traced to the post-Renaissance period in Europe. The European idea of "development" was exported globally through international trade and colonization between roughly the 16th century and the early decades of the 20th century.

It is interesting to notice that all three institutions originated in Europe at about the same time. Feudalism was replaced by capitalism. The states became the dominant political units. The religious world-view was challenged by a new materialistic philosophy based on natural science. It was also at this time that the Europeans started to conquer the rest of the world. A singularly expansive power complex came into existence (Friberg and Hettne 1985: 231–32).

In essence, science has claimed to be the final arbiter of truth. As the Enlightenment values that undergird science are consistent with those of modern political-economic systems, science and scientific discourse, economics, and politics constitute mutually reinforcing systems. Thus, modern states, bureaucrats, elites in positions of power, and scientist-technocrats using science have taken over the responsibility of deciding what is truth and what is not. Post-structuralists such as Foucault (1980) have posited that as a servant of the state, science has been used not just to explain reality, but to produce, control, and normalize. The process of normalization reduces heterogeneity by homogenizing individual feelings, desires, and actions.

Today, the "development machine" is very powerful because of its vast reach and institutional backing. Institutions that are partners in the enterprise of development include state bureaucracies, aid agencies, multilateral agencies, the global network of NGOs, private banks, technical consultancies, and research departments in universities (Crush 1995). The role of the elite and the state bureaucrat in developing countries has greatly enhanced the spread of this development model.

Left to its own, development would have made little headway across the globe. That it did eventually get moving was due purely to the coercive power of the new nation-states which now assumed, in addition to their earlier *controlling* function, a *conducting* function as well. Every nation-state stepped in voluntarily to force development, often with the assistance of police and magistrates (Alvares 1992: 226).

In addition, state-induced violence and authoritarianism is a well-known fact. Scholars such as Ashis Nandy (1992), posit that today the coercive power of governments to control their populations or wage war against others comes from the application of sophisticated scientific method. What sets the present development discourse apart from that of the past is that the state has entered *all* areas of life of its citizens and set up total systems for social and political engineering based on the theory of development and progress (Nandy 1992).

The dominant paradigm of development is inseparable from the concept of modernity (Ullrich 1992). This concept of modernity, also discussed in Chapter 3, has particular attributes:

> Its starting point is the assumption that unremitting diligence, constant progress in the production of material goods, the unbroken conquest of nature, the restructuring of the world into predictable, technologically and organizationally manipulable processes will automatically and simultaneously produce the conditions of human happiness (Ullrich 1992: 278).

We summarize some of the overt and covert biases of the dominant paradigm and its discourse. The list is not exhaustive, but rather should be seen as a start in the deconstruction of the dominant paradigm:

- Rationality and progress are synonymous with economic rationality and growth as articulated by the economic and political elite in the North, by multilateral organizations controlled by such elite, state bureaucrats, and by vested interests in the South (Braidotti et al. 1994).
- A higher and higher standard of living as quantified by indicators such as per capita income, per capita consumption of resources, and gross national product constitutes a key goal. The bias is not necessarily the "well-being" of an individual or community that would include the material and non-material aspects of life, but "well-having" that denotes maximum material consumption (Latouche 1992).
- The dominant discourse aided by the positivistic scientific method has claimed to speak the "truth" about development. Thus, assumptions and images of modernity and progress as exported from the industrialized West have been uncritically accepted by the leaders of many recipient countries (Foucault 1980). These assumptions

frequently have overruled other analyses, such as folk-scientific descriptions of nature (Alvares 1992).

- The prior histories of developing countries have been considered irrelevant to the enterprise of modernization. Communities have been stripped of their histories and cultures, and a technocratic plan has been constructed for their future (Crush 1995). Thus, objects of development are treated in a historical vacuum that precludes any analysis of previous initiatives and their harmful effects (Mitchell 1995).

- Development concepts, initiatives, and their presumed benefits have been guided by master geographies constructed by the dominant states and institutions. Thus, notions such as the Third World, Oriental, African, and North–South have become stereotypes. Third World countries or poorer enclaves within them are viewed as net receivers of development assistance. "That most of the benefits actually flow from the groups and areas 'targeted' to the capitals, wealthier enclaves, families and their technical advisers (through debt-servicing or absorption of the externalities of development), is not part of the map of development" (Hewitt 1995: 128).

- There is a strong biological metaphor in development discourse. *Entwicklung* or the process of social evolution was considered similar to the phylogenic changes in a biological organism. Over time, ontogeny imitated the irreversible and linear stages of phylogeny.

- The irrelevance of history leads to social problems that are interpreted as occurring naturally rather than as outcomes of politics, mismanagement, corruption, greed, or the exercise of power (Escobar 1995b; Wilkins 1999). "Natural" hazards such as famine and drought, are not regarded as possible outcomes of policy failure, failures of research paradigms or the crises of capitalist modernization ventures. "Rather, hazards are constructed as problems due to external factors beyond managerial control . . . . Hazards are situated, metaphorically, at the frontier, part of the un-finished business of modernization" (Crush 1995: 16; Hewitt 1995).

Consequences of the Dominant Paradigm of Development

Many of the consequences of the dominant paradigm, often negative, flow directly from the above biases. The stage theory of development and the linear bias of social change have straitjacketed objects of development into frozen states assumed to share common characteristics. "Not only are the objects of development stripped of their history, but they are then inserted into implicit (and explicit) typologies which define a priori what they are, where they've been and where, with development as guide, they can go" (Crush 1995: 9). Uprooted from their histories and cultures, Third World countries became pliable objects to be manipulated by the development experts. They all had a common and inevitable destiny. "The industrial mode of production, which was no more than one, among many, forms of social life, became the definition of the terminal stage of a unilinear way of social evolution" (Esteva 1992: 9).

As for the people and communities far removed from the center, developmentalism has eroded their control over their lifestyles and natural resources. The mantra of economic development has reduced most of these people into objects to be "developed" for their own good by the all-knowing development technocrat. In the process, local narratives, cultural meanings, and social arrangements have been devalued. Thus, development has resulted in the colonization of indigenous views relating to a "good life," sickness and death, the environment, and the cosmos. These views have been discarded without even a cursory inspection.

. . . the Western world-view has been presented as *the* world-view, claiming universal validity. All colonized or penetrated countries were stigmatized as inferior in culture, religion or race. Western man did not bother to listen to the African shaman, the Indian guru or the Chinese scholar (Friberg and Hettne 1985: 237).

In the name of development and progress, the state has unleashed violence against its citizens, especially on those who are powerless. Mega development projects such as hydroelectric dams, nuclear power plants, highways, and mines have displaced local people from their land, their livelihoods, and their communities. Often they have not even been rehabilitated or compensated for their loss. Examples of such groups include the Penans of Borneo, the Gond tribes in Central India, the local people in the Chotanagpur region of India, the rubber tappers in the Amazon, and the residents of Bhopal, India who faced the devastating effects of the leak of noxious fumes from the nearby Union Carbide plant (Fernandes and Thukral 1989; Sainath 1996; Shiva, 1992).

Sachs (1992) warns that the monoculture being spread by development "has eroded viable alternatives to the industrial, growth-oriented society and dangerously crippled humankind's capacity to meet an increasingly different future with creative responses" (p. 4). Other scholars caution that the present development model that is resource-intensive and polluting, is empirically untenable.

This voracious appetite for resources is demonstrated yet more clearly in the example of the United States: less than 6 percent of the world's population consumes about 40 percent of the world's natural resources. If one were to extend this industrial mode of production and lifestyle to all the people of the earth, five or six further planets like the earth would be required for resource plundering and waste disposal (Ullrich 1992: 280).

A major factor in the spread of the technocratic development discourse is the powerful, monolithic institutional structure that has been set up to promote it. The Bretton Woods conference put in place a powerful array of forces to steer the world past the pitfalls of underdevelopment. It is time now for a dismantling, or at least, a downsizing of these institutional forces. Addressing the multilateral, bilateral, and non-governmental development institutions, Honadle (1999: 141) points out:

They were innovative reactions to the cold war atmosphere of the immediate post World War II era. Their monolithic natures, their utilization and enhancement of civil engineering and neo-classical economic tools and perspectives, their rigid hierarchies and technocratic cultures, and their opaque organizational styles are no accident. Cold war origins made such attributes natural. The imperatives of the period dictated just such institutional responses.

However, the world of the 21st century is vastly different from the 1940s. Today, themes such as diversity, human welfare, community-oriented participatory initiatives, and transparent modes of collective action reflect the new priorities (Honadle 1999). The political and developmental realities of today call for a new set of institutional arrangements based on the conditions and priorities that exist in the new century.

The legitimacy of the dominant paradigm is being challenged on several fronts, ranging from critiques of its scientific and economic foundations, to critiques by fundamentalist religious movements, to the postmodernist, post-structuralist, and feminist revolts at the other end (Tehranian 1994). Fundamentalist religious movements, such as in Islam, are questioning the validity of the Western mode of modernity and advocating a return to their vision of a modern society, while the postmodernists, post-structuralists, feminists, and others point to the fundamental problems with the metadiscourse on development.

CRITIQUE OF THE ECONOMIC MODEL

There are many approaches to critiquing the overwhelming economic orientation of the dominant paradigm, based in neo-classical theories. For instance, Tipps (1973) makes three kinds of critiques. *Ideologically*, he shows the many ways in which modernization indicates an ethnocentric world-view in its assumption that the Western way is universal. *Empirically*, there is much evidence that modernization has failed to achieve its goals. This is related to the ideological critique in that successful projects must carefully consider local history and context. Finally, at the *metatheoretical* level, Tipps argues that the concepts of modernization are not parsimonious and vague; hence modernization is a weak theory.

In this section we organize our critique as follows. First, we detail some of the key empirical critiques, both at the macro level of economic statistics and at the micro level of the Third World household. Next we consider modernization's failure to address basic needs in its emphasis on economic indicators. Third, we discuss critiques of modernization's failure to address global power imbalances. Major areas of theory proposed to replace modernization are dependency theory and world systems theory.

Empirical Critiques of the Economic Model

Consistent with the Enlightenment-based scientific model, the neo-classical economic model was adopted during the First Development Decade that suggested a "trickle-down" approach to development benefits. This approach gradually began losing credibility in the 1970s. Dudley Seers (1977b: 3) documents some of the reasons for this:

1. The social problems of developed nations were spreading concern about the environmental costs of economic growth;
2. Despite substantial transfers of capital and technology from the developed nations to the Third World, the gap between the *per capita* incomes of the two blocs was growing;
3. Third World nations with impressive rates of growth did not achieve either the political status or social equity expected of them;
4. Income inequality was rising throughout the Third World;
5. Unemployment rates were refusing to go down in spite of impressive growth rates; and
6. Power was being concentrated among an elite coterie who benefited from the growth, then used that power to preserve the inequality in their societies.

In the dominant paradigm, economic growth was synonymous with development. Per capita incomes and GNP rates constituted reliable criteria to measure progress. However, there were other economic indicators that were equally important but given a short shrift in the "trickle-down" approach. Seers (1977a: 3) put it very well:

the questions to ask about a country's development are therefore: what has been happening to poverty? What has been happening to unemployment? What has been happening to inequality? If all three of these have declined from high levels, then beyond doubt this has been a period of development for the country concerned.

Unfortunately, progress in eradicating unemployment, poverty, and income inequality was dismal. Weaver and Jameson (1978) note that in each of these areas, the poor benefited very little, and their plight deteriorated during the 1950s and 1960s.

Unemployment. During the Development Decade of the 1960s, unemployment rates actually went up rather than going down. And, this was the period during which the economies of developing nations were doing very well. Available data indicate that the rate of increase of unemployment was concomitant with high rates of growth (Weaver and Jameson 1978).

Inequality. Income inequality increased all over the Third World. Weaver and Jameson (1978) documented the trend in several Third World countries such as Kenya, Brazil, Ecuador, and Turkey. In these countries, the share of national income was concentrated in the hands of a very small minority. For example, in Brazil in the 1960s, the top 5 percent cornered as much as 46 percent of the national income. While the trickle-down model encouraged some initial inequality as necessary to generate savings and incentives, the rate of inequality that actually emerged was dysfunctional to economic growth. Seers (1977a: 4) questioned the need to generate inequality for a later day trickle-down effect:

> I find the argument that the need for savings justifies inequality un-convincing in the Third World today. Savings propensities are after all very low precisely in countries with highly unequal distributions; the industrial countries with less concentration of income have, by contrast, much higher savings propensities.

Weaver and Jameson (1978: 36–37) constructed the Lorenz curve which could be used to compute Gini coefficient—a measure of income distribution. Figure 5.1 is the graph they obtained.

Figure 5.1
Lorenz Curve

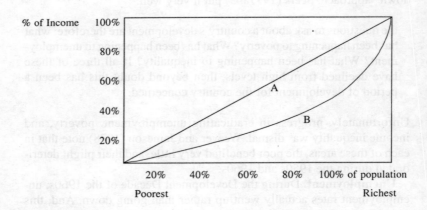

In Figure 5.1, the vertical axis denotes income distribution and the horizontal axis the spread of the population. Perfect equality of income distribution is denoted by the diagonal line. For example, 40 percent of the population will get 40 percent of income. However, actual data obtained would show points falling on a curved line, or the Lorenz curve. The closer the distance between the curved line and the horizontal axis, the greater the income inequality. Gini coefficient was computed by the ratio **A/(A+B).** Thus, if there were extreme inequality (i.e., area **A** covered the whole area of the graph), the Gini coefficient would be unity. If there were perfect equality (Area **A** was zero), Gini coefficient would be zero.

According to the theoretical assumption of the trickle-down model, the measure of inequality would reduce as economies grew. However, Weaver and Jameson (1978: 37), using data from Chenery (1974), showed (see Figure 5.2) that this was not the case. Income inequality, once established did not decline.

Figure 5.2
Relation between GNP and Income Inequality

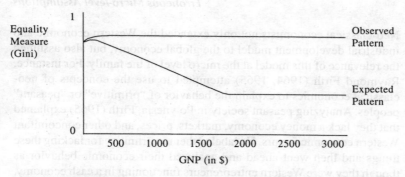

Poverty. This was intimately connected with unemployment and income inequality. Any negative growth in these two areas would have a detrimental effect on poverty rates. In this discussion, poverty is defined as the inability of people to meet basic necessities such as minimal food, clothing, footwear, and shelter. Studies found that as economic expansion proceeded, the income of the bottom 40 percent of people in developing countries fell not only relatively (which was to be expected during the initial period) but in absolute terms as well (Adelman and Morris 1973). In other words, the bottom half of the population in several countries such as Pakistan, India, Brazil, and Mexico, had less income (in absolute dollars) at the end of the 1970s than they had in the early 1960s (Adelman and Morris 1973).

In short, economic planning using modernization models brought about mixed results. Many developing nations showed very impressive increases in their GNP rates until the 1960s. Some even doubled and tripled the rates. For example, in Brazil, GNP rates showed a 7 percent increase every year from the mid-1960s, and in Korea, since 1974, GNP grew at 10 percent per year. However, unemployment, poverty, and income inequality were increasing as well. The poor, therefore, benefited very little from the economic growth in their countries.

As Weaver and Jameson (1978: 39) conclude:

> this model led to increasing inequality and also led to increasing poverty . . . what planning seems to have brought is an enhancement in the good life of a small elite class, while increasing the good life for the poor very little or perhaps even removing them further from the attainment of the good life.

Erroneous Micro-level Assumptions

Neo-classical economists not only extended the Western economic and industrial development model to the global economy, but also assumed the relevance of this model at the micro level of the family. For instance, Raymond Firth (1964, 1965) attempted to use the concepts of neo-classical economics to explain the behavior of "primitive" or "peasant" peoples. Analyzing peasant society in Polynesia, Firth (1965) explained that they lack a money economy, markets, prices, and other concomitant Western economic factors. He labeled them as primitive for lacking these things and then went ahead and analyzed their economic behavior as though they were Western entrepreneurs functioning in a cash economy. Daniel Thorner (1968) summarized how this approach equated the peasant household with a capitalist enterprise:

> When the "farm business" method is applied to analysis of peasant agriculture, the peasant's land and livestock, equipment, and other goods are equated with those of a small firm. The peasant's behavior is then treated in terms of the theory of the firm as developed for business enterprises. It is taken for granted that the peasant's aim is to rationalize his operations so as to obtain the maximum profit (Thorner 1968: 507).

In the above approach, the subsistence farm family's expenses for equipment and wages were deducted from the gross income to obtain the net profit. When the expenses exceeded the total income, the farm was said to be operating at a loss. This approach, then, failed to explain some obvious realities in developing nations. For example, as Thorner (1968) posited, how was one to explain why peasants in many developing nations survived despite engaging in "uneconomic farming" decade after decade?

Production and Consumption Approach. The classical economics approach to subsistence agriculture also was challenged by a team of Russian scholars: Kablukov, Kosinskii, Chelintsev, Makarov, Studenskii, and Chayanov. They based their arguments on data they had collected and analyzed from Russian peasants in the decades from 1880 and onward. They argued that the economic orientation of the peasant enterprise could not be treated as if it were a business firm. The primary motive of the family was to eat, make required payments, and somehow survive. It was not possible to impute money value to the labor performed by the peasant family. The sheer pressure exerted on the family made the members behave in ways that could be considered "irrational" according to capitalist business standards. If the consumption needs of the family demanded extra labor, the members would expend that labor even if the additional product that was obtained was very small. Since labor was in abundance, the family would rent or buy extra land regardless of its price. Chayanov argued that since hired hands were not employed, the concepts of classic and neo-classical economics could not be applied to peasant farm families (Thorner 1966).

One of the notable contributions of Chayanov to a clearer understanding of the peasant household economy was the labor–consumer balance. As he put it, "We can state positively that the degree of self-exploitation of labor is established by some relationship between the measures of demand satisfaction and the measure of the burden of labor" (Chayanov 1966: 81). According to this, the production and consumption decisions in the household economy were interrelated. Each household worked to the point where the household's subjective evaluation of the marginal disutility of work equaled its estimate of the marginal utility of the output gained. This statement is represented graphically in Figure 5.3.

In Figure 5.3, **AB** indicates the degree of drudgery of work; **CD** represents marginal utility of output (rubles). The curve **CD** cuts **AB** at the point **X** which corresponds to a sum of rubles 67 received per year. At this output level, the subjective evaluation of output obtained equals the subjective evaluation of the drudgery involved in the agricultural work. From this point onwards, as the curves indicate, each succeeding ruble will be evaluated lower than the drudgery of winning it.

Chayanov drew similar curves and showed how, for different families, the balance between demand satisfaction and "irksomeness" of work was influenced by the size of the family and the ratio of working members to non-working members. Thus, Chayanov and his colleagues demonstrated that the peasant exhibited a totally different rationality when it

Figure 5.3
Chayanov's Curves of Utility/Disutility of Output and Drudgery of Labor

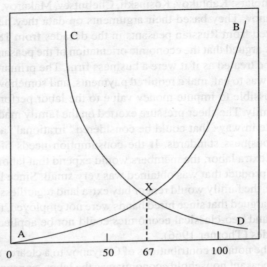

Source: Chayanov. 1966: 82. "Measure of Self-exploitation of the Peasant Family Labour Force." In D. Thorner et al. (Eds.), *The Theory of Peasant Economy.* © American Economic Association. Reprinted with permission.

came to questions such as adoption of innovations, subsistence farming, and risk-aversion. Kerblay (1971) noted that though Chayanov's thesis worked better for thinly populated countries, nevertheless, it was still relevant to peasant populations in other Third World nations:

> The problem raised over forty years ago by the leader of the Russian organizational school, and the basic approach focusing analysis of peasant economies on the dynamics and structures of family farms, are just as pertinent today for developing countries where peasant economies still predominate (Kerblay 1971: 159).

Subsistence Ethic. Several other scholars such as Migdal (1974), Scott (1976), Popkin (1979), and Hyden (1980) have raised concerns consistent with the findings of Chayanov, but go further in explicating a subsistence ethic. These scholars agreed on the precarious existence of poor people in the Third World: living dangerously close to the subsistence level. Scott posited: "If the Great Depression left an indelible mark on the fears, values, and habits of a whole generation of Americans, can we imagine the impact of periodic food crises on the fears, values and habits of rice farmers in monsoon Asia?" (Scott 1976: 2). He argued that the fear of food shortages in peasant societies had given rise to a *subsistence ethic*. This ethic was the consequence of living so close to the margin and could be compared to the ethic of peasants in 19th-century France, Russia, and Italy. Scott placed the subsistence ethic at the center of the analysis of peasant politics. The peasant family's major objective was to produce enough rice to feed the family, buy necessities, and pay land rents and taxes. Living dangerously close to the margin, where one bad crop meant starvation, the peasants had perfected ways of keeping alive. For example, the local tradition of seed varieties, planting methods, and timing were designed over centuries of trial and error to produce the minimum subsistence even under very difficult circumstances (Scott 1976). Scott (1976: 3) pointed out that several social arrangements served the same end:

> Patterns of reciprocity, forced generosity, communal land, and work sharing helped to even out the inevitable troughs in a family's resources which might otherwise have thrown them below subsistence.

Safety-first Principle. Scott (1976) asserted that it was the *safety-first* principle that anchored many of the social, moral, and technical arrangements of the peasant agrarian order. Given the imminent possibility of facing hunger, starvation, or malnutrition every year, it was reasonable to assume that the peasant would have a different perspective vis-à-vis adoption of risky innovations. In other words, the "peasant household has little scope for the profit maximization calculus of traditional neoclassical economics" (Scott 1976: 4). Thus, the objective was to stabilize returns and minimize risks even if this meant reduced returns for the labor expended:

> In decision-making parlance, his behavior is risk-averse; he minimizes the subjective probability of the maximum loss. If treating the peasant as a would-be Schumpeterian entrepreneur misses his key existential dilemma, so do the normal power-maximizing assumptions that fail to do justice to his political behavior. To begin instead with the need for a reliable subsistence as the primordial goal of the peasant cultivator and then to examine his relationships to his neighbors, to elites, and to

the state in terms of whether they aid or hinder in meeting that need, is to recast many issues (Scott 1976: 4–5).

Through his/her subsistence ethic and safety-first principle, the subsistence farmer was desperately trying to earn a *minimum income*. It is usual in advanced nations for the state to guarantee a minimal standard of living through social security, unemployment compensation, medical care, and so on. Most in the Third World do not have this safety net and it is therefore irrational for them to engage in innovative, achievement-oriented and profit-maximizing behavior.

The recent spate of suicides among subsistence farmers in central and southern parts of India is a grim reminder of the outcomes when impoverished farmers attempt to adopt risky farm practices or crops. More than 180 subsistence farmers in the states of Andhra Pradesh, Karnataka, and Maharashtra in India, committed suicide (by drinking pesticide) when their dreams of lucrative returns from cash crops (mostly cotton) were shattered due to crop failure resulting from weather-related problems and pests. These farmers had spent their life savings and also incurred huge debts from banks and moneylenders to pursue their dream of making profit by growing cotton (*Halarnkar* 1998).

Basic Needs Critiques and Approaches

The disenchantment with the trickle-down idea of development, as a result of observations at the macro and micro levels as discussed above, led to a focus on basic human needs beginning in the early 1970s, i.e., those necessities that are absolutely essential to maintain a decent quality of life. The usual indicators of development such as the GNP and per capita measures did not give adequate information on the quality of life of individuals at the bottom of the socio-economic ladder in developing nations. "The idea was to go beyond mere capital investment towards investment into human resources in the form of equitable distribution of wealth and income, social justice and improvement of facilities for education, health, social security and so on as salient features" (Braidotti et al. 1994: 17). Early proponents of the basic needs idea were Mahbub Ul Haq and Holis Chenery of the World Bank, Paul Streeten, a development economist, and James Grant of the Overseas Development Council.

The basic needs approach, which aimed to eliminate some of the worst aspects of poverty, drew support from a variety of sources: the World

Bank, the ILO, United Nations Economic and Social Council, the United States Congress and many national governments. Paul Streeten (1979: 48) summarized the main objectives of the basic needs approach:

1. Provide adequate food and clean drinking water;
2. Provide decent shelter;
3. Provide education;
4. Provide security of livelihood;
5. Provide adequate transport;
6. Help people participate in decision-making; and
7. Uphold a person's dignity and self-respect.

Thus, this approach emphasized both basic, fundamental needs of people and a respect for human rights. However, since basic needs may be met in ways that deny basic rights, and human rights may be practiced in ways that may reject basic needs, Streeten added one more human right: the socio-economic right to international resources. This included the right to universal primary education; the right to adequate food and health standards; the right to equitable employment; and the right to minimum wages and collective bargaining.

Several attempts were made to address the basic human needs problems in a quantifiable way (Grant 1978). One measure that was developed by the Overseas Development Council was the PQLI: the Physical Quality of Life Index. This index incorporated data on three factors—life expectancy at age 1, infant mortality, and literacy—into a single composite index having a low of zero and a maximum of 100. Morris (1979: 4) pointed out that while the PQLI did not measure important qualitative indicators such as freedom and justice, it attempted to measure how basic life-sustaining social needs of individuals were met by their societies. It was possible to use the PQLI to compare any changes between nations or between ethnic, regional groupings within nations. Grant supported the idea of using life expectancy, infant mortality, and literacy as indicators of quality of life:

A major advantage of consolidating these three indicators in the PQLI is that such a composite index usefully summarizes a great deal of social performance. It also encourages consideration of the interrelatedness of the policies that bear on each aspect of development and thus favors the emergence of broadly rather than narrowly conceived strategies of development. Use of life expectancy or infant mortality alone, for example, all too often leads to the mistaken conclusion that these problems should be left for medical practitioners alone to resolve. Together, however, the three indicators provide important information about how the benefits of development are distributed—about how well the worst aspects of poverty are being eliminated (Grant 1978: 9).

The basic needs approach, then, was a microanalysis attempting to eradicate the worst kind of poverty among the poorest of the poor in developing nations.

We note that through the 1980s and into the 1990s and beyond, basic needs critiques and rhetoric have continued to pervade the discourse of development, as it is obvious that pressing human needs remain unmet. The 1980s were punctuated with global recession in most of the industrialized countries along with serious economic difficulties in the developing world. The countries in the South faced serious balance of payments problems, loan repayment difficulties, drastically lowered prices for their exports, and a wave of protectionist tendencies among the Western industrialized nations (Young 1993). A neo-liberal economic model was employed to tide over the crisis. This sharply curtailed the role of the state and substituted instead an increased reliance on the market. The recommended solution of the donor banks and agencies was to impose structural adjustment policies (SAP) on the debtor countries to revive their sick economies.

Overall, the impact of SAP was disastrous. State expenditure in key social services such health, food subsidies, education, and social welfare was significantly reduced. Young (1993: 39) points out:

The neo-liberal solution to debt and other LDC economic problems— structural adjustment—puts enormous pressure on most sectors of the population, but especially on the poorest. As we saw, the South Commission noted that it is the poorest that suffer the most hardship; but among the poor, women are suffering disproportionately.

Due to its harsh effects on the Third World, many derisively refer to the 1980s as the lost decade of development. In the 1990s, the yo-yo-like shifts in economic policy are back to emphasizing basic human needs. "The idea that adjustment must be with a human face has gained currency in international development circles" (Young 1993: 36). This has meant a return to the basic needs rhetoric espoused in the 1970s.

Especially notable in the 1990s is the UNDP's introduction of the Human Development Index (HDI) and the Human Poverty Index (HPI). The HDI measures each country's *achievements* in three development dimensions—longevity (life expectancy), knowledge (a composite measure of educational attainment; adult literacy; and primary, secondary, and tertiary enrollment), and standard of living (real GDP per capita). The HPI measures *deprivation* in human development using the same measures as the HDI (see UNDP 1997).

We note that the basic needs perspective does have much surface appeal in deemphasizing capitalist interventions in order to address desperate concerns of poverty, health, and unemployment. Yet, as long as those who favor the neo-classical approach wield power in development, the basic needs approach cannot dominate. Considerations of national and global security and economics will always take priority. This is clear, for instance, in the fact that aid to Africa diminished with the end of the Cold War. Eastern Europe became the favored recipient for both military and economic aid. Further, Third World critics have feared that the real motive of basic needs proponents is to sustain global patterns of power by maintaining a "reserve army" of labor for capital, an "army" that is perhaps better fed, but still disempowered (e.g., Hoogvelt 1982: 101). Hence, attempts have been made to propose alternative economic development paradigms that directly challenge the power imbalances assumed by the neo-classical approach.

Critiques of Power Imbalances

The above discussion demonstrates that the trickle-down economic model has not alleviated the poverty of the very needy and poor in developing nations who constitute the majority of the population. A periodic emphasis on basic needs has not resulted in any real change. Many have argued that this is because the emphasis has been on economic growth via capital-intensive projects and *not* equitable distribution of the fruits of development. The focus on capital-intensive projects made capital cheap relative to labor. However, in reality, developing countries were labor-rich and capital-poor (Weaver and Jameson 1978). Thus, rising GNP rates, to the extent that they occurred, did not reflect a broad rise in income. Those who controlled economic and political power benefited from the growth.

It is not surprising that those few who benefited from the economic expansion of modernization would be slow to even out imbalances.

Instead, as Seers noted, "they will inevitably try to find ways of maintaining privilege, resorting (as dozens of historical examples show) to political violence [rather] than give it up" (Seers 1977a: 5). A fundamental problem was the trickle-down concept. In the Third World, it was difficult to "grow now and trickle-down later." The unequal structures and the concomitant economic and political power of those who controlled the rules of the game prevented redistribution of benefits. Moreover, the new profits and income were converted into goods such as expensive college educations, luxury houses, and imported cars, which could not be redistributed (Weaver and Jameson 1978).

Additionally, the profits and high incomes derived from economic growth were not adequately reinvested in the development process. Either they went into projects with low priority for development or they were sent abroad. And, these projects fueled the conspicuous consumption of goods and services with a high foreign exchange content. This proved dysfunctional to countries suffering from foreign exchange difficulties (Seers 1977a: 4).

Dependency Theory

Lenin (1939) theorized that imperialism is the highest or "monopoly" stage of capitalism. In this stage he predicted increases in the size of companies, the export of capital, the growth of monopoly ownership, and rivalry among capitalist nations for global resources. Marxian scholars continue to agree on these phenomena and their origins in capitalism, though they differ in their interpretations. Classical Marxists (including Marx and Lenin) assumed a dynamic and progressive role for capitalism and capitalist imperialism in creating the material preconditions for socialism (Brewer 1980: 16–17). Others, including dependency and world-system theorists, observed the failure of capitalism in much of the modern world. They rather described a world-system of exploitation, where the "core" nations exploit "periphery" nations, with the assistance of elite groups within the periphery nations.

In essence, members of the depedency school, such as Frank, Cardoso, Goulet, dos Santos, Baran, Sunkel, and Amin, observed that the main feature of the Third World is its dependent global economic position and they leveled serious criticisms against the power imbalances of the dominant paradigmatic model. Underdevelopment, according to these writers, was not a process distinctly different from development. In fact, they constituted two facets of the same process. The "development of underdevelopment" in Third World nations was and is related to the economic development of Western Europe and North America (Frank 1969). Frank argued that:

> underdevelopment is not due to the survival of archaic institutions and the existence of capital shortage in regions that have remained isolated from the stream of world history. On the contrary, underdevelopment was and still is generated by the very same historical process which also generated economic development: the development of capitalism itself (Frank 1969: 9).

Dependistas maintained that underdevelopment of Third World nations could be regarded as the consequence of the development of Europe and North America which satellized the former and exploited them in order to help their own economic growth.

In the dominant paradigm, Third World societies were conceived as autonomous with respect to changes that were thought to be due to internal forces. Portes (1976: 67) points out that:

> it fails completely, however, to provide a framework for understanding the insertion of individual countries in an evolving international system. Distinctions between core and peripheral economic regions are foreign to the theory. Nor does it grasp the possibility that "autonomous competitors" in the developmental race may be integral parts of transnational units in which weaker states are kept in place by a context of overwhelming political and economic forces.

The dominant paradigm denied history to developing nations. The assumption was that the Third World nations resembled earlier stages of the history of West European nations. Neo-Marxist scholars contend that this was not true. Underdevelopment in the Third World does not signify an earlier stage of European developmental history but instead "is in large part the historical product of the past and continuing economic and other relations between the satellite underdeveloped and the now developed metropolitan countries" (Frank 1969: 4).

Frank (1969: 9–13) posited several hypotheses in the theory of imperialism which he then supported using empirical and historical observations:

1. In contrast to the development of the world metropolis, which is no one's satellite, the development of the national and other subordinate metropoles is limited by their satellite status.
2. The satellites experience their greatest economic development and especially their most classically capitalist industrial development if and when their ties to their metropolis are weakest, and
3. The regions that are the most underdeveloped today are the ones which had the closest ties to the metropolis in the past.

The dependency paradigm later influenced the debate on the New International Economic Order and provided the critics of the dominant paradigm with useful arguments and a system of beliefs for their views.

World-system Theory

Wallerstein (1974, 1980), the main exponent of this theory, considers the world as a single economic system. This theory includes the tenet of the dependency theory that the world-system is capitalist in its orientation. However, Wallerstein departs from the dependistas and does not dwell on the development of the core and the underdevelopment of the periphery:

> Thus there is only one kind of capitalism, namely that of the world-system, although its various branches may manifest themselves differently. By avoiding the prerequisite polarization between center and periphery, Wallerstein circumvents another of the pitfalls of the dependency school: the idea of two different sorts of capitalism (Friberg and Hettne 1985: 213).

The world-system is dominated economically by a set of core states (e.g., the European Union, the US, and Japan), there are peripheral states (e.g., in Africa, Latin America, and Asia) that are weak and to some extent dependent economically on the core states, and there is a third type of state called the semiperiphery (e.g., oil producing countries and the tiger states of Southeast Asia) that lies in between the two. According to Wallerstein (1974), there is a division of labor between the states: tasks requiring higher levels of skill and greater capitalization are reserved for or controlled by the core states. The core states are able to maintain their supremacy as long as they maintain capital accumulation. There are no peripheries that are totally dependent on the center for their development, nor are there any states that are completely autonomous.

The state plays an important role in maintaining the world-system. What differentiates this paradigm from the dependency school is that "the focal point of pressure in the world-economy is the state structure. The state helps to stabilize capitalism by absorbing its costs and managing the social problems which it creates" (Waters 1995: 24). The political and economic elite and the military rulers in the peripheral states then play an important role in maintaining the world-system. "One of the techniques they use is to sell Western domination as the universalizing process of modernization which increases its palatability" (Waters 1995: 25). When viewed thus, the evolutionary universals (explained by the Parsonian functionalist theory) would be indicative of exploitation leading to underdevelopment rather than as adaptive mechanisms leading to greater development. As Portes (1976: 67) points out:

> Since colonial times, extensive legal and bureaucratic regulation of dependent territories has been employed by metropolitan centers as a means of ensuring their hegemony. The historical dialectics by which "modern" structural features serve to perpetuate weak and stagnant societies are not understood by proponents of the evolutionary perspective.

Network Society and the Digital Divide

Castells' three-volume analysis (also discussed in Chapter 2, and noted briefly in Chapter 3) predicts a global network system where power goes beyond the level of both transnational corporations and states (dependency and world-system theories), but rather is "diffused in global networks of wealth, power, information, and images" which transcend time and geographic space (Castells 1997: 359). Nonetheless, these networks will continue to generate profits that will sustain the reward structure of the market. In this new network/market system, the greatest financial benefits will still go to the privileged few. Castells also concludes that the network society will continue to increase global political, economic, and cultural gaps. However, these gaps will be defined less and less by geography (industrialized versus Third World nations) or by transnational economic structures, but rather by a *digital divide*, i.e., those with access to cyberspace and others without such access. Castells predicts, however, those without access will reside disproportionately in a "Fourth World," i.e., much of sub-Saharan Africa, South America, and Asia.

Sociology of Development and Psychosocial Models Revisited

Alongside—and in fact enmeshed with—the economic critiques of modernization, are criticisms of the sociology of development and the psychosocial models discussed in Chapter 3. Critiques of the sociology of development models have been directed at several fronts: their excess abstractness, failure to consider history, and poor selection of development indicators. The psychosocial models were clearly ethnocentric and insensitive to the cultural contexts of people's lives.

Sociology of Development Models

Excessively Abstract

The propositions based on the theories of social evolution were too abstract. While they served as a comprehensive tool for an understanding of social change in general, they had limited utility when applied to concrete problems of development in Third World countries (Portes 1976).

To make the diagnosis, for example, that social transformations occur in the passage from underdevelopment (backwardness, undifferentiation, and ruralism) toward modernization (industrialization, social complexity, and urbanization), is to beg the entire question. Such descriptions are not the end point of scientific inquiry into the problem but their beginning. The question is why such transformations occur in some societies and not others, why they take place at different rates and in different forms, and under what conditions they successfully overcome structural obstacles (Portes 1976: 64).

The bipolar theories presented ideal-typical extremes of the process of change without providing insight into the determinants and constraints of developmental processes (Portes 1976). Other theorists pointed out that actual developmental changes that took place in developing countries went against the empirical relationships proposed in the old paradigm.

Several countries in Central and Eastern Europe, Latin America, and Asia seemed to have reached at certain levels a negative correlation between such socio-demographic indices as literacy, spread of mass media, formal education, or urbanization on the one hand and the institutional ability to sustain growth or to develop libertarian or "rational" institutions on the other (Eisenstadt 1976: 36).

In other situations, the empirical facts were different from the relationships proposed in the paradigm, yet they led to the same conclusions. For example, India had very low urbanization and relatively little industrialization but still it was able to evolve a stable, viable, modern Western political system.

Ahistorical

The Rostowian thesis on economic growth was also found wanting. Some writers pointed out that Rostow had taken the prerequisites of economic growth from the historical experience of Western democracies and applied them as preconditions for growth in non-Western nations in the future. Also, the model distorted history:

> Rostow has compressed epochs of economic struggle in the history of nations into a neatly drawn five-stage model of transition that does not extend more than two centuries at the most . . . . Rostow's historical evidence is based on the limited experience of a few countries that constituted a highly homogenous sample (excluding Japan) (Abraham 1980: 47).

Others criticism of Rostow's model were directed at its unilinear evolutionary nature. He had proposed that every society would pass through the first four stages in his model in order to reach the golden age of mass consumption. However, the historically specific settings of the newly independent developing countries made it extremely difficult, if not impossible, for them to recreate the developmental path of the Western nations. As Abraham (1980: 47) notes:

> it is, however, highly unlikely that the developing societies of today with their history of colonial exploitation, current population explosion and a wide variety of geographical and cultural differences will be

able to go through the process of growth which developed countries treaded.

The sociology of development models invoked a very limited time perspective of 50 to 400 years at most. Going back further in history reveals that several countries, such as China, Egypt, India, Iraq, and Peru, were centers of sophisticated civilizations. Paul Harrison (1979: 33) puts it across very succinctly:

All three continents of what is now the Third World were home of sophisticated civilizations. Many of their cities were centres of fabulous wealth far in advance of anything their first European visitors knew back home. Mathematics, astronomy, medicine were all highly developed among the Arabs, the Indians, and the Chinese. It is wrong to call these civilizations backward. In an intellectual, moral and spiritual sense, several of them were far in advance of Europe. Europe was able to bring them all to their knees for one reason only: because she was more developed in purely material respects. She had achieved breakthroughs in the technology of war and of sea travels which were the basis of her military conquests. And she had developed industrial capitalism, along with its peculiar contempt for and exploitation of human beings and of nature.

The critical stimulus to investment which spurred economic growth in Western Europe was provided, to a great extent, by the surplus appropriated from the slave-plantation colonies (Williams 1964). It was the unlimited overseas market captured by British commerce through superior naval power that fueled the Industrial Revolution in England (Hobsbawm 1968). Also, *laissez-faire* philosophy was not in vogue at the time England was striving to be an industrial power. For instance, in the year 1700, British textile manufacturers had to be protected from the imports of textiles from India, which was at that time one of the biggest exporters of textiles. "Deindustrialization of India thus flowed from British industrialization" (Brookfield 1975: 4).

The underdevelopment of countries in Asia, Africa, and Latin America, therefore, was not by choice. Their colonized status resulted in either deindustrialization or a sustained state of underdevelopment—providing raw materials for the factories in Europe and remaining as captive markets for their finished goods. For example, on the eve of colonialism (c. 1500),

China, India, the Middle East, and Europe were at the same level of economic development. They were all agricultural communities and well-versed in the technology of that time— plough culture. However, by the year 1945, much of Asia, Africa, and the Middle East was still predominantly agricultural using the same technology of circa 1500, whereas European nations such as England and France had become military-industrial giants. "It is possible that industrial civilization might have emerged spontaneously in China or India. But it is futile to speculate; Europe evolved first as an industrial force, and that fact alone changed the entire situation, crippling what industry existed in Asia and giving Europe an advantage that would last at least two hundred years" (Harrison 1979: 38).

Incorrect Indicators

In the old paradigm, wrong dimensions were identified as indicative of development (Portes 1976). For example, Parsons (1964b) identified several "evolutionary universals" such as money, markets, and bureaucracy as strategic for development. However, for a majority of Third World countries, these "evolutionary universals" were nothing new:

> Minimal familiarity with Third World nations would indicate that, by these standards, most of them are already "developed." Such features as money and markets, extensive bureaucratic regulation, and formal legal systems have been long known and present in underdeveloped countries. It is perhaps for this reason that when the abstract discussion of "universals" reaches for concrete examples, it selects primitive tribal societies as poles of contrast to modern Western nations. Such comparisons are, of course, entirely irrelevant to the problem of national development. Third World nations, regardless of stereotypes dear to theorists, are not in the tribal stage (Portes 1976: 67).

Another evolutionary universal suggested by Parsons was a democratic form of government. However, many countries in Africa and Latin America that followed the path of West European nations and set up a democratic form of government achieved mixed results. "Democratic politics in these societies did not greatly increase the adaptive capacity of their social systems" (Portes 1976: 68). Instead, they perpetuated and even legitimized the inequality that existed due to internal contradictions and external subjugation of their economies into a dependent status (Zeitlin 1968).

Psychosocial Models Revisited

Chapter 3 outlined the theories of McClelland, Inkeles, Lerner, and Hagen on the relationship between personality structure of the individuals and modernization of their societies. These theorists conceptualized the attributes of the "modern" person, which comprised an ideal mix of certain belief systems, patterns of behavior, and attitudinal structure. All of these made modernization and economic growth in their societies almost automatic. These perspectives of development, also called value-enactment theories, were quite controversial and now have been largely discarded for a number of reasons.

Contextual Vacuum

The value-enactment theories did not address or take into consideration the influence of structural constraints on individual action. Theorists of this perspective resolutely avoided looking into the effects of political and economic interests at the national and international level on individual independence, action, and opportunities (Frank 1969). For example, the structural obstacles faced by black Africans in South Africa under Apartheid Rule, the lower caste in South Asia, and the racial minorities in the United States override and nullify whatever achievement motivation, aspirations, or empathy they may have had. Portes (1976: 72) notes:

> an active set of individuals, motivated by whatever psychological mechanism one may wish to posit, must still cope with existing economic and political arrangements. One way of doing so is to attempt to transform them, in which case "entrepreneurs" must organize themselves and enter the political arena in conflict with entrenched interest groups. The transformation of "modernity" or "n-achievement" into potential rebellion and ideologically committed elite is a possibility seldom contemplated in these theories.

Thus, McClelland's *n-achievement* may not be an independent variable but rather a dependent variable—dependent on the sanctions, norms, political and economic interest groups that prevail in a society. As Abraham (1980: 86) notes, "achievement motivation itself is a highly institutionalized function of a system of stratification that distributes motivation differently and unevenly over different social strata." Some critics argue that the existence of highly motivated achievers may be irrelevant or even harmful to a nation attempting to bring about socio-economic development. Portes (1976) suggests several possible dysfunctions arising from the role of such individuals: they may support unequal power structures within their societies; they may become managers of transnational corporations, as Marxian critics have observed; or they may choose to emigrate to industrialized nations, resulting in a "brain drain." Hence, these critics argue that what is important for a developing nation is not just a mass of individuals with high levels of aspirations, empathy, or achievement motivation, but articulating clearly the goals toward which the energies and creativity of such individuals are to be channeled.

Unrealistic Consumer Lifestyle

Additionally, a consumer lifestyle was simply unrealistic in most of the Third World. Lerner and Inkeles outlined several characteristics of a "modern" person: such an individual was to tailor his/her behavior, values, and lifestyles to be consistent with that of a Western person. Empathy was, after all, the ability to lift oneself out of the traditional environs and be placed in a Western urban-industrial society. However, this could very well lead *not* to a *revolution of rising expectations* among the people in the Third World nations but to a *revolution of rising frustrations* (Lerner 1958). This is because a developing nation cannot support the consumption patterns of individuals in Western countries. Rather, excessive consumption could be dysfunctional to a country with scarce and limited resources, which could be better used for long-term development. Portes (1976) cautions that the emphasis on consumption could also constrain the flexibility of governments in choosing between different development strategies. The temptation could be to succumb to immediate consumption which would produce mass political support, whereas the curbing of immediate consumption for long-term development objectives could result in mass protests and concomitant political problems.

Ethnocentrism

In much of the literature on modernization, a major blame for the relative backwardness of developing nations was attributed to the traditional behavior and attitudes of their people. The value-normative complexes of scholars such as McClelland, Hagen, Inkeles, and Rogers painted a rather grim picture of the anti-change attitudes and values of individuals in the Third World. As a group, the subsistence farmers or peasants were more often the subjects of study by social scientists. Everett Rogers described a *subculture of peasantry* that was characterized by 10 functionally related variables, all indicating that their ideas and behavior were irrational and that they constituted a formidable obstacle to modernization and change (Rogers 1969). All of these studies were focused on the individual. Consequently, the peasant was the locus of blame for the sluggish pace of progress and change in developing nations. A macro analysis of the entire society, its history, tribulations, social structure, and power relationships may have placed the blame elsewhere. For example, social-psychological variables such as mutual distrust in interpersonal relations, perceived limited good, dependence on and hostility toward government authority, familism, lack of innovativeness and limited aspirations of peasants, while seeming irrational at the individual level, would seem perfectly logical when one considered the long history of oppression and exploitation that poor majorities have suffered under the elites in their societies. Also these socio-psychological findings, to the extent they were valid at all, were probably the consequences rather than the causes of underdevelopment. Thus, while the objective was to understand better the lifestyles of the peasants, the findings of earlier research greatly distorted their image.

Finally, the development of peasant agriculture depends crucially on how one views the nature of subsistence farming and its enterprises. Earlier theories viewed the peasantry as a traditional sector, necessarily in conflict with modernization and change. Therefore, innovations had to flow from the outside into these *traditional* enclaves and somehow *modernize* them. This conceptualization on the nature of peasants and their enterprises was highly inaccurate and ethnocentric (Gusfield 1971; Schultz 1964; Tipps 1973). The failure of countless funded agricultural projects globally has revealed the inherent superiority of many indigenous agricultural systems that were replaced. Thus, there is a need to better understand the complex realities of subsistence families and their household resource allocation. Critiques of the micro-level economic assumptions of modernization reveal the irrelevance of the assumptions in many instances.

RELIGIOUS, GENDER, AND ENVIRONMENTAL BIASES IN THE DISCOURSE OF THE DOMINANT PARADIGM

While alternative frameworks such as dependency and world-system theory have attempted to challenge economic class assumptions inherent in the dominant paradigm, they have been less effective in addressing other concerns regarding the dominant paradigm, such as those raised from religious, feminist, and environmental perspectives. Hence, we briefly discuss critiques that have been raised from these perspectives.

Religious and Cultural Bias

Chapter 3 delineated the popular notion among sociologists and anthropologists regarding the normative structure of communities in Asia, Africa, and Latin America. The blame for relative economic backwardness in the Third World was ascribed to traditional values and institutions, especially the dominant religions. German sociologist Max Weber and a host of sociologists who followed him regarded Buddhism, Confucianism, Hinduism, and Islam as fostering values and beliefs that were incompatible with modern science, technology, and the ideology of progress (Singer 1966).

Since then, Weber's ideas, particularly in regard to Asian religions, have been criticized. Leading anthropologists argue that Weber downgraded the importance of political and economic factors in change, and that his ideas were simplistic and sometimes even ahistorical (Singer 1972; Srinivas 1973). For instance, Srinivas wondered why Weber chose the concepts of *samsara* (rebirth) and *karma* (fate) and not any other ideas as the dogmatic foundation of Hinduism. Srinivas even questioned the existence of a dogmatic foundation in Hinduism:

> Hinduism is so fundamentally different from Judaism, Christianity and Islam, the three Mediterranean religions, that ideas and biases carried over from them may stand in the way of understanding it. Hinduism is an acephalous religion. It has nothing corresponding to the religious hierarchy of Christianity or even Islam. It does not state that it is the only true religion and all others are false. There is no formal provision of conversion. It is not congregational. Crucial ideas such as *samsara*

and the sanctity of the *Vedas* have been rejected by one or another sect which has managed to remain within the Hindu fold (Srinivas 1973: 279–80).

Again, Weber projected a view of Asian religions in general and Hinduism in particular, as incapable of change. Critics charge that this view was patently ahistorical. Hinduism, the oldest continuous religion in the world, has been changing and adapting since 5000 BC. The ideas in the earliest holy text, the early *Vedas*, changed in the later texts, the later *Vedas* and the *Upanishads*. The dominant ethic of Hinduism changed since the days of the Indo-Aryans, who ate meat and drank liquor, to vegetarianism and abstinence from liquor among a great many Hindus today (Srinivas 1973). Also, during its long history, there have been several religious revivals. Importantly, Hinduism survived the enormous challenge posed by Buddhism (which had almost eclipsed Hinduism) to come back as the dominant religion of the region. Moreover, the fact that it survived almost 700 years of Islamic and then Christian rule in India speaks volumes of its adaptability and resilience.

There were other conceptual problems with Weber's thesis. He and other Western Indologists regarded Shankara's *advaita* philosophy as synonymous with Hindu theology. *Advaita,* which propagated asceticism and other-worldliness, is not the only school of philosophy or even the most important in Hindu theology. However, Indologists who regarded *advaita* as the dominant idea in Hinduism, criticized it for its other-worldly emphasis and asceticism. This neglected the diversity of religious ideas in Hindu theology. A substantial portion of Hindu texts, literature, and folklore, deal with duties and action in this world. For example, in the *Bhagavad Gita*, the holy book of the Hindus, a central concern is the problem of action. Srinivas (1973: 282) has noted:

It must be mentioned that there is in the *Gita* an undoubted emphasis on performing the duties of one's caste and status. Duty conscientiously performed, without attachment to the fruits of the action, leads to salvation . . . . Duty properly performed makes the entire life an offering to God. It is interesting that during the last 70 years or more, Indian leaders and intellectuals, including Tilak, Gandhi, and Aurobindo, turned to the *Gita* to justify their involvement in political and social action. It is difficult to understand why Weber failed to see that the *Gita* was a major scriptural source for a "work ethic" and for political and social activism . . . .

Also, attainment of salvation or eternal life in the other world was just one goal in Hindu texts. The other three goals stressed a person's obligations in the present world. They are *dharma* (morality), *artha* (pursuit of wealth), and *kama* (sex within marriage). Singer and Srinivas, who have conducted several studies in India, note that there is compartmentalization in that society. The office and factory symbolize modern life, whereas the home is a place for traditions. Indians are able to move quite easily between these two worlds. As one informant aptly put it, "when I put on my shirt and go to the factory, I take off my caste. When I come home and take off my shirt, I put on my caste." Thus, the advantages Hindus have is that they move from the traditional role to the modern without schizophrenia (Singer 1966). These observations indicate coexistence of traditional and modern lifestyles and cast doubts on the widespread belief among certain Western sociologists that traditional beliefs and practices are always obstacles to modernization.

Research conducted by anthropologists provides evidence that other religions such as Islam and Buddhism do not necessarily foster piety, resignation, or fatalism among the people. For example, the giving of *dana* (alms) in Buddhism and going on pilgrimages in Islam, while on the surface might seem economically irrational, serve to motivate very rational behavior. In order to fulfill these traditional obligations, individuals need to work hard and save (Goldthorpe 1975). Also, traditional forms, arrangements, and institutions are not an antithesis of development. Singer and Srinivas expose the fallaciousness of such arguments by showing how caste, joint family, and other traditions could contribute to profitable entrepreneurial behavior and rational bureaucracy:

> The joint family, for instance, provides a pool of trusted personnel for commercial and industrial activity in India today, just as in the rural setting it enables large farms to be managed at particular technological and organizational level. Since the running of big farms, commercial undertakings, and industries needs political backing and bureaucratic clearance, one or more members of the joint family are allowed to specialize in the cultivation of politicians, bureaucrats, and influence-peddlers (Srinivas 1973: 283).

All of the ensuing discussions bring us back to re-examine the utility of traditional institutions and arrangements vis-à-vis progress and change. The dominant paradigm of development took a very negative view of tradition. It had to be destroyed if the Third World nations and peoples wanted to modernize. This notion does not have many overt supporters in recent times. The importance of tradition in the process of development has been recognized. Eisenstadt points out that, "the mere destruction of traditional settings—the family, the community, or even the political order—led to disorganization, delinquency, and chaos rather than to a viable modern order" (Eisenstadt 1976: 35).

Additionally, the cultural critique in the dominant paradigm was riddled with contradictions. First, there was stereotypic emphasis on religion as an inhibiting factor in Third World countries. The stereotypes were often false. Goldthorpe notes many examples of Chinese, Muslims, and Asian Indian groups, who migrated to other lands and became associated with entrepreneurial zeal and innovative energy:

> For example, it is possible to explain the economic backwardness of China before the Communist triumph of 1964 in terms of passivity, the Confucian ideal of the cultivated man of the world, lavish expenditure on funerals and weddings, non-rational magical beliefs, and the like . . . . Yet, when Chinese migrated to Indonesia, Malaysia, Singapore, Thailand, or even Hong Kong they suddenly became energetic innovators whose industry and enterprise stimulated the economy of the region into new life; and it does not seem to have been the case that the religious beliefs and ritual customs of the overseas Chinese were in any important respect different from those of the homeland (Goldthorpe 1975: 236).

Another assumption that was uncritically accepted was the notion that a Western person was always rational. Yet traditional attributes such as particularism, favoritism, belief in astrologers, and lavish expenditures on social/religious occasions are widely prevalent in Western countries, whereas modern attributes such as universalism, secularism, and strict criteria for merit may be found in developing nations. For example, Abraham (1980: 76) noted that:

1. Several practices in the United States make the political system there very particularistic: influence of family tradition on voting; preferring individual candidates over political parties and letting elected officers such as the president or mayors to return political favors by rewarding friends with administrative assignments;

2. There is a preponderance of local news and local newspapers in American small towns making the value orientations of the average person very local-oriented. However, in the developing nations the average "traditional" person is universally-oriented since his/her regional newspaper is more national and international than local;

3. Serious contradictions prevail in terms of attributes fostered by traditional cultures vis-à-vis the value orientations instilled by modern societies. For example, even the most orthodox Hindu person exhibits religious tolerance and the belief that all religions ultimately lead to the same destination, thus exemplifying universalism of the highest order. However, many "progressive" individuals in Western nations exhibit particularism as reflected in their attempts at proselytization and conversion to their "true" religion;

4. Universities in many Third World countries, particularly in Asia and Africa, have a universalistic system of examinations where the student papers are graded by examiners from other schools or universities.

In addition to the above observations, several more could be posited to highlight the inconsistencies and contradictions in the cultural model proposed by the old paradigm. For example, the observation that top government officials in the Third World countries consult astrologers and look at the position of the stars in the constellation for planning of important projects is not something unique to developing countries. In the summer of 1988, mass media all over the world reported how US President Reagan consulted an astrologer in San Francisco to plan his duties and even marked his personal calendar with different colored pens to signify good, bad, and neutral days. Again, individuals in traditional cultures were faulted for spending huge amounts of money and other resources on social and religious ceremonies. This behavior is quite common in the West too, especially at Christmas time. Individuals shop months ahead of Christmas so that they may buy gifts for all relatives and friends. Many people go into debt to fulfill their gift-buying obligations.

All of these observations are intended to demonstrate that value-laden labels such as "traditional" and "modern" may be misplaced, and in many situations, the line driving the two could be very thin indeed. Later, in Chapters 7 and 8, we will more closely examine the positive, often crucial, role of religious tradition in supporting development.

Gender Bias: Women in Development Discourse

Earlier in this chapter we reviewed the scientific basis of modernization. Modern science developed in Europe at a time when the social, economic, and political contexts were governed by a strong patriarchal order. Women were excluded from scientific activity. Thus, many concepts that we use even today revealed a male bias. For example, nature was considered female, and women were assumed best suited for the private sphere of home and children. Women were thought to be more susceptible to subjective feelings and emotions and therefore less rational, whereas males were better equipped to use objective reason. Gradually, these beliefs became a self-fulfilling prophecy. Women and nature were relegated to the categories constructed for them. These biases had real consequences as the scientific method and its male-oriented concepts were used to guide the development process (Braidotti et al. 1994).

The role accorded to women in the dominant discourse has seen several shifts in the post-World War II period. Until the end of the 1960s, women were regarded as recipients of welfare; they entered the debate only as reproducers. Development planners assumed that men performed all productive work. While this approach revealed the patriarchal biases of modernization, it was also the result of total ignorance of women's productive roles, especially in agriculture. Ester Boserup's book, *Women's Role in Economic Development* (1970) has been considered groundbreaking in this area. Through her research focusing on sub-Saharan Africa, she demonstrated a failure to account for the productive roles performed by women, especially in agriculture. This omission along with the sex-role stereotyping and patriarchal biases inherent in the agricultural development projects, led to initiatives that favored the male farmers. The benefits of the modernization process had accrued exclusively to men who derived greater opportunities and resources while women were confined to the welfare sector. Relative to men, women were denied access to technical training, education, rights to land, and modernizing technology. Boserup's research was a clarion call to development planners and policy-makers to include women in development activities as producers and contributors to the economy. Some critics of Boserup pointed out that emphasis on just women and their relative deprivation due to development masked the crisis faced by all peasants, not just women (Whitehead 1990), while others criticized her for equating "development" and "economic development" (Mohanty 1988: 7). Still, Boserop's work was extremely important as an instigator of further study and organizational work globally.

Sub-field of Women in Development

In the 1970s, a number of global developments strengthened the new sub-field titled, *Women in Development* (WID). These included: the publication of Boserup's research as well as that of other scholars on the economic roles of women; the increased attention given to women by the United Nations through the sponsorship of the Decade for Advancement of Women (1975–85); and the disappointing effects of the development efforts of the 1950s and 1960s on women and the poor. Additionally, simple statistics demonstrated women's and girls' marginalization in development globally. While these were increasingly gathered and publicized beginning in the 1970s, present statistics show that there are still huge inequities for most basic needs as well as in political and organization access (see for example, Seager 1997; UNDP's *Human Development Report* 1997). In developing countries, there are still 60 percent more women than men among illiterate adults. Even at the primary school level, female enrollment averages 13 percent lower than male enrollment. All over the world wages are lower and unemployment is higher for women than for men. Women also constitute the vast majority of unpaid family workers (UNDP 1997). Controlling for other social divisions such as age and ethnicity reveals even worse conditions for women. Overall deprivation and gender disparities are the most extreme in sub-Saharan Africa (United Nations 1995).[5]

Spearheaded by liberal feminism in the North, WID started as a US-based chapter of the Society for International Development. The 1973 Percy Amendment to the United States Foreign Assistance Act to explicitly consider and include women in the development process, provided further encouragement to the efforts of WID (Tinker 1990). In the early 1970s, WID units were first created within the development bureaucracies in the North. The UN Decade for Women brought great visibility to WID during the period 1975–85. By the time the Nairobi Conference on Women, Development, and Peace was held to conclude the UN Decade for Women, WID units were also established within women's bureaus and development ministries in the countries of the South (Braidotti et al. 1994).

The work of WID specialists led to greater visibility for women's roles in development. The WID specialists sought to integrate women into the mainstream of economic development and lobbied to ensure that the benefits of modernization accrued to women (and not just men). Women's access to education, training, employment, credit, capital, and land were emphasized in this discourse. In terms of institutional response, USAID and the UNDP integrated WID objectives in their projects dealing with family planning, family health, child nutrition, and agriculture (Wilkins 1997). However, funding for WID still comprised only a small portion of these organizations' budgets; and WID considerations were virtually absent in many projects, as Kathleen Staudt (1985a) clearly demonstrated in her study of USAID.

In the 1980s, many studies focused on communication-related issues; they documented women's continued marginalization and even a worsened situation as a result of development. For example, female subsistence farmers produce 80 percent of the family food in much of sub-Saharan Africa. Yet, extension communication workers commonly bypass subsistence women farmers seeking out male farmers or wealthier women (Staudt 1985b).

Initially, WID had demanded equality between the sexes. However, this demand faced institutional resistance from male-staffed development agencies. By the mid-1970s, the call for equity was incorporated within the rubric of meeting basic human needs and poverty alleviation. This move addressed the issue of equity between the sexes without disrupting the male-bias in the development discourse:

Casting women in the role of managers of low-income households and providers of family basic needs retained a reassuring continuity with earlier welfare approaches . . . . However, it also incorporated the WID concern with women's productive roles by recognizing that these responsibilities had an economic component and therefore required income-enhancing measures (Kabeer 1994: 7).

Thus, the WID call for equity based on sexes was co-opted under the argument of economic efficiency (Moser 1989).

The WID approach has been criticized for subscribing to the dominant model of modernization and not critically addressing the structures of domination and patriarchy in the development discourse. Parpart (1995: 259) echoes the critique of postmodernists when she states that development practitioners "accepted the ideas that development for Third World women meant becoming more modern. For it is clear that development thought, in both its Marxist and liberal expressions, has been (and continues to be) the embodiment of Enlightenment thinking, and therefore does not reject the modernist paradigm."

Another source of criticism came from women's movements in the South. The point of contention between the First World women and Third World women rested on the nature of their goal. While the former were interested in bringing about greater equality between the sexes, the latter went beyond mere equality to questioning the structural inequalities that deprived women (and some men) of access to resources and power. In addition, women researchers from the South belonging to the group Development Alternatives with Women for a New Era (DAWN), questioned if women in the South really wanted to be integrated into a patriarchal Western mode of development (Sen and Grown 1987). The South–North linkage sensitized Northern women to a more pluralistic goal (i.e., to let the women in the South choose the type of development they desired), and stimulated them to think about alternative paths to development based on a feminist perspective (Braidotti et al. 1994).

Gender and Development

Since the mid-1980s, the Gender and Development (GAD) approach has received increased attention in academic literature, within aid agencies, and women's movements. The GAD approach goes beyond the creation of equality between the sexes to question the underlying assumptions of the dominant social, economic, and political structures that accord and perpetuate an inferior status to women relative to men. The conceptual framework of GAD incorporates important propositions:

> Women are incorporated into the development process but in very specific ways; that a focus on women alone was inadequate to understand the opportunities for women for agency or change; that women are not a homogenous category but are divided by class, color and creed; that any analysis of social organization and social process has to take into account the structure and dynamic of gender relations (Young, 1993: 134).

It became increasingly evident that the WID discourse of including women could not solve the fundamental inequities faced by women and girls. Additionally, females are already central to virtually all concerns of development, for instance, farming and meeting basic needs, sustaining the environment, and contributing economically. What is urgently needed is a restructuring of societies to accommodate women's needs and concerns. In fact, the improvement in the conditions of women's lives is statistically related to societal improvement. Gender inequalities are usually correlated with human poverty. Additionally, societal progress is correlated with improvement in the lives of women and girls (e.g., see UNDP 1997).

The GAD framework includes both a feminist analysis and a Marxian social analysis. It is both the ideology of male superiority as well as the control of valuable resources (capital) by men that is at the heart of women's disadvantage (Young 1993). Thus, the GAD analysis goes beyond the goal of equating women with men through more training and education to looking at the distribution of power in societies and its relationship to gender relations.

Also, GAD's objective of challenging society's socio-economic structures and empowering women poses a threat to large donor agencies that would rather not tackle issues of fundamental social transformation. However, the Canadian International Development Agency (CIDA) as well as the United Nations Development Fund for Women (UNIFEM) have incorporated the interests of GAD in their programs (Wilkins 1997). Overall, the results have been disappointing. Wilkins (1997) points out that both WID and GAD initiatives that target the productive roles (as opposed to reproductive roles) of women have attracted limited funding, thus signaling "a reluctance to engage these issues more aggressively" (p. 116). Therefore, the focus has not been on addressing macro-level structural issues in societies, but to continue targeting women as individuals and attempt to change their behaviors as reproducers. Thus, many of the projects that address women deal with health, family planning, and nutrition. Commenting on projects that focus on women's productive (as opposed to reproductive) roles, Wilkins (1999: 62) reports that "between 1975 and 1984, 27 percent of all projects attended to women, but this proportion subsequently dropped to 16 percent."

Some aid agencies, such as USAID, situate their aid policies within a privatized commercial structure. The institutional discourse of USAID is influenced by the foreign policy initiative of the United States that links modernity with the private sector (Steeves 2000; Wilkins 1999). This may affect the nature and scope of the projects and, quite often, they are confined to persuasive campaigns attempting to change individual attitudes and behaviors and individual consumption rather than tackling fundamental structural constraints in societies.

Global Feminist Movements

More recently, several scholars have considered the idea of international or global feminism(s) (e.g., Haraway 1991; Mohanty 1991a, 1991b). This trend attempts to recognize the diversity of women's experiences around the globe and yet also encourage coalition-building based on a "common *context* of struggle against oppression by gender, class, race, ethnicity, and nation, including colonization" (Steeves 1993: 222). The concept "imagined community" has been used by Chandra Mohanty to highlight the *political* motives for coalitions.[3]

In some ways, global feminism constitutes a new movement that could combat the increasing asexual character of postmodern societies. Postmodernist scholars have pointed out that,

> the process of assimilation of women into industrial or post-industrial societies is such that they have disappeared as sex-specific social agents. In other words, the post-industrial system makes oppositional politics utterly redundant, in a context of dissolution of political identities based on sex or class (Braidotti et al. 1994).

Haraway (1991) makes a useful critique of the international feminism concept. Dwelling on common interests or experiences of women (for example, their victimhood in almost all societies) is only a start. Haraway (1991) urges that, in the 1990s and beyond, feminists must use the concept of global sisterhood as a *political* tool for interventions and action. The emphasis in the post-industrial and post-millennial world should be on temporary and mobile coalitions of like-minded participants that are built on a foundation of common interests.

One problem that affects women globally is violence against women and girls in its many forms: battering, rape, child abuse, incest, child prostitution, and slavery. Gender violence has been a major focus of women in recent years. There have been two interrelated arguments. First, gender violence is a major obstacle to development as it affects women's participation in development activities (Carillo 1992; Heise 1992). Second, freedom from violence is an international human right. In 1979, the UN General Assembly adopted the Convention on the Elimination of All Forms of Discrimination Against Women (CEDAW), which remains as the most comprehensive international treaty addressing the human rights of women, including the right to freedom from gender violence.

So far 161 countries have ratified CEDAW, although at the time of this text's publication, the United States was not yet among them.

Environmental Challenges to the Dominant Discourse

The 1970s were a watershed of sorts. In the area of environment, the earlier premise of an open and unlimited global space for individual nation-states to explore and exploit for maximum economic growth was turning out to be empirically untenable. The finite nature of the global space and its limited carrying capacity received increased attention both in academic literature and the mass media. Environment was now part of a complex ecosystem, i.e., fragile and threatened by severe disruption from the competing forces of overpopulation, resource exploitation, over-consumption, and industrial pollution.

> The global ecosystem approach was not without competitors; but both the biocentric and the humanist perspectives were foreign to the perceptions of the international development elite . . . . And recognizing the offences against nature as just another sign of the supremacy of technological expansion over people and their lives . . . would go against the grain of development aspirations (Sachs, 1992: 27)

The discourse, then, moved to efficient management of environment to serve the needs of development.

Debate on Sustainable Development

The competing interests of protecting the environment and sustaining development were debated in several international fora starting with the 1972 United Nations Conference on Human Environment in Stockholm. The Brundtland Report (1987), *Our Common Future*, a document prepared by the World Commission for Environment and Development has remained the point of departure for anyone interested in this issue. Brundtland (1987) defined the term *sustainable development* as "development which meets the needs of the present without compromising the ability of future generations to meet their own needs" (p. 43). A controversial aspect of the Brundtland Report is its pro-economic growth recommendation to countries to avoid environmental disaster:

If large parts of the developing world are to avert economic, social and environmental catastrophes, it is essential that global economic growth be revitalized. In practical terms, it means more rapid economic growth in both industrial and developing countries (Brundtland 1987: 89).

To critics of the economic growth model, the Brundtland Report is, therefore, viewed as an apologist for mainstream development organizations such as the World Bank, the business community, and state governments. "The solutions to the crisis are seen by them to lie within the range of measures that contributed to the environmental crisis in the first place: more economic growth to pay for environmental recovery, more funds for environmental projects, more technology, and altogether better and more management of the environment" (Braidotti et al. 1994: 4). Sachs (1992) points out that this is the same tactic that was used in the early 1970s, when the magic that was promised by the trickle-down economic model failed to help the weaker sections of society. A new term "equitable development" was used then to make development more humane without necessarily changing the structural anchors of the failed model.

Continued economic growth, alongside higher levels of consumption, is viewed by many as unsustainable. Moreover, it will lead to greater pollution and environmental degradation. However, the Report's argument for continued economic growth has made the notion of sustainable development widely accepted within mainstream institutions, "because it does not fundamentally threaten the status quo, for which the imperative for continued economic growth is a crucial element" (Braidotti et al. 1994: 133). Therefore, to many critics of the dominant eco-cratic discourse, the bias in the Brundtland Report is to sustain the present development process by putting limits on nature through scientific management techniques (Esteva 1992; Sachs 1992; Shiva 1992).

Adams (1995), likewise maintains that the new discourse on sustainable development has deep roots in the mainstream environmentalist movement in the North. The technocentrist environmental discourse incorporates a "responsible" exploitation of the environment through technical instruments such as an Environmental Impact Assessment and keeping a wary eye on the balance between economic development and environmental cost. The Brundtland Report "picks up the same arguments about mutuality, multilateralism, and environmentally sustainable growth within a Keynesian-managed world economy. This is entirely consistent with the existing economic paradigms of the industrialized North"

(Adams 1995: 89). Thus, the language of the sustainable development model is consistent with the dominant modernization paradigm. There are no major departures suggested from the present economic system. The focus is really on better management, planning, and more effective monitoring to ensure the least disruption to the ecological system (Adams 1995). It is also a call to apply more rigorous scientific techniques to sustain the continued exploitation of nature without damaging it beyond repair.

Environmentalist Challenges to Sustainable Development

Social Ecology. This environmental movement has attracted a significant following in the North since the 1960s. It is regarded both as an alternative science and a new social practice. Murray Bookchin is considered one of the intellectual leaders of this movement. According to Bookchin (1982), the crisis of modernity is based on two factors: the distancing of humanity from nature, and the inherent hierarchical structure of human societies. Hierarchical structures give rise to dualistic and reductionist tendencies in feelings, thoughts, and reality. He believes that the relationship between society and nature should be built on mutualism and that human societies should emulate nature by modeling their societies on the principle of unity in diversity (Braidotti et al. 1994).

Social ecologists propose radical changes to the nature of modern societies. These changes include:

> The adoption of small, community-scale social arrangements, decentralization, participatory democracy and decision-making based on consensus, whereby ultimate authority is at the community level, the level of lived experience (Braidotti et al. 1994: 158).

Social ecological concepts challenge the mainstream sustainable development view by rejecting the instrumental way in which nature is treated, and the dominant–submissive relationship between nature and society. Also, the related concepts of hierarchy and dualism help illuminate the present crisis in the relationship between environment and development.

Deep Ecology. This strain of environmentalism owes its intellectual origin to Arne Naess. The deep ecology concept includes several other types of movements/ideas such as bioregionalism, Earth First! and the Gaia hypothesis. A strong theme in their critiques of development discourse is its anthropocentric bias. Adherents of deep ecology trace the present environmental crisis to the Enlightenment idea of humans' (and human cultures') superiority over nature. Deep ecologists propose replacing the anthropocentric bias with the concept of biocentric egalitarianism, a view wherein both humans and nature and all other living things have important roles to play (M.E. Zimmerman 1990). Deep ecologists consider:

> richness and diversity of life as values in themselves and assume that human beings have no right to reduce these, except to satisfy their basic needs. They also stress the need for cultural diversity and diversity in social arrangements as necessary preconditions for the survival of the planet (Braidotti et al. 1994: 150).

These ideas show the similarity in views between the deep ecologists and indigenous peoples who have been the traditional stewards of forests and other natural environments. Radical biocentrists share some of the views of deep ecologists vis-à-vis nature. This group includes neo-Malthusian environmentalists who support coercive population control measures to readjust the carrying capacity of the Earth. This radical strain has been criticized as "harsh deep ecology" (Lewis 1992). Deep ecology has contributed to an alternative view of development termed as bioregionalism:

> Bioregionalism is about re-inhabiting the Earth on new terms . . . the core of the bioregional idea of development is communitarianism, small-scale, self-sufficient development, and a definition of regional boundaries by natural features, such as watersheds, soil types, vegetation or climate. The organization of bioregional communities is described as non-hierarchical and participative. Instead of formal hierarchical structures of leadership, bioregional communities thrive on networking and organic change (Braidotti et al. 1994: 151–52).

Another outcome of deep ecology is the notion of the Gaia, a concept that describes the holistic and self-regulatory characteristic of the Earth (Braidotti et al. 1994; Lovelock 1979).

> The major tenet of the Gaia hypothesis is the assumption that Gaia is a total self-organizing and self-reproducing, organic, spatio-temporal and teleological system with the goal of maintaining itself. The focus is on the primary role of a constant disequilibrium, but at the same

time, stability maintained by diversification, co-operation, and mutualism (Braidotti et al. 1994: 153).

This view of the Earth is a major departure from the dominant paradigm's view of nature as a dead and brute matter. Not surprisingly, adherents of the Gaia hypothesis view all nature management as dangerous, as it interferes with the Earth's regulatory mechanisms and the survival of the Gaia (Braidotti et al. 1994).

Radical deep ecologists do not have much faith in social reform and institute a new kind of hierarchy: nature over humans. For example, some have attributed the underdevelopment in the countries of the South to high fertility rates and support harsh population control measures. The poor (i.e., women) who breed too fast have been seen as the culprits and held responsible for their own poverty, the relative under-development of their countries, and degradation of the environment. However their critics argue that:

> the problem with this line of argument is its simplistic view on cause and effect and the total disregard of other reasons for environmental degradation, such as the North's overconsumption of natural resources, trade policies, commodity prices, and so on which create poverty in the South. For example, population growth as a survival strategy of poor families is not analyzed, neither is there recognition of the fact that it is induced by poverty, rather than the reverse (Braidotti et al. 1994: 143).

Mamdani (1972), using examples from India, showed that people are not poor because they have too many children but rather that they have many children because they are poor. Beginning in the 1970s, the simplistic and coercive measures used to reduce fertility rates were criticized and a major shift in policy took place after the 1974 Population Conference at Bucharest. However, real change has not occurred and this continued to be a major theme in the 1994 Population and Development Conference in Cairo. More serious problems in health, education, and social service were recognized.

Green Feminism. This has served both as a theoretical position and a social movement (Braidotti et al. 1994). Also termed as ecofeminism, this idea/movement traces the present environmental crisis to the dominant development discourse in which dualistic hierarchies have resulted in enslaving both women and nature (Shiva 1988). These groups focus on the patriarchaial bias in the dominant epistemological framework:

> The male-centered (androcentric) ways of knowing, which account for the antagonistic, dualistic and hierarchical conceptions of self, society and cosmos are perceived to be at the roots of oppression. Most ecofeminists contrast dualisms, such as the subject–object split associated with patriarchal epistemologies, and the oppression of women and nature, with connectedness and mutualism perceived to be inherent in women's ways of knowing (Braidotti et al. 1994: 162).

Shiva (1988) invokes "the feminist principle of nature" and the notion of a caring and nurturing Mother Earth as countervailing principles against the dominant patriarchal and gender-related ideology of the dominant discourse to combat further ecological degradation (Adams 1995).

Challenges from Organizational Theory

George Honadle (1999) places context (geographical, temporal, and social) at the center of the critique of the present institutional strategies being employed for environmental protection and sustainable development. He points out that the "Quality Hypothesis" has been the dominant model since the Bretton Woods conference for managing the environment. "Globally, this logic supports a technocratic approach to environmental policy that places the World Bank and the Global Environmental Facility (GEF) in the apex position among institutions" (Honadle 1999: 135). This hypothesis, then, puts scientists and technocrats in the driver's seat and empowers technical expertise in the solution of problems.

The "Autonomy Hypothesis" has been the alternative approach. The response advocated is a team approach already common in NGOs, in some Third World villages, and in some restructured industrial organizations that make use of workgroups versus hierarchies (Honadle 1999: 136–37). The autonomy perspective is anti-elitist, anti-technical and anti-scientific in its orientation. The guiding principle of this alternative viewpoint is social proximity, small organizational structure and non-hierarchical relationship (Honadle 1999).

Honadle's "Context Hypothesis" argues that each unique set of circumstances should suggest resources and strategies that are needed for environmental protection. Yes, big organizations such as the World Bank and the IMF have roles to play, but so do the NGOs and other smaller players. Development success requires a creative mix of government- and private-sector input, and both small- and large-scale initiatives. However, it is the specific context that decides what mix of resources to use (Honadle 1999). Today, specific local circumstances and diversity are important factors that need to be addressed in policy and planning instruments. This will call for innovative, temporary networks of task forces that can best deal with the problems and challenges emanating from specific contexts.

CONCLUSION: ALTERNATIVE PERSPECTIVES ON DEVELOPMENT

Dependency and world-system theorists, religious activists, feminists, postcolonialists, environmentalists, grassroots workers, and others have articulated their visions for the future. A common theme in these visions is their critique of the ethnocentrism of the dominant Western development discourse and the violence inflicted upon local, non-Western, indigenous ways of life, cultural arrangements and knowledge structures. Braidotti et al. (1994) call for "locally sustainable lifestyles, participatory democracy, and recovery of dominated people's subjugated knowledge" (p. 170). Other groups such as social ecologists argue for a nature–society reconciliation. This calls for the elimination of hierarchical thinking and an end to subjugation of nature by human societies. Goulet (1973) explicated in detail his ideas of *real development*. This description of development was holistic and included a clean environment; growth with equity; provision of basic needs such as food, shelter, education, and medical care; meaningful employment and relationships with others; and a harmonious relationship between culture and change.

Wang and Dissanayake (1984a: 5) emphasized the protection of nature and culture. They defined development as:

a process of social change which has as its goal the improvement in the quality of life of all or the majority of people without doing violence to the natural and cultural environment in which they exist, and which seeks to involve the majority of the people as closely as possible in this enterprise, making them the masters of their own destiny.

Alternative approaches to development are pluralistic and indicate several new goals for meaningful and real development in the Third World.

1. **Equity in distribution of information and other benefits of development.** The emphasis is placed on the poorest of the poor. The widening hiatus between the advantaged and the disadvantaged has to be closed. *Growth with equity* was the clarion call of the 1970s and has been reintroduced in the 1990s under the banner of development with a human face.

2. **Active participation of people at the grassroots.** The objective is to involve the input of people in activities that are ostensibly set up for their benefit. This gives people voice and ensures that development plans and decisions are relevant and meaningful to them. Postmodern scholars point out that such efforts may revitalize local, subjugated knowledge/power systems thus providing valuable information on the lived experiences of people at the margins (Parpart 1995). Also, it "opens up new possibilities for the reconstruction of the South, away from one valid model of development towards polycentric and polyphonic developments" (Braidotti et al. 1994: 108).

3. **Independence of local communities (or nations) to tailor development projects to their own objectives.** The reliance would be on local skills and material resources, thus fostering greater self-reliance in development and leading to freedom from external dependency.

4. **Integration of the old and new ideas, the traditional and modern systems, the endogenous and exogenous elements to constitute a unique blend suited to the needs of a particular community.** This approach would consider the local culture not as something to be discarded but instead would benefit from the native wisdom to come up with a unique syncretization that incorporates critical traditionalism with critical modernism (Nandy 1987).

Local Organization for Development

In the dominant paradigm, the immediate value of information for individuals was emphasized, whereas its value as a catalyst for local organization was virtually ignored. However, some scholars point out that exogenous information will not affect a community unless it organizes the people and starts a process of autonomous development (Hornik 1988). Roling (1982) hypothesized that the rural poor are impoverished because they lack power. He argued for changing power relationships in the social system and increasing the countervailing power of the rural power relative to other groups:

> Reward systems ensuring creation of opportunities for the rural poor, and especially self-sustaining linkage relationships, can only be created when the rural poor involved acquire power over opportunity-building systems. The latter must somehow be accountable to the former (Roling 1982: 9).

How could the poor at the grassroots acquire the countervailing power and make the system at the top accountable to them? One method suggested is the formation of strong organizations at the grassroots capable of articulating and protecting the interests of people on the periphery. For instance, Barkan and McNulty (1979) noted that small-scale Self-help Development Projects (SHDP) in rural Kenya had, on many occasions, forced the center to enter into a bargaining relationship with the periphery. Reviewing the findings of 18 case studies on local organizations in Asia, Uphoff and Esman (1974) contended that there was a strong empirical basis for concluding that local organizations are necessary for speedy rural development, particularly the kind that bring about higher productivity and improved welfare of the majority of rural people. Some of the successful development objectives they cited were higher agricultural productivity and better rural welfare, i.e., health, nutrition, education, security, employment, political participation, and equity in income distribution. Barkan and McNulty (1979: 31) discussing the role of the SHDPs in Kenya pointed out the following achievements:

1. They produced a net transfer of resources from the center to the rural areas;
2. They appeared to foster a more equitable distribution of wealth within local communities;
3. They marshaled local initiatives and entrepreneurial skills in ways the state could not do by itself; and
4. Most importantly, they provided an organizational infrastructure at the grassroots without which the development of the rural poor was unlikely to proceed.

Other grassroots groups, women's groups, environmental groups, and religious groups have also suggested empowerment of the people through viable organizations, political mobilization, consciousness raising, and popular education (March and Taggu 1986; Sen and Grown 1987).

While it is important to recognize that local organizations could extract greater resources from the center and lead to greater equity in rural areas, they could also lead to greater inequality. Certain groups in the rural areas could acquire a disproportionate share of material goods and services. Also, local organizations could help some leaders become very powerful, creating an elite sector in areas where there was none before. And, it is also possible that powerful local organizations could exacerbate regional inequality between different communities on the periphery of the national political economy.

Re-emergence of Religion and Local Culture in Development

Religious groups offer complex examples of local activism and influence. At certain times, religious groups may support modernization. This support may help or harm women, minorities or the environment, depending on the context. At other times, religious groups may resist a modernizing influence. Again, the meaning of this resistance may be helpful or harmful with regard to particular demographic groups and the environment. There has been a renewed interest in studying the positive role of religious traditions and organizations in social change. The dominant paradigm has been criticized for the way it conceptualized the role of non-Western cultures, especially their religious traditions. Theorists believed that religion was necessarily in conflict with progress and change. This view is unrealistic (Gusfield 1971; Servaes 1999; Wang and Dissanayake 1984a). Wang and Dissanayake (1984a) posited that religion and local culture are essential not only for providing a context to development and change but also to maintain a certain degree of continuity. Denying the role of religion and culture would deny the continuity that it has provided during all periods of change and thus deny history and meaning to the people or nations involved.

Increasingly, there have been calls for new approaches to development that are more open-ended and flexible than the deterministic and per-scriptive models of the dominant discourse (Servaes 1999). Among other things, the newer approaches need to reconceptualize the role of religion and local culture in change. Grassroots activists argue for a regeneration of local people's space and local cultures in developing nations to counter the ill effects of development to communities at the grassroots. In Chapters 7 and 8 we explicate in some detail the positive role of religious traditions in social change.

In the remaining chapters, we continue to explore the theme of individual and community empowerment. In Chapter 6, we critically examine the role of communication under modernization and its failure to empower individuals and communities. In Chapters 7 and 8, we examine the positive role of religion in empowerment. In Chapter 9, we broaden our discussion of empowerment and the role of communication in facilitating these goals.

SUMMARY

It was roughly between the 16th and the 20th centuries when the European idea of "development" was exported to the rest of the world. Today, the "development machine" is very powerful because of its vast reach and institutional backing. The concept of modernity is central to the dominant paradigm of development. Many of the negative consequences of this paradigm, and associated structures and discourse, flow directly from its inherent biases. The stage theory of development and the linear bias of social change have straitjacketed objects of development into frozen states wherein they share common characteristics. Uprooted from their histories and cultures, communities in the Third World have become pliable objects to be manipulated by development experts. As for the people and communities far removed from the center, developmentalism has eroded their control over their lifestyles and their use of community and natural resources. In the name of development and progress, the state has unleashed violence against its citizens, especially those who are powerless. The monoculture being spread by the development discourse has eroded viable alternatives to the industrial, growth-oriented society and crippled humankind's capacity to meet an increasingly different future with creative responses.

The development process in the Third World countries did not fit the assumptions implicit in the dominant paradigm of development. The paradigm worked better as a description of social change in Western

Europe and North America than as a predictor of change in developing countries. The neo-classical economic model that suggested a *trickle-down* approach to development benefits started losing credibility in the 1970s. The worldwide recession of the 1980s and the neo-liberal economic reforms in the Third World countries left them further behind. Neo-Marxist scholars made serious criticisms of the dominant paradigmatic model. To them, underdevelopment was not a process distinctly different from development. In fact, they constituted two facets of the same process. The *development of underdevelopment* in Third World nations was and is related to the economic development of Western Europe and North America.

The criticisms of the sociology of development models were directed at the abstractness of the social theories, the ahistorical nature of the propositions, and incorrect nature of development indicators that constituted the "evolutionary universals." Additionally, the value-enactment models of McClelland, Hagen, Inkeles and Smith, Lerner, Rogers, and others were criticized for their ethnocentrism and for neglecting to account for the influence of structural constraints on individual action and enterprise.

The dominant paradigm was criticized further for its negative view of culture, especially religious culture, for its patriarchal biases, and for its androcentrism. In the mainstream view, cultural traditions had to be destroyed if the Third World nations and peoples wanted to modernize. This notion no longer has overt supporters, though modernization processes still function to destroy, appropriate, or absorb indigenous traditions. In the 1970s, a number of global developments strengthened the new sub-field titled, Women in Development (WID): the publication of Boserup's (1970) research as well as that of other scholars on the economic roles of women, the increased attention given to women by the United Nations through the sponsorship of the Decade for Advancement of Women (1975–85), and the disappointing effects of the development efforts of the 1950s and 1960s on women and the poor. The work of WID specialists gave greater visibility to women's roles in development. The WID specialists sought to integrate women into the mainstream of economic development. Since the mid-1980s, the GAD approach has received increased attention in academic literature and within aid agencies. The GAD approach goes beyond the creation of equality between the sexes to question the underlying assumptions of the dominant social, economic, and political structures that accord and perpetuate gender inequities.

In the area of environment, the earlier premise of an open and unlimited global space available for individual nation-states to explore and exploit for maximum economic growth was turning out to be empirically untenable. The competing interests of protecting the environment and sustaining development were debated in several international fora starting with the 1972 United Nations Conference on Human Environment in Stockholm. The Brundtland Report (1987) has remained the point of departure for anyone interested in this issue. A controversial aspect of the Brundtland Report is its pro-economic growth recommendation to countries if they need to avoid environmental disaster.

Alternative approaches to development tend to be pluralistic and indicate several varied goals for meaningful and real development in the Third World (e.g., see Servaes 1999). Among other things, the newer approaches need to reconceptualize the role of religion and other areas of culture in change. Grassroots activists argue for a regeneration of local people's space and local cultures in developing nations to counter the ill effects of development to communities at the grassroots. In these newer approaches, goals of individual and community empowerment are usually central. Concerns with spiritually, cultural, and grassroots organization provide a sharp contrast to modernization and the Marxist school's near-exclusive concerns with economic systems.

NOTES

1. Alvares (1992) quoting Sheshadri (no date) points out that the concept of efficiency (i.e., minimal loss of energy during a conversion) came from the law of entropy. This concept stipulated that such efficiency could be attained at very high temperatures only. This biased modern science and modern industry toward high temperature combustion techniques. Soon, it became the criterion for judging the relative efficiency of all modes of production both in nature and non-heavy industry areas. However, both in nature and traditional practice, the techniques for production and conversion are performed at ambient temperatures, for instance, cloud formation and desalinization, production of fiber by plants and animals, and the production of "gur" (as opposed to sugar) in rural India (Alvares 1992). Traditional techniques were considered primitive when judged by the efficiency criterion of modern industry. Development then incorporated the high temperature but highly polluting and natural resource intensive method of big industry and set it up as a standard to compare the efficiency of indigenous modes of production.

2. See also Steeves (2000) for an overview.

3. Mohanty borrowed the concept from Anderson (1983). Steeves (1993) drew on Mohanty's use of the term.

CHAPTER 6

CRITIQUE OF COMMUNICATION APPROACHES IN THIRD WORLD DEVELOPMENT

The answer is not just another series of projects, a bit more money
to send from developed countries to developing countries . . .
the answer clearly is knowledge, partnership and opportunity brought about by this new (knowledge and
digital) revolution.
James Wolfensohn, President, World Bank at the Second Global,
Knowledge Conference in Kuala Lumpur, March, 2000

I n this chapter, we take a critical look at the communication strategies
used to guide social change in Third World nations. We begin by
looking at the period when big media were used to both prescribe
and direct development efforts. This period spanned from the early 1950s
through the 1980s, though a bias for mass media is evident even now.
Many of the criticisms we highlight overlap with criticisms of modernization in general, discussed in Chapter 5. We then focus on the diffusion
of innovations approach used to disseminate modernizing innovations
in the areas of agriculture, health, and family planning. This approach
continues to be used, though later applications have sought means of

narrowing the communication gap between different social classes. Some tenets of diffusion theory have been borrowed by the increasingly popular social marketing campaigns that are employed to change people's knowledge levels, behaviors, and actions in areas such as AIDS prevention, responsible sexual relationships, family planning, health, nutrition, social harmony, national integration, and many other related themes.

We then describe the newer roles assigned to communication in development. Starting in the early 1970s, the exclusive emphasis on the mass media was complemented by interpersonal and organizational networks of communication. In addition, there was a newer interest in local cultures. This led to a re-examination of the traditional media as vehicles for information, persuasion, and entertainment. We conclude by describing and critiquing the present interest in using information communication technologies for rural development in the Third World.

MASS MEDIA AND MODERNIZATION APPROACH: A CRITIQUE

As discussed in Chapter 4, the general note of optimism that reigned in the 1950s and the 1960s regarding the role and potential of the mass media in the development process in the Third World turned sour in the 1970s. Administrators and researchers realized that the development process was not as straightforward and clear-cut as it was earlier conceptualized. There were too many extraneous variables that affected the process. The mass media, far from being independent variables in the change process, were themselves affected by extraneous factors.

The following comments from Beltran (1976: 19) conveyed the concerns of scholars from the Third World:

1. An overall change of the social structure is the fundamental prerequisite for the attainment of genuinely human and democratic development;
2. Communication, as it exists in the region, not only is by nature impotent to cause national development by itself, but it often works against development—again, in favor of the ruling minorities; and
3. Communication itself is so subdued to the influence of the prevailing organizational arrangements of society that it can hardly

be expected to act independently as a main contributor to profound and widespread social transformation.

By the 1970s, it became increasingly clear that the American communication models and research designs were seriously flawed, leading to numerous gaps, biases, and failures. Research in Asia and in Latin America showed that political-economic constraints diminished and even eliminated the influences of media in overcoming development problems (Rogers 1976b). The neglect of these constraints may be traced directly to ideological biases exported from the West. Regardless, project failures quickly showed that for many reasons mass media were not modernizing Third World nations, as anticipated.

Critique of the Models and Research Design

Critics have pointed out serious problems with the conceptual underpinnings, the models, and the underlying assumptions of the mass media and modernization approach. For example, research in the 1950s and 1960s conceptualized mass media as having direct and powerful effects on receivers in developing nations. This was essentially a recreation of the *bullet theory* of communication. However, the notion of an all-powerful mass media acting on defenseless receivers was tested extensively in the 1940s and 1950s in the US and found to be incorrect, as discussed in Chapter 4. Thus, rejected theories were recycled in analyzing the effects of mass media in developing nations.

Much of the earlier research, especially Lerner's classic study in the Middle East, was done at the height of the Cold War between the United States and Soviet Russia. While the communist nations were criticized for their propaganda and indoctrination, the direct effects model of Western researchers was welcomed, even though it attempted to manipulate people into discarding traditional values and behaviors and adopting modern ways (Golding 1974; Samarajiwa 1987). There were other inconsistencies in the underlying assumptions. For example, the 19th century notion of the *mass society* was overwhelmingly rejected in the West by the 1940s. The mass society concept stated that in an industrial society, people are isolated from each other, suffer anomie, and do not have meaningful ties to other individuals. However, this was shown to be incorrect. Even within an "impersonal" industrial society, people belonged to important social groups and had close interpersonal relationships with others in their subgroups. However, when turning to developing nations, researchers implied a mass society phenomenon wherein people, lacking significant group ties, were readily available for conversion by the mass media.

In the theories on modernization, the mass media were regarded as the independent variables. Was this an accurate assessment of the nature and role of mass media in developing nations? Probably not. Beltran (1976) noted serious problems in regarding the mass media as independent causes of social change. However, other propositions were not tested adequately. The mass media could have been treated as dependent variables, affected by variables such as the political structure or elite ownership of media institutions. Later studies showed that the mass media are intervening variables in the process of change. The antecedent or independent variables were literacy, education, social status, age, and cosmopoliteness; while the dependent variables were empathy, achievement motivation, educational and occupational aspirations, innovativeness, and political awareness. Fjes argued that it could have been possible that "the antecedent characteristics correlate directly with the consequent characteristics. A high degree of media exposure could very well be just another attribute of what is defined as a *modern* person" (Fjes 1976: 11).

There were other methodological concerns. The partial correlations used to indicate the intervening nature of mass media exposure were not significantly different from direct or zero-order correlations. This raised questions about the results. Also, as Rogers acknowledged, the correlational analysis did not reveal the time-order nature of these relationships. Part of this problem was the nature of correlational data, the abundance of one-shot cross-sectional surveys, and the relative lack of experimental designs in development communication studies (Rogers 1969).

While communication was conceptualized as a process, the models used failed to show that clearly. Early models of communication were one-way, top-down, and linear. Diaz-Bordenave (1977) called this the *transmission mentality*, a conceptualization that did not incorporate the transactional or the multidimensional nature of communication.

Finally, there were numerous problems with operational definitions for concepts such as empathy and fatalism. Lerner's "empathy" measure is a common example. Lerner's (1958) nine-item scale asking respondents "what would you do if you were . . . ?" was essentially meaningless in the context of their lives. Earlier, Gans (1962), showed that American slum-dwellers whom he called *urban villagers* scored very low on empathy scales. Golding (1974) concluded that for the American slum-dwellers as well as for the Third World peasant such as Lerner's Balgat shepherd, "the perception of massive structural constraints against upward mobility mitigates against 'role empathy' far more than does an inert imagination" (Golding 1974: 47). Lack of empathy rather than being the cause of fatalism was actually the result of frustrated experience. Thus, operational problems with key concepts were largely due to the researcher's poor knowledge of the respondents and their cultural milieu. It was really the Western researchers who lacked empathy with their respondents and their cultures.

Political, Economic, and Social-Structural Constraints on Change

In his classic study, *The Passing of the Traditional Society* (1958), Daniel Lerner showed that there was a strong correlation between the indices of the mass media and the socio-economic and political development of a nation. In other words, he showed that the mass media were both an index and agent of modernization in societies. However, Lerner implied causality among the variables based on the strength of the correlations (Fjes 1976). Correlation measures are necessary but not sufficient indicators of causality. In fact, other attempts by researchers to show causality among the various indices of development and media availability have not proved successful (Schramm and Ruggels 1967; Shaw 1966). Golding (1974) and many others noted the ethnocentrism in considering the Western-style democracy as the dependent variable in Lerner's model. Any failure to attain the Western form of political arrangement indicated underdevelopment (Douglass 1971; Fjes 1976).

A factor that was largely ignored in the modernization approach was the unequal power relationships within Third World countries. Consequently, many dependent variables of modernity such as leadership, cosmopoliteness, and reference groups lacked face validity. Beltran, reviewing the research of Cuellar and Gutierrez, noted that the political-economic situation in a Third World society gave a totally different meaning to several variables. Thus,

the concept of "leadership" hides "elite" or "oligarchy," that "cosmopoliteness" disguises the connection of interests between rural and urban power-holders, and that the term "reference group" may serve to dilute the reality of "internal domination" which victimizes the peasantry (Beltran 1976: 21).

Lerner, Schramm, and Lakshmana Rao described a dual society in Third World nations: a traditional sector existing alongside a modern entity. The traditional sector not only preceded the modern sector in temporal sequence, but it was backward because of its traditionalism. They visualized the day when the modern sector would, through diffusion, dominate and get rid of the traditional society. However, a lack of interest in studying social-structural constraints obfuscated the reality in developing nations. Fjes (1976: 25) cautioned that:

> often times it is not in the modern sector's interest . . . to modernize the so-called traditional sector. Rather than being isolated from the modern sector, the so-called traditional sector often exists in a relationship of oppressive dependency, its human and material resources being exploited for the benefit of the modern sector. Rather than the traditional and modern sectors existing as two distinct systems, each more or less separate from the other, the modern and traditional systems exist within one system of economic, political, and social relationships, with the modern sector dominating the traditional.

Thus, quite often, the perpetuation of the traditional sector served the interests of its modern counterpart.

Serious ethical problems have been identified in the way Lerner's study was conceptualized and executed (Samarajiwa 1987). Lerner's classic study was not originally intended as a study of the relationship between empathy and development. Instead, as Samarajiwa (1987: 10) pointed out, "the objective of the project was audience research in the broader sense of identifying target audiences, as well as in the narrow sense of obtaining *nuts and bolts* information about how Voice of America (VOA) broadcasts were received and how the VOA was evaluated in relation to competing broadcasters." Samarajiwa also pointed out that the United States Department of State, at the height of the Cold War, funded Lerner's study. Thus, there was more than academic interest in the role of mass media vis-à-vis social change. One of the clandestine objectives was to identify vulnerable audience segments within the Middle East populations and then to target VOA propaganda messages at these groups.

Individual as Locus of Change

An important conceptual problem in the theories of modernization was the level at which change was sought to be introduced. The unit of analysis was predominantly centered within the individual, also discussed in Chapter 5. The underlying theme in this approach was that the benefits of modernization would accrue by changing the traditional attitudes, values, and aspirations of individuals in developing nations. Exposure to new ideas and practices, usually through the mass media, could help remove traditional attitudes that were impediments to progress (Lerner 1958; Shore 1980). This psychological bias in research, Rogers stated, could be traced to the fact that several early scholars in communication had psychological backgrounds, and so it was obvious that their views of communication and change neglected the influence of social structural variables that affect communication (Rogers 1976a). Much of the early research, therefore, placed an exaggerated emphasis on the individual as the locus of control for change to the neglect of the group and also the relations between sources and receivers. This resulted in the individual constituting the unit of response, the unit of analysis, and consequently the unit of change (Coleman 1958; Fair 1989; Rogers 1976a).

There were other reasons for the individual orientation besides the psychological bias. The research design used favored the individual approach. The survey design usually involves a random sample of individuals rather than of groups. Most often the respondents chosen were the presumed "heads of households," obfuscating some very real social realities. It biased the data to the views of one individual in a family and ignored the views of all the other members, especially females. The sample survey method also obscured on-going interactions between people as it ripped the individual from his/her social-structural context:

> Using random sampling of individuals, the survey is a sociological meat grinder, tearing the individual from his social context and guaranteeing that nobody in the study interacts with anyone else in it. It is a little like a biologist putting his experimental animals through a hamburger machine and looking at every hundredth cell through a microscope; anatomy and physiology get lost; structure and function disappear and one is left with cell biology (Barton 1968: 1).

The survey was clearly an inadequate research tool. It did not record the relational and transactional aspects of society. It was only in the 1970s that the level of analysis moved from the monad to the dyad or network of individuals, largely through network analysis and general systems approaches (Beltran 1976; Rogers 1976a).

It is important to point out that the individual approach to change certainly has its roots in the individual bias of American empirical research. This bias was carried into the Third World without checking whether individuals were the right unit of response. In much of the rural Third World, individual decisions are not common and are usually overruled by the decisions of the reference group. So, the overuse of the individual as the locus of change may have masked the fact that the unit of response and analysis could have been the group, such as the immediate family, clan, tribe, caste, or some other subgrouping of individuals.

Ironically, the individual-centered approach ran contrary to the dominant theoretical position:

> One of the significant achievements of American communications research is that it has shown, contrary to the expectations of mass society theorists, that within a highly developed industrial society the individual is not an isolated, atomized entity, but an ongoing, active member of one or a number of the pyramid of social subgroups that exist . . . . However, in turning their attention upon the peoples of the underdeveloped world, communication researchers tend to ignore this insight and view underdeveloped populations as being homogenous, atomized, and lacking any significant group ties (Fjes 1976: 12).

Individual-blame

A consequence of the psychological, methodological, and individual bias in communication research was that it held the individual responsible for all problems. Little or no attention was given to investigating the anomalies of the system. "Person-blame rather than system-blame permeates most definitions of social problems; seldom are the definers able to change the system, so they accept it. Such acceptance encourages a focus on psychological variables in communication research" (Rogers 1976a: 213). A high degree of person-blame was present in studies pertaining to communication and development. Beltran succinctly summarized this thinking in much of the earlier diffusion research: "If peasants do not adopt the technology of modernization, it is their fault, not that of those communicating the modern technology to them. It is the peasantry itself which is to be blamed for its ill fate, not the society which enslaves and exploits it" (Beltran 1976: 25). Much of the earlier communication research, with its exaggerated emphasis on the individual-blame causal hypotheses to social problems, obfuscated the social-structural, political, and institutional constraints acting against the individual's efforts to change. Thus, the use of the individual as the unit of response and analysis led to the use of the individual as the unit of change and consequently the unit of blame.

Economic and Political Barriers to Change

Starting in the 1980s, communication research gave increasing attention to the role of larger economic and political structures in a particular society rather than individual factors in the development process. It was observed that these structural constraints produced unequal distributions of resources, such as wealth, land, skills, and information among the people (Narula and Pearce 1986). These inequalities had a deleterious effect on the nature of innovation diffusion and who among the recipients reaped the advantages and disadvantages of such change (Rogers 1976a). It was found that the socio-economic structure invariably favored adoption of innovations by individuals with higher socio-economic status, i.e., those who owned more land, had higher economic and educational status, and ample mass communication access, thus resulting in greater inequality (Beltran 1976; Rogers and Adhikarya 1979). In short, in developing nations, the mass media communicated innovations down the social structure leaving the structure of power intact.

The influence of social structural variables as mediating factors in communication and change led to a reconceptualization of the role of communication in national development. What was apparent, "from the results of research in rural development over the past two decades, is the need to consider communication not as a simple independent variable but as both dependent and an independent variable in a complex set of relationships with social, economic and political structures and processes" (Shore 1980: 21). Also, the influence of the social structure on the individual adopter pointed to the fact that the main barriers to development, at least in Latin America, were not psychological or primarily informative, as assumed, but mainly structural, and that a restructuring of society was a prerequisite for the achievement of humane development (Beltran 1976; Diaz-Bordenave 1976; Eapen 1973; McAnany 1980b; Rogers and Adhikarya 1979).

Research also showed that in the Third World, quite often the people who were supposed to be the prime beneficiaries of development were not reached at all (Lenglet 1980). Access of marginalized people to media resources was a crucial constraint in many developing countries:

Those farmers with higher education, higher reading ability, greater exposure to other media, and higher standards of living (half of whom were already well-informed and had less need for the information) attended programs (media shows) more frequently than those with less education, less reading ability, limited exposure to other media, and a lower standard of living (Shingi and Mody 1976: 94).

These findings confirmed that the highest attendance was usually among those who had access to other sources of information. The rural poor in developing nations had very limited access to mass media, as most media were concentrated in urban areas. Research indicated that there was an important imbalance within rural areas, where the elite, disproportionately male, had better access and exposure to media sources (Beltran 1974; Eapen 1975; Khan 1987; Shore 1980).

The quality and content of the mass media messages too left much to be desired. The urbanites and other elite sources controlled the modern media in most Third World nations and the quality and content of messages were not well suited for rural audiences (Beltran 1974; Eapen 1975). Also, very little time and space was accorded to developmental information in the mass media. Shore (1980) quoted studies on the content of newspapers, radio, and television which suggested that information relevant to development was given less preference than trivial and non-development-oriented subjects. The poor, disadvantaged sections in rural areas of the Third World lived in a state of "undercommunication."

Attempts to improve this situation, however, faced political constraints. Though the rural poor needed all the help they could get, local governments did not have the political will to ameliorate their condition. McAnany (1980a) pointed out that though communication projects for rural people promised to save money, the costs were usually based upon comparisons with delivering information to urban audiences or the highly motivated elite and not the most disadvantaged rural masses. He concluded, "the approach to a 'solution' to the problems of the rural poor is a political one, rooted in the history of the country and the structures that continue to support the status quo" (McAnany 1980a: 11).

McAnany's comment deserves attention, particularly when reviewing the history of many developing nations in Asia and Africa. These nations gained their independence from European colonial powers only in the last 35–50 years, and the political structures that exist today have been largely developed after their independence. The histories of these nations were distorted by the colonial powers, and restoration to an independent status only created new problems (Eapen 1973). National geographic boundaries were drawn arbitrarily by the colonial powers, leading to frequent factional fights and boundary disputes between neighboring countries. Also, the governments and political structures left behind in many of the new nations did not fit into the traditional mold, giving rise to complex problems.

Ideological Constraints

Why was there a benign neglect of political-economic constraints on development in the mass media and modernization theories until the 1970s? Latin American scholars argued that this neglect was neither conspiratorial nor accidental. Instead, in developing nations, the field of scientific thought in general, and communication research in particular, was influenced by *alien premises, objects and methods* (Beltran 1976). The definitions of concepts, the role and functions of the mass media, indeed the field itself was incompatible or irrelevant to the needs and problems of the Third World.

Latin American scholars such as Beltran and Diaz-Bordenave noted that much of the initial work in the discipline of communication was done in the United States, and mostly by psychologists, political scientists, and sociologists. The study of communication was strongly influenced by the disciplinary perspectives of these other social sciences. In the infant stage, communication models stressed political persuasion and propaganda. The problems were uniquely American, i.e., World Wars I and II. The mass media were used for gaining internal support and cohesion and for propaganda against the enemy. However, after World War I, the knowledge gained in media effects was applied to other important objectives in peacetime America. It was used to improve commercial advertising techniques, raise radio ratings, and to win elections.

In the 1950s and 1960s, American communication models were exported to the Third World nations. Quite clearly, however, the scientific knowledge, research, and models that were exported were best suited to the socio-economic, political, cultural, and structural arrangements in the United States, at least from the perspective of those in power. Beltran (1976: 23) noted:

What kind of society hosted these remarkable scientific experiments and advancements? Was it an unhappy one burdened by poverty,

> afflicted by social conflict, and shaken by instability? Not at all. It was
> basically a prosperous, content, peaceful and stable society .... It was
> also a society where individuality was predominant over collectivism,
> competition was more determinant than cooperation, and economic
> efficiency and technological wisdom were more important than cultural
> growth, social justice, and spiritual enhancement.

Obviously, the knowledge generated by such a society would strive to
achieve conformity of individuals to the dominant norms and behaviors.
In other words, it would be a science striving to maintain the status quo.
The discipline of communication had similar objectives. If the need was
to help individuals adjust to the dominant social ethic, "communication
scientists had to find those personality traits which would render them
amenable to persuasion. Accordingly, they had to invent media and message strategies able to produce in them the desired behaviors" (Beltran
1976: 23).

Thus, the emphasis was on curbing individual aberrance and on
persuasion. The early, influential communication model of Lasswell was
obsessed with receiver persuasion (Chapter 4). The social context, however, was irrelevant. The functionalistic paradigm of Merton and other
American sociologists further supported the need to persuade individuals
to conform to the existing arrangements in the society. The locus of change
then was not the society but the aberrant individual.

The scenario in Latin America and the newly independent nations in
Asia and Africa was quite different from that of the US or Western Europe.
These nations were afflicted by poverty, gross inequality among their
citizens, rigid social structures, political instability, and other negative
consequences of their earlier colonized status. The models of adjustment,
conformity, and persuasion of individuals toward a status quo were clearly
incompatible and irrelevant to the problems these nations were facing.
The locus of attention was to be the entire society. Beltran (1976: 26)
outlined several relevant questions that the mass media had to address in
the Third World nations:

> Who owns the media today and to which interest groups are they
> responsive? Are there ethical limits to persuasion proficiency? Must
> feedback forever remain no more than a tool for securing the intended
> response? Does the state exert any control over North American com-
> munication interests overseas? How far should advertising be allowed

to keep exacerbating consuming behavior in a time of serious economic crisis?

Diaz-Bordenave (1976: 54) posited other concerns:

How autonomous or independent is the country from external forces that affect its economy and its political decisions? How is the rural structure organized and what influence does it exert over individual decision-making? Who controls the economic institutions, particularly the market, credit, and input supply organizations?

At least in Latin America, scholars raised questions suggesting that the main problem was not maintaining the status quo but a restructuring of the socio-economic policy so that it could better serve humane development objectives. This analysis was never voiced by American communication scholars in the 1950s and 1960s, such as Schramm and Lerner. Schemes which appeared successful for the Western nations were recommended for developing nations. Thus, the Third World was told that more mass media were needed for speedy modernization without making sure whether mass media were actually needed in such numbers. This dubious argument was supported by the American-influenced UNESCO's minimum standards for every 100 persons in developing countries: 10 copies of a daily newspaper; five radio receivers; two cinema seats; and two television sets (Schramm 1964).

This was clearly the American notion of media development. As Tunstall pointed out, "typically only daily newspapers were mentioned although their relevance in rural areas of many poor countries is small, since a daily paper may in any case take several days to arrive from the nearest big city" (Tunstall 1977: 211). The weekly newspapers and magazines were more relevant to the conditions in these countries and they also helped to conserve precious newsprint. Tunstall noted that the UNESCO figures for the electronic media were even more doubtful. "The two cinema seats and two television sets per 100 population would obviously be concentrated in urban areas, whereas the five radio sets per 100 was too low to emphasize the possibility of making radio available to almost the entire population" (Tunstall 1977: 212). In short, the UNESCO recommendations considered socio-economic change in Third World to be synonymous with development of media hardware.

The hard sell of Western communication models inhibited local ideas and planning more relevant to the conditions in developing countries. To quote Tunstall (1977: 212) again, "for at least some nations in Africa and Asia an alternate set of targets might have stressed a high ratio of weekly papers and magazines per population, a complete halt on cinema and television expansion, and a high ratio of radio sets to population . . . these are some possibilities among many—but the failure of UNESCO to state such simple alternatives was a serious weakness." Thus, the Western communication models overvalued communication technology as a solution for social problems in the developing nations of Asia, Africa, and Latin America.

Critique of the Role of Mass Media in Development

An implicit assumption running through the literature in the dominant paradigm was that the mass media (especially the electronic media) in developing nations carried a strong pro-development content (Douglass 1971; Rogers 1969). Therefore, increased exposure to mass media messages would obviously create the "climate for modernization" in the villages in the Third World (Lerner 1958; Schramm 1964). This view of pro-development content of media messages was not entirely correct. Larry Shore cites research in Latin America, mostly on the content of newspapers, and some on radio and television, suggesting consistently less preference for information relevant to development than for the trivial and non-development-oriented subjects such as sports and entertainment (Shore 1980).

The main architects of the communication approach in the modernization paradigm, such as Schramm (1964), Lerner (1958), Pye (1963), and Frey (1966), did not examine the relationship between the institutional structures of the media and their impact on the media content. This was consistent with the underlying bias of examining the mass media devoid of their relationship with larger structural factors. Thus, it was likely that messages preaching conspicuous consumption may have been a part of the larger construct of social-structural and economic dynamics that hindered humane development in the Third World (Fjes 1976; Hamelink 1983). In fact, Rogers (1976b: 135) made an astute observation concerning this phenomenon:

By the late 1960's and the 1970's a number of critical evaluations were being made of the mass communication role in development. Some scholars, especially in Latin America, perceived the mass media in their nations as an extension of exploitative relationships with the U.S.-based multinational corporations, especially through advertising of commercial products. Further, questions were asked about the frequent patterns of elite ownership and control of mass media institutions in Latin America and the influence of such ownership on the media content.

Even if governments in some developing countries actively promoted pro-development content in their mass media, it had to be viewed from the perspective of the total program structure prepared for each medium and the total time allotted to each type of program. For example, although the broadcasting authority in India was committed to rural development and carried rural radio programs that were clearly pro-development, the total percentage of such programs was very low. In "home-service" radio programs, only 5.8 percent of total program time was devoted to rural programs while 40 percent of broadcast time was claimed by music and 24.8 percent by news (*India* 1982). Thus, there was the anomaly of rural programs being pro-development but the total time accorded to such programs being rather insignificant.

Also, even assuming that many media messages in developing nations were pro-development, there was still reason to be concerned with other factors. First, there was the question of selective exposure of the audience to particular media messages because, more often than not, such selectivity was towards messages that were not pro-development. As Rogers observed on one of his visits to a village in a developing nation, "the only radio in the village, owned by the president of the village council, was tuned to music rather than to news of the outside world" (Rogers 1969: 96). Second, there was the question of comprehension of the media content even if the farmer chose to listen to pro-development programs. The absence of programming in all regional languages or major dialects and the irrelevant content due to the largely urban control of media production in many developing nations made the programs unsuitable for rural audiences (Masani 1975). Development communication literature made very little contribution to the understanding and solving of these problems (Vilanilam 1979). Finally, while the media were successful in raising people's aspirations, Third World governments were not capable of satisfying the new wants. Thus, what resulted was a *revolution of rising frustrations* (Lerner 1958). Lerner had posited that exposing individuals in developing nations to media images of modernity would bring about a *revolution of rising expectations*. However, by avoiding a thorough examination of the structural constraints in developing nations, the scholars made faulty use of mass media. Exposing people to images of the West without the same conditions as in the West created a serious imbalance in the want/get ratio (Fjes 1976).

In many developing nations, the mass media in their present form are not suited for the kinds of developmental tasks they have to perform, and in some instances are becoming even less suitable than in the past (Eapen 1975; Heath 1992; Masani 1975; Steeves 1996). Heath (1992) documents diminished radio programming for the rural poor in Kenya. As the Kenya Broadcasting Corporation (KBC) has acquired new and expensive television technologies, it has also acquired debt. Debt repayments require profitable services, i.e., television entertainment programs that can attract advertising. A result has been cutbacks in indigenous language radio broadcasts in rural areas. In general, an adequate response to the challenging task of rural development in developing nations would:

> involve a re-consideration of the structure of the broadcasting system, the location of transmitters and studios and the language and content of programs . . . . It is clear that unless policies are changed, the services expanded and decentralized there is little chance of the mass media playing a significant role in bringing about rural change (Masani 1975: 2).

Knowledge Gap Hypothesis

In developing nations, the mass media—like other social institutions—can reinforce or increase existing inequities between the advantaged and disadvantaged sectors of the population. The "increasing knowledge gap" first proposed by Tichenor et al. (1970) remained largely unexamin-ed in early development communication research. They hypothesized:

> As the infusion of mass media information into a social system increases, segments of the population with higher socio-economic status tend to acquire this information at a faster rate than the lower status segments, so that the gap in knowledge between these segments tends to increase rather than decrease (Tichenor et al. 1970: 159).

The existence of this gap did not mean that the lower status population remained totally uninformed or even absolutely worse off in knowledge, but rather that they became relatively lower in knowledge, thus giving rise to the gap.

The authors posited several reasons for the knowledge gap to occur and widen with increasing media flow: (a) differential levels of communication skills (that is, persons with more formal education had higher reading and comprehension capabilities); (b) amounts of stored information or existing knowledge due to prior exposure to the topic (such receivers of communication were better prepared to understand the next communication); (c) relevant social contact (there could be a greater number of people in the reference groups of the more advantaged sector, and also these receivers may have had greater interpersonal contact with other information-rich individuals); and (d) selective exposure, acceptance and retention of information (higher education could be related to greater voluntary exposure to communication). Thus, to the extent that the above factors were operative, the gap would widen as a heavy mass media influx continued (Tichenor et al. 1970).

This knowledge gap could be socially significant. Differentials in knowledge could lead to greater tension in a social system, giving rise to greater disparities between sectors of a population:

> In developing countries like India, most development benefits have tended to accrue to better-off segments rather than to the downtrodden for whom they may ostensibly have been intended. A much-discussed case in point is the so-called Green Revolution that benefited the larger farmers and widened existing socio-economic gaps. Given their higher levels of knowledge, capital and social contact, it is not surprising that the "haves" achieve greater effects from exposure to most interpersonal and mass media information sources (Shingi and Mody 1976: 83).

Shingi and Mody (1976) carried out an experiment that suggested some modification in Tichenor et al. (1970) conclusion that media increase information inequities among their audiences. They discovered that media (in this case, television) could narrow the knowledge gap, but this would obviously require exposure using proper communication strategies. It appeared that the sections of the audience that were high on ignorance before the programs, gained most in absolute terms from the television programs, although they still had a little less knowledge than the pre-exposure higher-knowledge audience. The researchers called this the "ceiling effect." By selecting messages that were redundant or had little potential value to the large farmer, the media could narrow and even close—rather than widen—the communication effects gap. The significance of this study was that it proved that the knowledge or communication effects gap is not inevitable. In fact, the gap could be narrowed if appropriate communication strategies are used in campaigns (Shingi and Mody 1976: 97):

1. Low knowledge (and other small) farmers should be encouraged to see television shows and given access to a receiver set;
2. Message content should be simple and easily understandable to non-elite audiences. Technical jargon, if any, should be simplified and sources of high credibility and understandability should be utilized; and
3. The salience, appeal, and presentation of information should be such that lower-knowledge audiences could "catch-up" with higher-status counterparts who would probably find lesser value and interest in such messages due to its redundancy and "ceiling effect."

These strategies, however, would need to be built into a flexible, on-going development support project, and such a venture would have to be institutionalized. One-shot approaches to development communication, such as, the Indian Satellite Instructional Television Experiment (SITE), may not result in any significant behavior change among receivers. Such ventures, which provide intensive information support for a short period and then are discontinued, can be likened to the analogy of sending a child to school for a short while then taking him/her out but still expecting the child to retain all that he/she has learned. What is necessary is an institutionalized, ongoing, and flexible strategy. As we will show next, this has not always been the case with projects based on diffusion or social marketing models.

CRITIQUE OF DIFFUSION OF INNOVATIONS RESEARCH AND PRACTICE

As presented in Chapter 4, the predominant model that guided local-level development communications planning from the 1950s into the early 1970s was the diffusion of innovations model. The critique of this approach is categorized under three heads: (i) Theoretical biases in diffusion of innovations research; (ii) Methodological biases; and (iii) Social-structural constraints to diffusion of innovations.

Theoretical Biases in Diffusion of Innovations Research

Communication Effects Bias

Consistent with the environment from which it arose, the predominant concern of communication research through the 1960s was the effects of a particular source, medium, message, or a combination of these elements on the receiver. The focus on communication effects in the modernization process was also present in much of classical diffusion research. The communication effects orientation gave undue importance to the question of exposure to mass media. "Larger mass media audiences, accompanied by high levels of mass media exposure per capita, can be expected to lead those exposed to more favorable attitudes toward change and development, to greater awareness of political events, and to more knowledge of technical information" (Rogers 1969: 101).

Inattention to Message Content

The obsession with effects of mass media on behavior alteration through increased exposure to mass media gave little consideration to the content of the messages to which the audience was exposed. In fact, there was an implicit assumption that any kind of mass media exposure would lead to development:

> Nor does our measure of exposure consider the specific nature of the messages received from the mass media—whether musical, news, or technical content. It should be remembered that exposure, not influence or *internalization*, of mass media messages is what is being dealt with here (Rogers 1969: 101).

The methodology, therefore, in much of the classical diffusion of innovations studies revealed a serious shortcoming. As no attempt was made to discover the types of media messages audiences were exposed to, little or no attention was given to the content and quality of information, or knowledge and skills emanating from the messages. The corollary to this was that there was no attempt to investigate whether the content of the messages was internalized by the audience, i.e., whether the messages were consumable, reliable, and efficient, leading to internalization of the messages. The mass media exposure index was constructed thus: the respondents' indications of degree of exposure to each medium, in terms of number of radio shows listened to per week, and so on, contributed to form a standard score (Rogers 1969). This quantitative approach to media exposure revealed nothing of the respondents' media message preferences: the respondent could have been listening to music, news, plays, talk, or even static noise from the radio set. Hence, researchers gathered little information on types of programs preferred, whether these programs were pro-development, neutral, or anti-development in content, the quality and relevance of the programs, and differences in their use and perception (Golding 1974).

The lack of interest in the content of media messages and, consequently, individual or group differences in their use and perception, led to a lack of interest in the *cognitive* dimension of communication effects. Most diffusion of innovations studies focused predominantly on the *behavioral* dimension of communication effects. They posed questions such as: "Has there been any effect of the media on respondents' behavior? If so, what has been the nature and direction of that effect on adoption behavior?" Very rarely did research seek to investigate the cognitive dimension, or what audience members know. Diffusion studies did not posit questions such as: Did the communication attempt have a relatively greater effect on the cognition of certain receivers than on others? Why? Whereas the first question asked about effects on adoption behavior, the second question directed communication research to the differential levels of cognition among receivers and to the possible concern with knowledge gaps (Shingi and Mody 1976). The early research, therefore, did not reveal the potential inequalities media exposure could create among different segments of the audience, particularly the disadvantaged sections low in socio-economic status.

Women constitute one major audience segment ignored in most diffusion studies. Yet women usually have less access to media than men. For example, in most Third World countries, women's illiteracy levels are higher than men's, obviously limiting women's access to print media (United Nations 1995). Also, in some cultures, men control the use of the radio in the household (Manoff 1985). On average, women are poorer than men, reducing their economic ability to purchase media (United Nations 1995). Additionally, fewer women than men have opportunities to work in media organizations or otherwise participate in media decision-making (see Steeves 1996). Therefore, critiques and analyses must consider the relative occurrence and context of media exposure:

This implies a need for more feminist analyses of media representations and roles, particularly comparative research to understand differences in societies with different political and cultural histories. Also, more research is needed to learn how women and men in developing countries are processing media content, how these perceptions mesh and clash with their cultural values, and how they relate to national development goals (Steeves and Arbogast 1993: 250).

The newest innovation for which women's access is restricted is the Internet. Globally, males dominate the use of the Internet (also see the last section of this chapter). The gender ratio for Internet access and use has remained at 63 percent males and 37 percent females for several years (Panos 1998a). If the new information and communication technologies, such as the Internet, are going to play a significant role in information transmission and retrieval in the future, it is essential that women and other traditionally marginalized groups participate fully in cyberspace.

Shallow Depth of Knowledge

The important dependent variable in most diffusion studies was the adoption of non-traditional innovations. In the measurement of this consequent variable, however, most studies revealed methodological and conceptual weaknesses. Insufficient attention and treatment were given to the amount and depth of knowledge and skills the respondent possessed prior to the adoption decision. Shingi and Mody (1976) report that diffusion studies used the easily measurable concept of awareness of new practices rather than deeper concepts tapping knowledge of innovations. The empirical definition of the awareness of an innovation was confined to "Have you heard of . . . ?" kinds of queries and did not measure the "how-to" knowledge consisting of information vital to use an innovation efficiently, and "principles-knowledge" dealing with the fundamental principles underlying an innovation. Shingi and Mody cautioned that,

the long-range competence of farmers to evaluate and adopt (or reject) future innovations is not directly facilitated by mere awareness of a great number of innovations . . . . In our opinion, the innovation-decision process is considered to be initiated not when the individual is merely exposed to information on the innovation but when he gains some understanding of how it functions (Shingi and Mody 1976: 95).

Methodological Biases in Diffusion of Innovations Research and Strategy

The lack of innovativeness among diffusion researchers in employing experimental and panel study designs in place of the familiar post-hoc one-shot surveys gave rise to three overlapping methodological and campaign biases identified by Rogers (1976a): (*i*) a pro-innovation bias, (*ii*) lack of a process orientation, and (*iii*) neglect of causality. Melkote (1984, 1991) delineated several additional biases: (*i*) one-way message flow bias, (*ii*) pro-persuasion bias, (*iii*) pro-source bias, (*iv*) pro-literacy bias, and (*v*) in-the-head variable bias. A discussion of these interwoven biases will be useful.

Pro-innovation Bias

An implicit assumption running through diffusion tenets was that adoption of non-traditional innovations would be advantageous to all potential adopters. While this assumption was true in a few cases, it could not be justified in a majority of cases in the rural Third World where the innovations were clearly ill adapted to local conditions (Rogers 1976a; Roling et al. 1976). An example of the incompatibility of technological innovations with local practices was in the area of traditional subsistence farming. Scholars noted that diffusion researchers arrived in rural communities with a built-in bias toward Western ideas of agricultural practice with its orientation to permanent commercial enterprises concerned with plant population per unit area, planting distances, fertilizer use, and other technologies primarily developed for single-crop systems (Bortei-Doku 1978; Horton 1991; Whyte 1991b). The mixed cropping and shifting agriculture practiced in developing countries were considered backward. In fact, the very nature of mixed-cropping prevented the easy application of scientific recommendations about planting distances, crop protection, and the application of fertilizer and pesticides. So, the farmers were persuaded to adopt the single-crop system with all its attendant technologies to ensure increased productivity. In a few cases in Mexico and Colombia, the farmers were persuaded to adopt innovations that would poten-tially cut the value of their crops in half (Whyte 1991b). In other cases, the innovation was not only incompatible with local conditions, but also too complex for the subsistence farmers to sustain. If the small farmer was reluctant to adopt the innovation, it was not because he/she did not care to increase his/her productivity with the new techniques. Instead, there were many factors favoring practices of traditional farming:

The truth of the matter is that traditional farm practices are based on the farmer's concept of the most efficient use of his land, given his available resources. Lacking financial resources not only to invest in cash crops but also to tide him over till they mature and produce food-purchasing means for himself, his priority crops became those which guaranteed him his subsistence with minimum risk. To make sure he has a good supply in the early part of the growing season, he mixes his crops, planting, for example, early millet with some later maturing crops. Lacking the labor to clear and maintain large tracts of land, he farms on small manageable plots, mixing his crops to ensure himself self-sufficient variety . . . . Unable to obtain a loan to purchase a plough or hire a tractor for deep ploughing, he scrabbles the land with a hoe, dibbling corn on it with a pointed stick (Bortei-Doku 1978: 4).

Thus, adopting the new innovation or adapting it to the traditional system was too risky. Experimentation could lead to relative success, but there was also a greater likelihood of crop failure due to inadequate knowledge of modern technologies and methods.

A discussion of the pro-innovation bias brings to the surface an issue that has not received much thought among diffusion theorists: the painful contradiction between diffusion theory and its practice. Early diffusion research delineated the characteristics of the innovation itself that would affect its rate of acceptance (or rejection) by the potential adopter. Some of these factors were (as we explained in Chapter 4): relative advantage, compatibility, complexity, divisibility, and communicability. Rogers, who coined these terms, underlined their importance:

It matters very little whether or not an innovation has a great degree of advantage over the idea it is replacing. What does matter is whether the individual perceives the relative advantage of the innovations. Likewise, it is the potential adopter's perceptions of the compatibility, complexity, divisibility, and communicability of the innovation that affect its rate of adoption (Rogers 1962: 124).

Yet, from some of the examples above it may be surmised that diffusion practice gave limited critical attention to innovations before they were diffused. No study has looked into this anomaly. Therefore, the pro-innovation bias has been, in essence, a failure to assess the innovation itself.

Absence of a Process Orientation

There was a misalignment between what the researchers theorized and what they actually measured. Though communication has always been conceptualized as a process, the research designs in diffusion studies mostly consisted of analyses of cross-sectional data collected through surveys at a single point in time (Rogers 1976a). The dynamic process conceptualization of communication was thus obscured in this approach:

> Very few communication researchers include data at more than one observation point, and almost none at more than two such points in time. So almost all communication research is unable to trace the change in a variable over time; it deals only with the present tense of behavior. Communication thus becomes, in the actuality of communication research, an artificially halted snapshot (Rogers 1976a: 209).

Mainstream diffusion researchers did not just obscure the concept of communication as a process. They, in fact, distorted the communication process itself. Contrary to the assertion of Rogers in the above quotation, diffusion research dealt not with the present tense, but the past tense of behavior. In the correlational analyses, the dependent variable of innovativeness was measured with recall data about past adoption behavior. Diffusion research, therefore, examined recipients' adoption histories and constructed not an "artificially halted snapshot," but an artificially constructed movie or biographical history of the adopter.

The pro-innovation bias coupled with an overwhelming use of post-hoc survey design confined the focus of diffusion research to testing of strategies of *what-is* or reaffirming current practice rather than *what-might-be* or testing alternative strategies. Since the innovation was thought to be good for the adopter and the present process of diffusion satisfactory, the survey design was used to replicate the status quo. There was no attempt to use field experimental designs and go beyond current practice to gain knowledge of effective means to reach an alternative, desired state (Roling 1973; Roling et al. 1976).

Neglect of Causality

Researchers used the terms "independent" and "dependent" variables, borrowed from experimental designs in an incorrect and ambiguous way in correlational analyses. In an experimental design, an independent variable X could change a dependent variable Y if, (*i*) X occurs before Y in a temporal sequence, and (*ii*) they co-vary. In most diffusion studies, as Rogers noted, the only aspect that was investigated was whether the independent variable co-varied with the dependent variable (i.e., innovativeness). The use of the post-hoc one-shot survey design prevented the determination of time-order sequence between X and Y. Thus, it was seen that the dependent variable of innovativeness was measured with recall data about past adoption behavior, whereas the independent variables were measured in the present tense. This virtually resulted in independent variables following the dependent variable of innovativeness in temporal sequence and yet leading to adoption of an innovation (Rogers 1976a). In short, this was methodologically incorrect and, in practice, impossible.

A discussion of the foregoing methodological and conceptual biases reveals the post-hoc preoccupation of diffusion research with already diffused innovations. The diffusion tenets, Ascroft noted, "provided researchers with few insights about strategies for 'pushing' the process, for 'causing' it to occur more rapidly, reliably, efficiently and completely" (Ascroft and Gleason 1980: 3). The dearth of experimental designs in diffusion theory, therefore, gave rise to biases such as a lack of process orientation, a pro-innovation bias and ignoring of the issue of causality.

One-way Message Flow Bias

An implicit assumption in diffusion research was that changes within developing nations happened exogenously. It was only through continuing contact with Western ideas and technology that Third World nations could become modern (see previous chapters). This one-way approach, to quote Rahim, "has tended to block the researcher from seeing the reverse flow of ideas and innovations from the poor to the rich, from the less developed to the more developed, from the peasants to the technicians, administrators, and scientists" (Rahim 1976: 224). Thus, in diffusion research there was not only a North to South communication flow between nations, but even within a nation, there was a top-down message flow from administrators, scientists, and donor agencies, to farmers (Whyte 1991a). Thus, in short, the flow of communication was from a Northerner to a North-like-Southerner[1] within developing nations, and from him/her to the rural peasants. This one-way message flow, illustrated earlier with the example of the multicropping agricultural system, could not recognize the virtue of traditional methods. An FAO report had this to say about multicropping:

There are increasing indications that such systems should not be rejected wholesale as primitive and uneconomical. In fact, it appears that past research aimed at improving cropping systems had not shown enough attention to some of the techniques developed by small farmers, and that a scientific approach to such systems can sometimes give better results than the use of technology primarily developed for single-crop systems (FAO 1977; Whyte 1991b).

So, as Bortei-Doku pointed out, instead of finding ways to adapt new technology to existing patterns of farming, efforts were made instead to train a whole new generation of farmers through agricultural institutes. "Such trainees, however, hardly ever returned to the farm to apply their new knowledge. They went instead in search of government jobs as field assistant and technical officers, leaving the problem of the development and improvement of traditional agriculture largely unsolved" (Bortei-Doku 1978: 4). Instances such as these could have been avoided to a great extent if diffusion research had accommodated the reverse flow of ideas and practices from farmers to scientists or donor agencies.

The neglect of a broad framework which considered the diffusion of ideas and practices as a multi-way flow between individuals at the micro level and between nations at the macro level has been a serious conceptual and methodological weakness of diffusion research.

Box 6.1
Flow of Innovations can be a Multi-way Process

Our solid American citizen awakens in a bed built on a pattern which originated in the Near East but which was modified in Northern Europe before it was transmitted to America. He throws back covers made from cotton, domesticated in India, or linen domesticated in the Near East, or silk, the use of which was discovered in China. All of these materials have been spun and woven by pro-cesses invented in the Near East. He slips into his moccasins, invented by the Indians of the Eastern woodlands, and goes to the bathroom, whose fixtures are a mixture of European and American inventions, both of recent date. He takes off his pajamas, a garment

(Box 6.1 contd.)

(Box 6.1 contd.)

invented in India, and washes with soap invented by the ancient Gauls. He then shaves, a masochistic rite which seems to have been derived from either Sumer or ancient Egypt. Returning to the bedroom, he removes his clothes from a chair of southern European type and proceeds to dress. He puts on garments whose form originally derived from the skin clothing of the nomads of the Asiatic steppes, puts on shoes made from skins tanned by a process invented in ancient Egypt and cut to a pattern derived from the classic civilizations of the Mediterranean, and ties around his neck a strip of bright-colored cloth which is a vestigial survival of the shoulder shawls worn by the seventeenth-century Croatians. Before going out to breakfast he glances through the window, made of glass invented in Egypt, and if it is raining puts on overshoes made of rubber discovered by the Central American Indians and takes an umbrella, invented in Southeastern Asia. Upon his head he puts a hat made of felt, a material invented in the Asiatic steppes. On his way to breakfast he stops to buy a paper, paying for it with coins, an ancient Lydian invention. At the restaurant, a whole new series of borrowed elements confronts him. His plate is made of a form of pottery invented in China. His knife is of steel, an alloy first made in southern India, his fork a medieval Italian invention, and his spoon a derivative of a Roman original. He begins breakfast with an orange, from the eastern Mediterranean, a cantaloupe from Persia, or perhaps a piece of African watermelon. With this he has coffee, an Abyssinian plant, with cream and sugar. Both the domestication of cows and the idea of milking them originated in the Near East, while sugar was first made in India . . . . When our friend has finished eating he settles back to smoke, an American Indian habit, consuming a plant domesticated in Brazil in either a pipe, derived from the Indians of Virginia, or a cigarette, derived from Mexico . . . . While smoking he reads the news of the day, imprinted in characters invented by the ancient Semites upon a material invented in China by a process invented in Germany. As he absorbs the accounts of foreign troubles he will, if he is a good conservative citizen, thank a Hebrew deity in an Indo-European language that he is 100 percent American (Linton 1936: 326–27).

Pro-persuasion Bias

The preoccupation with one-way effects, as illustrated in earlier sections, implied that the aim of communication research, including diffusion research, was to determine the persuasiveness of messages in changing respondents' behavior. An important task for diffusion researchers was to change the multitudes of ignorant farmers from a "traditional" to a "modern" way of living, mostly through persuasion. However, by using the persuasion approach there was an implication that farmers were resistant to change. This approach influenced a dichotomous categorization of respondents into the *persuasible* and the *recalcitrant*. An investigation of the analysis of adoption curves would show that those who were successfully persuaded to adopt non-traditional innovations were, compared to recalcitrants: more literate, had higher social status, and had exposure to more channels of communication. The resistant group had access only to the most localite sources of information and were generally ignorant of the process of modernization (Rogers 1962).

There is a logical inconsistency in this finding. How could a group with little information on new methods or of the modernization process be resistant? Logically, an individual can effectively resist a new idea or practice if he/she has sufficient knowledge about it and can logically and rationally argue against its acceptance. This preoccupation with effects and persuasion, therefore, did not assure that receivers knew enough about innovations to start with. Did the receivers understand what change was expected of them? Did they have sufficient information and knowledge to adopt a non-traditional innovation? These kinds of initial queries were not made. Those who were most resistant to change were also found to be the most ignorant. However, the test of resistance cannot be made until the pro-persuasion approach is preceded by a pro-information strategy.

Pro-source Bias

While diffusion literature discussed elaborately the weaknesses, shortcomings, and deficiencies of receivers impeding the adoption process, little or no research focused on the shortcomings and deficiencies of the source or initiator of innovations. The source was considered to be faultless and blameless and any anomaly in the diffusion process was attributed to the recalcitrance of receivers. There was even an explicit assumption that the source knew what kind of change was desirable for the adopter. This can be seen in the manner in which a change agent was defined: "A change agent is a professional who influences innovation decisions in a direction deemed desirable by a change agency" (Rogers 1969: 169). This pro-source bias also had its roots in the influence of the dominant paradigm on diffusion research. The top-down, one-way, linear model of message flow in the dominant paradigm, by its very nature, favored the source over the receiver. Diffusion research emerged from this framework and therefore revealed the same bias.

History reveals disastrous consequences of the pro-source bias. For instance, for a thousand years the people of Bali practiced ancient rituals to coordinate the irrigation and planting schedule for the island. In the 1970s and 1980s, the Indonesian government and the Asian Development Bank spent $24 million on a new system. As the negative side effects of the new system became evident, researchers at the University of Southern California used a computer model to show that the traditional system had been a perfect model of resource management (Cowley 1989). Additionally, the on-farm research program reported by Whyte (1991a) and Horton (1991) provide numerous examples of the inventiveness and rationality of the small farmers in Latin America. Many times, their methods of cultivation and seeds were superior to the innovations diffused by outside experts.

Pro-literacy Bias

A large number of people in the lower socio-economic status (SES) groups in the Third World are illiterate. Yet, development communication research and strategy often inappropriately has assumed literacy (Melkote 1984; Rogers and Adhikarya 1979). Thus, most development benefits have accrued to the large farmers and other elite groups (Gaur 1981; Shingi and Mody 1976). This pro-literacy bias has functioned as a major constraint to diffusion of information to preliterate audiences. It has prevented strategies of percolating information, knowledge, and skills to an illiterate audience that forms the bulk of the population in rural areas. Meanwhile, it has led to easier information access for elite groups in the rural and urban areas.

The pro-literacy bias is defined as the tendency of a communication source to encode messages in terms of symbols, either written, printed, or verbal, which imply literacy and numeracy skills on the part of receivers, even when they are known to lack both skills. In an investigation of communication strategies of the World Bank-sponsored Training and

Visit Extension system in south India, Melkote (1984) identified several symbols in extension messages to illiterate farmers that required knowledge of the native language as used by the literate, knowledge of English, the Western calendar, weights and measures in the Metric or Imperial systems, statistical terms such as averages, percentages, means, and technical terms in agriculture, agronomy, and agrobiology.

If the objective is to reduce socio-economic status and knowledge gaps between people in the developing nations, then it is absolutely essential that the pro-literacy bias be identified and removed from all development-oriented communication strategies.

In-the-head Variable Bias

Much of the diffusion research was preoccupied with psychological traits of receivers such as empathy, familism, and fatalism, about which little could be done. As Roling (1973) noted, such an orientation resulted in diffusion research dwelling at length on the relationships between variables that were not manipulable. Diffusion literature, partly because of its post-hoc orientation, usually aimed at reaching conclusions about peasant communities instead of discovering methods and techniques of changing these communities. Carefully delineated campaign goals and longitudinal research designs could have revealed a number of more measurable and helpful variables. One such variable, for example, was receiver knowledge, the lack of which was a crucial constraint to adoption. However, much of diffusion research chose to study non-manipulable variables in current practice and seldom about what would happen if one tried to change current practice (Roling 1973).

Network Analysis of Diffusion

The inadequacy of the monadic analysis in diffusion research to capture the transactional and relational nature of communication between individuals led to an increasing interest in network analysis. This approach was based on the convergence model of communication, which defined it as "a process in which participants create and share information with one another in order to reach a mutual understanding" (Rogers and Kincaid 1981: 63). In the network approach, the communication relationship between two or more individuals constituted the unit of analysis (Rogers 1976a; Rogers and Kincaid 1981). The sample research design was a total census of all eligible respondents in a system, rather than the earlier method of sampling scattered individuals in a population. Sociometric data about communication relationships were utilized besides the usual personal and social characteristics of individuals and their communication behavior studied in earlier monadic analyses. The data were then subjected to various types of network analyses to determine how social-structural variables affected diffusion flows in a system:

> This advance allowed the data analysis of a "who-to-whom" communication matrix, and facilitated inquiry into the identification (1) of cliques within the total system and how such structural subgroupings affected the diffusion of an innovation, and (2) of specialized communication roles such as liaisons,[2] bridges and isolates thus allowing communication research to proceed far beyond the relatively simpler issues of studying just opinion leadership (Rogers 1976a: 215).

Researchers hoped that the network analysis would lead to a greater focus on understanding the role of social structures on diffusion flows. While this was an improvement over the monadic analysis, there were other problems. There was an inadequate fit between the network analysis and the convergence model of communication that guided this approach. The convergence model views human communication as a dynamic and cyclical process, but the communication network analysis does not have this capacity (Rogers and Kincaid 1981). One of the major shortcomings of network analysis has been its inability to describe the flow of influence at each point in time. Communication flows, as represented by network structure existing at the time of data collection, are assumed to be stable over a decade after that date. This is a questionable assumption. Also, the total census method restricts the size of the aggregate that can be selected, as it is not feasible to handle a very large aggregation of individuals. The network approach is expensive, the analysis is complex and time consuming, and all this again limits the number of people it can include.

In general, the dimensions of analysis in the network approach have been very limiting. Most of the data collected have been soft and individualistic communication variables such as "who talks to whom." Unless economic, health, family-related, and other data are also included, it is not possible to get a comprehensive view of development.

Political-economic and Social-structural Constraints on Diffusion of Innovations

The classical diffusion model was originally conceived in the industrial-ized countries of the West, where the socio-economic, political, and cul-tural conditions were substantially different from those in Asia, Africa, and Latin America (Beltran 1976; Diaz-Bordenave 1976). Yet the model was uncritically applied to Third World nations. Latin American com-munication scholars pointed out some of these presumptions:

(1) Communication by itself can generate development, regardless of socio-economic and political conditions, (2) increased production and consumption of goods and services are the essence of development, and that a fair distribution of income and opportunities will necessarily derive in due time, and (3) the solution to increased productivity is technological innovation, irrespective of whom it may benefit and whom it may harm (Beltran 1976: 18–19).

The neglect of political and economic structures in the diffusion of innovations produced negative results. Some researchers even showed how diffusion practice widened socio-economic gaps between recipients of innovations. For instance, Roling, Ascroft, and Chege (1976) found that development agencies provided intensive assistance to a small number of innovative, socio-economically advanced, and information-seeking progressive farmers. The assumption was that innovations would ultimately trickle-down to the other less progressive or traditional farmers. This strategy actually led to less equitable development.

In many developing nations, extension agents are in short supply and they reach only a fraction of farmers (McAnany 1980a). This constraint, coupled with the progressive farmer strategy of diffusion practice, gave undue importance to opinion leaders. It was these leaders, who are actually the rich, educated, progressive, and usually male farmers, who came into direct contact with extension agents. The basic tenet of diffusion research was that innovations would diffuse autonomously from pro-gressive farmers to other members of the community. In reality, however, diffusion of innovations from the progressive farmers was mostly homo-philous. Information, therefore, did not reach the subsistence farmers who were not integrated into their interpersonal networks of communi-cation. Also, the messages that managed to reach the small farmers were usually distorted. This was largely because diffusion research considered the innovation itself as the message. No effort was made to carefully construct messages to promote the innovation as it diffused, so as to prevent distortion. As Allport and Postman (1947) pointed out, messages lose fidelity very soon, so it may be unlikely that information received second-hand could provide as specific, detailed and reliable information as messages received first-hand (Roling et al. 1976).

Diffusion practice benefited the advantaged sections of rural populations because (Roling et al. 1976: 69–71):

1. Early adopters (usually the rich farmers) reaped "windfall profits";
2. Having available funds relatively earlier than others permitted acquisition of additional resources when they were still relatively cheaper;
3. The adoption of an innovation usually required slack resources in order to adopt;
4. The focus on progressive farmers tended to create a fixed clientele over time; and
5. Credit was provided to farmers who could provide collateral, so costly and therefore profitable innovations could be more readily adopted by those who were relatively better off.

Thus, diffusion processes turned out to be imperfect equalizers of development benefits due to the unequal distribution of resources.

In an effort to overcome these inequities, the World Bank introduced the Training and Visit (T&V) system in the 1980s (Benor and Harrison 1977). This system required that well-trained extension specialists make regular visits to "contact farmers" (essentially carefully chosen opinion leaders), who were then expected to spread the information to their friends, consistent with two-step flow theory. As the contact farmers met in groups with the extension specialists according to a fixed schedule, the system aimed to address extension difficulties in covering vast geographic distances.

Unfortunately, follow-up research indicated that the system has not been effective. Most developing countries have not had the resources for intense and up-to-date specialized training, agents have not been able to sustain their "fixed" travel schedules, and the information disseminated has not spread to poor farmers as hypothesized. Women especially have been neglected in the system, as we will discuss shortly.

As indicated in the above examples, by the early 1970s it was fairly clear that the political-economic constraints on development often did not yield to the indirect influences of the media (Rogers 1976b). All this pointed to the fact that the main barriers to development in many parts of the Third World, particularly Latin America, may be structural versus informative, and that a basic restructuring of society might be needed to make the diffusion of innovations more functional in the development process (Beltran 1976; Diaz-Bordenave 1976; McAnany 1980b; Rogers and Adhikarya 1979). Structural change is difficult to achieve and often unrealistic (Gran 1983; McAnany 1980a). In the 1970s, however, there were some successful efforts to research and plan diffusion campaigns more effectively to the benefit of the poor and without major structural changes at the macro level.

In most diffusion campaigns the treatment of the messages for low SES audiences had been exactly the same as those meant for higher SES audiences (Melkote 1984, 1987, 1989). Research began doing a better job of assessing audience needs and tailoring messages to these needs. Research indicated that it is not practical or feasible for people with little or no formal education to learn everything about an innovation through one or two instructional radio or television programs or a couple of visits by the field extension agent (Rogers and Adhikarya 1979). Diffusion of an innovation to these disadvantaged groups would therefore need to adopt a sequential approach, with message content built according to the level of complexity of innovation and comprehension of receivers. Also, the communication content would need to be tailored to cater to farmers with different levels of cognition of innovations.

The Tetu Extension Project in rural Kenya provides a good example of a campaign that successfully adopted such a "gradual stages" approach to the diffusion of agricultural innovations (Ascroft 1971). In the first stage, the farmers were taught simple useful techniques such as row cropping, equal spacing, contouring, and weeding. None of these innovations involved any complex technology. Once the farmers had learned these innovations and were comfortable using them, the diffusion process moved on to the second stage. Here, the farmers were told how to harvest crops and dry them. Still no highly complex innovations were introduced. In the next stage, the farmers were given hybrid seeds and taught techniques of thinning and of applying fertilizers and insecticides. It was only in the last stage that concepts of farm management and administration such as bookkeeping, a careful rearrangement of plots, and growing a balanced set of crops were introduced. Such a sequential adoption process, spanning a couple of years, helped these farmers to successfully adopt complex innovations.

The Tetu example shows that where complex innovations (such as miracle rice or hybrid maize, requiring 14 explicit steps for successfull yield) are intended for particular recipient groups, diffusion strategies should be sequential and research-based in order to be successful. Just one component of the innovation should be introduced at a time, with the content and methodology carefully selected. Of course, successful diffusion does not necessarily mean that project was appropriate in the first place. Assuming an innovation is appropriate, project success requires careful demographic research and strategic planning.

Diffusion and Women's Access to Information

Although the operationalization of the diffusion model has changed over time in an attempt to reach more rural people, research beginning in the 1970s showed that women remained disproportionately neglected. While much has been written about the Training and Visit (T&V) Extension System, Jiggins (1984) noted that the system favored male farmers. Due, Mollel, and Malone (1987) found that in northeastern Tanzania, extension agents visited significantly fewer female farmers than contact farmers (who were all male) or non-contact male farmers. The T&V focus on specialized training for agricultural agents (usually male) worked to the detriment of any training for home economics or other kinds of agents (who are often female), and who may be best able to reach women farmers with the information they need.

In Africa, as elsewhere, most change agents are men (FAO 1988), and the few studies that have been reported indicate that these men are not reaching poor women farmers. Despite the fact that women grow most food in Kenya, research has shown that women are disadvantaged in visits by extension agents. In the mid-1970s, Staudt (1985b) studied a sample of female-managed and jointly managed farms. She found that female-managed farms received the poorest service, and that the gaps were greatest for the most valuable types of services. Ten years later, the situation remained essentially the same (Ruigu 1985). Staudt and others emphasize the need to train and hire more female extension agents. Ruigu (1985) gives employment data for the Ministry of Agriculture in Kenya, showing very few women in any professional and subprofessional divisions. Other suggested remedies that are being implemented include providing agricultural training for female home economics agents, placing more emphasis on group extension (as opposed to individual home visits), providing gender-sensitivity training for male extension agents, and making more use of existing women's groups and networks (Steeves 1996).

Conclusion

The pro-innovation bias of diffusion research implied that everyone should adopt all innovations because they were beneficial. But often agricultural research benefited the progressive farmers, usually elite males. This was mainly because the farmer profiles available to the researchers were based on generalizations from a non-representative and purposive sample of progressive farmers (Roling et al. 1976). This process usually resulted in innovations inappropriate for small farmers. Thus, the progressive farmer strategy coupled with the pro-innovation, pro-source, and pro-literacy biases worked against poorer farmers. The diffusion process, in short, usually produced a vicious circle. Easier information access by progressive farmers led to successes and greater efficacy which in turn led to more information seeking and more successes. Lack of information access, on the other hand, led to failure and diminished need for information seeking. The small, traditional farmer, crushed by forces from all sides over which he/she had no control, was obviously fatalistic, lacking aspirations and innovativeness. "Fatalism, mutual distrust, and so on, on the one hand, and modernity, information-seeking, and the like, on the other, may be actual consequences rather than causes of behavior" (Roling et al. 1976: 72).

The biases of diffusion alongside an analysis of the realities of the rural poor—social-structural and political constraints to change, the knowledge gap, and the role of diffusion in widening the socio-economic and gender benefits gaps—provide much insight into the failures of diffusion campaigns. It is clear that insufficient innovation information, knowledge, and skills have percolated to the disadvantaged sections of rural populations either from the mass media or interpersonal channels of communication. There are sharp gender and class inequities within rural areas and a gross imbalance of information disseminated between the urban and rural areas. The quality of the information also leaves much to be desired. The innovations disseminated to subsistence farmers are frequently irrelevant, the information unreliable, and the campaigns sometimes leave farmers worse off than before. In light of this, it is obvious why the small or traditional farmer has been resistant to adopt innovations.

New strategic methodologies of social marketing have improved on the diffusion model by formalizing the importance of systematically considering the needs and contexts of various audience segments. All decisions about interventions and modes of communication follow this careful research. In reality, however, many of the same biases evident in diffusion have been reproduced in social marketing campaigns.

CRITICAL APPRAISAL OF COMMUNICATION CAMPAIGNS IN STRATEGIC SOCIAL CHANGE

As discussed in Chapter 4, strategic social marketing applies the principles and steps of commercial marketing to achieving socially desirable goals (Andreasen 1995; Kotler 1984; Manoff 1985). A great deal of formative market research is assumed necessary to define problems from the perspective of those who experience the problems, properly segment the audience, determine appropriate products and messages for the various segments, assess communication and commercial market channels, assess audience uses of these channels, and develop campaign strategies. Evaluation and feedback are important throughout the process. There is no question that many social marketing campaigns to improve health and nutrition, reduce teen pregnancy, encourage girls' education, prevent HIV/ AIDS infection, protect the environment, and more, have contributed a great deal to improving people's lives. In this section we do not critique the theoretical intent of social marketing, nor its positive effects in many instances globally. Rather we are concerned with the individualistic assumptions (as in diffusion campaigns) that ground social marketing, and the ways in which commercial biases may compromise the pro-social goals, especially where commercial products are involved.

As in many of the diffusion of innovations campaigns, most strategic communication interventions in social change have been confined to the individual as the locus of change. A few social marketing campaigns have addressed local norms and still fewer have tackled larger structural issues. Information and associated products are treated as the missing link. The appropriateness of the information and products is not always systematically assessed at the outset, as assumed necessary by the social marketing model. Individuals are therefore provided with "pro-social" messages with the anticipation that they will adopt a product or practice, or change their attitudes or behaviors in the direction desired by the campaigners. The communication model is usually top-down with the receivers treated as targets for persuasion and change. This goes against newer models and perspectives that call for participatory approaches where the receivers are participants in the communication intervention efforts.

Large or powerful organizations and not the recipients of innovations usually have the opportunity to frame social "problems" in campaigns. As in the modernization approach that we critiqued earlier, organizations control the process of social change by selecting certain themes as "problems" or "solutions." Thus, too many children are a problem in a family planning campaign and not the structural conditions that contribute to family economic difficulties and high child mortality rates in Third World settings. The power to frame issues needs to be problematized. "Without question, this power resides disproportionately with government, corporations and other institutions possessing legitimacy, social power and resources and access to the mass media" (Salmon 1989: 25). Marginalized groups such as women, the poor, and ethnic minorities, lack the social power to frame issues that are constraining them and instead serve as targets of campaigns organized by paternalistic sources. Many of the problems faced by marginalized groups are caused by complex social contexts, yet campaigns do not usually address social-economic and political constraints:

> Particularly in the case of public information campaigns, for which the government is the primary source of funding, it is unusual for funds to be disbursed to change the system rather than changing individuals responding to the system. It is because of this that most campaigns can be viewed as efforts to induce evolutionary rather than revolutionary changes (Salmon 1989: 27).

In addition to mass media, traditional communication channels are used to disseminate the views and prescriptions of a dominant class and thus maintain the status quo in an unequal society. Kidd (1984) described the Song and Drama Division (SDD) of the Ministry of Information and Broadcasting, Government of India, to highlight its approach to social marketing. The SDD is controlled either by the central government from the nation's capital or by the respective state governments. The chief role of the SDD is to use folk media such as theater, mime, song, and dances for modernizing people's attitudes and behaviors through entertainment (Parmar 1975). Basically, the SDD acts as a publicity unit informing the people about services and programs made available by the government and then, via the folk media performances, persuade the audiences to accept the modern ideas and change their attitudes and behaviors accordingly. The model is top-down and highly prescriptive. The SDD performs the valuable function of creating awareness among the rural people of new services and programs provided by the government specifically for their benefit. The folk performances also provide useful information on topics such as a balanced diet or where to get a loan. However, the underlying bias is to blame the receiver for his/her backwardness. The skits usually point out that a person is backward because he/she: has too many children, is lazy, does not eat healthy food, or fails to maintain hygienic surroundings. While some of these reasons may be true they reflect only one dimension of the reality.

These easy slogans fail to address, for example, (*a*) the economic circumstances (needed for labor and old-age security) forcing people to have large families, (*b*) the issue of transportation itself, (*c*) the exploitation of rickshaw pullers, (*d*) the red tape and corruption involved in getting a development loan, and (*e*) the underlying political-economic conditions which often leave people without any diet, let alone a balanced diet. Instead of giving a broader picture of people's material conditions, the political-economic structures creating those conditions, and the obstacles they face in taking individual or collective actions, an easy technical solution is offered (Kidd 1984: 119).

Thus, the power to frame social problems most often comes with the authority to identify the causes and suggest solutions. In societies with sharp inequities in incomes, living conditions, and other social relations, the power to identify problems and suggest solutions can be reduced to social engineering by the government or the elite.

Methodology Problems in Enter-education Approaches

As we indicated in Chapter 4, the cross-sectional survey has been a commonly used design in entertainment–education campaigns and approaches. This limits the utility of the research findings of successful campaigns due to serious threats to internal validity. Several artifacts such as history, subject selection, and maturation are not controlled and may contaminate the effects, thus producing spurious relationships (Campbell and Stanley 1963; Wimmer and Dominick 2000). The problem associated with the contaminating effects of history presents an interesting conflict. Soap operas are not expected to be stand-alone but, rather, complementing a multimedia strategy in a campaign. As such, it is difficult to unravel the effects of history from the real effects of the soap operas (Sherry 1997). In addition, there has been limited use of advanced statistics that could be used to filter out the extraneous variables contaminating the proposed relationships. For example, in situations where regression and path analysis techniques were used besides simple frequency distributions, the results were not as dramatic as in cases where only simple statistics were used (Sherry 1997). Sherry (1997: 93) provides an excellent critique of the methodology used in pro-social soap operas:

1. Data on exposure to radio and television soap operas are impressive but it is difficult to interpret the results beyond sheer numbers. There is limited information about who the viewers are and the intended target audience. It may be likely that the audience consists of people predisposed to development-oriented messages.
2. The soap operas are effective in creating involvement with the principal characters in the story. However, the audience members, especially the lower socio-economic groups, identify with characters that are different from what the writers intended.
3. Time series analysis support results that show change in behaviors but, as indicated earlier, the data are confounded by extraneous variables such as history and other campaign effects.
4. Finally, knowledge and attitude change may not necessarily mean change in behaviors.

Organizational Context of Strategic Interventions

The structural and normative conditions of organizations and their relationships and dependence on funding sources have a profound effect on the nature of their work. For example, USAID, which funds a large number of projects in the areas of health, nutrition and family planning, is influenced by US foreign policy. Thus, USAID prioritizes working with the private sector in the promotion of health care and health promoting measures (Hoy 1998; Steeves 2000; USAID 1982; Wilkins 1999).

In addition, the intervention strategies of the USAID stress persuasion (of individuals) versus addressing structural issues and constraints (Wilkins 1999). Persuasive strategies dominated by a social marketing approach detract from a focus on critical structural factors.

In Bangladesh, Rashmi Luthra (1988, 1991) examined USAID's multi-million-dollar social marketing project to make non-clinical modern contraceptives widely available, particularly to the urban and rural poor. Luthra found considerable evidence that commercial marketing conventions neglected both the project's social mission and women's needs. For example, she found evidence of error and bias in market research indicating that because men in Bangladesh do the shopping and are the primary mass media users, men should be the targets of campaign information. She also noted that the market research had ignored the effectiveness of informal media in reaching the women. There was an overuse of the mass media despite their low penetration among the target audience. This omission, Luthra felt, was related to biases toward working with advertising agencies and reaching the largest possible audience through formal mass media, a bias that clearly privileged the urban wealthy in this instance. While it seems that contraceptive projects might be particularly vulnerable to technological and patriarchal biases (Jaquette and Staudt 1985), it also seems likely that wherever traditional marketing practices and commercial interests predominate, a sensitivity to gender and class interests as well as to other important systems dynamics, may be neglected.

Nancy Worthington (1992) reported findings consistent with those of Luthra in her analysis of an HIV/AIDS awareness campaign in East Africa, particularly Uganda. The "AIDS in the workplace" theme targeted urban men, who constitute the majority of paid workers in Uganda. The use of mass media in the campaign also supported a class, gender, and urban bias. An expensive entertainment education video, entitled "It's Not Easy," reinforced these biases, as it was meant to be shown primarily to groups of workers and managers.[3] To the extent that the video was shown on television, the wealthier groups with television access were privileged. Additionally, the video represented women as passive victims, with few options beyond hoping their husbands would remain faithful and consider the use of condoms.

In general, social marketing has a commercial marketing orientation that often privileges mass communication and neglects informal communication channels that may be most salient to poorer sectors in society, especially those in rural areas. Women are especially neglected in these campaigns. A marketing orientation is rapidly spreading to NGOs, which increasingly are the implementers of bilateral and multilateral aid. Some NGOs are actually created with the assistance of bilateral grants in order to perform consistent functions. An example of this is the Ghana Social Marketing Foundation. This NGO based in Accra was started with the assistance of USAID. It seeks funds from multilateral, bilateral, and other aid organizations, which allow it to hire consultants and other resources for social marketing research and campaigns. All of this contributes to a commercial orientation in development that is often class, gender, and urban biased and also neglects traditional forms of communication in the process (Steeves 2000).

A video produced by the Academy for Educational Development on a USAID social marketing nutrition project in Bolivia provides another good example.[4] The video demonstrated ways in which the purchase and consumption of imported, subsidized soy beans were promoted via the steps of social marketing. Mass media, especially radio, were used in the campaign. The videotape failed to explain why protein-rich crops could not be grown locally or what the project consequences would be for local farmers and vendors. The evaluation research findings presented in the video were not persuasive in substantiating the project's success. Therefore, there is clearly a need for critical evaluations of the many types of social marketing projects and their uses of media in social change.

Communication Interventions in HIV/AIDS Prevention

As noted above, most strategic, social marketing campaigns are concerned with individual behavior change. As sweeping structural change in society is not always realistic, individual change may be significant in gradually leading to progressive social change. However, social divisions such as class, gender, and race need to be adequately considered in research and strategies (Goswami and Melkote 1997; Luthra 1991; Melkote et al. 2000; Worthington 1992).

Race, Gender, and Class

According to Schneider, race, class, and gender largely determine a person's health status: "In concert they will affect perception of health and illness, kinds and availability of care, [and] modes of delivery . . . . This unequal distribution of access to health care mirrors the manner in which social and political power, resources, labor and services are distributed in society" (Schneider 1992: 21). Quinn (1993) exploring the interaction of race, class, and gender in the context of AIDS preventive behavior, found that social factors push risk reduction behaviors outside the control of certain individuals. For example, the use of condoms assumes an equal distribution of power in sexual relationships: the woman may have the intention and the self-efficacy to adopt this behavior, but the actual act requires the active co-operation of the male partner (Fee and Krieger 1993; Kashima et al. 1992; Peterson and Marvin 1988; Quinn 1993). Poor women are especially vulnerable to their male partners' views, since they are economically and emotionally dependent on them (Bandura 1994). Other scholars have noted that poor women are limited in their choices about relationships and living situations in ways that middle-class women may not be, and that they may not experience the freedom to regulate sexual practices or to separate from their husbands. Concerns regarding food, shelter, and care of their children may be more important, certainly more immediate and visible, than worries about AIDS.

Developing countries offer a conducive environment for HIV to flourish. In Asia and Africa, poverty, malnutrition, unemployment, illiteracy, lack of infrastructural and basic primary health care systems, rural–urban migration, unemployment, poor sanitation, cultural factors (such as the low status accorded to women), and war, among other factors, create a favorable setting for the large-scale spread of HIV. The social impediments to safer sex and knowledge regarding AIDS are also prodigious. In Zimbabwe, Kenya, South Africa, and Zaire, the increasing financial insecurity that exists among a large number of female-headed households make transactional sex a "rational means of making ends meet" (Gill and Mohammed 1994: iii). Further, women in these societies generally have smaller landholdings, less income, and less access to agricultural training which sometimes make the exchange of sex for money their only survival mechanism. Low economic and social status of women is also widespread in parts of Asia and Latin America where similar factors may operate to constrain individual behavior change (Bhawani and Gram 1994; Rai et al. 1993). While the world attention has been focused on Asia and Africa, the number of HIV infections have also been growing rapidly in Latin America (Snell 1999). Brazil, Mexico, Ecuador, and other countries in the region face the threat of an AIDS epidemic but are ill-equipped to do much due to poor economies, lack of infrastructural facilities, and poor data collection methods.

Therefore, the social context is an important mediating factor in shaping individuals' behaviors and attitudes related to HIV/AIDS (Goswami and Melkote 1997; Melkote et al. 2000). Also, AIDS is not just a health issue nor a sexual behavior-related issue. At present, the emphases in communication campaigns usually are on short-term goals: get tested, use condoms, choose partners carefully, communicate with partners, etc. While these goals are very important for containing the spread of AIDS, they are not sufficient. An effective strategy for HIV/AIDS prevention will require long-term and sustained strategies that should also address the social, cultural, economic, and political factors that influence the spread of AIDS.

Participatory Strategies

Media campaigns that just deliver accurate and comprehensive HIV/AIDS knowledge from a medical and immunological point of view and do not address the subjective images that individuals hold about AIDS may have less of a chance of reducing perceptions of risk than those messages and educational strategies that also deal with people's subjective concerns (Melkote and Muppidi 1999). While we support calls for a theory-based persuasive message design that incorporates an analysis of audience needs and beliefs, we would go further and recommend participatory communication strategies where the beneficiaries of campaigns and projects play an active role in message construction and design. Fee and Krieger (1993) argue that the subjective truths of those directly affected by the epidemic constitute authentic knowledge and are as valuable for understanding AIDS as any objective biomedical account. Granting legitimate status to people's knowledge requires involving the intended beneficiaries of media campaigns in the planning, design, and construction of message strategies (Melkote and Muppidi 1999). This would ensure that health education campaigns are compatible with people's own modes of understanding and are relevant to their needs (Fee and Krieger 1993).

NEW ROLES FOR COMMUNICATION IN DEVELOPMENT

In development literature, mass communication media have been considered the prime movers in social development. This view was much stronger in the 1950s and 1960s when the central focus was on the big mass media to the neglect of interpersonal/organizational networks and indigenous channels of communication (Tehranian 1994). Mass media such as newspapers and the radio were saddled with the important task of spreading information as widely as possible. Government authorities, subject experts, and extension agents would go on the radio or visit villages lecturing on how to have smaller families, increase agricultural yields or how to live healthier lives. Communication flows were hierarchical, one-way, and top-down. People were regarded as passive receivers of development information. This scenario started to change somewhat in the 1970s, as we have discussed previously.

Communication in Self-development Efforts

The idea of self-development gained popularity in the 1970s. In other words, user-initiated activity at the local level was considered essential for successful village-level development. Thus, the emphasis was not so much top-to-bottom flows of information and messages from a government official to a mass audience, but importantly, bottom-up flows from users to sources, and horizontal communication flows of communication between people. People need to have open discussions, identify their needs and problems, decide on a plan of action, and then use a specific medium of communication and an information database most appropriate to their needs. Thus, while the mass media were helpful and often necessary, they were not sufficient for the tasks at hand. The emphasis was not on big media but appropriate media. Along these lines, Havelock (1971) suggested a *problem-solving* model that put the spotlight on the needs of users and their diagnosis of their problems. In this model, the needs of the users, as well as their problem-solving strategies, were studied intensively. The need for information, then, was the prerogative of the user at the village level rather than an authority at the top.

In these approaches, the role and place of communication in social and behavioral change was radically different from the postulates of the modernization paradigm. Early communication models implied that mass mediated information was absolutely essential regardless of evidence as to whether it was appropriate. Communication processes took place in a social and cultural vacuum and environmental variables were not given much consideration (McQuail and Windahl 1981). This was despite research in the sociology of mass communication that indicated, as early as 1959, that mass communication is but one social system among many others in a society. Riley and Riley (1959) had shown that mass communication should be regarded as an important social process among other equally salient social processes. While the mass media affected individuals and society, they were themselves influenced by other environmental variables.

Self-development implied a different role for communication from what was conceptualized and operationalized in the modernization paradigm. Development agencies still had to perform a service function in terms of collecting technical information, but it was no longer prescriptive. Communication flows were now initiated in response to articulated needs of the users. Several examples may be provided of successful self-development efforts.

The Indian experiment with Radio Farm Forums is a case in point. The radio station provided an organized listening group in a village with useful information on agriculture and other related matters. This was the top-down component of information flow. However, the listening group was the final deciding authority. The group discussed the new information, its relevance to their needs and problems, and then decided whether to seek more information. Thus, horizontal flows of communication were very important and any help requested was clearly at the initiative of the users (Masani 1975).

Again, in Fogo in New Foundland, Canada, the income from the once lucrative fishing business was all but destroyed. Many young people left the village. The residents decided to act on their own using a loaned portable video recorder from the Canadian Broadcasting Corporation. They initiated discussions and debates of what the problems were and what ought to be done. All of this was videotaped. The people then viewed the tape, collectively decided on a plan of action, and with external help, made their village prosperous again (Schramm 1977; Williamson 1991). The Fogo process was replicated with some success in Nepal. Here, a video camera was used to facilitate the participation of women in issues of interest to their community (Belbase 1987). Also in Tanzania, there was useful information exchange between the people and experts. When villages in the Arusha region decided to construct latrines, they borrowed relevant audiotapes from the local communication center, which helped them with expert knowledge from the project authorities (Hedebro 1982). Thus, in this project, the idea was not to persuade the people to do something specific at the initiative of the experts but rather to allow the users decide what ought to be done and then seek expert information, if necessary.

Box 6.2
Radio Station in a Briefcase

Two young men from India, Vikas Markanday and Dayal Singh, have put together their own radio station in a briefcase. Basically, this is a low-cost FM radio transmitter that is capable of receiving its signals from a radio station, a microphone, or even a cassette. Weighing a little more than a regular laptop computer, this transmitter may be used for narrowcasting signals within a 10–15 kilometer (6.25–9.4 miles) radius. A prototype of this product was shown to the public at a conference in New Delhi and carried a hefty price tag: about Rs 200,000 or US$ 5,000. However, the duo, using components purchased locally, have assembled the radio station for about US$ 225. The two men work for Nutra Indica Research Council, a non-profit NGO in Rohtak, India. This versatile product should come in handy once India decides to open up its airwaves to community radio stations. Neighbors Nepal and Sri Lanka have demonstrated the beneficial impact of such locally administered radio stations. The briefcase radio transmitter presents a low cost alternative to narrowcasters to beam locally useful and relevant programs.

Source: Compiled from a report by Frederick Noronha, "India Duo Put Together a 'Dirt Cheap' Radio-Station-in-a-Briefcase," July 24, 2000, fred@goal.dot.net.in.

Rogers (1976b: 141) summarized the chief roles of communication in self-development efforts:

1. Provide technical information about development problems and possibilities, and about appropriate innovations, in response to local requests; and
2. Circulate information about the self-development accomplishments of local groups so that other such groups may profit from the experience and perhaps be challenged to achieve a similar performance.

The role of mass media, then, in self-development efforts was of a catalyst in change rather than the sole cause. Importantly, the communication channels initiated a dialogue between the users and the sources, helping them to "talk together." Schramm (1977: 3) summarized it succinctly:

Only when communication can build itself into the social structure, is it going to show any real hope of extensive results. Only when media channels can mix with interpersonal channels and with organization in the village, are you going to have the kind of development you will like.

Role of Folk Media in Development

For a long time, traditional or folk media were ignored in development literature. In the modernization paradigm, anything that was even remotely connected with the local culture was to be eschewed. Since the traditional media are extensions of the local culture, they were regarded as vehicles that would discourage modern attitudes and behavioral patterns and instead reinforce cultural values of the community. Lerner (1958) had predicted that the direction of change in communication systems in all societies was from the oral media to the technology-based mass media. Also, the mass media were hailed as indices and agents of modernization. Thus, all resources were devoted to the strengthening and growth of radio and television. The period from the 1950s to 1970s, therefore, was characterized by a benign neglect of the traditional media.

The newer concepts of development that we discussed in Chapter 5 emphasized, among other things, the re-emergence of culture as a facilitator of development and the integration of traditional and modern systems. This shift in focus put the spotlight on indigenous channels of communication or the folk media that were relegated to relative oblivion in the modernization paradigm. Folk media are products of the local culture, rich in cultural symbols, and highly participatory. In addition, they have great potential for integration with the modern mass media (Casey 1975).

In the early 1970s, several international conferences addressed the idea of using folk media to promote development: the Expert Group Meeting sponsored by the International Planned Parenthood Federation and UNESCO in London (1972); the New Delhi Seminar and Workshop on Folk Media sponsored by the UNESCO and the Indian Ministry of Information and Broadcasting (1974); and the East–West Communication Institute Seminar on Traditional Media (1975).

Folk media consist of a variety of forms: folk theater, puppetry, story telling, folk songs, folk dances, ballads, mime, and more. They have served as vehicles of communication and entertainment in Asia, Africa, and Latin America for centuries: "Through the use of dialogue, action, music, song, and dance the stage has presented a vitally important view of the cosmos which has implanted basic beliefs and behavior patterns in rural audiences" (Van Hoosen 1984: 127). Wang and Dissanayake (1984b: 22) define folk media as a "communication system embedded in the culture which existed before the arrival of mass media, and still exist as a vital mode of communication in many parts of the world, presenting a certain degree of continuity, despite changes." Ranganath (1975: 12) defines the traditional media as "living expressions of the lifestyle and culture of a people, evolved through the years." These definitions reiterate the origin and nurturing of the folk channels in and by the richness of the indigenous culture.

The traditional uses of the folk media were primarily entertainment, social communion, and religious activity. However, folk forms also became vehicles for persuasive communication wherein modern messages exhorted the audience members to limit the size of their families, live in harmony with their neighbors, or lead more healthy lives. Newer concepts of development such as self-help, grassroots participation, and two-way communication led to a re-examination of the advantages of traditional media as vehicles for these purposes. Clearly, folk media have several advantages: they are part of the rural social environment and, hence, credible sources of information to the people. They command the audience as live media and are ideal examples of two-way communication. They have proved useful in generating grassroots participation and a dialogue between the performers and the audience. Many of the folk media formats are flexible (to be discussed), thus facilitating the incorporation of development-oriented messages in their themes. This makes them useful and credible channels for promoting planned change. Additionally, they are relatively inexpensive and, in almost all cultures, command rich and inexhaustible variety both in form and theme. The timeless traditional media, therefore, present inexhaustible alternatives for experimentation in development communication (Ranganath 1980).

Excellent examples of the value of highly participatory, traditional theater in Africa for consciousness-raising and problem-solving are provided by Morrison (1993) and Mda (1993). In Burkina Faso, the popular "forum theater" is used to help rural people think critically about their health problems. Morrison (1993) discusses a play entitled "Fatouma the Baby Machine," which portrays conflict between a husband and wife over family size. The wife does not want more children, yet the husband resists the notion of limiting family size, ultimately throwing his wife out of the house. When the play ends, the audience is invited to reenact how they think the characters should have behaved. Everyone has equal access to the stage (including women) and the role-playing helps facilitate the consideration of otherwise sensitive topics. Mda (1993) discusses the Marotholi Traveling Theater in Lesotho, which also makes use of traditional forms of expression and problem-solving. Ideas for plays come from problems raised by community members. The plays aim exclusively to act out the problems, not to present solutions. Following a play, the audience analyzes the reasons for the problems and suggests solutions. The audience controls the actors, directing them to play roles, almost as though the actors are puppets of the audience.

Critical Issues in Using Traditional Media for Development

There are some important concerns in using folk media for development. Ethical questions may be raised about inserting development content in folk media, as it is possible these media may be fundamentally changed or even destroyed in the process. Appropriating folk media for development is a delicate task requiring an intimate knowledge of the nature of traditional communication channels (Mane 1974). Ranganath (1980) cautions that preparation of a book of basic data, or a comprehensive account of all the known traditional media in a particular region/country should be given the highest priority. In the book of basic data, Ranganath suggests that the following characteristics of every folk form should be recorded under the following categories:

(a) Form (audio, visual, and audio-visual)
(b) Thematic content
(c) Flexibility in accommodating development message
(d) Cultural context

In terms of flexibility, Ranganath (1980) suggests that it is possible to categorize all the media as: rigid, semi-flexible, and flexible. The rigid forms are usually ritualistic, very religious, and reject all foreign messages. Some examples are *Yellamma* songs, *Vydyarakunitha* (both of south India) and Chinese revolutionary opera (Chiao and Wei 1984; Ranganath 1980). The semi-flexible media might permit the limited insertion of foreign messages through certain characters or situations. Examples here would be rural dance drama such as *Yakshagana* of south India, leather puppetry such as *Wayang Kulit* of Indonesia, and religious forms such as *Jatra* of north India. The flexible media provide unlimited opportunities for inserting development messages, assuming careful consideration of ethical issues. Examples would be puppet drama such as *Wayang Orang* (Indonesia), ballads such as *Lavani* and *Gee Gee* of south India, and *Chamsoun* (United Arab Emirates); some forms of theater such as *Katha, Bhavai* and *Tamasha* of north and western parts of India, *Kakaku* of Ghana, and the Caribbean *Calypso*.

More research needs to be done to comprehensively examine and categorize all of the folk media in terms of the above criteria—form, theme, and flexibility—before being used as vehicles to carry development-oriented messages. Otherwise, there is a danger of harm being done to the folk form and the inserted message (Ranganath 1980). One example is the *Yellamma* songs, a rigid form. The songs are popular with devotees of *Yellamma*, the goddess of worship in the state of Karnataka in India. Research showed that the devotees were poor and had large families:

> It was considered that these songs could be harnessed to carry pre-determined messages on various aspects of the population theme . . . the field reaction to the message-bearing medium was disturbing; it even became hostile . . . the new content of the songs to them was not merely incongruous but sacrilegious (Ranganath 1980: 21–22).

Thus, while folk media have great potential in communicating development-oriented messages to rural audiences, they should be employed judiciously. This requires intimate knowledge and context-based research.

Another important issue involves the integration of folk media with mass media. This could work to the mutual advantage of both: it gives the folk media a wide geographical spread while providing the mass media with a rich array of information and entertainment themes from the local culture. However, there are dangers to both media if proper methods of integration are not used. A case in point is an experiment conducted in Taiwan for integrating bag puppetry with television (Wang 1984). Like other folk media, the popularity of once famous bag puppetry was on the decline, mainly due to competition from television. However, by adapting it to fit the needs of television, there was a revival of this ancient Chinese folk form. Television, too, benefited from this since it was able to draw a record number of viewers who were interested in watching the puppet shows (Wang 1984). In the end, however, the bag puppetry was changed so much to fit the needs of television that it lost its original character. The extempore dialogue was replaced by a written script, the traditional Chinese language gave way to popular slang, Chinese classical music was replaced by a hybrid of Chinese and Western rock music, and even the symbolic face-painting of the puppets was de-emphasized (Wang 1984). Soon, televised bag puppetry was no longer the medium that attracted people historically. The changes had done serious harm to the form and theme of bag puppetry.

However, adaptation need not necessarily change, destroy, or reduce the original popularity of a folk form (Chander 1974; Chiranjit 1974). Examples of successful integration are many: the Indian television and commercial films have successfully integrated elements of folk theater, songs, and dances (Agrawal 1984, 1998; Krishnaswamy 1974); Iran's *Barnameh* has been successfully adapted to radio and television; *Kakaku* of Ghana has become a successful serial over radio and television; and the Caribbean *Calypso* is a hot favorite on the stage, film, and television (Ranganath 1980). In fact, integration of folk media may be necessary to legitimize television among rural viewers, and may be inevitable to the future of the waning folk media. Efforts, however, should be made to preserve the originality of each folk form (Yount 1975).

INFORMATION AND COMMUNICATION TECHNOLOGIES FOR RURAL DEVELOPMENT

Since the mid-1970s, there has been a steady growth in information and communication technologies (ICTs) and their application in development. The US and several West European countries have become information societies, i.e., countries in which the production, processing, and distribution of information software and hardware are the main activities (Rogers 1986). The ICTs may be described as "electronic means of capturing, processing, storing, and communicating information" (Heeks 1999). Digital ICTs store the information as ones and zeros and transmit the data through telecommunication networks. The "older" communication technologies such as the radio and television are analog systems in which information is held as electric signals and transmitted through electromagnetic waves. Examples of digital ICTs include, among others, telephones, wireless cellular phones, communication satellites, computers, and the Internet. There has been a significant proliferation of each of these technologies in the Third World since 1975. The Satellite Instructional Television Experiment (SITE) in India, the Palapa Experiment in Indonesia, and experiments with satellite-based rural telephony in Peru are some of the examples of ICTs in the 1970s and 1980s.

A recent phenomenon has been the spread of public call offices (PCOs) that provide payphone services, as well as fax and photocopying services. The PCOs have proliferated in most urban areas and some rural areas in the Third World. The model of a telecenter is not common yet. A telecenter extends the functions of a PCO by the addition of a computer with Internet link. This provides email facilities, and sometimes web browsing. Most large cities in the Third World have a telecenter or cybercafe, but this model is still rare in rural areas. The PCOs and telecenters, wherever available, have proved to be useful in providing much-needed telecommunications connectivity and other communication services in rural and urban areas in the Third World (Talero and Gaudette 1996).

Supporters of ICTs have advocated integrated rural development through telecommunications by highlighting many of their uses and applications in developing countries (Barr 1998: 154–56):

- Finding markets for farm produce, fishery catches, and handicraft products; negotiating prices, and arranging for transportation.
- Arranging for the delivery of inputs such as raw materials, supplies, and tools.
- Obtaining and distributing information rapidly on markets, prices, consumption trends, and inventory.
- Carrying out financial transactions such as making money deposits, paying bills, and obtaining cash.
- Facilitating rural and eco-tourism.
- Expanding educational opportunities such as distance learning.
- Promoting telemedicine. This will include dissemination of medical information, diagnosis, training of staff in remote health centers.
- Facilitating quick and easy ways to stay in touch with family members, relatives, and friends.

Role of the Internet in Rural Development

In the 1990s, the Internet was "exported" to Third World countries. Though its penetration is very low in many developing countries and it is still very much an urban-based ICT, it has significant potential for rural development in the Third World. At present, given the socio-economic situation in most developing countries, the advantages of the Internet will accrue not to individuals in the rural areas but to inter-mediaries such as small to medium enterprises, NGOs, development officers, rural health centers, and other development-related organizations (Richardson 1998b).

The Internet may be used to support rural development in many areas (Richardson 1998b: 173–77):

1. In the area of agriculture, the Internet can serve as a gateway to global markets and information. Well-organized user groups can access information relevant to local needs and realities. New information can be fed into the community through existing channels such as the community radio, bulletin boards at local co-operatives, stores, and interpersonal networks Internet can serve as an information resource as well as a research tool.

2. In the area of community development, the Internet could be employed to "develop locally appropriate applications and services; provide knowledge about successful development strategies; enable efficient regional, national and global organization efforts; . . . and enable rural young people to learn about computers and to have access to the technologies and information available to their urban peers" (Richardson 1998b: 174). In addition, development support functionaries such as local NGOs can use the Internet as a window to the outside world and publicize their work and seek donors while the health workers can use the Internet to access technical information. Easy access to information coming into the community and information going out about the community are valuable resources and the Internet makes this possible. The use of the Internet by the Chiapas Indians in Mexico to garner international support for their cause is an example of its power.

3. Participatory communication approaches place a great value in bottom up flows of information and delivering research results from the rural areas to the policy-makers in urban centers. The Internet can be used to effectively document local knowledge practices and

share it with outsiders as well as facilitate horizontal flows among rural communities and organizations.

4. Small businesses can exploit the Internet to get information on new markets and access critical business and financial information.

5. Lastly, the Internet may be used to share news among developing countries. A major criticism of the existing international news flows has been that they are usually from the Western capitals to the Third World countries and not vice versa. There are few effective channels to share information and news among developing countries. The Internet provides an opportunity for newspapers, communities, and special interest groups in the Third World to relay their views, ideas, and news to the outside world and at the same time access news and information from the outside.

Case Studies of the Use of Information Technology

The promises offered by the Internet and other new information technologies will remain incomplete until they are deployed to cater to people on the other side of the digital divide. Some local-level projects have attempted to tailor the newer technologies to serve the information needs of the "digital have-nots" in developing countries. In India, the National Association of Software Services Companies (NASSCOM) provided email service with video to connect immigrant taxi drivers in the city of Mumbai with their families in the state of Uttar Pradesh, about 500 miles away. A majority of the taxi drivers are illiterate and it was a pleasant surprise for them to see their relatives and speak with them for a price cheaper than a telephone call (Project Mass Communication 2000). Another instant messaging system besides the Internet that is being implemented in India is the satellite mail. Over 200 towns in India have been connected through a network of 35 earth stations providing satellite mail facilities such as fax, pager, and telephonic messages to any place in India. Under this scheme, short messages can be sent for a mere 50 cents per message. Delta Innovative Enterprises, the company responsible for this service, plans to connect about 3,000 towns and 40,000 villages over the next three years. To facilitate easy access, the company is also creating 100,000 message collection centers to cover a large number of areas all over India. The service is available only in English but the company's software is capable of using several Indian languages (Adhikari 2000).

In early 2000, the government of the state of Madhya Pradesh in Central India, launched an experiment to bring the benefits of information technology to the residents of rural areas. Essentially, it was a push by the state to find low-cost alternatives to overcoming lack of infrastructure and poor conditions in rural areas. In 2000, this project won the Stockholm Challenge Award for Public Service and Democracy. Under this project, an Intranet network gives over five million villagers, spread over 600 villages in Dhar district, easy access to vital information. This Intranet system provides information to previously information-poor residents on commodity rates in local and regional markets, information about government welfare schemes, copies of land records needed to obtain agricultural loans, and rural water supply schemes. An area where the residents have benefited directly is in getting accurate and timely land-ownership records without going through corrupt and inefficient inter-mediaries. The Intranet has made it possible to obtain grain produce rates quickly and for as low as 10 cents for the service. There have been direct financial benefits. Farmers with better knowledge of market rates were able to ship their produce to centers where they could fetch prices that were as much as 40 percent higher than local outlets. This project is being imitated in other states in India and the central government in New Delhi is considering expanding it nationwide. This is a good example of the benefits of information technology involving common people especially in the rural areas in India (Lloyd 2000).

In another project, the benefits of e-commerce have been made avail-able to rural areas of Warana and Baramati in the state of Maharashtra in India. In Warana, about 70 villages have been wired to the Internet. Due to this, co-operative dairies in this agro-rich area of rural Maharashtra have started to market their products on-line. Many milk collection centers have been turned into cyber cafes providing access to the Internet. Sugar farmers now have a choice of marketing their products both regionally and globally. The sugar farmers in Warana have even opened an outlet in Europe for direct marketing of their products (Farmers too Reap the Rewards of e-comm. 2000).

In Kotmale, Sri Lanka, villagers are able to access the Internet through their local community radio station (Seneviratne 2000). The Kotmale Community Radio (KCR) was established in 1989 as a low-powered, community-based radio service to serve the surrounding areas with devel-opment-oriented messages. Kotmale became part of the cyber world in 1998 when a UNESCO-supported project established an Internet hub which included a local server and five computer terminals. The KCR has regularly used material from the Internet to supplement its programs. Thus, this station is serving as a gateway to cyberspace for rural Sri Lankans.

Box 6.3
Slum Kids Surf the Internet

Children can become familiar with the Internet and pick up basic literacy with the computer with little or no training according to Sugatha Mitra, senior vice president of NIIT, a prominent computer education institute in India. The *Economic Times* reported that Mitra has won international recognition for his experiment in encouraging children living in slums in and around Delhi, India, in using the computer and surfing the Internet with very little direct intervention of a teacher or an adult.

A computer housed in an all-weather kiosk was placed in a neighborhood close to a slum and children living in the area were allowed to access it through a touchpad. The children were not provided with any instructions and literally had to find their way around. A camera monitored the moves of the children as they used the computer. It was only a short while before the kids discovered the relationship between the mouse and the computer screen, and were successfully surfing the Internet. Within a few months, the children were downloading MPEG3 files to play "bhajans" or Hindu devotional music for their mothers, and downloading horoscopes for their fathers.

The children had no knowledge of English and some had never attended a school. Yet, in spite of these handicaps, the kids became computer savvy in a very short while. Mr. Mitra noted that there is a unique relationship between a child and the computer that adults do not seem to understand. In a few months, the children had attained the competency of people attending a top training school that would typically charge high tuition fees.

Source: "Slum Kids Break Language Barriers, Get Web-Savvy." 2000. http://www.economictimes.com/today/07tech01.htm.

During the first half of 2000, KCR broadcasted a one-hour program every weekday to introduce the Internet to the local community. During the regular programs, listeners were encouraged to contact the station for more information from the Internet. The requested information was obtained by the station and broadcast in summary form. Listeners were also encouraged to visit the radio station and explore the World Wide

Web (WWW). The KCR is also setting up computer terminals in public libraries in Kotmale and Gampola to increase community access to the Internet (Seneviratne 2000). Thus, experiments such as the Kotmale project are providing a model of best practices in terms of making the new information technologies easily accessible to rural populations in developing countries.

Another prominent example is the Grameen Telecommunications Project in Bangladesh. This was established by Professor Yunus to provide a nationwide cellular network. In this project, a woman who is a registered borrower in the Grameen Bank scheme, is appointed as the village "telephone lady." All the 68,000 villages in the country are covered under this project. The telephone lady operates a cellular pay phone business with some of the most competitive rates in the world. Thus, all residents of that village have access to a telephone without the need to construct large and expensive telephone exchanges throughout Bangladesh (Singhal and Rogers 2001).

Are ICTs a Boon or Bane for Development?

So far, we have provided information on the usefulness of ICTs in rural development. However, given the socio-economic and political structures in most rural areas in the Third World, the examples provided above should be seen as the *potential* contributions of the ICTs. Serious constraints exist that will inhibit the use of ICT-based information by the rural residents in Third World countries. Unfortunately, there is too much hype about the benefits deriving from ICTs and very little discussion about their negative effects. More important, there is very little analysis of the challenges faced by the rural poor in effectively harnessing the benefits derived from the use of ICTs:

> It is driven on by the hype from ICT vendors and the media that makes ICTs an icon for modern development, turning use of ICTs within development into an end in itself rather than a means of achieving other development goals. The main development objective becomes bringing as much technology to as many people as quickly as possible so that they can obtain the claimed benefits it provides (Heeks 1999: 15).

Our analysis of the challenges faced by the rural poor, small entrepreneurs, and other actors in using ICT-based information is summarized in Figure 6.1. This analysis has benefited from the critiques of Heeks (1999), Richardson (1998a, 1998b), Panos (1998a), and Hudson (1998).

Figure 6.1
Constraints in the Use of ICT-based Information by the Poor

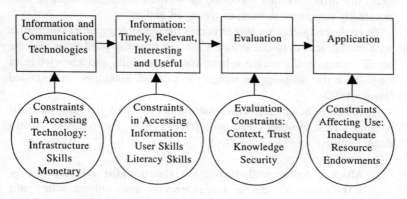

Source: Compiled from Heeks 1999.

Technological enthusiasts are pushing ICTs vigorously under the guise that technology per se is development. However, we have to separate the technology from the information it produces and examine people's capacities to receive, process, use, and transmit information. The rural poor and small- to medium-size entrepreneurs face many resource constraints that may prevent them from accessing the technology. These constraints include "a telecommunications infrastructure to make the ICTs work, a skills infrastructure to keep all the technology working, and money to buy or access the ICTs" (Heeks 1999: 7). In low-income countries, the access to telephone lines is very low in general and highly unequal between the urban and rural areas (Crishna et al. 1999). There is less than one line per 100 people overall in these countries while in urban areas connectivity is confined to about five lines per 100 people (Hudson 1998; ITU 1995). In addition to very low teledensity, there are hardly any Internet nodes in the rural areas of developing countries. Almost all the nodes are situated in the urban areas, and this may involve making long-distance calls to connect to the Internet if one lives outside the capital city or a big urban center (Panos 1998a). In addition, the quality of telephone lines is very poor, especially in the rural areas, and the costs to connect to the

Internet are prohibitive for the average user in a developing country (Mehta and Akthar 1999). In Africa, the lowest priced Internet account could cost at least $65 per month and the total could exceed $100 per month when the cost of telephone calls is added (Panos 1998a). Costs certainly affect women's access, as women are disadvantaged economically compared to men, as we noted earlier.

Once the recipients are able to access the technology, other constraints will inhibit access to the information put out: the rural poor and the small entrepreneurs may not have the usage skills and knowledge of English or the language in which the Internet messages are encoded (Heeks 1999).

At the stage at which the information is evaluated, the rural poor encounter a host of other constraints (Heeks 1999; Panos 1998b; World Bank 1998):

1. Much of the received information is meaningful and relevant only if the source and the receiver share a common culture, status, and the same set of priorities. Unequal class status or incompatible cultures make a huge difference in finding common ground in communication, a problem that has been discussed extensively by scholars writing about participatory action research and about feminist method.

2. Some prior knowledge is necessary to locate and evaluate the importance, utility, and relevance of the information received.

3. A certain amount of trust between the receiver and source is necessary to accept new information. "For most entrepreneurs, sufficient trust to justify business decisions will mainly be created through personal contact, through interaction and, ideally, through a shared context/proximity" (Heeks 1999: 9).

4. Last, the receiver must feel secure enough to be able to take the risk of using the new information.

Finally, the rural poor may not have sufficient resources to actually use or apply the new knowledge. Resource inequalities can include monetary resources such as starting capital, maintenance costs and taxes, and infrastructure resources (inadequate production capacity, lack of skilled personnel, etc.). As in other resource areas, poor, often illiterate women are among the least likely to have Internet access (e.g., Gersch 1998; Steeves 1996).

Challenges at the Macro Level

There are several challenges at the macro level that need to be carefully analyzed to assess the overall benefit of the new communication technologies in rural development (Panos 1998a). These will comprise development opportunity costs, technology opportunity costs, and socio-economic and political costs (Heeks 1999: 15–16). Development opportunity costs means that money for development of ICTs comes at the cost of some other inputs for development:

> The debate centers on prioritizing need; how important is Internet access in an area without safe water or even an affordable telephone service? While some health workers praise the satellite system that has brought them e-mail connections and cheap access to health information, others complain that Internet connections will not pay for aspirin or syringes (Panos 1998a: 1).

Technology opportunity costs means that in the race to install the Internet or other newer ICTs in developing countries, other technologies that are already in place may be ignored. For example, radio covers about 75 percent of the population in Africa while the Internet has a penetration of about 0.1 percent (Panos 1998a). Therefore, in the near future, the radio should be the vehicle for information dissemination and community networking in African countries. "Radio, TV and newspapers have all been used to disseminate agricultural, educational and business information to the poor. These technologies have capacity, interactivity and ownership limitations the new ICTs do not. However, in access and coverage terms they beat ICTs hands-down now and for the foreseeable future" (Heeks 1999: 16).

The socio-economic and political costs relate to the issue of power. People, countries, and organizations with power can present ICTs as the panacea for development. Thus, the attention of the populace may be deliberately drawn away from social and economic inequalities. Technology advocates will underplay the larger social/political/economic resource inequality issues in the process of marketing the ICTs as the new weapons in the war against underdevelopment.

The great optimism about the potential of the new telecommunications technology for development is, in many respects, similar to the crusade for the mass media in the 1950s and 1960s. The advocates of the mass media believed that exposure to the new media would bring about speedy development of the Third World. Yet, today, the plight of the urban and rural poor in the Third World has become, if anything, somewhat worse than it was in the 1960s, despite the widespread adoption and use of radio and television. In the absence of drastic changes in international and national economic, social, political, and legal structures, one wonders whether the effects of information and communications technologies in accelerating development will be any different from that of the mass media.

Another challenge at the macro level deals with the issue of technology planning. It is no longer a local affair. The process of globalization is largely determining the field for actors even at the local level. Global negotiations such as the GATT round in Uruguay in the 1990s, will have significant impact on national technology planning processes (Hamelink 2001). This means that in the future national technology planning will be influenced by trade-related policies developed by the World Trade Organization (WTO), a successor to the GATT. As a result, local planning has to take into account the effects of global forces. Hamelink (2001) cautions that unless the developing countries are well-prepared and coordinated, they will have to continue to accept policies framed by countries of the North. It is, therefore, important that the countries of the South participate more effectively in the global negotiations dealing with technology planning. "This asks for policy coordination among developing countries . . . this can be done effectively when planners in the periphery mobilise resources and join a constituency that counteracts the northern dominance in global planning" (Hamelink 2001). With the passing of the UNCTAD, a global forum friendly to the developing nations, to global institutions such as the WTO, World Bank, and IMF, the need for a well-coordinated policy response by the South has become more pressing and urgent.

Role of Intermediary Organizations

In the near future, it is unlikely that the rural poor will be able to directly use information technologies. The greatest potential for the use of ICTs in rural development, then, lies with intermediate organizations:

> These intermediaries are needed to bridge both the overt and the social resource endowment gaps between what the poor have and what they would need in order to use ICTs. Indeed, ICTs currently have a far

greater enabling value in building capacity within intermediary institutions than in directly affecting the poor (Heeks 1999: 18).

Academic and research institutions and progressive organizations such
as the Association of Progressive Communications (APC), GreenNet,
and the Institute for Global Communications were some of the early
users of ICTs, and these networks provide links to NGOs and local civil
society groups in developing countries. They also provide links between
like-minded individuals and groups in the First and Third Worlds.
Planning and follow-up efforts by women's groups for the Fourth World
Conference on Women in Beijing, made extensive use of the Internet
globally. These intermediary organizations in turn have championed the
causes of greater democracy, social equality, and environmental protection
(Panos 1998a). However, Heeks (1999) cautions that the locus of control
of ICTs should reside in organizations within the communities. "Poor
communities with the highest 'social capital' of effective institutions
will therefore be the most effective users of ICTs. Initiatives in which
technical and contextual knowledge are disconnected, with intermediaries
and control located outside the community, are more likely to fail" (Heeks
1999: 18). At some point in the future, though, it is imperative that the
people them-selves or their organizations directly control the use of ICTs
and be able to design and interpret the information systems and the
attendant tech-nologies to derive the greatest benefit.

SUMMARY

By the 1970s, it became increasingly clear in Asia and in Latin America
that socio-economic structural constraints greatly diminished the power
of mass media in overcoming problems of development. The process of
development was not as straightforward and clear-cut as conceptualized
earlier. And the mass media, far from being an independent variable in
the change process, were themselves affected by many extraneous factors.
Much of the earlier communication research, with its exaggerated
emphasis on the individual-blame causal hypothesis regarding underdevelopment obfuscated the social-structural, political, and institutional

constraints acting against the individual's efforts to change. Scholars contended that there was a benign neglect of social-structural and political constraints on development because "alien premises, objects, and methods" influenced the field of communication research. The mass media, in particular, were criticized for (*i*) their trivial and irrelevant content; (*ii*) giving rise to a *revolution of rising frustrations* in developing nations; and (*iii*) increasing the knowledge gap between the advantaged and disadvantaged sectors of the population.

Diffusion of innovations research and campaigns, which emerged from the modernization and communications effects frameworks, were criticized for (*i*) an overemphasis on individuals' exposure to mass media with less attention to message content; (*ii*) a pro-technological bias; (*iii*) a pro-source bias; (*iv*) a pro-persuasion bias; (*v*) a one-way message flow bias; and (*vi*) a pro-progressive farmer bias, among other criticisms. Diffusion actually served to exacerbate socio-economic and communication gaps between the progressive and subsistence farmers. Poor women were most neglected in diffusion projects and campaigns. The failures of diffusion necessitated more attention to careful research on particular audience segments in planning message and media strategies for persuasive campaigns. Models of social marketing emerged as useful guides for campaign research and planning, and many of these campaigns have done much to improve people's lives.

As in many of the diffusion of innovations campaigns, social marketing campaigns have tended to focus on the individual as the unit of analysis. Although social marketing theoretically begins with a thorough analysis of local needs, campaigns often have been largely top-down with receivers treated as targets for persuasion and change. The power to frame social problems typically comes from those with the authority to identify the causes and suggest solutions. In societies with sharp inequities, this power can be reduced to social engineering by the government or the elite.

The role accorded to communication in the development process changed significantly in the 1970s. Communication was used increasingly in self-development activities. In other words, user-initiated activity at the local level was considered absolutely essential for successful development at the village level. Revised concepts of development communication, such as self-help, grassroots participation, and two-way communication, led to a re-examination of the advantages of traditional media as vehicles for information, persuasion, and entertainment of rural people.

Since the mid-1970s, there has been a steady growth in information and communication technologies (ICT) and their application in development. Supporters of ICTs have advocated integrated rural development through telecommunications by highlighting many of their uses and applications in developing countries. However, there is very little analysis of the challenges faced by the rural poor in effectively harnessing the benefits derived from the use of ICTs. The rural poor and small- to medium-size entrepreneurs face many resource constraints that may prevent them from accessing the technology. In the near future, it is unlikely that the rural poor will be able to directly use information technologies. The greatest potential for the use of ICTs in rural development, then, lies with intermediate organizations. At some point in the future, though, it is imperative that the people themselves or their organizations directly control the use of ICTs and be able to design and interpret the information systems and the attendant technologies to derive the greatest benefit.

NOTES

1. The elite in Third World countries.
2. Defined by Rogers as an individual who links two or more cliques in a system (Rogers 1976a: 221).
3. "It's Not Easy," produced by AIDSCOM, USAID, and Uganda Television 1990.
4. "Marketing Ideas, Selling Nutrition," produced by the Academy for Educational Development for USAID and the US Department of Agriculture.

IV

LIBERATION PERSPECTIVES ON DEVELOPMENT

CHAPTER 7

LIBERATION THEOLOGY AND DEVELOPMENT

... if the religions of the world can recognize poverty and oppression as a common problem, if they share a common commitment to remove such evils, they will have a basis for reaching across their incommensurabilities and differences in order to hear and understand each other and possibly be transformed in the process.

Knitter (1987: 186)

Whether grounded in critical theory (from Marxism) or modernization theory (from neo-classical economic theory), or a combination of these approaches, most discussions of development take place within an overall *economic* framework concerned with how material resources are allocated in society. While critical arguments do at times express concern about ideological influence (for example, issues of cultural expansionism and imperialism, as previously discussed), these arguments are usually subordinate to larger questions of power and control over capital resources.

Non-material considerations that move development to a different depth, i.e., to the realm of the spiritual, are seldom priorities in the scholarship or practice of Western development aid. Few of the writings on development communication in mainstream traditions consider the impact of religion and spirituality. At best, development communication texts provide just passing references to religion, i.e., Christianity, Islam, Hinduism, Buddhism, etc., and often as a simple demographic or in a negative sense, as an obstacle to development. In Chapters 3 and 4 we noted that Buddhism, Hinduism, and Islam, among other religious frameworks, are usually perceived as barriers to development under the dominant paradigm of modernization. In Chapter 4, in particular, we used Hinduism as an example of some of the biases and errors inherent in these perceptions.

Despite widespread negative attitudes toward religion, most who spend time in developing countries observe that religious affiliations and spiritual motivations frequently play key roles in project success. For instance, Sipho Masilela (1994) examined communication strategies of NGO-sponsored development projects within a fixed geographic area in Kenya, assuming a high degree of participatory communication in these projects compared to those funded and administered by bilateral or multilateral organizations. He observed that NGO status alone was not quite as important as assumed. Also, NGO size and motivation played more significant roles. The larger the sponsoring NGO, the greater the level of corruption and the lower the recipient participation. The projects with the most community participation and dialogue and the least corruption were the smaller ones carried out at the grassroots by organizations with religious affiliations. Both authors of this text have made similar observations in South Asia and in sub-Saharan Africa.

These observations are difficult to reconcile with the overwhelming secular orientation of Western scholars and practitioners, who often assume a separation between material and spiritual concerns. The unspoken modernization assumption is that economic aid addresses material needs, whereas religion speaks primarily to spiritual needs, needs that may be in conflict with material gain. Material development goals require a set of communication strategies to assist in achieving objectives. In large projects, communication campaigns often are scientifically planned via social marketing research as discussed in Chapters 4 and 6. The idea that religion may play a positive role is seldom considered. Rather, if anything, religion usually is considered a barrier or a "resistance point" that needs to be overcome by creative strategizing.[1] Religion is considered more problematic than helpful in much of critical or Marxian thought. It is the "opiate of the masses," blinding people to material inequalities and injustice.

There is no question that women's and men's lives *are* often seriously constrained by religious beliefs that legitimize, rationalize, or deny those constraints. Much theological writing and practice indeed focuses on spiritual issues with little or no attention to social injustice. Yet, a closer look shows a more complex picture. The practice of *hermeneutics*, that is, the interpretation of sacred texts within historically specific contexts and by subjective individuals, shows that no religion may be reduced to a stereotype. Within every major religion there are branches with intellectual and spiritual leaders making strong theological arguments for development as a process of liberation from injustice, discrimination, and prejudice wherever they occur, including within religious organizations.[2] These arguments—and accompanying faith—frequently catalyze activism and provide important openings for individual and community empower-ment, openings that have led to real social change.

In this chapter, we discuss the meaning of development from spiritual perspectives and the nature of the arguments within different religious traditions. The type of theology that actively supports development for personal and collective empowerment often is called *liberation theology*. While liberation theology has been traditionally associated with Christianity, there are, in fact, emancipatory—or "liberation"—arguments within every major religion, arguments that speak about the specific issues of poverty, racial, ethnic, and sexual discrimination. These arguments are quite consistent in drawing on sacred texts to reject exploitation and injustice, and promote compassion and tolerance. Proponents often work together for common goals, as described in Farid Esack's (1997) discussion of the anti-Apartheid Movement in South Africa. As Selwyn Gross (1990: 2) notes:

> It is not uncommon for religious believers in the struggle to discover that they have more in common, theologically speaking, with comrades from very different religious traditions than they have with members of their own communities who are not involved in the struggle.

In this chapter, aside from Christianity, we summarize liberation perspectives expressed within Buddhism, Hinduism, Islam, and Judaism, as these are among the most significant belief systems that affect development. Together, they comprise nearly three-fourths of the world's people. We recognize that other religious organizations, beliefs, and motivations play important roles in development, including Baha'i, Shintoism, Taoism, Sikhism, Jainism, indigenous North American and

African religions, and more, but space does not allow an exhaustive discussion. We additionally discuss the relationship between Marxism and liberation theology, as the two systems of thought have been mutually reinforcing. At the same time, areas of conflict and contradiction remain. In Chapter 8, we show how arguments from liberation theology translate into communication strategies of development projects.

CHRISTIAN LIBERATION THEOLOGY

Christianity emerged from the teachings of Jesus of Nazareth and his followers approximately 2000 years ago. It is a monotheistic religion, which is grounded in the God of Abraham in the Old Testament. Hebrew scriptures prophesied that a Messiah (Christ) would be sent by God to teach and save humanity. Christians believe that God sent his son, Jesus Christ, to earth in fulfillment of these prophecies. They further believe that Jesus lived, taught, suffered, and died to atone for the sins of humanity. The life and teachings of Jesus are contained in the New Testament of the Bible, including the four Gospels, written by disciples of Jesus. A central Christian doctrine is that of the Trinity, that one God takes three forms, Father, Son, and Holy Spirit. Jesus is believed to be the incarnation of God, i.e., the manifestation of God in human form: "The Word became a human being" (John 1: 14).[3] Later, after Christ's crucifixion, God sent the Holy Spirit to dwell within all who proclaim the Christian faith. Hence, Christians believe that individuals as well as Christian communities serve as God's temple (1 Cor. 3: 16–17). Jesus supported the Ten Commandments of the Old Testament, but additionally taught that the greatest commandments are to love God and to love one's neighbor.

Today, Christianity is the largest global religion, embraced by nearly two billion people worldwide. The three major branches are Roman Catholicism, the largest; Protestantism (numerous denominations); and Orthodox Christianity (including Greek, Russian, and Ethiopian Orthodox churches). The assumptions that ground Christian liberation theology come substantially from the New Testament's emphasis on a life of prayer and service to one's neighbor, appropriate to the context of each situation. Hence, it is important to emphasize that liberation theology must begin with an analysis of the specific context involved, then respond with prayer and active service in a contextually appropriate manner. The Christian liberation theology movement gained initial momentum in Latin America, in large part because it is a continent characterized by majority identification with Christianity, primarily Roman Catholicism. However, there have been Christian liberation movements on every continent, in response to the specific circumstances of oppressed groups, usually identified by some combination of class, caste, gender, race, ethnicity, religion, or nation.

The origins of key elements of Christian liberation theology are impossible to pinpoint. For instance, numerous Christian writings through the centuries since Christ (e.g., the writings of St. Augustine) have been context-based, that is, inspired by and directed to particular historical and political-economic contexts of oppression. Additionally, many clerics and lay workers within Christian traditions have followed the tenets of liberation theology in their identification with and activism on behalf of the poor and oppressed. A prominent example is Bartolomé de las Casas, a priest who dedicated his life to protecting the rights of the indigenous peoples of South America from 16th century Spanish conquest and exploitation (Casas 1992).

A key event that catalyzed the 20th century liberation theology movement in Latin America was the Second General Conference of Latin American Bishops held at Medellín, Colombia in August 1968. The overwhelming preponderance of poverty and injustice in Latin America was the major theme, and the idea of the *Christian base community* as one response was formally sanctioned (to be discussed in Chapter 8). In 1971, Gustavo Gutiérrez, a Peruvian priest and theologian, synthesized the arguments that grounded the liberation theology movement in the 20th century in his groundbreaking book, *A Theology of Liberation* (1973).[4] Gutiérrez points out that liberation theology derives most significantly from unjust suffering, not from abstract arguments. The struggles for survival of millions of Latin American Christians prompted their religious leaders to rethink Biblical teachings and their priorities in light of those teachings. The overwhelming emphasis of liberation theology is *practice*, i.e., direct work with the poor and oppressed. It is impossible to understand liberation theology without practicing it. Along with this experience, selected Biblical passages and prayer can provide further enlightenment and support, especially in group contexts. Liberation theology is a combination of work with and activism on behalf of the poor, Bible study, and prayer.

Box 7.1
Biblical Arguments for Christian Liberation Theology[5]

1. *God is very close to humanity.* "The Biblical God is close to man; he is a God of communion with and commitment to man" (Gutiérrez 1973: 190). This theme is abundant in the Old Testament. God's presence is especially evident in the Exodus story, where God literally frees (via Moses) the Jewish slaves and leads them to the Promised Land. Much of the Old Testament emphasized God's presence in special places such as mountains, the Ark of the Covenant, and later the temple. Yet at the same time it was believed that God could not be contained in any one place, as He is transcendent and universal. God is most present in the hearts of individual men and women. This idea that the human being is the temple of God is reinforced and extended throughout the New Testament, as noted earlier.

2. *We encounter God via commitment to justice for all.* Again, this theme is evident throughout both the Old and New Testaments. To despise, harm, or exploit one's neighbor is an offense against God. Additionally, God is encountered via service to others. Gutiérrez concedes that in the Old Testament the neighbor often means a member of the Jewish community; however, references to other groups appear to point to broader interpretations. These broader interpretations are greatly extended in the New Testament, which repeatedly says that Christ came to save all, and that Christians must seek justice for all. Probably the most famous text cited by advocates of liberation theology is the chapter in the Bible, Matthew 25: 35–36, which describes the final judgment gathering of all people from all corners of the earth and God's criteria for salvation: "I was hungry and you fed me, thirsty and you gave me a drink; I was a stranger and you received me in your homes, naked and you clothed me; I was sick and you took care of me, in prison and you visited me." Gutiérrez notes that there have been varying interpretations of this passage, but that most agree the passage directs all to love and serve all, regardless of religion, ethnicity, or nation. Finally, it is important to highlight

(Box 7.1 contd.)

> *(Box 7.1 contd.)*
>
> the societal versus individual interpretations of love of neighbor in liberation theology. The neighbor should be viewed as more than a specific needy individual but additionally includes social patterns and structures of injustice. This suggests concrete action beyond the individual act of the Good Samaritan, and includes activism to transform society.
>
> 3. *A spirituality of liberation is inseparable from and catalyzes the work of liberation.* The work of liberation arises from and is closely linked with spiritual experience. Hence, a spirituality of liberation requires conversion to God and to the oppressed. "Conversion means a radical transformation of ourselves; it means thinking, feeling and living as Christ" (Gutiérrez 1973: 205). Conversion leads to what Gutiérrez calls a sense of gratuitousness, that is, a sense that God's love is a free gift and must be shared freely with others. Prayer is key to experiencing (and subsequently sharing) gratuitousness (Gutiérrez 1973: 206).

Gutiérrez (1973) systematically cites the Old and New Testaments of the Bible to weave this argument. The specific tenets of his argument and selected supporting passages are summarized in Box 7.1. There are essentially three assumptions: that God is close to and committed to humanity; that to love God is to love your neighbor and vice versa; and that spiritual practice is essential to catalyze and sustain the love of God and neighbor. It is important to recognize that similar arguments and many of the same passages are cited by other advocates of Christian liberation theology, whether in reference to Latin America or other continents and contexts. Especially relevant for development communication and development education are the views of the Brazilian educator Paolo Freire, first articulated in *Pedagogy of the Oppressed* (1970), and discussed in greater detail in Chapter 8. Beginning with the assumptions of Latin American liberation theology,[6] as described above, Freire argues that development communication/education should not involve a one-way flow of persuasive and informational messages, but rather initiate a *dialogue for liberation*, a dialogue that is supplemented by religious practice. The result is expanded consciousness and power for everyone involved.

In the geographical context of Latin America, there are other emerging liberation theologies. Independent of the liberation theologies of the settler groups, the indigenous people and the black population have turned toward other empowerment theologies anchored in their earlier spiritual ideas and their histories. Other overlapping arguments also include feminist liberation theologies globally, African American liberation theology in North America, and anti-Apartheid liberation theology in South Africa. These context-based variations are clearly illustrated in two overviews by Deane William Ferm (1986a, 1986b).[7] Certainly in each context, Biblical passages that were highlighted and strategies of response (discussed in Chapter 8) have evolved as culturally and politically appropriate to the situation.

JEWISH LIBERATION THEOLOGY

Judaism, also a monotheistic religion, is the foundation of Christianity, as described above. It originated in the Middle East around 1900 BC, and the earliest texts of the Old Testament appeared around 1300 BC. The Jews were persecuted by the Romans during the early years of Christianity, and therefore departed to create a Jewish Diaspora. Israel was established as a Jewish state in 1948 following the Holocaust of World War II. Judaism is often considered an ethnicity as well as a religion, as Jews have been labeled and persecuted regardless of their religiosity. Approximately 4 million Jews live in Israel, and millions more live elsewhere in the world, predominantly in North America and Russia. Although Jews make up a small percentage of the world's people (there are about 12.8 million Jews living worldwide), Judaism is important to include here because of its historic significance and the strong voices for liberation within Judaism.

Arguments for a Jewish liberation theology have emerged in recent decades primarily as a result of the Holocaust. Ellis (1990) and Lerner (1991) trace this history, pointing out the common roots of Jewish and Christian liberation theologies, as well as issues unique to the Jewish population. Certainly there exists a continuity of Judeo-Christian beliefs and traditions. The Exodus story is central to Jewish liberation theology and has also had a strong influence on the development of Christian liberation theology, as discussed above. Ellis notes the many ways in which the Exodus tradition inspired Latin American liberation theology, as well as African American liberation theology, e.g., "The songs of African slaves in nineteenth century America calling on God for freedom echo the lamentations of the Jews in Egypt" (Ellis 1990: 1).

In that liberation theology arises from the context of human experience, Holocaust theology emerged to address questions of survival and empowerment in the aftermath of the genocide. Ellis argues that new forms of Jewish liberation theology are needed to deal with ethical concerns of the present, yet in the light of contributions of Exodus and Holocaust theologies focusing on Jewish survival and empowerment. Particularly significant is a recognition of Israeli expansionism and its consequences for oppression globally (Ellis 1990).

Ellis provides considerable evidence of efforts to operationalize a new Jewish liberation theology, a theology that moves beyond Exodus and Holocaust survival themes to emphasize inclusivity, i.e., to negotiate and transcend the "tension between particularity and universality as a self-critical voice that comes from the depth of Jewish tradition and seeks to serve the world" (Ellis 1990: 111). These examples of Jewish "renewal" or liberation praxis include acts of civil disobedience to protest nuclear weapons tests, American and Israeli involvement in Central America, and Apartheid in South Africa. Additionally, feminism has influenced these movements, as in the Israeli peace movement seeking to end the oppression of Palestinians.

ISLAM AND LIBERATION

Muhammad, born in Mecca in AD 570, is regarded by Muslims as God's final prophet. Muhammad received messages from God via the angel Jibra'eel (Gabriel) outlining fundamental principles for life, as well as more nuanced rules for spiritual practice. Muslims believe that the Qur'an was written by God and revealed to Muhammad. The Qur'an guides and inspires over a billion Muslims living worldwide. The five major principles or pillars for regulating the Muslim life are especially significant. The Muslim must first and foremost believe that there is no God but Allah, and Muhammad is His Prophet. Second, every Muslim must pray five times per day and Friday afternoons in the Mosque. Third, Muslims must give alms to the needy. Fourth, Muslims who are physically and economically able must fast from dawn to dusk throughout the holy month of Ramadan. Finally, if possible, each Muslim should make a pilgrimage to Mecca once in his or her lifetime.

Muslims believe that the Qur'an is not merely a divinely inspired work, but rather the direct speech of God as revealed to Muhammad. Yet, like the Old and New Testaments of the Bible and other sacred texts believed to contain the speech of God, the Qur'an reflects the context in which it was written. It is generally accepted by Qur'anic scholars that its contents are "vitally related to the taste and temperament, the environment and history and customs and usages of Arabia" (Maududi 1988: 26–27). Further, Esack (1997: 59) observes contextually meaningful differences and contradictions between certain verses written in Mecca and Medina. In addition to contextuality, history shows that every generation and branch of Muslims has produced its own perspective on the Qur'an, consistent with its experiences and observations.

Beyond agreement that the Qur'an remains relevant as God's word and reflects the historic context in which it was written, contemporary interpretation and subsequent practice vary widely. Some groups have used the Qur'an, like the Bible, to justify oppression and violence, as in the case of the Taliban government of Afghanistan's systematic persecution of women, and a few governments' formal adoption or informal tolerance of extreme punishments (e.g., amputations, hangings, and beheadings) for crimes such as robbery and adultery. Unfortunately, these are the images of Islam that dominate the imaginations of many in Western industrialized countries. Yet alongside these extreme traditional interpretations exist a range of more liberal interpretations, reflected in Islamic practice by the majority of the world's Muslims.

In addition, many scholars and activists draw on the text to argue persuasively for a Qur'anic theology of liberation, a theology that reflects the concerns of the interpreter. Malcolm X preached and practiced a form of Qur'anic liberation theology on behalf of African Americans during the Civil Rights Movement of the 1960s. Fatima Mernissi (1987) and Leila Ahmed (1992) have made gender-sensitive interpretations of the Qur'an, contributing new perspectives on women's role in Islam.

Farid Esack (1997) details a Qur'anic hermeneutic of liberation in the context of South Africa, though his analysis applies to struggles in other contexts of oppression as well (see Box 7.2). Through both his own careful reading of the Qur'an and his analysis of other progressive interpretations, Esack draws a number of overlapping conclusions that are remarkably similar to those of Gutiérrez (1973). He argues that Allah (i.e., God in

Arabic) is very close to humanity, especially the oppressed, and that God's central priority is justice for the oppressed. Further, religious enlightenment necessitates work on behalf of the oppressed in that prayer and progressive involvement with people are dialectically linked.

Box 7.2
Qur'anic Tenets for Islamic Liberation Theology[a]

1. *Allah is constantly involved in the affairs of humankind* (Esack 1997: 54, 94–95). This is demonstrated via the progressive sending of prophets to deliver His Word, appropriate to the demands of the situation in question. This may be referred to as the "principle of progressive revelation," also assumed by most Biblical scholars. Additionally, throughout the Qur'an there is a great deal of evidence that God identifies with people, and is an ongoing source of sustenance as they seek meaning in their lives.

2. *Allah is concerned with justice for the oppressed, both believers and non-believers* (Esack 1997: 98–106). Allah's central concern is justice for all people, beginning with the most marginalized and oppressed. Esack carefully documents the varied Arabic terms used to refer to the oppressed, Muslim, non-Muslim, those responsible for their condition, and those not responsible. Regardless, it is clear that God identifies with and prefers the oppressed, even those who have rejected Him, and denounces the wealthy and powerful who reject com-passion and sharing. Additionally, the Qur'an shows that the oppressed are hermeneutically privileged, i.e., favored to have a better understanding of the text. Evidence includes the fact that all of the Prophets, including Muhammad, came from peasant backgrounds. The only exception, Moses, spent many years in the desert to prepare for his destiny as Prophet (Esack 1997: 99). Further, the initial followers of the Prophets, including Muhammad, were the poor and weak. Although the aristocracy of Mecca offered to convert to Islam if Muhammad would re-ject these undesirable followers, Allah condemned such offers.

3. *A full understanding of the Qur'an's support for the oppressed requires full commitment to and engagement in the struggle for*

(Box 7.2 contd.)

(Box 7.2 contd.)

liberation (Esack 1997: 87–90, 257). "The Qur'an bears testimony to the idea that it is a book of understanding through praxis, rather than one of doctrine and dogma" (Esack 1997: 157). Muhammad's own journey toward and during Prophethood demonstrates this. Esack shows how the Qur'an constantly links relations with others and with God. The term *taqwa* is frequently used as an ethical call to know God via service to others. The Qur'an calls for both individuals and communities "deeply imbued with *taqwa* who will to carry on the Prophet's task of transformation and liberation" (Esack 1997: 87). A commitment to all of God's people cannot be separated from a commitment to God. As the engaged interpreter participates in the struggle, he or she is personally transformed. A combination of prayer and praxis is crucial in this process. The term *jihad* is commonly understood to mean sacred warfare. Yet, Esack points out that *jihad* has varied meanings and has been used more frequently to refer to the struggle to transform both self and society, in Esack's words, both "struggle and praxis" (p. 107). Hence, the Qur'an calls the believer to *jihad*, as a means of knowing God and eradicating injustice.

In addition, Muslims who are committed to the liberation of the poor and oppressed must work closely with similarly committed non-Muslims. An acceptance of pluralism is necessary for the realization of democratic, non-sexist, and non-racist society (Esack 1997: 258). The Muslim can do this while still constantly seeking inspiration and strength from the Qur'an. Esack (1997) acknowledges that there may be limits to a postmodern theology of pluralism, as such a perspective begins to threaten traditional rituals, for instance. Hence, there is a need for ongoing interpretive work to consider categories of inclusion and exclusion under different circumstances.

GANDHIAN LIBERATION THEOLOGY

Liberation theology in the Hindu tradition is often credited to Mahatma Gandhi, who remained staunchly Hindu, but borrowed key ideas from Christianity, ultimately influencing the development of Christian liberation theology as well. The practice of borrowing ideas from other religions is completely consistent with Hindu thought, as Hindus accept the validity of other religions, recognizing that there are many paths to God.

Hinduism is perhaps the oldest religion in the world, and the religion is unusual in having no original founder. It emerged in the Indus Valley from indigenous Indian religions around 3500 BC, and evolved via contacts with other peoples and religions over the centuries. In fact, one of the central qualities of Hinduism is its tolerance of and active interest in other religious perspectives. The Hindu accepts the reality and validity of other perspectives, and may borrow and incorporate elements of other perspectives. Today, there are over 800 million Hindus living worldwide.

Hinduism has a number of sacred texts. The most significant are the four *Vedas* and *Upanishads*. There are many Hindu sects. The doctrine of *karma* is central to Hindu belief. *Karma* assumes that the human soul transcends human life, and is reborn in multiple physical forms. However, as a way of life, Hinduism focuses on three ends: *dharma*, or virtue; *artha*, the acquisition of material things guided by the principles of *dharma*; and *kama*, the gratification of the senses, governed by a cultivated mind. If these three are rightly pursued, the end result is *moksha*, or salvation. The main goal of a devout Hindu is release from reincarnation by practicing yoga, following the scriptures, and seeking the counsel of a personal guru. Numerous deities are worshipped, including Brahma the creator, Vishnu the preserver, and Shiva the destroyer (Knott 1998; Social Studies 1969; Summary of World Religions).

Mahatma Gandhi is the central figure in Hindu liberation theology in recent history and he has had a powerful influence on other liberation theologies and on development. Therefore, we briefly summarize his life, insights, and accomplishments. It is important to acknowledge, however, that there certainly have been others struggling for liberation, equality, and justice within the Hindu tradition.[9] These include activists on behalf of women and dalits (untouchables), as both groups have experienced discrimination and oppression (Knott 1998: 81–94).

Mohandas Karamchand Gandhi (later known as Mahatma or "great soul") was born in 1869 in western India. He was the youngest child of deeply religious merchant class parents. His parents placed great value on truth and devotion to family. They also respected other faiths and openly discussed their religious beliefs. It was common for Hindu and Muslim religious leaders to visit and engage in dialogue with Gandhi's father (Jesudasan 1984: 8–9).

At the age of 18, Gandhi went to England for legal studies. While there, he also systematically studied other religions and was especially impressed by the Bible and themes of non-retaliation and non-resistance. Shortly after completing his legal education, he was invited to go to South Africa as a legal interpreter for an Indian company. He eventually spent 23 years in South Africa (1891–1914), developed his liberation theology and became a champion of South African Indians. Among other successes, his movement gained legal recognition for Hindu marriages, overturned laws limiting the economic and civil rights of Indians, and ended indentured immigration from India.

Gandhi's theology and methodology were shaped both by his comparative study of religions and his experiences and observations of oppression. The life of Jesus made an impact on Gandhi, but he was not impressed by the dogmatism of most Christians and their ignorance and intolerance of other religions. The universal compassion of the Buddha also played a role in Gandhi's evolving consciousness, as did the teachings of Islam and its emphasis on serving the poor. Eventually, Gandhi was led back to Hinduism, though his interpretations certainly were influenced by his studies.

In South Africa, Gandhi increasingly simplified his life, owning nothing beyond necessities, praying, meditating, and practicing physical labor daily. Though married, he took a vow of celibacy at the age of 35 years. His increased identification with the poor led him to cancel his life insurance policy and direct all his savings to community service (Jesudasan 1984: 14–16). While in South Africa, Gandhi developed the two concepts of *swaraj* and *satyagraha* that would direct his later activism in India. The concept of *swaraj* or liberation was first developed in Gandhi's book *Hind Swaraj*, written in 1908. Eventually this became Gandhi's central idea in his fight for the liberation of India. Put simply, swaraj meant a democratic, self-determined society, grounded on belief in God, tolerance of multiple faiths, and rejection of all forms of oppression and exploitation. Gandhi's emphasis on spirituality and rejection of oppression led him to condemn modern civilization, including modern professions, as materialistic and exploitative. In 1910, he gave up his law profession permanently and started a communal farm near Johannesburg. Residents gained strength for the liberation struggle via daily disciplines of spiritual practice and communal work (Jesudasan 1984: 19).

The concept *satyagraha* served as Gandhi's primary philosophical and methodological guide in achieving swaraj. Satyagraha combined the two Sanskrit words "satya" (truth) and "agraha" (firmness or force). Hence satyagraha means the force (or firmness) of truth. Satyagraha grounded Gandhi's leadership in many acts of passive resistance and civil disobedience against laws and practices that discriminated against Indians (Jesudasan 1984: 18–21). Additional component concepts were *ahimsa* (non-violence) and *tapaya* (self-suffering). Ahimsa that has Buddhist, Jainist, and Hindu origins, combines an attitude of love with rejection of injury to living beings. It assumes that truth is impossible without love. Tapaya is an extension of ahimsa and means that an acceptance of self-suffering may be necessary to achieve love and non-violence. One willingly accepts suffering as preferable to inflicting pain on others (Jesudasan 1984: 95–98).

In 1914, Gandhi returned to India and led the struggle to free India from British control. His dream to achieve India's independence was realized on August 15, 1947. In 1948, he was assassinated while being escorted to a prayer meeting. As the leader of India's independence movement, he promoted a number of strategies consistent with satyagraha, including the mass education of laborers and villagers, boycotts, and acts of civil disobedience. Gandhi strongly believed that India could not be free without economic self-sufficiency and a rejection of oppression and discrimination within the country. Hence, he developed three pillars or themes in his movement toward swaraj or liberation, to be achieved via satyagraha. First, was the promotion of daily hand-spinning (khadi). This supplied a daily discipline while also reducing the need for foreign cloth. Second, was the removal of untouchability. Gandhi argued that no one can be free until the suffering of the most oppressed is alleviated. He saw sanctioning untouchability (via interpretations of karma) as a sin. The third was encouraging peace and unity between Hindus and Muslims, as an internally divided nation cannot effectively rule itself. He urged the forgiveness of past offenses and forging unity based on mutual respect and common goals.

Gandhi's historic global influence cannot be underestimated. His life and work transcended religious, ethnic, and political boundaries and has served as an inspiration to many other religious leaders committed to liberation ideals.

BUDDHISM AND LIBERATION

Buddhism is a younger religion than Hinduism and has its origins in India. Its founder was Gautama Buddha, who lived in ancient northern India in the 5th and 6th century BC. The name Buddha means "enlightened one." The Buddha's birth name, however, was Gautama Siddhartha. He was born to a royal Hindu family and had a privileged upbringing, but felt dissatisfied with the extravagant lifestyle of the royal court and eventually chose to dedicate his life to seeking enlightenment. The Buddha spent several years practicing meditation and asceticism, none of which eased his mental suffering or led to enlightenment. Finally, at the age of 35, he decided to assume a lotus position and remain there until he attained enlightenment. His deep meditations in this position eventually led to his discovery of a true path to liberation from suffering. This was a "middle path," a path of neither extravagance nor asceticism (Mahathera 1998).

It is important to note that the Buddha was not a god and never claimed to be one. He was a human being who become enlightened. By following his tenets, Buddhists believe that many others may became Buddhas as well. As a religion, Buddhism does not believe in the idea of worshipping a central creater or God. Nor does Buddhism have a dogma. Rather Buddhism is a process of spiritual growth leading eventually to enlightenment, i.e., deep insight into the ultimate mysteries of life.

The Buddha's primary concern was life as a process of suffering, and the steps necessary to overcome suffering, ultimately resulting in nirvana. As the Buddha sought to simplify life, he rejected much of the Hindu teachings of the time as outlined in the *Vedas*, especially regarding caste categories and sacrifices. He also started an order of monks that aimed to be a model of simplicity and democratic organization.

Today there are several sects of Buddhism. There are over 300 million Buddhists worldwide, living mostly in Sri Lanka, Myanmar (Burma), Laos, Cambodia, Thailand, China, Bhutan, Mongolia, and Japan. All adhere to the Four Noble Truths taught by the Buddha: that life is characterized by suffering; that the cause of suffering is human desire—for pleasure, material gain, recognition, etc.; that suffering can be ended only by achieving freedom from human desire; and that there is a Noble Eightfold Path that may end suffering. The Noble Eightfold Path specifies right views, right thoughts, right speech, right action, right livelihood, right effort, right mindfulness, and right concentration. Additionally, the Buddha emphasized the importance of four lofty states of mind, or qualities of heart, essential to successfully follow these steps and achieve the highest spiritual level. These are *metta* (loving kindness), *karuna* (compassion, or the wish to free others from suffering), *mudita* (sympathetic joy in the happiness of others), and *upekkha* (equanimity, or tranquillity under pressure) (Mahathera 1998).

Buddhism's central concerns with compassion for all, with suffering and liberation from it, translate readily to a Buddhist liberation praxis, often called *engaged Buddhism*. Although some Buddhists may seek to bypass concern with human suffering via focusing on nirvana (as Christians may focus on heaven), many others centralize liberation perspectives. The key is to find sufficient hope in suffering for systematic involvement with oppressed groups. Engaged Buddhism is often associated with Sulak Sivaraska, who started an indigenous NGO movement in Thailand by creating a variety of grassroots social welfare and development organizations (see e.g., Rothberg 1993b). These organizations reject Western consumerism in favor of traditional culture and they also emphasize spiritual practice. Sivaraska also helped start the International Network of Engaged Buddhists, which now includes hundreds of members and groups working in 33 countries.[10] Another key leader in the engaged Buddhist movement has been the social activist and exiled Vietnamese monk, Thich Nhat Hanh. Also in this category is the Sarvodaya Sahramadana Movement of Sri Lanka (see Ariyaratne 1987; Liyanage 1988), to be discussed in detail in Chapter 9. This countrywide movement is now 40 years old, and has spread to other countries as well. It is a grassroots, village-level self-development movement that aims to simultaneously awaken and empower individuals and address pressing issues of rural poverty.[11]

Beyond small group empowerment and social change, some Buddhists have engaged dramatically in protest and freedom struggles, even paying the ultimate price in the service of liberation. Examples include the activism of Buddhist monks against the dictatorship of Ngo Dinh Diem during the 1970s in South Vietnam. Protests even included self-immolation to mobilize global resistance against brutality and exploitation (Wielenga 1999). More recently, Tibetan Buddhist nuns have actively resisted the Chinese occupation of Tibet, as portrayed in a film by Ellen Bruno: "Satya: A Prayer for the Enemy."[12] Countless nuns have been imprisoned and tortured for their non-violent demonstrations favoring Tibetan independence and against religious oppression and human rights abuses by the Chinese State.

LIBERATION THEOLOGY AND MARXISM

Liberation theology's historic association with Marxism requires some discussion as it has been controversial, resulting in statements of condemnation and concern from the Vatican (Turner 1999). Liberation theology's call for social action on behalf of the poor requires political involvement and activism in collaboration with other groups that challenge oppressive social structures. This collaboration additionally necessitates consideration of the political-economic theory that grounds the actions of these groups. As Zweig (1991: 16) notes, "The call to confront institutional sin brings theology fully into the secular world as an active, conscious agent and requires of theology some familiarity with the doctrines of social science."

It is important to recognize that regimes grounded in every social science or religious doctrine have sanctioned oppressive and brutal social policies and acts. Every doctrine is open to varied interpretations, distortions, and consequent actions. However, many proponents of liberation theology find far more common ground with Marxist philosophy than with mainstream, capitalist models. This is because mainstream economics is based on values of individualism and individual opportunities to accumulate capital, discussed in Chapter 3. As a result, "it is blind to the social relations established in economic processes and can only promote the blame-the-victim conclusion that those who suffer economic privation do so voluntarily or in some way through their own fault" (Zweig 1991: 28). In contrast, Marxist economics foregrounds an analysis of social relations in their proper historic context (see Chapter 5). The individual cannot be understood except as a social creation. The relations of economic production have an especially important bearing on the quality of human existence.

An alignment between liberation theology and Marxism recognizes that they share common ground yet provide unique insights in the struggle against oppression. Most fundamentally, both emerged from observations and experiences of social injustice, especially by economic class. Both have taken sides favoring the exploited poor. Both favor remedies beyond the charitable actions of individuals, recognizing that social problems require collective actions. Despite these commonalities, there has been much resistance to collaboration. Some conflicts have historic origins. For example, Zweig (1991) points out that organized religion has a long history of hostility to science, including biology, astronomy, and even the social sciences. Moreover, religious leaders have often been aligned with the oppressive ruling elite that Marxists, or others (including those within the same religion operating from a liberation framework), have sought to overthrow.

Additional conflicts between liberation theology and Marxism have been primarily in three areas (Turner 1999; Zweig 1991). First, is the place of God. God is central to most religious beliefs; yet Marxism embraces atheism and rejects religious claims about the role of God or any spirit in the material world. This and related problems are confronted via extensive criticisms of Marxism's economic determinism—by neo-Marxists such as Althusser and Gramsci, as well as by liberation theologians. These groups and others point out that a major flaw of orthodox Marxism is its simplistic base-superstructure assumptions, that the economic "base" drives society, including all political and cultural phenomena that comprise the "superstructure." They additionally argue that non-material facets of society including media representations, popular culture, and religion have the potential to catalyze or contribute to change (Zweig 1991: 40–41).

Second, many resist Marxism's call to revolution on ethical grounds, as a part of a general rejection of violence. They argue that the practice of Marxism must be guided by ethical norms. Most liberation theologians who align with some of the tenets of Marxism promote non-violent remedies for social change. Key examples are Mahatma Gandhi and Martin Luther King, Jr. (Zweig 1991: 43).

Third, many say that Marx goes too far in assuming the social (e.g., class) determination of the individual, therefore denying the unique value of each individual. Vatican documents, for instance, argue that social structures are human products, and that the individuals must be freed from sin before social structures can be reformed. Individual acts of charity constitute the keys to reform (Turner 1999). Advocates of Marxism, however, argue the other way: that the excess individualism in capitalism denies individuality by failing to recognize that individuality is meaningless except in the context of community. Obviously, Marx was most interested in relations among people in processes of economic production. He argued that capitalist production is dehumanizing and alienating, separating workers from one another and from the products of their labor. Social change of any significance requires collective effort, not isolated individual acts. Likewise, liberation theology is concerned about the plight of the individual in a web of historically grounded social relationships, with the assumption that individual oppression cannot be resolved without simultaneously considering the larger social context.

Today most recognize that Marxist theory has serious weaknesses that have resulted in failed social experiments, as it became abundantly evident in 1989 with the fall of most socialist states. Contemporary theorists and activists continue to grapple with the weaknesses of Marxism. Yet, the tradition still provides a basis for social action in collaboration with others who share Marxism's fundamental concerns. These collaborators include followers of liberation theology.

FORMING ALLIANCES

This chapter has shown that within every major religion, and nearly every religious tradition, there are groups concerned with social injustice who make contextual interpretations of sacred texts. These interpretations yield common and overlapping conclusions, notably, that humans fundamentally need human and divine relationships, that oppressive social and psychological conditions often thwart these crucial relationships, and that overcoming oppression requires a combination of spiritual practice and political action.

These interpretations yield political and spiritual alliances with like-minded religious groups concerned with injustice and oppression, evident in numerous organizations. Current organizations that represent global or regional alliances include: the Ecumenical Association of Third World Theologians (EATWOT), the World Council of Churches, and ecumenical organizations specific to particular regions, e.g., the Conference of Churches in Asia (CCA). Alliances often go beyond diverse religions to include more traditionally secular groups such as Marxists and feminists. For instance, in 1971 the Christians for Socialism Movement was initiated in Chile when 80 Latin American priests met to find common ground between Christianity and Marxism, leading to continued dialogue between Christians and others concerned with the excesses and abuses of capitalist systems that privilege wealthy minorities (Christians for Socialism 1986). Just as liberation theologies challenge religious traditions that emphasize spirituality without social awareness, many who identify with Marxism and feminism deviate from their anti-religious peers by acknowledging the importance of spirituality as a resource for challenging class, gender, and other forms of oppression. In short, many advocates of liberation theology additionally identify with Marxism or feminism or both. How these labels are defined, however, and even whether they are used, varies with the history and context of each situation.[13]

It is clear that every major belief system and social movement is complex, with many interests and concerns. Hence, there is no one simple characterization. Additionally, common concerns across systems and movements often yield creative forms of collaboration and mutual influence. In Chapter 8, we will see how liberation motivations may be conceptualized and operationalized in development communication projects, many of which involve collaborative efforts by a number of organizations.

SUMMARY

Few writings on development communication in mainstream (modernization) traditions consider the impact of religion and spirituality, except in a negative sense, as an obstacle to development. Yet observations and experience in developing countries show that religious organizations and motivations are often crucial for project success, especially projects that aim to empower people. The theology that supports development as a process of liberation from injustice, discrimination, and oppression is called liberation theology. While liberation theology has traditionally been associated with Christianity, especially in Latin America, there are liberation theologies in every major religion. Religious feminists also have made liberation interpretations. Liberation activists from different religions often work together toward common goals.

This chapter examines context-inspired liberation interpretations of sacred texts central to Christianity, Judaism, Islam, Hinduism, and Buddhism. These interpretations yield a number of overlapping conclusions: (*i*) God (ultimacy) is actively involved in human affairs; (*ii*) Humans fundamentally seek freedom from internal and external forms of oppression; (*iii*) Oppressive social and psychological conditions and suffering in general constitute barriers to relationships with others and with God, or with ultimacy (in the case of Buddhism); (*iv*) Social and divine relationships are dialectically linked, such that spiritual practice inspires service to the oppressed, and God is discovered via this work; (*v*) Service to the oppressed includes recognizing the role of corrupt institutions in sustaining oppressive conditions; and (*vi*) Political actions to confront institutional evils may be necessary as a part of this divinely sanctioned work. In essence, liberation theology involves work with and activism on behalf of the poor, the study of sacred texts, and spiritual practice. The combination of progressive involvement with people and spiritual practice is crucial, as these two endeavors are assumed to be dialectically linked and both are essential for spiritual enlightenment.

We close with a critical discussion of liberation theology's historic association with Marxism. Both emerged from observations and experiences of social injustice, especially by economic class, and have taken sides favoring the exploited poor. Both also recognize that solutions require collective action, appropriate to the social context of the situation. Conflicts include (*i*) religion's historic aversion to science, including social science; (*ii*) Marxism's historic aversion to religion; (*iii*) orthodox Marxism's support of revolutionary remedies for injustice, whereas most liberation activists promote non-violent means of achieving social change; and (*iv*) Marxism's excessive focus on class determination of individual, therefore denying the unique value and power of the individual.

NOTES

1. See examples in Manoff (1985), especially Chapter 10, "Case histories," and Chapter 11, "Cultural and structural impediments to social marketing."

2. However, the ability of these theologies or intellectual and spiritual leaders (whether they be Christian, Muslim, Hindu, or Buddhist) to make a lasting impact on the conditions of practice will depend on both historical and geographical considerations. Thus, the practice will differ from region to region and from one historical period to another. Our intention is to identify and describe elements of liberation theology in the different religions and not to imply that they are a force to reckon with in every religion, region, or historical period.

3. This quote is from the Gospel of John in the Bible. For more information, see *Good News Bible: Today's English Version* (1992).

4. His book was first published by CEP in Lima, Peru in 1971, titled *Teología de la Liberación, Perspectivas.*

5. See Gutiérrez, 1973: 190–208. For specific quotes from the Bible, see *Good News Bible: Today's English Version* (1992).

6. For a discussion of the theological foundations of Freire's work, see Thomas (1993).

7. Additionally, for a discussion of feminist liberation theology in Latin America, see Isasi-Diaz and Tarango (1988). There is quite a large literature of Christian feminist theology challenging women's oppression in religious organizations, e.g., Rosemary Radford Ruther's many books. Some, not all, of this literature focuses primarily on issues of poverty and women's rightful place in liberation movements. For overviews of feminist liberation movements, see Grey (1999) and Brubaker (1991). For a discussion of Christian Liberation Theology in Asia, see Ateek (1990). For an overview of African American liberation theology (the North American context) see Cone (1969). The South African perspective is articulated by Boesak (1987).

8. For more detail, see Esack (1997). For specific quotes from the Qur'an, see *Al-Qur'an* (1984).

9. For example, Tilak, Aurobindo, and Annie Besant were activists who used tenets from Hinduism.

10. For more information and sources, see the website for the International Network of Engaged Buddhists: http://www.bpf.org/ineb.html.

11. For an overview of Buddhist liberation movements in India, Sri Lanka, Thailand, Tibet, Taiwan, Vietnam, and Japan see Queen and King (1996).

12. For more information, contact Film Arts Foundation, 396 Ninth St. 2nd Floor, San Francisco, CA 94103, USA.

13. As Grey (1999) points out, the term feminist theology is seldom used outside of North America and Europe. Elsewhere, the labels that women choose and their priorities vary considerably. Even in North America, the term Womanist theology refers to the theology of African American women and Mujerista theology, the theology of Hispanic women.

CHAPTER 8

COMMUNICATION AND SPIRITUALITY IN DEVELOPMENT

Critical and liberating dialogue, which presupposes action, must be
carried on with the oppressed at whatever the stage of their
struggle for liberation. The content of that dialogue can and
should vary in accordance with historical conditions
and the level at which the oppressed perceive
reality. But to substitute monologue, slogans,
and communiques for dialogue is to attempt
to liberate the oppressed with the
instruments of domestication.
Paolo Freire (1970: 47)

In Chapter 7, we summarized theologies of liberation from major
religious traditions. In this chapter, we will give examples of movements and projects that are grounded in liberation theologies and
describe how these foundational beliefs shape development communication practice.

In general, projects motivated primarily by emancipatory philosophical
and spiritual concerns share certain overlapping characteristics, regardless
of the religion involved. First, goals of individual spiritual growth and
empowerment are as important as alleviating material needs; the two

areas of need are assumed to be dialectically linked. Second, these projects reject the development diagnoses of outsiders and insist on a process of community discussion and decision-making, consistent with the community's cultural and spiritual values. Third, this process necessarily includes an important role for religious leaders and religious practice. Fourth, the projects ideally involve people from varied economic classes and other social strata, assuming that all are in need of spiritual awakening in a manner that can contribute to addressing broad social problems. Finally, while outside governmental and non-governmental organizations, and their funds may be involved in project support, fundamental values must not be compromised as a result of this involvement.

PAOLO FREIRE AND LIBERATION THEOLOGY

Probably the most influential scholar to apply liberation theology specifically to education and communication practice in development contexts is Paolo Freire (1970, 1973).[1] Although his ideas emerged primarily from Christian liberation theology, he drew upon the writings and actions of liberation leaders from other traditions as well, especially Gandhi (1967). The impact of Freire's arguments and methodologies has been broad, beginning in Latin America and spreading globally. Freire's signature work, in which he outlines his central argument for a pedagogy of liberation, is *Pedagogy of the Oppressed* (1970). Following from liberation theology, Freire's assumptions about what development communication should do are radically different from the assumptions of development projects under modernization, which emphasize the transmission of messages to support a persuasive goal, a goal believed to be in the best interests of "target" audiences.

First, from liberation theology, particularly Teilhard de Chardin,[2] Freire assumes that people innately want to become fully human, which means free from internal and external forms of oppression. Hence, the central purpose of development should be liberation from oppression. But what is oppression? Oppression is not the same as dissatisfaction or unhappiness, but rather is complex and systemic. It has been defined as the state of being caught among systemically related "forces and barriers" that restrict one's options, "immobilize," "mold" and "reduce" (Frye 1983: 2).

Sources of oppression are many; they are external, internal (psychological), and they are often closely entwined in that externally imposed limitations may affect one's internal sense of empowerment.

Large organizations that aim to persuade and/or to make a profit constitute one significant source of oppression, as their success depends on maintaining a class system such that the privileged few exploit the labor and material needs of the majority. These organizations may certainly include multilateral, bilateral, or non-governmental aid organizations that follow the modernization paradigm. Another major source of oppression, critiqued extensively in Freire's writings, is the traditional system of education, called "banking education," where "knowledge is a gift bestowed by those who consider themselves knowledgeable upon those whom they consider to know nothing." In this system, students are empowered to do little beyond "receiving, filing and storing the deposits" (Freire 1970: 53). This system regards people as passive, malleable beings, who should be prepared to do little beyond adapting to their surroundings via categorizing and applying the knowledge fed to them. Creativity and critical thought are discouraged in banking education, as such capabilities might lead to challenging the status quo and role relations within the system. Banking education works alongside other institutions, including the social welfare system, to maintain class and power relations that do not threaten the positions—or possessions—of the oppressors (Freire 1970).

Freire (1970) argues that teachers, communication specialists, and others who participate in oppressive organizations are just as oppressed as their victims, because such individuals do not realize that acts of domination are dehumanizing; therefore, they dehumanize themselves in the process. In reality, a teacher's—or communication specialist's—credibility can never exist on its own merit. "The teacher's thinking is authenticated only by the authenticity of the students' thinking" (Freire 1970: 58). It is against authentic human nature to relate from a position of repressive control.

Given these and additional assumptions, Freire builds an argument for a *dialogic* process of liberation. Consistent with liberation theology, he argues that individuals have the internal capacity to develop themselves on their own terms, but need relationships to recognize and act on this capacity. Relationality is never instantaneous, but requires a process of communication (or education). Communication involves shared meaning between people. It also includes spiritual practice, or communication with ultimacy according to the religious tradition involved. As a relational process, communication may be unequal and exploitative, or it may be equitable and empowering for all participants.

Therefore, according to Freire, development communication should be practiced *not* as message communication but rather as emancipatory dialogue, a particular form of non-exploitative, egalitarian dialogue, which is carried out in an atmosphere of profound love and humility and which progressively examines contexts and experiences of oppression. Freire's concept of dialogue emerged largely from Martin Buber's work, especially Buber's book *I and Thou* (1958). In this book, Buber distinguishes between the *I–Thou* and the *I–It* relationship. The former relationship involves equality, openness, and mutual affirmation, both in conversation and in action:

It is in the actual reaching out to the other, in the affirmation of the otherness of the other, that genuine dialogue takes place. And the act of dialogue is the act of making oneself whole, of freeing oneself from the shackles of individualism and emerging in the full personhood in a community (Thomas 1993: 53).

The latter, the *I–It* relationship, is the opposite, a relationship of inequality, distance, and detachment. Buber (1958) argues that the experience of acceptance and affirmation in the *I–Thou* relationship liberates and strengthens the participants to act. It also leads to communion, which is crucial to the community and to the liberation and development of the community. In contrast, the domination of the *I–It* relationship merely reinforces existing power relations.

Freire (1970) assumed that genuine dialogue in the spirit of Buber's *I and Thou* ultimately frees people and communities to determine their own futures. Freire labeled this radical outcome *conscientização* (conscientization), which has been translated from Portuguese to mean, "learning to perceive social, political, and economic contradictions, and to take action against the oppressive elements of reality" (Freire 1970: 17). Ideally, participants in dialogue should include not just so-called disadvantaged groups, but everyone involved in systems of oppression. However, participation in emancipatory dialogue is not easy if taken seriously, as expanded consciousness leads to potentially transformative choices, hence risk, change, and loss.

So, for Freire, development communication ideally is emancipatory dialogue that leads to expanded consciousness and power. Freire assumed that once people got in touch with their sources of oppression, as well as their sources of power, they would then be able to determine their own solutions—both collectively and individually. His many books specify varieties of interpersonal and small group methodologies that enable participants to identify and explore issues that have meaning for them.

It is important to recognize that many people who draw on Freire remain secular in their assumptions. Additionally, consistent arguments are made by feminists and Third World scholars who believe in the importance of context-based dialogue as a means of challenging unequal power relations, as we will discuss in some detail in Chapter 9.[3] Yet, the theological origins of Freire's ideas are clear. For development communication practice, the central focus should be face-to-face emancipatory dialogue. The success of the awakening process via dialogue requires spiritual practice, which is also communication, though a form of communication seldom examined by Western communication specialists. The assumption, from theology, is that spiritual practice by individuals and groups taps resources that provide the necessary energy and motivation for change. Awakening via face-to-face dialogue is crucial. But, awakening suggests personal change that requires divine as well as human assistance.

This chapter shows just how central the combination of dialogic communication, spiritual practice, and other forms of religious communication may become in development strategy. Three examples are discussed in some detail below. The first two are broad umbrella movements with regional, national, and grassroots components: the Base Ecclesial Community (CEB) Movement in Brazil, a movement motivated by Christian, usually Roman Catholic, religious beliefs; and the Sarvodaya Movement in Sri Lanka, grounded in Buddhist and Hindu beliefs, and including other traditions as well. The third example is an ongoing "Family Life Education" project in Ghana, involving numerous religious organizations, each of which largely determines project goals and strategies. The focus in this chapter is on the Muslim component of the project.

BASE ECCLESIAL COMMUNITY MOVEMENT IN BRAZIL

In Latin America, liberation theology is largely manifest in the emergence of *base ecclesial communities* or *comunidades de base* (CEBs). These communities of worship, social analysis, and activism have played important roles in development for liberation throughout the continent. Dawson (1999) emphasizes that the evolution and character of these communities have varied from country to country. Brazil provides a good case study of some of the key factors involved, as it eventually produced many of the greatest intellectual and activist leaders of the liberation theology movement, including Paolo Freire.[4]

For many decades, Roman Catholicism gained steady headway in Brazil and was transmitted unchallenged to new generations. The post-World War II years of the 1950s brought rapid urbanization and accompanying demographic shifts, as well as population growth in general. Protestantism began securing converts, especially among the wealthier classes. Additionally, the Cold War plus the geographic proximity of Cuba resulted in a perceived communist threat by both the government and the church hierarchy (Dawson 1999).

A severe shortage of priests accompanied all these changes. As priests are essential to the sacraments in Catholicism, people in outlying areas often had to wait months to practice key elements of their faith. To both address the priest shortage and help sustain Catholic tradition and communities, a "catechetical experiment" was initiated in the 1950s. The experiment involved selecting and training lay people to gather the faithful several times per week and lead prayer meetings, called "priestless masses." Crude houses were built for these meetings. As time went by, these buildings were used for much more than prayer. The broad secular community increasingly used them for many additional purposes, including food co-operatives and non-religious social events. The catechetical experiment initially produced around 475 such meeting houses in Brazil (Dawson 1999).

Dawson (1999) and Cook (1985) trace how the proliferation of meeting houses combining religious and non-religious events under lay leadership was very important in setting the foundation for the base ecclesial community as a place combining Christian faith and social activity. The Second Vatican (Vatican II) Council in Rome (1962–65) under Pope John XXIII further reinforced an enhanced role for the laity in church leadership, and called for greater participation by all via the reduced use of Latin and increased use of local culture in religious practice. Especially significant was Vatican II's call for the decentralization of large parish structures to foster greater intimacy, i.e., the creation of communities within communities. Vatican II was followed by the issuing of follow-up documents and responses, showing how the church on each continent and in each country would implement the new ideas.

In Latin America, the idea of the Christian base community was formally sanctioned at the Second General Conference of Latin American Bishops held at Medellín, Colombia in August 1968. Hence, in much of Latin America, including Brazil, plans were drawn up to transform large parishes "into a confederation of small base communities," a confederation already established in many places because of the earlier experiments. Hence, these base communities now were considered official church infrastructure. In Brazil, by the mid-1970s, there were an estimated 40,000 base communities in about 40 dioceses (Dawson 1999: 114). This number grew to more than 100,000 by the mid-1980s (Cook 1985).

The political and activist role of the base communities in Brazil began evolving in the late 1960s through the mid-1970s following the coup of 1964, which replaced a democratic government with a repressive military dictatorship. Thousands were arrested and tortured or killed, unions were banned, and censorship became absolute. Hence, traditional avenues for protest were completely closed. Pastoral workers at the base increasingly recognized the importance of spiritual communities for political consciousness-raising via biblical analysis, as well as meeting ongoing spiritual and material needs. It was not sufficient to merely pray and carry out church rituals, but to connect words and rituals to social organization and change.

In 1975, the first national meeting of base community leaders in Brazil was held.[5] This and subsequent national meetings helped reveal common issues and transform the base communities into a national movement that lobbied for progressive social change. Additionally, intellectuals, including Leonard Boff, Carlos Mesters, Gustavo Gutiérrez, and many others attended these meetings as both students of the movement and advisers. The meetings helped them further articulate the tenets of liberation theology, foregrounding the needs of the poor and minimizing the role of church tradition and hierarchy. Two highly influential books that emerged from papers developed as a part of these meetings were *Ecclesiogenesis: The Base Communities Reinvent the Church* (Boff 1986); and *Defenseless Flower: A New Reading of the Bible* (Mesters 1989). Ultimately, the CEB movement played a major role in overthrowing the military government of Brazil and restoring democratic elections by 1986.

As Dawson, Cook, and others describe, the intellectual, spiritual, and political leaders of the liberation theology movement in Latin America and elsewhere have embraced their positions in opposition to the government on the one hand, and the church hierarchy on the other only at great sacrifice and personal risk. During the period from the mid-1960s to the mid-1970s, many activist educators and pastoral leaders were imprisoned and martyred for their opposition to the government. Paolo Freire was among those arrested for subversive activities following the military coup of 1964.[6]

Although the Catholic Church initially supported the CEB movement and associated theological writings, this began to change as theologians increasingly criticized church hierarchy. For instance, Leonoardo Boff (1986) was censured and silenced by the Catholic Church for arguing for the application of democratic principles to church structures (Dawson 1999).

The CEB practice in Brazil has changed somewhat over time. Protestant base communities that have much in common with Roman Catholic CEBs have emerged (Cook 1985, 1994).

Additionally, following open presidential elections in 1986 and increased democratization in general, issues of party politics and unionization have moved away from CEBs to other, more appropriate channels in society. These changes have led many to describe CEBs today as less concerned with political than with spiritual issues. Nonetheless, the CEB movement continues to have considerable grassroots and national relevance in Brazil. As Dawson (1999: 124) points out, Brazil's "politics of democracy continues to rest upon the unbridled exploitation of the many by a small minority." Brazil continues to struggle with a large poor population in rural areas and in cities. In contrast to the elite and middle classes, these impoverished millions experience unemployment or inadequate pay, poor housing, poor schooling, illiteracy, and inadequate health care. A large number of homeless children struggle daily to survive in contexts of violence and with few sources of material or spiritual support. Hence, there remains an important grassroots and national role for the CEBs in Brazil, as elsewhere in Latin America.

The CEB process is profoundly non-hierarchical. Typical meetings use a three-part methodology, following an opening prayer. In addition, meetings involve a process of dialogue consistent with Freire's teachings. The three-part methodology, first encouraged at the Medellín conference of 1968 has been called "See–Judge–Act" (Cook 1985; Dawson 1999). In the seeing phase, each individual is invited to share his or her concerns or troubling experiences from the previous week. These concerns are often communal in nature, including issues of malnutrition, illness, sanitation, or poor working conditions. Next, in the judging phase of the meeting, a passage from scripture is typically read aloud and discussed in light of experiences shared in phase one, especially experiences of hardship, suffering, and oppression. The judging phase is further extended by a reflection given by one member of the community, who synthesizes and summarizes the points made in the previous discussion. Another follow-up discussion seeks to further examine the scripture for ideas on how to address the community's need via short-term and long-term actions.

If the seeing and judging phases are successful in providing spiritual and community acceptance, encouragement, affirmation, and inner strength, these phases are naturally replaced by an action phase in the days following the meeting. Individuals become motivated to apply their new insights in concrete action in their neighborhoods. They no longer perceive themselves as passive victims, but feel confident to act, based on the collective experience and energy provided by the CEB and the shared belief that this is what the gospel demands.

This simple description of CEB process masks the very real difficulties encountered in actual practice. Carlos Mesters (1983) outlines some of the obstacles that must be overcome, obstacles that Freire also wrote about in his many books. Illiteracy is a major constraint, as Bible reading and analysis are central to the CEB process. There are many ways to overcome this, including using traditional forms of communication such as songs, stories, pictures, and plays. Another obstacle is a "slavish literalism" in interpreting the text. It takes much practice before participants understand how to make interpretations that are sensible for their own circumstances. Most participants come to the CEB meetings expecting to be taught in an authoritarian manner, as in their past experiences with clergy, teachers, and other experts. Often they actively resist the idea that they might have knowledge and information of value:

> You often hear people say something like this: "I don't know anything. You or Father should do the talking. You're the ones who know things. We folks don't know anything" (Mesters 1983: 125).

Freire similarly describes the self-deprecation of the poor:

> They call themselves ignorant and say the "professor" is the one who has the knowledge and to whom they should listen. The criteria of knowledge imposed upon them are the conventional ones. "Why don't you," said a peasant participating in a culture circle, "explain the

pictures first? That way it'll take less time and won't give us a headache." Almost never do they realize that they, too, "know things" they have learned in their relations with the world and with other women and men. Given the circumstances that have produced their duality, it is only natural that they distrust themselves (Freire 1970: 45).

It is only as the oppressed begin to both recognize their own areas of strength and experience and the vulnerabilities in their oppressors, that they gain confidence in their own interpretations and conclusions. These insights are attained through a process of prayer and critical dialogue, followed by action. This is the process of critical pedagogy, grounded in liberation theology. It is also the CEB process, with Biblical scripture as the catalyst.

SARVODAYA SHRAMADANA MOVEMENT IN SRI LANKA

Like the base ecclesial movement in Latin America, the Sarvodaya Shramadana Movement in Sri Lanka has been well established for decades at the village level throughout the country. It is grounded in a mix of Sinhalese Buddhism, and Gandhian interpretations of Hinduism.

Certainly other, more recent movements based on engaged Buddhism could be selected for examination here. The indigenous NGO movement in Thailand, started by Sulak Sivaraska, would be an especially good choice because of Sivaraska's extensive use of media and grassroots communication empowerment strategies[7] (for descriptions of nine contemporary Buddhist movements in Asia, see Queen and King 1996).

We think the Sri Lankan Sarvodaya Movement remains a useful case study because it has been lauded by many as a model of grassroots, egalitarian, participatory, and environmentally sensitive development, though admittedly it is in crisis now because of the Civil War in Sri Lanka, resistance to its goals by the government, and other internal problems of increased bureaucratization (with growth and the acceptance of foreign aid) that compromise its philosophy. The Movement has been given some attention in development communication as well, where it has been referred to as "beyond development communication,"[8] an "ethical approach," and "a Buddhist approach."[9] It has also been portrayed both in its websites and by scholars as supportive of gender equality and women's advancement.

The Movement began in 1958 when A.T. Ariyaratne first organized a *shramadana* (labor assistance) camp in a poor village. Today the Movement is active in more than 8,600 villages in Sri Lanka, about a third of the villages in the country, and involving many thousands of volunteers and specialists.[10]

The goals and processes of the Sarvodaya Shramadana Movement have many similarities to those of the CEB movement. In essence, the primary goals are individual and collective awakening. These are accomplished via the voluntary sharing of time, resources, and labor. Spiritual practice involving meditation in the Buddhist tradition is an important feature of the Movement. Yet, the Movement also aims to be inclusive and affirming of all religious traditions.

Inclusivity as a central feature of the Sarvodaya Shramadana Movement may be traced directly to Mahatma Gandhi, who first coined the term *sarvodaya*, meaning "welfare for all."[11] As discussed in Chapter 7, Gandhi remained a Hindu, but his philosophy and activism drew on his deep knowledge of several religious traditions and certain universal truths that cross most religions. For Gandhi, sarvodaya was based upon the concept of *swadeshi*, which expresses the spirit of service in the context of one's immediate surroundings in order to help and to elevate the lives of one's neighbors. His "gospel" of sarvodaya emphasized the unity of all people and the need to serve one's neighbor as a necessary part of spiritual life. Gandhi did not believe that spiritual law works in a field of its own. It is actually operationalized through the ordinary activities of life thus impacting the economic, social, and political arenas.[12]

Adopting both the name and philosophy of Gandhi's sarvodaya, the Movement in Sri Lanka uses it in conjunction with the Sinhalese and Sanskrit term *shramadana*, meaning "the voluntary sharing of time, resources, thoughts, energy and labor."[13] As we will narrate below, the idea of *shramadana* came first, and was joined with *sarvodaya* in the early years of the Movement's evolution.

Ariyaratne: The Founder of the Movement

Ariyaratne, the founder of the Sri Lankan Movement, was born on November 5, 1931, the third of six children and first son born to Ahangama Tummahewage Hendrick Jinadasa and Roslina Gajadeera Arachchi.

Ariyaratne's father Jinadasa was a well-educated and deeply religious businessman from the village of Unawatuna, near the southern tip of Sri Lanka; and his mother also came from a respectable family in the village of Pelana in the central part of the island (Liyanage 1988). While Roslina was pregnant with Ariyaratne, an astrologer predicted that her third child would be a son, that he would be sickly as a child, and he would eventually serve the world in important ways—but as a layman, not as a Buddhist monk (Liyanage 1988).

As predicted, Ariyaratne was a frail child. He was also bright and devoted. He attended the Sinhala Buddhist Mixed School through third grade, learning quickly and also spending much time at the temple. In 1939, Ariyaratne's father moved the family to the town of Meddekanda near Colombo, where Ariyaratne advanced quickly at Sinhala Buddhist Mixed School, skipping several grades. After graduation he enrolled at the Buona Vista College at Unawatuna, where he began studying English and also developing an interest in social welfare issues and communist politics (Liyanage 1988). In 1952, Ariyaratne obtained a teaching post at Buona Vista College to assist with his family's finances. Later, he was invited to study economics at Matara and earned a degree, after which he entered the Teachers' Training College at Maharagama, a suburb of Colombo, in 1956 (Liyanage 1988).

Ariyaratne's primary interest in community development (versus teaching) began crystallizing at the Teachers' Training College and in his subsequent teaching position at Nalanda College. Inspired by the Indian philosopher Krishnamurthy, among others, and while still studying to be a teacher, Ariyaratne started an organization called the Council for the Development of Underdeveloped Communities. Later, at Nalanda College in Colombo, Ariyaratne was elected vice-president of the Social Service League and proposed a program to help villages. He carefully selected an impoverished, isolated, low-caste village named Kanatoluwa and began preparing his students to assist with the project. In December of 1958, hundreds of shramadana workers arrived at Kanatoluwa to begin work, including digging wells, building roads and schools, improving agricultural productivity, and starting small businesses. The success of this camp and accompanying publicity led to similar camps in Sinhala areas and later in the Tamil areas (Liyanage 1988).

Despite the success of these early projects, Ariyaratne was not fully satisfied with their philosophical foundations and methodologies. Hence, in 1959, he went to India for advice from leaders and educators drawing on Gandhian philosophy. There he became acquainted with the concept of sarvodaya, quickly realizing that "this term could well reflect a Buddhist conception of human emancipation" (Liyanage 1988: 57). In April 1960, Ariyaratne officially changed the name of the movement to "Lanka Jatika Sarvodaya Shramadana Movement" (Liyanage 1988: 67), which is usually shortened to Sarvodaya Shramadana Movement or simply the Sarvodaya Movement.[14]

Sarvodaya Philosophy, Goals, and Practice

As noted at the outset, the Movement has spread throughout Sri Lanka, encompassing a third of the villages in the country. Sarvodaya philosophy, goals, and practice have evolved over the years and are now firmly grounded in Buddhist values and encoded in a set of goals and a series of recommended stages.

Buddhist teachings that undergird the movement include those discussed in Chapter 7, especially three key principles of reality that enable individuals to find a "Middle Path" to happiness: that life involves suffering, that the cause of suffering is human ego and desire, and that suffering can be ended only by achieving freedom from human desire. In addition to recognizing these truths, those involved in the Movement are encouraged to follow the Eight Noble Steps to achieve enlightenment and relief from suffering: right views, right thoughts, right speech, right action, right livelihood, right effort, right mindfulness, and right concentration. In order to successfully follow these steps and achieve the divine state, the Buddha stressed the importance of certain qualities of the heart: *metta* (loving kindness), *karuna* (compassion), *mudita* (altruistic joy), and *upekkha* (equanimity) (Mahathera 1998). All of these Buddhist tenets constitute key reference points for the Sarvodaya Shramadana Movement (Kantowski 1980; Liyanage 1988). At the same time, it is assumed that the central idea of sarvodaya, i.e., welfare for all, is at the core of all religions. Therefore, the Movement is not just for Sinhala Buddhists, but for everyone:

> Hindus, Muslims and Christians all belong to this common national culture. They have lived in friendship and harmony except on a very few occasions when foreign interests have promoted dissensions among them. Every human being is fundamentally recognized as an equal with any other human being under the Buddhist principle of *Samanath-matha* or equality (Liyanage 1988: 153).

Liyanage outlines the goals in detail. The primary objectives of the Sarvodaya Shramadana Movement are fourfold:

1. develop the [character and priorities of] youth in keeping with the values of the culture and ongoing cultural change;
2. awaken rural communities to . . . social change and help them become agents of such change in keeping with their own culture and interests;
3. achieve national integration by giving opportunities for all irrespective of caste, race, religion or language to contribute their share in the common effort of nation-building based on the principles of truth, non-violence and self-denial and for the objective of realizing fundamental human rights and social justice; and
4. bring about collaboration with people and communities with similar ideas and progressive programmes [globally] for world peace, human brotherhood and development cooperation between basic groups (Liyanage 1988: 143–44).

To accomplish these goals, particularly the first, individual personality development is crucial, called *paurushodaya*. This entails two forms of liberation. The first is liberation from internal character flaws ("defilements") and from feelings of low self-worth. Second, paurushodaya means a growing consciousness of unjust socio-economic forms of oppression that keep the poor majority from improving their lives and experiencing freedom. Liyanage points out that the Sarvodaya Shramadana Movement cannot succeed without the leadership and participation of individuals fully dedicated to their own personal liberation, as well as the liberation of others. Consistent with liberation theology, the Movement assumes that individual and collective liberation requires a combined process of spiritual practice and direct service to those in need (Liyanage 1988).

The process of combining spiritual practice and voluntary shared labor is operationalized primarily at the village level, where the goal is community self-sufficiency and empowerment (Ratnapala n.d.). Sarvodaya Shramadana's website details the five-stage village development model, with numerous examples and photographs[15] (see Figure 8.1).

At stage 1 of the model, the beginning of the project, a village requests assistance, and Sarvodaya volunteers arrive to introduce the philosophy and goals of the Movement and the concept of shared labor camps. Additionally, leadership and participation are encouraged. At stage 2,

Figure 8.1
Five-Stage Model of the Sarvodaya Shramadana Movement in Sri Lanka

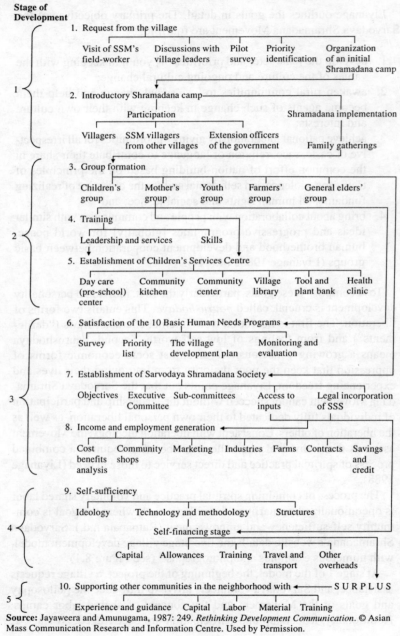

Source: Jayaweera and Amunugama, 1987: 249. *Rethinking Development Communication.* © Asian Mass Communication Research and Information Centre. Used by Permission.

functional groups are formed according to demographics that meaning-fully indicate share needs. Typical groups are mothers, children, youth, elders, and farmers. Training programs are developed consistent with the cultural values of each of these groups. Special attention is given to the youth group with the establishment of a youth development center. At stage 3, a legally registered Sarvodaya Shramadana Society emerges to coordinate the activities of all groups. Groups prioritize their basic needs, assess their resources, and launch work projects accordingly. Beyond basic survival needs, the Sarvodaya Society generates projects to increase community employment and economic development. At stage 4, the community becomes increasingly self-sufficient due to the creation of income-generating activities, alongside social development programs to meet basic needs. At the fifth stage, the community has become econom-ically self-sufficient. An economic surplus results and is used to assist other communities that are not yet as far along in the Sarvodaya process.

In essence, the Sarvodaya camps aim to find ways to address a com-bination of spiritual needs, basic survival needs, and economic needs, eventually leading to community self-sufficiency. The community is also able and motivated to assist other villages that are beginning the process. Sarvodaya recognizes that economic development cannot be sustainable unless individuals undergo a personal transformation as well. Hence, personal awakening is a fundamental goal and accomplished via the com-bination of spiritual practice and shared work. Every day at the Sarvodaya Shramadana camp begins and ends with sharing and meditation. In fact, sharing and mediation are assumed important throughout the day and are inseparable from shared work. As is also true of the Base Ecclesial Community Movement, Sarvodaya recognizes the dual importance of addressing internally and externally imposed oppression, and the role of shared spirituality and shared work in the development process.[16]

Sarvodaya and Women

The Sarvodaya Movement has taken place in a country where women are considered inferior to men and are encouraged to focus on traditional roles as wives and mothers. This comes from centuries of Sinhalese tradition and mythology that assume that females are of lower birth than males (Risseeuw 1988: 273). These traditions also prescribe "virtues of submissiveness, motherhood and self-effacing caring [as] the highest ideals attainable in womanhood" (p. 273). Additionally, there are many examples in Sinhalese history of "woman transgressing her womanly boundaries, asserting her sexuality, her will-power and her desire to rule, and thereby leading to the downfall of her family or even her people" (Risseeuw 1988: 273). These traditions have remained pervasive even though women played an active role in anti-colonial and anti-imperialist struggles and there has been an active, though marginalized, feminist movement in Sri Lanka (Abeysekeera 1991; Jayawardana 1986; Pace 1993: 53).

In 1978, a separate "Women's Unit" was set up to address gender issues in the movement, following the realization that 75 percent of the unpaid Sarvodaya volunteers were women. This was also a result of influence of the UN Decade for Women. In 1990, the unit became legally independent as the Sarvodaya Women's Movement with the following objectives: to empower women and strengthen their capabilities in their many roles; to provide gender-sensitivity training for Sarvodaya workers; and to increase female representation among Sarvodaya leadership.[17]

Sarvodaya's website says that "Sarvodaya has always fully involved women in its development process." The evidence indicates that this statement is both true and false, depending on the meaning of full involvement. While women constitute the majority of the unpaid volunteers, they remain the minority (12 percent) of District Coordinators. Also, Women's Movement goals as articulated on the website highlight women's traditional roles as mothers: "to ensure the mental and physical well being of children . . . to bring about the total development of women as mothers, social workers, income generators and spiritual leaders."

Thus far, there have been few studies of women's roles in Sarvodaya. Johana Macy spent a year living and working in Sarvodaya Shramadana villages in 1979–80. She reported her own ethnographic research on the overall movement and also the result of an unpublished 1979 study on the role of women by the Sarvodaya Research Institute (Macy 1983). Both studies conclude that "the Movement has succeeded in giving women a prominent role in the 'awakening' of their villages," even while acknowledging that the movement "functions in a patriarchal society, where women have been traditionally discouraged from playing a public role in community affairs" (Macy 1983: 79). Both Macy and the Sarvodaya Research Institute conclude that the work camps often provide women their first opportunity to work side by side with men outside of their extended family circle. The Sarvodaya meetings—including both women only and mixed meetings—encourage women to speak up and share their views. Women also participate actively in leadership training at district centers (Macy 1983: 80–82).

Macy argues that the religious nature of the organization is important in attracting and sustaining women's participation. She gives six reasons for this. First, the Movement's social ethic highlights historical and scriptural evidence of the dignity and equality of women in early Buddhist history and their roles as saints, nuns, and scholars. Second, women have historically been closely associated with local temples in attending rituals, assisting clergy, and maintaining buildings and grounds. Women traditionally have been active in traditional ritual forms of communication that are also used in shramadana camps, including rituals to observe particular days, religious parades, and uses of visual symbols and decorations.[18] Third, Sarvodaya has tried to remain non-partisan. This attracts women, as their fathers and husbands discourage them from becoming involved in partisan organizations. Fourth, the involvement and presence of clergy at camps and meetings reassure parents that it is safe for their daughters to be involved without danger to their reputation or virginity. Fifth, as Sarvodaya does not tolerate drinking or gambling, which are common among men in other settings, women and their families are more drawn to and feel safer in these settings. Sixth, Sarvodaya has started income-generating projects that help women economically (Macy 1983: 82–88).

An unpublished master's thesis based on field research to study both Sarvodaya philosophy and interview women in the Movement reached more complex and nuanced conclusions and suggested the need for further analysis (Pace 1993). The study found that the philosophy is conservative with regard to gender roles. While the Movement does emphasize the necessity of personal transformation for societal transformation, it also idealizes village life, including traditional family life and gender roles therein.[19] These values are evident in Sarvodaya's official literature, including the website for the Women's Movement, noted earlier, and in Ariyaratne's speeches.[20] They are indicated in the fact that women's predominant historic involvement with the Movement is via the overlapping concerns of the mother's group, preschools, and the youth group. The study concluded that the movement is somewhat contradictory. It "remains radical in terms of its ideology around issues of spiritual and community development, yet it is conservative with regard to its perspectives on prescribed roles for men and women. As an organization Sarvodaya has not begun to investigate seriously changing gender constructs in Sri Lankan society" (Pace 1993: 73). Additionally, while village-level income-generating projects have been of genuine economic benefit to individual women, these new responsibilities are merely added to women's domestic and subsistence responsibilities with no change in gender roles. Pace found that these projects reflect a women-in-development versus a deeper, more critical gender-and-development approach to social change and are somewhat out of sync with Sarvodaya's critique of a marketplace economy. Yet the fact that Sarvodaya emphasizes village self-reliance, human development, and ecological balance, constitutes an ongoing challenge to some of the macro-level causes of women's exploitation, even if women are not aware of this. Also women's involvement and leadership in new roles are personally empowering even if these experiences do not result in feminist activism.

Pace's study was preliminary and did not focus explicitly on communication processes within the movement. Also her study did not interview men about gender issues. Further, Pace did not look at Sarvodaya partner organizations. These function to spread the values of the organization and inspire similar efforts in different contexts, as well as to provide financial and technical assistance. For instance, Sarvodaya USA provides a clearinghouse, network, and support resource for all individual and group initiatives that foster the ideals and activities of Sarvodaya.[21] One ongoing Sarvodaya USA endeavor is the creation of "partnership projects" between individual donors in the United States and Sri Lankan women, who wish to start or expand small businesses. The American donor provides $100 or less and the Sri Lankan woman provides the work. Although these investments are essentially donations, the Sri Lankan women treat them as loans and gradually repay them to the Sarvodaya Bank. Repayments allow loans to other women, so that the effects of one donation may be multiplied throughout a community.[22] It seems likely that these partner organizations and resulting global Internet connections between women have had mutual effects that warrant investigation. Women's roles in encouraging a recently launched Sarvodaya peace initiative would be important to look at as well, especially given evidence elsewhere of women's rejection of violence locally and globally.

Peace Initiatives

Finally, we note that Sarvodaya has recently tried to find ways to encourage peace in Sri Lanka, which has endured a long Civil War between the Sinhalese majority and the Tamil minority. On August 29, 1999,

Sarvodaya launched a national peace effort in the form of a "Peace Meditation Programme" with over 200,000 people participating in the program. This project assumed that the key to national peace is fostering inner peace within individuals: "Persons and groups lacking peace of mind hang onto [parochial attitudes relating to] nationality, language, religion, politics, ethnic groups, high status, low positions, etc., and engage themselves in anti-society acts of crime, terrorism, and war."[23] Hence, the project aimed to publicize and lead mass peace meditation sessions that encouraged a meditational focus on values such as non-violence, loving kindness, honesty, temperance, generosity, and daily spiritual practice. Additionally, Sarvodaya's peace efforts have moved beyond meditation to concrete involvement in potentially volatile situations. For instance, on December 21, 1999, presidential elections was held without major incidents of violence. Over 500 Sarvodaya volunteers risked their lives in joining other volunteers (from the Peoples Alliance for Free Elections) to help safeguard the peace during the voting process.[24]

Communication Process

In sum, the Sarvodaya Movement, like the Base Ecclesial Community Movement in Brazil and elsewhere in Latin America, aims for personal and communal awakening as prerequisites for liberation and self-sufficiency. Development communication cannot be separated from the Buddhist values and spiritual practices that ground the Movement. Hence, communication means the sharing of oneself via daily meditation, dialogue, and communal work, *not* the imposition of messages and goals by outsiders. Dissanayake compares the Buddhist model of communication as used in the Sarvodaya Movement with the typical Western or Aristotelian model. It is schematically represented in Table 8.1.

The table reveals an interactive, dynamic two-way process, contrasting sharply with the one-way, top-down Western model introduced by Berlo (1960), among others. Thus, in every way, the Sarvodaya Shramadana Movement, like the Base Ecclesial Community Movement in Latin America, represents a very different approach when compared to conventional models used in development. The individuals involved in the sharing process and their context determine whether and how the five-stage process evolves, as individual awakening and community self-sufficiency cannot be achieved otherwise.

Table 8.1
Western and Buddhist Models of Communication

Aristotelian Model	Buddhist Model
1. Emphasis on communicator	1. Emphasis on receiver
2. Influence a key notion	2. Understanding a key notion
3. Focus on control	3. Focus on choice
4. Emphasis on outward process	4. Emphasis on both outward and inward processes
5. Relationship between communicator and receiver asymmetrical	5. Relationship between communicator and receiver symmetrical
6. Stress on intellect.	6. Stress on empathy

Source: Dissanayake 1984: 49. "A Buddhist Approach to Development." In Wang and Dissanayake (Eds.), *Continuity and Change in Communication Systems.* © Ablex Publishers. Used by permission.

FAMILY LIFE EDUCATION IN GHANA

Next, we focus on the Muslim component of a nationwide Family Life Education Project involving religious organizations in Ghana. The Project differs from the previous two case studies in that it is not a movement initiated at the grassroots by liberation leaders. Rather it is a Project initiated and funded by the UNFPA, a multilateral funding agency. However, the Project is defined and sustained by the commitment of religious leaders with liberation motivations. The Project focuses centrally on issues involving women, including family size, family health, and women's and girls' education. In a 1993 report, the UNFPA gave reasons for initiating the collaboration with religious organizations. These include the fact that almost all Ghanaians are active members of religious organizations, that religious leaders are by far the most credible and influential opinion leaders in Ghanaian communities, and that religious organizations had in the past shown more reliability and accountability with aid money than secular organizations (Amoa and Assimeng 1993).

The Project began in 1990 with three religious groups. Since 1994, the number of groups involved has remained at eight.[25] The Project views religious organizations as active collaborators in the struggle for family welfare, which may include population intervention. It recognizes that most people in developing countries, including women, are profoundly involved with the religion of their community. Therefore, religious roles and experiences must be affirmed and centralized in Project support. It additionally challenges conventional views that mainline religions oppose interventions in family issues, and shows that many religious leaders and their followers are practical, care deeply about inequality, are open to new ways of thinking, and may be motivated to find new ways of interpreting religious theologies and attitudes.

When the Muslim component of the Project began in 1990, it was considered taboo to discuss family planning or anything to do with sex in a Muslim community in Ghana. Also, Muslims have often focused considerable attention on the Prophet's command to multiply so he would have many followers by the Day of Judgment. Yet, Muslim leaders were very concerned about the marginalized status of most Muslims in Ghana, and the extreme poverty that characterizes most Muslim communities. In these communities, family sizes are typically very large and there are high rates of teen pregnancy, child delinquency, drug and alcohol abuse, HIV infection, malnutrition, and school drop-out, especially among girls. The Project began by gathering together Islamic scholars and teachers to discuss what the Qur'an says about gender roles, family responsibilities, family size, and health issues of concern to Muslims. The initiative for these discussions came from Muslims, not the UNFPA. This is a critical difference from many other projects that have tried to engage religious leaders as opinion leaders, but not at their initiative and not in a manner grounded in the sacred text of the religion.[26] While most of the Islamic scholars and teachers who met to study the Qur'an were men, some leaders of Muslim and national women's groups were involved in the discussions as well.

All of this analysis led to a number of conclusions. First, the leaders agreed that while the Prophet does want many followers on the Day of Judgment, there is also evidence that he wants *quality* followers and not illiterate drug addicts and delinquents. It is faith and justice that will reap rewards not many children. Additionally, Allah prefers fewer people of faith and character to vast numbers of "unbelievers."

The leaders found nothing in the Qur'an that forbids limiting family size. Rather, they found additional verses that can be interpreted as support for family planning, especially verses that mandate parents to raise healthy, well-educated, and responsible children, neglecting none, and to avoid taking on more than they can manage.[27] This may mean delaying marriage and childbearing, and not having more children than can be properly cared for. Likewise, polygamy may result in an unmanageable household. Further, the leaders found nothing in the Qur'an that indicates a preference in education or vocational training for boys. And they found absolutely nothing supporting practices that may threaten the health of girls such as teen marriage or female circumcision. Rather they interpreted the Qur'an as directing parents to treat their children equally, meaning that girls and boys have an equal right to life, health, education, and training. They even extended this to training in sports and self-defense, an unusual stance in a country where girls in general are not encouraged to play sports.[28]

Below is a quote from just one of many speeches to Muslim leaders in Ghana by Chief Alhaji Baba Issa, who directs the Project. The speech contains many references to chapters and versus in the Qur'an:

Parents are held responsible for the social, cultural and moral training of their children, as well as for their . . . health care. Those unable to undertake these responsibilities should postpone marriage as admonished by the Holy Qur'an . . . . Islam enjoined us to have children but it insists at the same time that they should be good and righteous which requires an intensive effort to raise them correctly. The ability to raise children correctly is an inherent requirement of marriage in Islam. It is high time for Muslim communities to accord the Muslim woman her rightful place in society. We can only succeed in this effort by giving the Muslim girl the requisite education and training without discrimination. It is also our duty as Muslim leaders to disabuse the minds of some uninformed Muslims of the misconception they have about the status of women in Islam. The future of the Muslim community depends on the health, intelligence and quality of its children. It must therefore be emphasized that Muslim children should be born healthy and to healthy mothers and should be correctly raised with adequate education. These tenets can be met more adequately when the family size is manageable . . . . Family planning in this sense is not incompatible with nature and it is not disagreeable to the national conscience, and it is not forbidden by religious law.[29]

Following considerable dialogue to make and document these interpretations and to establish tentative goals,[30] the Project has continued to hold regular workshops in every region of Ghana for Muslim community leaders, including Imams and leaders of women's and youth groups. These leaders in turn facilitate discussions among members of their own constituency groups. The many workshops and discussions aim to provide an environment for open dialogue about religious and personal values, especially in relation to family size, female circumcision, HIV/AIDS, and gender inequality in education and health care. As with the CEB groups in Brazil, where the Bible is discussed, community members have the opportunity to critically discuss the Qur'an, often for the first time, and to openly consider new interpretations that may challenge their traditional views and lead to a better life.

Imams are especially important in these discussions as they meet with community members at neighborhood mosques five times a day for prayer. On Fridays, they meet at a larger mosque for a longer service and a sermon. Imams are encouraged to use these daily prayer meetings and the Friday gathering as opportunities for dialogue about family issues and problems and perceived connections to Islam. Leaders of Muslim women's groups are crucial as well, as most women in the community belong to them and meet regularly. Also, volunteers from the community are recruited and trained to work with families directly in providing counseling, as well as contraceptives if requested. Women are preferred as volunteers. Imams, women's leaders, and other volunteers additionally speak in schools and other group settings using a variety of communication strategies, including dialogue and discussion, counseling sessions, drama, storytelling, and song, plus more conventional forms of communication like posters, brochures, and films.

In sum, like the CEB movement in Brazil, and the Sarvodaya Shramadana Movement in Sri Lanka, the Muslim Family Life Education Project in Ghana (and the projects of the eight other religious groups) centralizes religious values and religious practice in the process of facilitating individual and community awakening and development. The Project recognizes that issues of family tap fundamental values that in Ghana, as elsewhere, are enmeshed with religious belief. Religious leaders, in turn, have been willing to reconsider family values that have been attributed to Islam and that harm and oppress Muslims and Muslim communities, especially women and girls. They have been willing to openly examine how family problems are experienced by different groups in their community and analyze the sacred text of Islam in light of these problems. They have actively reconsidered the stories and messages in the text, and have found persuasive openings to challenge conventional beliefs about family size, gender equity, and gender roles. Following reinterpretation, they have been willing to go further and collaborate with leaders of women's and youth groups to engage in dialogue and consciousness-raising with the larger community. Contexts for dialogue have included prayer meetings, workshops, schools, counseling centers, and private homes. Strategies have been numerous and certainly have included spiritual practice as all meetings begin with prayers. Muslim women's groups and their leaders have been active collaborators in the Project.

There are many questions about this Project that require further investigation. For instance, there are numerous groups besides the UNFPA and Muslims involved as partners in this Project, including other nongovernmental organizations, and multilateral and bilateral aid agencies.[31] Some of the contradictions and conflicts between the motives of the groups involved and their consequences for women need examination. For example, one of the groups involved is the Ghana Social Marketing Foundation, which obtains funding and supplies from aid organizations (such as the USAID and the UNFPA), assists with local research, packaging and promotion (e.g., of contraceptives), and informational materials, such as brochures and posters. This organization aims primarily to promote contraceptive sales, not necessarily to engage in dialogue about religious values and family roles. The conflicting motivations have resulted in some tensions and conflicts in carrying out some components of the Project. Additionally, Muslim leaders have found the brochures and posters inconsistent with Muslim images and values and have recruited their own artists to design and pretest new, more culturally relevant materials.[32] These and other problems show that the acceptance of outside funding and input means that projects may create, as well as challenge, barriers to liberation. Hence, individual and communal resistance is a continual struggle not just against the more readily identified sources of oppression, but a struggle to distinguish friend from foe within projects and movements as well.

CONCLUSION

The Base Ecclesial Movement in Brazil, the Sarvodaya Shramadana Movement in Sri Lanka, and the Muslim Family Life Education Project in Ghana all struggle toward common underlying goals—of individual and community awakening, liberation and self-reliance—in ways appropriate for their needs, their cultural contexts and their faith. These goals can never be completely achieved. They constitute ideals for ongoing struggle.

The case studies presented here offer important lessons for development planners and communication specialists. Few would disagree that the consideration of cultural and community context must include religious context. However, religion is not a resistance point to be overcome; nor is it a cultural tool for manipulation in persuasive campaigns. It is an integral part of individual and community identity, offering powerful resources for liberation and change. Successfully tapping and directing, these resources must involve a process of dialogue at the grassroots, dialogue that is egalitarian and inclusive, as Freire so eloquently conceptualized and outlined in *Pedagogy of the Oppressed* and his many other works.

SUMMARY

The tenets of liberation theology, discussed in Chapter 7, have been effectively translated for development communication and education practice by Paolo Freire (1970). As liberation theology assumes that attaining full humanity means freedom from oppression, in both its external and internal forms, Freire begins with the premise that the purpose of development is liberation. Liberation requires a process of *conscientização*, i.e., the individual's increasing awareness of oppression and accompanying actions to overcome it. Freire proceeds from there to argue that major sources of oppression are educators and communicators who aim to bestow their knowledge on ignorant and passive recipients or students, i.e., "targets." This system of "banking education" merely reinforces existing power structures and does nothing for the empowerment, awakening, and liberation of either the oppressors or the oppressed. Freire proposes replacing banking education, persuasive communication, and similar processes with emancipatory dialogue, dialogue grounded in equality, mutual trust, and affirmation. To the extent that oppressors participate in dialogue, they will be liberated as well, as the oppression of other human beings is dehumanizing to all involved. The success of the awakening process, i.e., the process of conscientization, requires spiritual practice alongside emancipatory dialogue, as a source of direction, insight, motivation, and energy to pursue change and resist oppression.

It is important to recognize that the most basic and fundamental expressions of religious practice, including prayer and meditation, *are* forms of communication. Most people globally do find these modes of communication perhaps the most empowering in sustaining faith and hope, and providing the inspiration and strength for action. Religious practice also provides a framework for community participation and plays a major role in defining communities. Hence, prayer and meditation require consideration, respect, and attention for their roles in the sustainability and viability of many projects and programs. Yet, these forms of communication, as practiced individually and in groups, are seldom examined by development communication scholars and practitioners. This chapter has sought to begin addressing this gap in the literature.

The case studies examined in this chapter show how the values of four major belief systems, Christianity, Buddhism, Hinduism, and Islam, have been used to ground liberation approaches to development and development communication in Brazil, Sri Lanka, and Ghana, respectively. While the origins, political-economic contexts, and other circumstances of the case studies vary considerably, along with the religions involved, all three prioritize individual and community awakening via dialogue at the grassroots. Religious leaders with liberation motivations have played crucial roles in facilitating dialogue and accompanying actions. Spiritual practice is central to each as well. Also, all have resisted the input of outsiders with inconsistent values. Finally, as indicated in the Sarvodaya case study, gender equity does not always accompany progressive spirituality. Social disparities in society usually require extra effort and attention to be adequately addressed by development planners and participants.

1. Others who applied liberation ideas to communication processes in development include Ivan Illich, Juan Diaz-Bordenave, and Francis Berrigan. However, few would disagree that Freire is the most well-known. Freire passed away in 1997.

2. See Thomas (1993) for a discussion of the theological and philosophical under-pinnings of Freire's ideas. Teilhard de Chardin was among many who influenced Freire's thought.

3. For feminist arguments, see hooks (1984, 1989) and Weiler (1988).

4. It is not our intention to suggest that the Base Communities in Brazil are the only groups engaged in such transformative social change. There is a rich variety of other movements. For example, grassroots groups such as the Movement of Landless Peasants in Brazil are prominent actors working toward empowerment goals.

5. This conference was held at Vitória (Espírito Santo), January 6–8, 1975.

6. Freire spent 70 days in jail and was subsequently expelled from Brazil. Freire began his first book while in prison, *Education as the Practice of Freedom* (published later as *Education for Critical Consciousness* 1973).

7. See Servaes (1999) for an excellent discussion of communication and culture, including Buddhist culture, in Thailand.

8. A.T. Ariyaratne (1987).

9. W. Dissanayake (1984)

10. See Sarvodaya, "The Sarvodaya Shramadana Movement of Sri Lanka," http://www.sarvodaya.org/index.html. Previous essays on the Movement in the context of development communication include: Ariyaratne 1987 and Dissanayake 1984, 1991.

11. In Sanskrit, *Sarva* means all and *Udaya* means awakening. Gandhi's translation was "the welfare of all." The works have similar meanings in the Sinhala language as well (Liyanage 1988).

12. See Sarvodaya, "The Gospel of Sarvodaya," http://hagpuronline.com/momgbook/Chap45.html. See also Gandhi (1967).

13. See Sarvodaya, http://www.sarvodaya.org/Library/Pamphlets.pamphlet1/name.html.

14. Lanka refers to Sri Lanka and *Jatika* means national. Hence the new name was Sri Lanka National Sarvodaya Shramadana Movement.

15. See Sarvodaya, http://www.sarvodaya.org/index.html. See also Ariyaratne (1987).

16. See Sarvodaya, "A Day in a Sarvodaya Shramadana Camp: Sharing and Meditation," http://www.sarvodaya.org/virualshramadanacamp/sharingandmeditation.html#top.

17. See Sarvodaya, "Project 2000," http://www.sarvodaya.org/Project2000/index.htm.

18. See Colletta, Ewing, and Todd (1982) for a detailed discussion of popular participa-tion in traditional religious activities in Shramadana camps.

19. Buddhist scholar George Bond has also charged that Ariyaratne idealizes village culture and romanticizes ancient village life.

20. An analysis of his speeches, however, shows that they have changed over the years, to show a greater recognition of gender inequality and how traditional roles sustain inequality (Pace 1993: 14, 64–65).

21. See Sarvodaya, "The Mission of Sarvodaya USA," http://www.sarvodaya.org/SUSA/susa.html.

22. See Sarvodaya, "Sarvodaya USA Partnership Projects," http://www.sarvodaya.org/partnerships/index.htm.

23. See Sarvodaya, "Sarvodaya Peace Meditation Programme," http://www.sarvodaya.org/PeaceInitiative/MeditationProgram.htm.

24. See Sarvodaya, "Sarvodaya and the Elections in Sri Lanka," http://www.sarvodaya.org/PeaceInitiative.

25. The three that started the Project are the Muslim Family Counseling Services, the Christian Council of Ghana, and the National Catholic Secretariat. By 1993, seven others were involved: the Adventist Development and Relief Agency; the Ahmadiyya Movement in Islam; the Church of Pentecost; the Ghana Pentecostal Council; the Islamic Research and Reformation Centre; of the Salvation Army; and the Seventh Day Adventists (Amoa and Assimeng 1993). A report dated June 1996 that extended the UNFPA project funding from June 1997 to June 2001, says that the following eight groups have been funded since 1994: the Muslim Family Counseling Services, the Community Development and Youth Advisory Center (for Muslim Youth), the Ghana Pentacostal Church, the Christian Council of Ghana, the National Catholic Secretariat, the Seventh Day Adventist, the Adventist Development Relief Agency, the Salvation Army, the Church of Pentecost, and the Ahmadiyya Muslim Movement (Government of Ghana 1996).

26. For example, see Khan's (1976) discussion of training Imams to be teachers at a rural development academy in Bangladesh.

27. See verses 6:151 and 17:31 in the Qur'an. Additionally, verse 31:14 encourages mothers to nurse for two years, a result of which is greater spacing between children. We credit Ahmed, Amoak, and Sakyi (1996) for assistance in locating verses used to support a manageable family size. See *Al Qur'an* (1984).

28. This was in an address by Alhaji Imoro Baba Issa delivered at the One-day Workshop on Muslim Welfare, Health and Development for Muslim Leaders (n.d.).

29. Welcome address by Alhaji Imoro Baba Issa to the UNFPA/MFCS (Muslim Family Counseling Services) Follow-up Workshop for Muslim leaders in Accra 1996.

30. Goals of the Project have been to educate the Muslim population about the benefits of family planning, about criteria for responsible parenthood, about the causes and prevention of AIDS and other sexually transmitted diseases, and about the benefits of education and vocational training for women and girls. The Project has also aimed to effect behavior change related to educational goals and to set up income-generating projects for women.

31. Other organizations that play roles include the Planned Parenthood Association of Ghana, which reviews budgets and carries out evaluations under the UNFPA, the Inter-Africa Committee for the Eradication of Traditional Practices affecting the Health of Women, the National Council for Women in Development, the Ghanaian Association for Women's Welfare, the Ghana Ministry of Health, and the National AIDS Control Program.

32. Interview with the Chief Alhaji Imoro Baba Issa, who directs the Muslim component of the Project, July 30, 1996.

COMMUNICATION AND EMPOWERMENT

CHAPTER 9

COMMUNICATION STRATEGIES FOR EMPOWERMENT

> People cannot be liberated by a consciousness and
> knowledge other than their own.
>
> Fals-Borda (1991: 14)

In this chapter, we will explore the construct of empowerment. We will examine how the organizational value of communication (as opposed to its transmission value) may be harnessed to help empower marginalized groups and communities. We begin by outlining an ethical perspective on development, also reviewing many points made in previous chapters. We move from there to introduce communitarian theory, as an umbrella framework that may include liberation perspectives, and that also encourages participatory strategies in social change. In particular, we examine participatory action research. We find this approach fruitful as it incorporates liberation assumptions in its methodology, is oriented to social action, and works towards the achievement of empowerment-related outcomes. We seek to find roles for communication in increasing the countervailing power of marginalized people. We will sketch a nomological framework for development support communication (DSC), and suggest a niche for DSC in activities that will empower individuals, groups, and communities situated at the periphery in Third World countries.

ETHICS AND DEVELOPMENT

Presently fewer and fewer individuals, families, and groups are consuming more and better goods and services. The consumption basket of the richest 20 percent of the people globally is very different from the basket of the poor majority. It takes more and more of scarce resources to fill rich persons' baskets while their baskets are also growing bigger. Over 20 years ago, Dasgupta noted that in the United States (which constituted about 6 percent of the world's population) the upper-middle class controlled about 40 percent of the world's resources (Dasgupta 1979: 5). Global inequities have increased since then. Also, great inequities exist within industrialized nations, in that between 7 and 17 percent of people within industrialized countries are poor:

> Inequalities in consumption are stark. Globally, the 20% of the world's people in the highest income countries account for 86% of total private consumption expenditures—the poorest 20%, a minuscule 1.3%. More specifically, the richest fifth consume 45% of all meat and fish (the poorest fifth consume 5%); consume 58% of total energy (the poorest fifth use less than 4%); have 74% of all telephone lines (the poorest fifth have 1.5%); consume 84% of all paper (the poorest fifth use less than 1%) (UNDP 1998: 2).

It has been increasingly evident that the process of development is associated with greater poverty levels. The premise has been that when nations *develop*, they reduce poverty. This has not been the case, suggesting that it is the *nature* and *method* of development (as it has been conceptualized and carried out) that is associated with increasing poverty levels. Rather than decreasing the poverty of the majority, development has served to increase the affluence of the few. Some nations or individuals benefit from the development process. Their standards of living and consumption levels rise. However, for the majority of nations or peoples in them the outcome is continued poverty. The relative state of the nations today and the stratification of people within them are an indication of this (Seager 1997; UNDP 1997, 1998; World Bank 1999).

Box 9.1
A World that is Out of Balance

The Worldwatch Institute in its annual report called, "*State of the World 2000,*" reported that 1.2 billion people around the world go to bed hungry. This is the largest number recorded in human history. However, the annual study also reported that about 1.2 billion people are either eating too much or eating the wrong kinds of foods. This study, therefore, revealed that the number of overfed people equals the number of hungry and underfed people. In 1999 in the United States, about 400,000 liposuction procedures were performed. This is a procedure where fat is surgically removed from the human body. The number of overweight people is increasing in Third World countries as well. The Worldwatch report indicated that in Brazil, China, and Colombia the percentage of overweight people has seen a significant jump. The report also indicated that about 2 billion people are in another category that overlaps with the hungry and the overfed. In this group, the people are well-fed but the body lacks essential minerals and vitamins.

Theorist and Policy-maker: A Grand Coalition

How did the process of development emerge as a scheme producing deprivation and human misery, especially in the Third World? Did policy-makers have a rationale rooted in theories of socio-economic, political, and cultural development, or were they functioning in a theoretical vacuum? Clearly, policy-makers were not acting in isolation. They had the full support of scientists and theorists. Three key qualities of modernization theory and practice (see Chapter 3) that have contributed to this situation are reviewed below, beginning with blaming the victim.

Blaming the victim is an ideological process, an almost painless evasion among policy-makers and intellectuals all over the world. It is a process of justifying inequality in society, by finding defects in the victims of inequality.

> . . . the generic process of *Blaming the Victim* is applied to almost every American problem. The miserable health care of the poor is explained away on the grounds that the victim has poor motivation and lacks health information. The problems of slum housing are traced to the characteristics of tenants who are labeled as "Southern rural migrants" not yet "acculturated" to life in the big city. The "multiproblem" poor, it is claimed, suffer the psychological effects of impoverishment, the culture of poverty (Ryan 1976: 5).

As an ideology, blaming the victim, unlike biological theories of the early 1900s, did not put the spotlight on the victims' genetically inferior nature. Ryan commented that the ideology instead focused on the victims' social origins. The shortcoming, however, was still located inside the victim. The victim blamer could thus criticize the social stresses that produced such defects, but yet turn a blind eye to the repeated onslaughts of the victimizing social forces on the individual. "It is a brilliant ideology for justifying a perverse form of social action designed to change, not society, as one might expect, but rather society's victim" (Ryan 1976: 8).

Social Darwinism, a second enduring quality of modernization stems from Darwin's work on evolution, which provided material for social theorists such as Herbert Spencer and William Sumner. They interpreted, or rather distorted, Darwin's work to explain the survival of the fittest in the social arena. Social Darwinists believed that government interventions on behalf of the poor would have catastrophic results since they would interfere with the laws of natural selection.

> Spencer and his followers publicly deplored poor laws, state-supported education, regulation of housing conditions, and the protection of the consumer against dangers and deceptions. They also found anathema any state-enforced effort to achieve equality, even equality of opportunity, because evolution depended for its force on inequality (Reich 1982: 34).

This cold-blooded rhetoric was not the product of demagogues or quacks. It flowed from the temples of learning and scholarship: "It came directly from the lectures and books of leading intellectual figures of the time, occupants of professional chairs at Harvard and Yale . . . such is the power of an ideology that so neatly fits the needs of the dominant interests of society" (Ryan 1976: 22).

Social Darwinism, though a product of the last three decades of the 19th century, has not been totally discredited or discarded. Today's victim blamers talk of cultural deprivation instead of the earlier notion of race and class differences in intellectual ability, and laziness is often replaced by a new term: culture of poverty.

A third key quality of modernization that is very difficult to overcome is its capitalist interest in **sustaining class structures of inequality.** From the notion of culture of poverty—which included, among other things, provincial orientation, low formal participation, a lack of integration into national institutions, a strong present time orientation, inability to defer gratification, and fatalism (Lewis 1961)—it was a small theoretical leap to the "subculture of peasantry." Writing about the peasants in the Third World, Rogers (1969: 25) posited that "they possess certain traits that make them members of a 'peasant culture' which transcends national boundaries."

Much of the work in social theory, policy planning, and action has served to maintain the present inequality in societies. Blame-the-victim ideologists, social Darwinists, and the top-down experts of development, among others, have aimed to change the individual but leave the structure of dependency within and between societies intact. The intellectuals, policy-makers, and planners have sought to legitimize the oppression and human misery caused by extreme inequality through *scientific* and *rational* explanations of subcultures: groups of individuals who are doomed to be backward because of their *cultural deficiencies*. In other words, the effect of a focus on individual-level cultural deficiencies has been to sustain the *status quo* within and between unequal societies and thus delay change.

Poverty can be viewed as lack of money. According to Ryan (1976: 122–23), "poverty is an economic status etiologically related to the absence of both monetary input and access to income generating resources." Conceptualized thus, the strategy for overcoming poverty would be to bring every poor person above the poverty line through transfer of resources. Ryan argued that in the US about 2 percent of the GNP would be sufficient for this purpose. However, poverty has not been viewed as simply lack of money, but rather the result of the *lower-class culture* of the poor or the *traditional* culture of the peasants. The solution, therefore, is not distribution of resources. Instead, the spotlight is on how to transform the "way of life" of the poor, including deep-rooted cultural beliefs and lifestyles.

Berger (1974) has argued that basic human needs include two categories: physical requirements and requirements for an ideologically meaningful existence, rooted in one's culture and traditions. Hamelink (1983) goes even further, arguing that cultural diversity, which is being replaced or irreparably altered by modernity, is essential for human survival, as it reflects the ways humans have differentially adapted to their environments. Therefore, from an ethical perspective, what have been the consequences of weaning people away from their *traditional* structures and habits and drawing them toward the *modern* system? This process has further impoverished the vast majority, as the traditional social support structures that had provided security for many hundreds of years are being destroyed.

An Ethical Perspective of Development

The dictionary definition of ethics is the "branch of philosophy dealing with values relating to human conduct, with respect to rightness and wrongness of certain actions and to the goodness and badness of the motives and ends of such actions." We have attempted to reveal and critically reconsider key themes and assumptions in modernization, noting the moral underpinnings of human actions in the theory and policy-making realms. This raises questions that we briefly re-examine in this context.

What is development? The dominant paradigm assumes an ethnocentric conception of what progress should be. It describes the type of modernization that has been achieved in West European and North American countries. Also, it has looked at development from a macroeconomic perspective, viewing development as economic growth obtained through greater industrialization and accompanying urbanization. Development performance has been gauged via measures such as GNP and per capita income levels.

Missing in this definition has been a broad-based conception of development. Any discussion of development must include the physical, mental, social, cultural, and spiritual growth of individuals in an atmosphere free from coercion or dependency. Also, greater importance must be given to preserving and sustaining traditional cultures, as these constitute the media through which people at the grassroots structure their reality. Local cultures in developing nations and elsewhere are not static.

The fact that they have survived centuries of hostile alien rule speaks volumes of their dynamic nature. Local cultures also may harbor solutions to many of the problems at the grassroots. To talk, therefore, of uprooting local cultures is not only naïve but also ethically indefensible.

Development at what level? Much of the work has been at the level of the nation-state. Even research at the micro level has been concerned with bringing the nation, or some region thereof, into modernity. Missing here has been the recognition that individuals, groups, and communities require different strategies for development. If development is not to create greater misery for the majority at the periphery, then we need a process by which not only the *mythical* concept of the nation is developed but individuals and communities are also given the opportunity to create the type of society they want. As Barken and McNulty (1979: 12) point out, development is "a set of judgments about what constitutes the good society and about the institutions and processes through which the good society is achieved." Societies have different value systems and goals, and must be free to determine their own definitions of the good society— at each level of society—and how it may be achieved. This leads to the next question.

Who within society determines whether or when a definition of development is acceptable or unacceptable? The elites in every nation, usually men, have always had the prerogative of deciding what their country needs. In most developing countries, economic and political power is concentrated in the hands of a small elite. In such circum-stances, any definition of development by elites will be in a direction opportune to their interests.

Missing in this approach has been the participation by the people at the grassroots. People who are the objects of policy need to be involved in the definition, design, and execution of the development process. Parti-cipation, in such a bottom-up orientation, would need to be more poly-phonic. The concept of participation favored by bottom-up strategies with labels such as Participatory Communication Systems and Inter-mediate Technologies has been narrow: achieve widespread co-operation in adopting better health care practices, increased agricultural production, etc. True participation, however, would go beyond such goals to raise awareness and catalyze activism to confront and reform unequal social and spatial structures.

Who reaps the benefits of development and who bears the risks? We believe that any policy that continues to exploit the masses to the benefit of the rich and powerful is morally indefensible. Development must aim for more egalitarian distribution of benefits as well as risks across all social and economic classes. The Western model as enunciated in the dominant paradigm is inappropriate for most developing nations. This model, emphasizing capital-intensive technology and centralized planning, has served to increase the power and wealth of elites. It has led to much corruption as well. An alternative model that stresses decentralized development planning with effective local participation would be more appropriate.

What are the moral implications at the policy-making level? The focus of policy-making needs to be on human development, i.e., to reduce human suffering and not increase it. Berger (1974: xiii) describes succinctly some of the implications at the development policy-making level:

> Most political decisions must be made on the basis of inadequate knowledge. To understand this is to become very gingerly toward policy options that exact high human costs . . . the most pressing human costs are in terms of physical deprivation and suffering. The most pressing moral imperative in policy making is a calculus of pain.

What is badly needed today is such a self-examination by every intellectual and policy-maker concerned with development.

COMMUNITARIAN THEORY

In previous chapters we have highlighted three development frameworks that are also evident in the literature of development communication: modernization, critical perspectives (such as dependency theory), and liberation perspectives. A fourth, communitarian theory, is of relatively recent vintage. In this perspective, preservation of the community and emancipation from oppressive structures and external dependencies are the dominant themes. Liberation, feminist, environmental, and some Third World movements have made arguments consistent with the tenets of communitarian theory (Tehranian 1994). The communitarian perspective attaches a:

higher value to human agency than either culturally or economically determinist views of social change. Culture and cultural constructions of reality, however, assume a central position in the communitarian perspectives. Restorations of one kind or another—of nature, of cultural identity, of the lost sense of community—play a critical role in the emancipatory projects of communitarian movements (Tehranian 1994: 286).

In addition, at various times in human history, the discourse of social change has been dominated by the following models: supernatural, mechanical, organic, cybernetic, and linguistic (Tehranian 1994). A change from one model to another has had a profound effect on social science discourse:

> Briefly stated, the shift from pre-scientific to mechanical, organic, cybernetic, and linguistic metaphors and models corresponds to the transition from traditional and pre-scientific world-views to the paradigm shifts in natural sciences from Newtonian physics to Darwinian evolutionary theory, to the rise of computer technologies, cybernetics and General Systems Theory, and finally to a transition from information theory to communication theory as reflected in the rise of semiotics, post-structuralism, and post-modernism (Tehranian 1994: 287).

Today, the post-structuralism and postmodernism embraced by leading theorists challenge universal truths and our notions of objective social reality. Epistemological plurality is the favored outcome in these approaches, which also assume that language actively constructs (versus merely conveys) meaning and that it is more valuable to discover representational meaning than to find explanations. At the same time, political economists, socialist feminists and others with Marxist leanings have cautioned against going too far in rejecting theories and methods of the social sciences to the neglect of real material structures that also—along with ideological factors—contribute to social inequalities, as well as to progressive change (e.g., Barrett 1999). For development communication as conceptualized here, the combined effect of all these trends has been to encourage the acceptance of multiple meanings, symbolic rationality (or irrationality), cultural specificity, change through human agency, communicative action and structuration, deconstruction of dominant ideology of power, and the strengthening of critical consciousness among the people in a community (Jacobson and Kolluri 1999; Servaes 1999; Tehranian 1994).

In general, the intellectual ferment in the humanities and social sciences (with ethical, practical, and philosophical implications) has increasingly favored participatory approaches in development communication, as appropriate for each unique context. The assumptions include the following:

- The scientific method and the knowledge that it has generated are value-laden, reflecting the economic–political–cultural contexts involved. In general, there is a suspicion of logocentric views. One major area of criticism relates to notions of objectivity and causality.
- As all knowledge systems and the scientific method are value biased, the accumulation of "objective" knowledge by such methods is a futile exercise. Universally valid explanations are nothing more than probabilistic explanations that have finite range and scope limitations (Jacobson 1993).
- Given the oppression of large groups of people—women; the poor; ethnic, racial, and linguistic minorities; refugees; and other marginalized people—ethical and practical concerns should take precedence in social science over principles of objectivity and detachment.
- Therefore, the goal of research should be the liberation of the oppressed rather than the generation of objective generalizations (Servaes and Arnst 1999) or the search for the ultimate truth, which is only a mirage.
- Research then should be problem-solving, "involved, relevant and activist, not afraid to tackle problems, take positions, or intercede on behalf of certain interests and intrude on the state of nature" (Rosenau 1992: 173).

PARTICIPATORY STRATEGIES IN SOCIAL CHANGE

Post-structuralism, postmodernism, and communitarian theory together provide an assumptive basis for participatory strategies. Attempts at operationalization of the term "participation" range from those that reflect the dominant paradigm—*the participation-as-a-means approach*—to those that genuinely represent the case for a context-based paradigm—

the participation-as-an-end approach (Ascroft and Masilela 1989: 12; Dervin and Huesca 1997). The participation-as-an-end approach has received support from many scholars and administrators (Alamgir 1988; Bamberger 1988; Diaz-Bordenave 1989; Kothari 1984; Tehranian 1985). They argue that participation must be recognized as a basic human right. It should be accepted and supported as an end in itself and not for its results. The need to think, express oneself, belong to a group, be recognized as a person, be appreciated and respected, and have some say in crucial decisions affecting one's life, are as essential to the development of an individual as eating, drinking, and sleeping (Diaz-Bordenave 1989). And, participation in meaningful activities is the vehicle through which the needs described above are fulfilled. Diaz-Bordenave (1989: 3) states it cogently: "Participation is not a fringe benefit that authorities may grant as a concession but every human being's birthright that no authority may deny or prevent."

The "participation-as-a-means to an end" approach could be visualized along a continuum: ranging from attempts at mobilization of the populace to co-operation in development activities, to empowering people so that they may articulate and manage their own development. In the former, the people may not be expected to participate in identifying the problem or designing a development program. In such situations, participation becomes shallow, reduced to a process whereby people are externally manipulated to serve the ends of authorities in charge of such programs (Ascroft and Masilela 1989; Diaz-Bordenave 1989; Nair and White 1987). Participation as a process of empowerment, though politically quite risky, is our favored approach. Here, individuals are active in development programs and processes; they contribute ideas, take initiative, articulate their needs and problems and assert their autonomy (Ascroft and Masilela 1989).

Participatory Research

There is great diversity in participatory research methodologies and practice. The following description brings together many of its tenets (Kronenburg 1986: 225):

1. It rests on the assumption that human beings have an innate ability to create knowledge and that this is not the prerogative of "professionals."

2. It is an educational process for the participants in the research program as well as for the researcher. It involves the identification of community needs, awareness regarding constraints, an analysis of the causes of glitches and the designing and execution of solutions.

3. There is a conscious commitment of the researcher to work for the cause of the community. Thus, the traditional scientific principle of neutrality is rejected in this research.

4. It is based on a dialectical process of dialogue between the researcher and the community. Dialogue provides a framework which guards against manipulation from outside and serves as a means of control by the community over the direction of the research process.

5. It is a problem-solving approach. The aim is to discover the causes of problems and mobilize the creative human potential to solve social problems by changing the underlying conditions to those problems.

6. Its major asset is its heuristic value. The close co-operation between the researcher and the community fosters an atmosphere in which all participants analyze the social environment and formulate plans of action.

Participation and Communication

Communication constitutes an indispensable part of participatory approaches. If development is to have any relevance to the people who need it most, it must start where the real needs and problems exist, i.e., in the rural areas, urban slums, and other depressed sectors. People living in such peripheries must perceive their *real* needs and identify their *real* problems. To a large extent, these people have not been able to do so due to a lack of genuine participation in development strategies ostensibly setup to ameliorate their problems. Alternative, bottom-up communication strategies have often turned out to be mere cliches, lacking in substance.

Many scholars and partictioners over the past three decades have favored active participation of the people at the grassroots. On the surface, these signaled a positive departure from the earlier overly top-down and prescriptive approaches. However, the structure of elite domination was not disturbed. Diaz-Bordenave (1980) noted that in these new approaches, the participation that was expected was often directly by the sources and change agents. In these so-called bottom-up approaches to development, people were induced to participate in self-help activities, but the basic solutions to local problems were already selected by the external development agencies. The participation of the people was directed because, often the aim of the development projects was to achieve widespread co-operation in increasing agricultural production, improving formal and non-formal education, limiting family size, etc. Thus, people at the grass-roots were co-opted in activities that, in the end, would make consumers of them for industrial goods and services. Participation, therefore, was a means to an end: the end being greater dependence of the people on a market controlled by the elites, both national and international. This remains the case in many social marketing projects today, as we have noted in earlier chapters.

True participation, however, should go beyond such pragmatic goals as higher productivity, higher formal education, or high consumption patterns to social and political action by the people at all levels. The goal of participation efforts should be to facilitate *conscientization* of marginalized people globally of unequal social, political, and spatial structures in their societies. It is through conscientization and collective action that they perceive their needs, identify constraints to addressing these needs, and plan to overcome problems.

Paulo Freire (1970) first introduced the concept of conscientization, as discussed in Chapter 8. He was disappointed with the educational systems in Brazil and Chile and advocated their "replacement with a more liberating type of communication education that would contain more dialogue and would be both more receiver-centered and more conscious of social structure" (Diaz-Bordenave 1976: 46). He called this process conscientization. Armed with new knowledge of their existential situation, the people could then come up with action plans to liberate them from their dependent and exploited status.

Hence, in this approach communication channels are used to generate dialogue, to help people understand each other and identify their collective problems. Communication is thus a vehicle for liberation from mental and psychological shackles that bind the people to structures and processes of oppression. Used in this way, communication is performing its true function—*communicare* or building commonness among the members of a group or community striving to change their present situation.

Box 9.2
Marginalized Languages are Disappearing

Thousands of marginalized languages are dying around the world due to intolerance, cultural repression, and globalization. In 1999, an international panel of experts met in The Hague to hold public hearings on cases of significant threat to linguistic human rights. Experts estimate that about 90 percent of oral languages in Asia, Africa, and the Americas will disappear in the next century. Two languages that are especially vulnerable are Kurdish and Creole. Kurdish is the native language of about 25 million Kurds living in Iraq, Iran, Syria, and Turkey. Creole is the spoken language in many Caribbean countries. Both these languages face severe restrictions in the countries where they are spoken. Professor Hamelink at the University of Amsterdam pointed out that people should have a fundamental right to use their language in educational settings or at least have their minority language protected. Linguistic diversity is as essential to human future as biological diversity.

Source: Branko Milinkovic, "Languages Die of Globalization and Intolerance." *Junio*, 1999: 33.

Communication as Empowerment Programs

In this section we wish to show the links between empowerment and attempts at democratization of communication through popular communication practices as carried out by NGOs and other communities all over the world. The organizations that we describe below have been prominent in experimenting with and exploring empowering communications and issues such as access to resources and local control of the development process. The World Association of Community Radio Broadcasters (AMARC) based in Montreal, Canada, is an umbrella organization supporting community radio broadcasters all over the world. It has been in the forefront to make radio a community-oriented medium that responds to the community's needs and contributes toward the development of the community. The AMARC has encouraged a role for radio as a vehicle for expression and participation of the community (Mayo and Servaes 1994). Worldview International Foundation (WIF) is another NGO that has placed great importance to the idea and practice of giving people a voice in their own development. The WIF has employed communication strategies in projects in Asia, Africa, and Latin America dealing with food production, community development, health education, women/child related issues, environment, and sustainable development issues. The World Association for Christian Communication (WACC) is yet another NGO that supports communication activities through funding, workshops, seminars, publications, and consultancy services. Most of its programs are in the developing countries. Mayo and Servaes (1994) posit that values such as participation, dialogue, cultural integrity, community development, and a concern for the marginalized people in society are the important criteria for funding by the WACC. In the area of news dissemination, the Inter Press Service (IPS) is an international co-operative of Third World journalists that is committed to a South–South and South–North information flow of especially development-related issues; development information, infrastructure building, and professional and technical support in the developing countries. The IPS's services reach over 500 media outlets worldwide (Mayo and Servaes 1994). The Women's Feature Service (WFS) is an offshoot of the IPS. The WFS covers development issues and is specifically interested in giving women and women's issues a voice in mainstream media. There is a presence of other organizations involved in communication for empowerment objectives such as Panos, Association for Progressive Communications, Videazimut, and Voices (*Dhwani*) some of which we have described in other chapters.

Other projects have specifically supported a variety of media empowerment outcomes in the developing countries. The Mahaweli Community radio, a project of the Sri Lanka Broadcasting Corporation, was a trailblazer in the development of community-based, two-way communication with emphasis on participation. It used community-based radio programming to involve farmers and others in the Mahaweli settlements in Sri Lanka in a process of self-reliant development. Radio Enriquillo in the Dominican Republic is a radio station sponsored by European and US NGOs. Its goal is to create a communication channel for the local farmers and community groups, to support their development initiatives, and encourage local cultural expression (Mayo and Servaes 1994). This program is characterized by a strong participatory approach in the management and production of radio programs.

Participatory Action Research

Participatory Action Research (PAR) has emerged as a forceful methodology cum action approach, principally as a reaction to the degradation of the economic and social conditions of poor and marginalized groups. It is dedicated to resuscitating both the power of marginalized people and their popular knowledge. The knowledge that PAR attempts to generate is specific, local, non-Western, and non-positivist. Importantly, it is used to initiate collaborative social action to empower local knowledge and wrest social power inherent in knowledge away from the privileged (Friesen 1999).

Domination of the poor and marginalized comes about in at least three ways: (*i*) control over the means of material production, (*ii*) control over the means of knowledge production, and (*iii*) control over power that legitimizes the relative worth and utility of different espistemologies/ knowledges (Rahman 1991a). Those who have social power will legitimize their knowledge and techniques of knowledge generation as superior. As long as there are inequalities in knowledge relations between different sections of a society, there will be inequities in the relations of material production. In an earlier chapter, we discussed how local narratives, popular knowledge, cultural meanings, and social arrangements have been devalued in the dominant development discourse. Nearly all of the knowledge of the oppressed and the marginalized has been disqualified as inadequate and unscientific by the dominant forces (Foucault 1980). Therefore, in PAR an important objective to achieve the liberation of the poor and the oppressed is to recapture their knowledge and narratives:

It is absolutely essential that the people develop their own endogenous consciousness-raising and knowledge generation, and that this process acquires the social power to assert vis-à-vis all elite consciousness and knowledge (Rahman 1991a: 14).

Thus, the basic ideology of PAR is that endogenous efforts and local leaders will play the leading role in social transformation using their own praxis.

Since European enlightenment, the scientific method has been used to further knowledge generation and also legitimize particular types of knowledge. A key argument used to support the superiority of the scientific method is its lack of bias, or objectivity, and the detachment of the scientist. This is not necessarily the most important indicator for social verifiability of new knowledge. In the epistemologies of the poor, an important criterion for social verifiability may be community consensus achieved through collective and democratic processes (Rahman 1991a):

In this sense the people can choose or devise their own verification system to generate scientific knowledge in their own right. An immediate objective of PAR is to return to the people the legitimacy of the knowledge they are capable of producing through their own verification systems, as fully scientific, and the right to use this knowledge as a guide in their own action (Rahman 1991a: 15).

The PAR approach, then, by resuscitating and elevating popular knowledge, attempts to create a counterdiscourse, disrupts the position of development as articulated by the dominant discourse as problematic, causes a crisis in authority (Gramsci 1971), and creates a space for marginalized groups to influence social change (White 1999).

PAR Methodology. The PAR encompasses an experiential methodology. In this process, the people on their own develop methods of consciousness-raising or critical awareness of their existential situation; the knowledge that is generated or resuscitated is by collective and democratic means; and, this is followed by reflection and critical self-evaluation, leading to endogenous participatory social action. This in essence forms the praxis (see Figure 9.1).

Figure 9.1
Praxis in Participatory Action Research

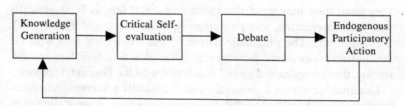

The PAR takes place in a local context, uses local material/non-material inputs, and is dominated by local people and their organizations. The role of the outsider, if helpful at all, would be as a facilitator. The dialectical tension created by differences in knowledge or style of the external facilitator and the local people and their leaders may be resolved in two ways (Fals-Borda 1991): (*i*) practical commitment of the external facilitator to the goal of social transformation. This may be achieved by the immersion of the facilitator in the praxis adopted by the community; and (*ii*) by the rejection of an asymmetrical relationship between the external facilitator and local people (i.e., subject–object) and its replacement by a subject–subject relationship. These steps are not easy or easily achievable. Hence, some have argued that the individual personality and motives are crucial in PAR, and that few are capable of sufficient sensitivity, humility, and self-reflexivity to do this work (e.g., Patai 1991). In the end, the external facilitator's role will become redundant. A successful PAR effort means that the social change process will move forward without the presence of the external agent. Successful PAR efforts will lead to the acquisition of countervailing power by the people's organizations and groups. Thus, the outcome of PAR is to "enable the oppressed groups and classes to acquire sufficient creative and transforming leverage as expressed in specific projects, acts and struggles" (Fals-Borda 1991: 4). The process, however, is continuous.

Knowledge-sharing on a Co-equal Basis. The symmetric (subject–subject) relationship atriculated in the PAR approach allows for exchange of information between equals. The emphasis is on symmetric knowledge-sharing rather than top-down information transmission or teaching (Ascroft et al. 1987; Ascroft and Masilela 1989). The communication model that is set up for this kind of interaction should, of necessity, be interactive. It should allow for the following features: multiplicity of ideas, decentralization, deprofessionalization, deinstitutionalization, and symmetrical exchange with interchange of roles between senders and receivers. This orientation of the new communication model, contrary to the oligarchic communication models of the 1950s and the 1960s, is fundamentally two-way, interactive, and participatory at all levels (McQuail 1983; Servaes 1985). The pluralistic nature of this model fits well with the *multiplicity in one world* paradigm; it also implies a more dialectic mobilization, thus complementing and consistent with the Freirian Approach.[1]

Communication on a co-equal basis is ethically preferable and practically more relevant and useful. By promising a more democratic forum for communication, it supports the *Right to Communicate*, a basic human right recognized by the United Nations charter affording access to communication channels to all people at the national and local level. Practically, it is important too. By allowing a symmetrical exchange of ideas between senders and receivers, it provides access to the storehouse of useful information and ideas of people at the grassroots. Some development agencies have benefited from such knowledge. Alamgir (1988: 98) notes that "the International Fund for Agricultural Development has found that much that is innovative in rural development stems from the traditions and practices of the poor themselves, who have experience in the demands of survival in harsh environment." However, in development communication the experts and policy-makers have often neglected to listen, understand, and incorporate the innate wisdom and knowledge of the rural and urban poor concerning their environment, with which they are intimately familiar (Alamgir 1988). The diffusion of innovations research reinforced the stereotype constructed earlier by modernization theories that the rural people in developing nations had little useful knowledge or skills to contribute to real development.

In the 1980s, however, development scholars discovered the complexity, depth, and sharpness of rural people's knowledge:

> Rural people's knowledge is often superior to that of outsiders. Examples can be found in mixed cropping, knowledge of the environment, abilities to observe and discriminate, and results of rural people's experiments. Rural people's knowledge and modern scientific knowledge are complementary in their strengths and weaknesses. Combined they may achieve what neither would alone. For such combinations, outsider professionals have to step down off their pedestals, and sit down, listen and learn (Chambers 1983: 75).

Knowledge-sharing on a co-equal basis will mobilize the large knowledge resource in rural areas that has remained underutilized. Rural people's knowledge, then, could serve as countervailing power to the presumed superiority of outsider's knowledge.

PAR and Self-development Initiatives

The process of individual and collective empowerment via PAR is complex and reveals different forms and outcomes. The types of actions initiated by organized groups as a result of participatory action research have, therefore, varied depending on the socio-economic, cultural, and political contexts. The outcomes of PAR may be categorized under four interrelated types. These include activities related to macro-level change as well as initiatives to achieve local self-development outcomes (Tilakaratna 1991: 140–42).

Defensive Actions. These are aimed at protecting existing resources that are under threat of encroachment, erosion, or outright takeover. Examples include displacement or loss of cultural communities and lifestyles due to big development projects such as hydroelectric dams or mines, or adverse effects on local communities due to industrial pollution. Defensive actions may include protests, making representations to authorities, and resorting to legal remedies, sometimes with the assistance of sympathetic legal experts.[2]

Assertive Actions. These refer to situations where the poor and marginalized groups lack access to resources and opportunities to better their lives and the lives of their communities. Often, many of the resources are legally entitled to them. For example, certain government-approved agricultural loans and support programs, poverty-alleviation benefits and minimum wages may not be adequately accessible to legally entitled groups. Through local organizations, these groups have attempted to access legitimate entitlements or blocked resources. Assertive actions also include the creation of alternative organizations (such as cooperatives) to recapture lost or diminished economic surpluses.

Constructive Actions. These constitute self-help development projects initiated and organized by the community to satisfy local needs. Grassroots organizations mobilize their own resources and skills with or without the help of external agencies such as the state or NGOs. Self-development projects include agriculture-related projects, health-related initiatives, shelters and other forms of assistance for victims of domestic violence, infrastructure-related projects, small-scale industrial initiatives, or cultural activities.

Alternative Actions. These actions comprise initiatives that are alternative to mainstream development projects. They could include projects that are ecologically sustainable and more suitable to the local context, such as organic farming or biogas plants, indigenous health care schemes, or actions to resuscitate local cultural practices, including indigenous forms of communication.

The above examples of constructive actions and alternative actions constitute types of self-development projects initiated under the PAR approach. In the rural African context, where class distinctions and polarizations are not sharp or where access to land is not a big constraint, PAR initiated self-development projects have thrived. Examples of successful projects have been documented in Senegal, Burkina Faso, Rwanda, and Tanzania (Rahman 1991b). In these projects, the local people's collective actions have confronted:

> those state bureaucracies and technocracies that seek to impose their ideas of "development" (modernization)—ideas that typically are alien to the people's way of life and culture and are often also destructive of the physical environment. The people's own initiatives seek to promote their authentic self-development, which takes off from their traditional

culture and seeks to preserve the physical environment with which they have an organic association (Rahman 1991a: 16).

The types of actions described above demonstrate the versatility of the PAR approach. It accommodates people's self-directed development initiatives as well as macro-level structural outcomes. However, PAR is better known for increasing the countervailing power of oppressed or marginalized groups through defensive and assertive actions described above. In Latin America and Asia, where land and other resources have been more keenly contested and where class and ethnic divisions are sharp, marginalized groups and their organizations have used PAR more often for macro-level, empowerment-related movements and outcomes.

Co-optation of the Liberation Movement

In the last 10 years, the work of NGOs in Third World development has grown significantly (Mayo and Craig 1995; Rahman 1995). This is a result of the dismal record of conventional development programs initiated by state agencies in alleviating poverty. This has led to small-scale and decentralized projects, funded mostly by foreign donors, to promote self-development efforts using popular participation approaches (Rahman 1995). At present, such participatory self-help development projects organized by NGOs (with foreign monetary assistance) are becoming the norm. One consequence of this trend has been the dilution of empowerment and liberation themes articulated by the PAR approach:

> Participatory development (PD) is far from being adopted in practice anywhere in a way which leads to major structural reforms and the transfer of resources away from those vested interests that control dominant social and political structures towards underprivileged people. Dominant lobbies in Southern countries are accepting PD as at best a poverty alleviation strategy, to be implemented sporadically at the micro-level (Rahman 1995: 26).

Thus, the participatory development projects run by the NGOs have co-opted the liberation ideal of the PAR approach (Mayo and Craig 1995; Rahman 1995; Rozario 1997). These projects are not challenging the status quo that prevails in most Third World countries. What they are providing is a "safety net" (in some geographical areas and among certain target groups) and not a critical appraisal of the fundamental inequities in the distribution and access to resources that have led to large-scale poverty and underdevelopment in the first place.

RECONCEPTUALIZING THE ROLE OF DEVELOPMENT SUPPORT COMMUNICATION: A FOCUS ON EMPOWERMENT

After nearly 50 years of research, some scholars have already written an obituary for development support communication (Hornik 1988). Is there no useful role for communication specialists in social change? Or, are we declaring the wrong patient dead? It is our contention that it is premature to declare development support communication dead. What really needs an overhaul is the conception of the omnibus term, "development."

Presently, much of the current academic work in development support communication is premised on pluralistic and participatory approaches as opposed to the top-down perspective transmission models of the past. However, even now, many of the frameworks offered for understanding social change in the newer approaches do not differ significantly from the earlier models in the dominant paradigm as they do not aim to alter the structures and processes that maintain power inequities in societies. We recognize that revolutionary structural change is usually unrealistic, especially given the globalization of economic structures, but we believe that progressive grassroots change can improve people's lives and gradually create openings for broader macro-level change.

We therefore attempt to sketch a nomological framework for development support communication. We will define what should be the outcome for research and practice in this field, examine the relationships and differences between constructs (for example, *development communication, development support communication, participatory communication*, and *empowerment*), consider the practices or exemplars, and explicate the role implications for communication media and communication practitioners in intervention processes. The focal point is the concept of empowerment. It is important that we account for power in development theory and practice. A premise throughout this chapter is that real change is not possible unless we directly address power inequities among individuals and groups. The construct of empowerment identifies the underlying constraints in Third World development and helps to articulate a more appropriate and useful role for development support communication (DSC) and DSC personnel. We advocate a departure from the "social equilibrium" model that has influenced approaches until now to a "social system change" model for DSC. We discuss the current trends and conclude by suggesting a niche for DSC professionals and agencies within the "social system change" model.

Explication of Constructs, Processes, and Outcomes

A major reconceptualization in academic literature and professional praxis was the transition from *development communication* to *development support communication*. Development communication was guided by the organizing principles of the dominant paradigm. Initially, the emphasis in this approach was on economic growth as the main route to development. Later, as disenchantment with this notion grew, people-oriented development variables were included under the umbrella of the paradigm. Development Support Communication, a term that was coined and popularized by practitioners (Childers 1976), was the response of fieldworkers to the realities in developing countries. With this term, the emphasis changed from viewing communication as an input toward greater economic growth to visualizing communication more holistically and as a support for people's self-determination, especially those at the grassroots (Ascroft and Masilela 1994; Jayaweera 1987). The development communication model and the development support communication model are compared in Table 9.1

Table 9.1
Differences Between Development Communication and
Development Support Communication

Development Communication	Development Support Communication
Structure:	
Top-down, Authoritarian (Subject–Object relationship)	Horizontal knowledge-sharing between participants (Subject–Subject relationship)
Paradigm:	
Dominant paradigm of externally directed social change	Participatory paradigm of an endogenously directed quest to maintain control over basic needs

(Table 9.1 contd.)

(Table 9.1 contd.)

Development Communication	Development Support Communication
Level: International and national	Grassroots, Local
Media: Big media; TV, Radio, Newspapers	Small media, Video, Film strips, Traditional media, Group and Interpersonal communication
Effects: To create a climate of acceptance by beneficiaries for exogenous ideas and innovations	Create a climate of mutual understanding between participants

Source: Adapted from Ascroft and Masilela 1989.

Participatory Decision-making

The idea of *development support communication*, after some initial resistance, gained acceptance among several multilateral agencies such as the UNDP, UNICEF, and the FAO. An FAO (1977) report urged the integration of multimedia with interpersonal communication approaches and strongly recommended participatory communication strategies. However, the DSC strategy has never really taken root among development agencies, partly due to the unwillingness of the experts to give up control over the process, and partly due to the inability of development support workers to appreciate and operationalize true participatory communication approaches at the grassroots. "Few understand its implications because few, very few, have ever been directly involved in projects in which theirs was the task of operationalizing the concept and implementing it in real life situations" (Ascroft and Masilela 1994: 281).

Meanwhile, the term participatory communication has been frequently misunderstood and misused, as noted previously. Participation has been defined and operationalized in many ways: from pseudo-participation to genuine efforts at generating participatory decision-making (Alamgir 1988; Ascroft and Masilela 1989; Bamberger 1988; Diaz-Bordenave 1989; Freire 1973; White 1994). There is a great deal of confusion about the outcomes desired and a contradiction between exemplars (or best practices) and phenomena of interest (or outcomes). While the practice of participatory communication has stressed collaboration between the people and experts, a co-equal knowledge-sharing between the people and experts, and a local context and cultural proximity (all of which fall under the empowerment model), the outcome in most cases has not been true empowerment of the people, but the attainment of some indicator of development as articulated in the modernization paradigm (see Table 9.2). Thus, participatory approaches have been encouraged though the design and control of messages, and development agendas usually have remained with the experts. Also, issues of power and control by the authorities, structures of dependency and power inequities have not been addressed adequately within Third World settings (Wilkins 1999). Thus, most of the participatory approaches have been essentially old wine in new bottles.

The reality of the social and political situation in most developing countries is such that the urban and rural poor, women, and other people at the grassroots are entrapped in a dependency situation in highly stratified and unequal social and economic structures. The low status accorded to these groups impedes their awareness of newer approaches such as the participatory strategies or the knowledge-sharing model described above. In the absence of tangible efforts to empower these "unequal" partners, the terms "participatory" or "co-equal knowledge-sharing" will remain mere clichés.

Paradigm of Empowerment

Much work has been done on empowerment in fields such as community organization, education, and community psychology, and we may do well by borrowing and adapting these concepts to development support communication. The construct of empowerment has been mentioned quite often in the communication and development literature, but the terms, exemplars, levels of analysis, and outcomes have not been thoroughly explicated. Thus, the material in Table 9.2 attempts to articulate elements for a conceptual framework; it compares and contrasts the development communication model that was informed by the dominant paradigm with development support communication, that has been influenced by goals of empowerment.

The basic premise guiding theory and practice in development communication (as articulated in the modernization paradigm) has been the notion that human societies are just and fair in their distribution of resources to individuals and groups within them, and that all people, with some effort and help, can achieve the benefits that societies have to offer. Thus, as articulated in the dominant paradigm of development, if an individual or group does not possess "desirable" attitudes, opinions, behaviors, or other attributes, or does not participate effectively in a society's

Table 9.2
Comparison of Development Communication in the Modernization Paradigm with Development Support Communication in the Empowerment Paradigm

Development Communication in the Modernization Paradigm

Phenomenon of Interest/Goal: National and regional development, People development, Community improvement

Belief: Underdevelopment due to economic, political, cultural, geographic, and individual inadequacies; Existence of a single standard (as articulated by experts)

Bias: Cultural insensitivity, environmentally unsustainable, standardization

Context: Macro and micro settings

Level of Analysis: Nation, Region, Individual

Role of Change Agent: Expert, Benefactor, Non-participant

Communication Model: Linear, Top-down, Transmission of information

Type of Research: Usually quantitative (surveys), some use of focus groups, contextual or evaluation research

Exemplars: Prevention of underdevelopment; Remedy through/by experts; Blame the victim; Individual adjustment to a dominant norm; Use of the mass media to spread standardized messages and entertainment; Message that are preachy, prescriptive and/ or persuasive

Outcomes Desired: Economic Growth, Political Development, Infrastructural Development

Development Support Communication in an Empowerment Paradigm

Phenomenon of Interest/Goal: Empowerment of people, Social Justice, Building capacity and equity

Belief: Underdevelopment due to lack of access to economic, political, and cultural resources; Underdevelopment due to lack of power and control on the part of the people; Diversity of standards

Bias: Cultural proximity, Ecological, Diversity

Context: Local and community settings

Level of Analysis: Individual, Group or organization, Community

Role of Change Agent: Collaborator, Facilitator, Participant, Advocate for individuals and communities, Risk-taker, Activist

Communication Model: Non-linear, Participatory, Used to convey information as well as build organizations

Type of Research: Quantitative and qualitative, Longitudinal studies, Labor-intensive participatory action research

Exemplars: Activate social support systems, social networks, mutual help and self-help activities; Participation of all actors; Empower community narratives; Facilitate critical awareness; Facilitate community and organizational power; Communication used to strengthen interpersonal relationships

Outcomes Desired: Increased access of all citizens to material, psychological, cultural and informational resources; Honing of individual and group competence, leadership skills, useful life and communication skills at the local level; Honing of critical awareness skills; Empowered local organizations and communities

affairs, it is the individual who is deficient and thus needs to be taught skills and provided help. The earlier development communication models have accepted such a victim-blame bypothesis. However, large sections of the population in the Third World continue to be impoverished and lack access to necessities that would make a qualitative improvement in their lives.

The concept of empowerment is heuristic in understanding the complex constraints in Third World development. It clarifies the empowerment-oriented outcomes we should seek and provides a useful niche for DSC.[3] Further, what sets empowerment apart from the models informed by the modernization paradigm is that the locus of control in this process rests with the individuals or groups involved and not with the experts, the DSC professionals or the sponsoring organizations. While the professionals may have a role to play in designing intervention strategies, they are not the key actors. The key players are the people handling their problems in local settings and learning and honing their competencies in the concrete experiences of their existential realities.

Power and Control in Development

It is important to provide a context for our discussion of empowerment by explicating carefully the concept and practice of power and control in Third World social settings. A review of literature from both theory and practice in community organization and Third World development indicates the following:

1. Power is exemplified through organized money or organized people (Alinsky 1971), or through connections with such entities.
2. Power is exercised through control of important economic, political, cultural, and informational resources. These resources are necessary in some measure for individuals, organizations, and communities to make qualitative improvements in their lives and, in developing countries, this could also imply the fulfillment of basic needs.
3. Entities that wield power can also reward or punish targets by withholding or decreasing access to important resources (Gaventa 1980; Polsby 1959; Speer and Hughey 1995).
4. Power is exercised through control of the development agenda, i.e., what gets included or excluded in policy statements, development plans, or public debate is carefully controlled. Entities with power can stymie participation or slant perspectives by erecting

many barriers: control the topics of discussions, the timing of discussions, discussion participants, and the range of issues discussed (Speer and Hughey 1995; Steeves 1996).

5. Power is also exercised by influencing or shaping the shared consciousness of a people, community, or nation. This may be operationalized through the propagation of myths, stories, ideology, or outright control over sources of public information (Lukes 1974; Speers and Hughey 1995). Thus, power is the ability to create, interpret, or tell stories about an individual, a group, community, or nation (Rappaport 1995). There are numerous examples globally of marginalized groups who have had their stories appropriated by outside entities.

Definitions of Empowerment

While empowerment as a construct has a set of core ideas, it may be defined at different levels: individual, organization, and community; and operationalized in different contexts (Rowlands 1998). Several working definitions of empowerment are available. However, given the nature of our work, which can be described as directed social change, and given the power inequities in societies that are posited as the major impediments to achieving meaningful change, it is important that the working definitions be linked directly to the building and exercise of social power (Speer and Hughey 1995).

The following definitions and descriptions of the term empowerment are useful. According to Fawcett, et al. (1984: 146), "community empowerment is the process of increasing control by groups over consequences that are important to their members and to others in the broader community." Rappaport (1987: 121) describes empowerment as "a psychological sense of personal control or influence and a concern with actual social influence, political power, and legal rights. It is a multilevel construct applicable to individual citizens as well as to organizations and neighborhoods; it suggests the study of people in context." Another definition describes empowerment as "an intentional, ongoing process centered in the local community, involving mutual respect, critical reflection, caring and group participation, through which people lacking an equal share of valued resources gain greater access to and control over those resources" (Cornell Empowerment Group 1989: 2). In summary, empowerment is the "manifestation of social power at individual, organizational, and community levels of analysis" (Speer and Hughey 1995: 730).

Empowerment is the mechanism by which individuals, organizations, and communities gain control and mastery over social and economic conditions (Rappaport 1981; Rappaport et al. 1984); over democratic participation in their community (Rappaport 1987; Zimmerman and Rappaport 1988); and over their stories. While we read scholarly papers or theses about local peoples' stories, we seldom get to listen to their actual voices (Rappaport 1995). Local stories document individual or community narratives about their own or others' lives, histories, experiences, and values. Like all other resources, the power to create, select, and tell stories about one's self, one's group, or other people is controlled by elites through their organizations, networks, agents, or genres. These groups or individuals also usually control the mass media and information channels that bombard communities with selective stories, messages, or mainstream populist entertainment fare. Thus, minorities, women, the poor, and local communities lose control of an important cultural resource: the right to tell their own stories to their children and to significant others. Community empowerment attempts to restore grassroots control over this resource. Peoples' right to communicate their stories should be at the heart of the participatory strategies leading to empowerment.

As a process, empowerment may have different outcomes. For some it could lead to a perception of control over their lives while for others it may mean actual control (Rappaport 1987; Young 1994); it could be an internalized attitude or an externally observable behavior; it could be an individual achievement (Zimmerman 1990; Zimmerman and Rappaport 1988), a community experience (Chavis and Wandersman 1990), or a professional intervention using strategies that are informed by local realities. The process itself defies easy definition and may be recognized more easily by its absence: "powerlessness, real or imagined; learned helplessness; . . . (and) alienation" (Rappaport 1984: 3).

Usually, a starting point in the process of empowerment is a realization on the part of an individual, group, or community of its inequitable position, its powerlessness in the system, or the relative neglect of its needs by the larger society. Biegel (1984) suggest criteria for the notion of equity:

the principle of equity is defined by citizens in two ways: whether their investment (objective or subjective) is equal to their return; and whether their neighborhood organization is getting its fair share of resources as compared to other parts of the city (Biegel 1984: 123).

The investments or costs perceived by the citizens could include various dimensions: financial, psychological, physical, political, cultural, and emotional. The return would constitute needs met, resources accessed or offered, and opportunities made available.

Perspectives on Interventions

Thus far we have argued that it is usually futile and may be unethical for communications and human service professionals to help solve minor and/or immediate problems, while ignoring the systemic barriers erected by societies that permit or perpetuate inequalities among citizens. Certainly sustainable change is not possible unless we deal with this crucial problem in human societies: lack of economic and social power among individuals at the grassroots. Over 25 years ago, Latin American communication scholars such as Beltran (1976) and Diaz-Bordenave (1976), among others, observed the oppressive social, political, and economic structures that exist in developing countries and that constitute barriers to progressive social change. Yet, most of the models and strategies that followed have failed to directly address these constraints. Individuals are impoverished or sick or often are slow to adopt useful practices, not because they lack knowledge or reason, but because they do not have access to appropriate or sustainable opportunities to improve their lives. This is an issue of power. Unless we are willing to recognize this and act on it, our work will either be ineffective or superficial, functioning as temporary Band-Aids for far larger problems. If DSC is to continue to play an effective role in social change processes, researchers and practitioners have to address fundamental problems of unequal power relations.

The focus on unequal power dynamics has a direct consequence for the traditional objective of development communication, i.e., the delivery of new information and technology innovations. This is insufficient. Empowerment requires more than just information delivery and diffusion of technical innovations. The objective of DSC professionals is to work with the individuals and communities at the grassroots so that they eventually may enter and participate meaningfully in the political and economic processes in their societies. This calls for grassroots organizing

(Kaye 1990) and communicative social action on the part of the poor, women, minorities, and others who have been consistently and increasingly marginalized in the process of social change. The implication for DSC, then, is a reconceptualization of its role. Greater importance will need to be directed to the organizational value of communication and the role of communicative efforts in empowering citizens. In essence, what we are advocating for DSC is a move away from effecting "development" (as articulated by the dominant paradigm and the helping professions) to assisting in the process of empowerment.

Hence, we advocate a *social system change* model (as opposed to the *social equilibrium model* of the modernization paradigm). This is not an easy task. It not only requires dealing with enclaves of power and influence that are deeply anchored in global and national structures, but also the active participation of individuals and communities in intervention efforts affecting their welfare (Swift 1984). However, it is the right thing to do if we are truly interested in appropriate and sustainable social change. This role is in consonance with the role of the DSC practitioner (see Table 9.2) as an advocate of the people at the grassroots and as a risk-taker (Wolff 1987).

Guiding Tenets for Practice

Speer and Hughey (1995), prescribe three tenets in their analysis of community organizations. First, empowerment is achieved through *organizational effectiveness*. Many external forces such as the government, development organizations, and other outsiders (both individuals and groups) act upon local communities and individuals. Some of these interactions are positive and beneficial and sanctioned by community consensus. However, many of the interventions may be coercive and not approved by the community as a whole. External (or internal) organizations are most often operating in their own self-interest. There are several competing self-interests, and usually the most powerful groups prevail. Thus, more marginalized groups need effective organizations of their own that work for their self-interest, network with similar organizations, and compete effectively for resources. Externally, effective organizations serve as important constituencies and as sources of countervailing power for participants, while internally they serve as a laboratory wherein leadership skills, political skills, group problem solving abilities, peer support, and motivation skills are tested and honed (Kieffer 1984). A reliance on the organizational process has implications for DSC practice. Local leaders may need help in forming (or strengthening) organizations, in developing communication and problem-solving skills, and in information gathering and networking.

The second tenet specifies that effective organizations are sustained by *strong interpersonal relationships* (Speer and Hughey 1995). Viable and self-sustaining organizations are built ground-up through interactions with people based on shared values. Indigenous and long-term organizations, including religious organizations (Chapters 7 and 8), are superior to ad hoc organizations built on temporal issues, however important the issues may be. In fact, research on women in development has indicated that it is more effective to involve indigenous organizations than to create new ones (e.g., Esman and Uphoff 1984; Hoskins 1980). Relation-focused organizations with historic purpose do not atrophy when an immediate issue goes away, nor are they as vulnerable to takeover by individuals with personal agendas. Again, all this has useful implications for DSC personnel. They can identify existing organizations that wield power locally. These may include organizations that formed originally for economic, political, cultural, or religious purposes. The DSC professionals can assist in supporting and strengthening relationships through one-on-one communication. They can also facilitate processes of group problem-identification via the use of contextually appropriate communication channels, whether indigenous media or modern media—such as video cameras, as in projects carried out in Nepal and the Fogo community in Canada (Belbase 1994; Williamson 1991)—or new information technologies.

The third tenet relates to individual empowerment and involves the concept of *action-reflection*. Individuals must activate their critical consciousness (Freire 1970, 1973), however, they need to go beyond reflection to social action as part of an organization. Organizations provide a context and process for cognitive and emotional insight, for challenging new ideas and for testing and evaluating actions and behavior (Kieffer 1984; Speer and Hughey 1995; White 1994; Zimmerman 1995; Zimmerman and Rappaport 1988). Over time, increased participation and reflection on the part of individuals are associated with their empowerment, as illustrated in liberation-oriented religious organizations in the case studies in Chapter 8. The communication and organizational implications of this tenet are immense for DSC practitioners. For instance, grassroots groups in India, Africa, and the Philippines have used drama and other traditional media to facilitate critical awareness, identify real constraints, and plan collectively to overcome problems (Kidd 1984; Mda 1993; Van Hoosen 1984). The DSC practitioners working with religious organizations must certainly consider and make use of religious forms of communication in their work.

Action for Cultural and Political Change (ACPC), an organization of lower-caste agricultural laborers in Tamil Nadu, India, believes in social transformation.[4] Drama occupies a central part of a socio-economic and political transformation process involving conscientization, organization, and struggle (Kidd 1984). For ACPC, "the cause of poverty and under-development is not the inadequacies and ignorance of the poor; it is the structural relationships which keep the poor powerless, subservient, and exploited" (Kidd 1984: 118). Thus, their "backwardness" is more a symptom rather than the cause of their situation. Organizations such as the ACPC consider conventional development strategies analogous to treating wounded soldiers with Band-Aids, then sending them back to war. The ACPC is attempting to do something about the "war." The organization sees no merit in giving token handouts to victims of an unjust and inequitable structure. Such remedies may provide short-term relief, but do nothing to solve the problem.

The organizing process of the ACPC consists of a number of stages: (*i*) getting into, accepted, and grounded in an area; (*ii*) adult education and literacy classes; (*iii*) leadership-training and action committees; (*iv*) cultural action programs and mass meetings; and (*v*) struggle and movement (Kidd 1984: 107). Unlike the conventional development approach that is essentially an exercise in top-down propaganda and bureaucratic paternalism, controlled and run by development planners, the ACPC approach is a self-reliant, people's movement at the grassroots. The main vehicle of conscientization, organization and struggle is the drama. The plays,

grow out of the situations, experiences, and analysis of the actors who are themselves villagers. They aren't handed centrally produced, pre-packaged scripts and told to perform. They create their own dramas out of their own collective analyses of their immediate situation and the deeper structures in which they are embedded. This is a genuine expression of the people (Kidd 1984: 117).

The ACPC approach is a good example of how people living in the periphery perceive their *real* needs and problems through active participation. Through reality-based village plays, people are encouraged to develop a critical awareness of the realities of their situation, identify *real* constraints, and plan collectively to overcome problems. What we see here is a self-reliant, grassroots movement that truly understands its problems and is attempting to achieve its goals.

The ACPC is not the only village-based group doing such work. Several grassroots community groups in the Philippines such as *Kulturang Tabonon Sa Debaw* of Davao and the *Kabalaka Mobile Theatre* also advocate dramatic conscientization (Van Hoosen 1984), as do the indigenous theater group in Africa discussed in Chapter 6. These groups are attempting to bring awareness to villagers of some of the socio-political factors affecting their lives. Other notable examples of participatory grassroots movements include the *Bhoomi Sena* movement in India, the *Mother's Club* in Korea, the *Ujaama* in Tanzania, and several community groups in Colombia, Mexico, Brazil, and Chile.

Role for DSC Professionals in Interventions

Who is a DSC professional? Ascroft and Agunga (1994: 310) state that, "it is a role which in the ultimate analysis, must be able to create the situational and psychological conditions in which development benefactors and their intended beneficiaries can participate together in mutual coequality in making development decisions." The role is yet to be systematically codified. However, attempts have been made to describe the qualities and functions of this person (Agunga 1997; Ascroft and Agunga 1994; Ascroft and Brody 1982). The DSC professional is not a development specialist like agricultural extension or health extension workers. Extension workers are primarily subject matter specialists in agriculture, health, or nutrition, usually with only a smattering of training in social-scientific communication techniques. They also lack a sufficiently broad education in the social sciences and humanities to observe and appreciate socio-economic and cultural barriers to empowerment. This makes most extension personnel ineligible to act as advocates for the people. In many development projects, the DSC person is seen as a functionary of the project, the development agency, or the government. Ascroft and Brody (1982) caution that this role reduces DSC personnel to mere mouthpieces of development, doing the bidding of the development planners. In this mode, the DSC practitioners, while attempting to improve the efficiency and effectiveness of development agencies, may not necessarily be promoting the real interests of people.

Niche for DSC Professional in Empowerment
Support Communication Initiatives

The previous discussion of power and control in development delineated several ways in which powerful groups or individuals could dominate. In order to effectively counter this, marginalized individuals/groups should have the capacities:

- to perceive and articulate their social, cultural, historical, economic, and political realities;
- to operationalize their needs;
- to identify resources they need;
- to identify, articulate, and operationalize possible solution alternatives;
- to identify and gain access to individuals, agencies, or organizations that are crucial to meeting their needs or solving their problems;
- to build communication skills such as: presenting issues cogently, conflict resolution, negotiation, and arbitration; and
- to organize and lead.

When individuals, groups, or communities lack some or all of these skills, there is a niche for DSC professionals to act as facilitators or enablers by strengthening such capacities.

The model shown in Figure 9.2 may be used to anchor the role of the DSC professional. The DSC professionals act primarily as communication channels and advocates for people, i.e., the marginalized individuals and groups that need to access resources and solve security problems. The DSC professionals can assist groups/organizations in identifying and articulating possible solution alternatives, identifying resources that may solve their security problems, and identifying and gaining access to relevant authorities that are crucial to meeting their needs or solving their problems. Thus, the DSC professional can help extend people's environment by acting as a collaborator, facilitator, and importantly as an advocate. As a development support communicator, he/she is uniquely qualified to organize and lead groups and has the communication skills to train people to present issues cogently, negotiate, arbitrate, and resolve conflicts. The DSC professional should be more than just a communication specialist: he/she should be a social worker trained in community organization skills; an anthropologist and a social scientist trained in research methods, problem-solving strategies, implementation, and evaluation of social action programs; and a management person trained in organizational development and strategic planning methods (Biegel 1984).

Figure 9.2
Role of DSC Professional in the Initial Stages of Empowerment Process

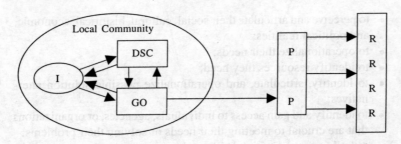

I = Individuals
GO = Grassroots Organizations
DSC = Development Support Communication Professional/External Researcher
P = Power Holders/State Bureaucracy/Technocracy
R = Resources

Fawcett, et al. (1995: 686–87), provide a list of activities for facilitating the process of community empowerment. An abbreviated version of this list is reproduced below and provides an excellent inventory of activities for DSC personnel.

1. Activities that enhance experience and competence. Encourage listening sessions to identify local issues, resources, barriers, and alternatives; conduct surveys to identify community issues, concerns, and needs; create an inventory of community assets and resources; determine the incidence and prevalence of identified problems; provide training in leadership skills; provide technical assistance in creating action plans; provide consultation in selection, design, and implementation of early projects.

2. Enhancing group structure and capacity. Provide technical assistance in strategic planning; help develop an organizational structure; provide technical assistance in recruiting, developing, and supporting members and volunteers; provide technical assistance in securing financial resources.

3. Removing social and environmental barriers. Conduct focus groups to assess interests of community members; make selective use of social marketing techniques to promote contextually appropriate programs, policies, and practices; provide training in conflict resolution; develop media campaigns to counter arguments of opponents.

4. Enhancing environmental support and resources. Provide ongoing information and feedback about community change, behavior change, community satisfaction, and community-level outcomes; help locate and develop ties to existing community sectors, organizations, and groups; reinvent innovations to fit local needs, resources, and cultural traditions; arrange opportunities for networking among those with relevant experiential knowledge; provide access to outside experts on matters of local concern.

Rappaport (1981) suggested in the early 1980s that human service professionals should discover empowerment tools through research, and then replicate and make these available to the public. Fawcett (1984), illustrated such a role for human service professionals in creating, using and replicating tools to facilitate individual and community empowerment. They illustrated how professionals and agencies developed several tools such as: a concerns report of basic needs, a self-help guide, the consequence analysis method, the study circle method, and a policy research project. These enabled them to: (*a*) increase knowledge of community problems and solution alternatives; (*b*) increase knowledge of possible consequences of public projects among people most affected; (*c*) involve consumers in the redesign of social programs to fit local needs and resources; and (*d*) develop and communicate research to increase the likelihood of actions taken regarding problems affecting the poor or otherwise disadvantaged.

Locus of Control in Empowerment Activities

The locus of control in empowerment activities rests with the community members. The DSC professional has important roles to play, however, in the intervention process. The roles will include that of a facilitator and consultant throughout much of the process and that of an initiator and a leader in the initial stages. As should be the case with the external facilitator in participatory action research discussed earlier, the DSC professional's role eventually should become redundant and he/she should withdraw. Figure 9.3 illustrates the ideal scenario in the later stages of the process, when the DSC professional is no longer needed.

Figure 9.3
Likely Scenario in the Later Stages of Empowerment Process

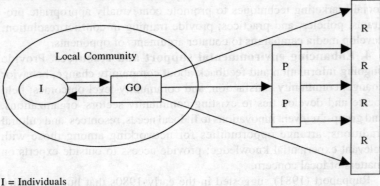

I = Individuals
GO = Grassroots Organizations
P = Power Holders/State Bureaucracy/Technocracy
R = Resources

CONCLUSION

Development as understood in the modernization paradigm usually aims for national, community, and individual economic betterment (Fawcett et al. 1995). While the objective is to bring about a beneficial change, the locus of control rests with people and organizations *outside* the community. "Community empowerment," on the other hand, signifies change where members of the community increasingly influence the agenda, design, and processes.

However, there are some important caveats, however. First, empowerment is a long-term process. The structures of domination and their cumulative effects on societies cannot be removed in a short-term frame. Second, empowerment is not something that can be acquired in a quick seminar or workshop setting. It evolves through practice in real-life situations. It is constructed "primarily through actions in, and on, the environment" (Kieffer 1984: 27–28). Third, it is a labor-intensive process. Last, the DSC professional may be important, but is never the central figure in the empowerment activities. The role of the DSC professional is that of a facilitator, collaborator, and advocate.

Social change is a complex, disordered, unstructured, and, quite often, an uncontrollable process. Empowerment is a process that is well suited to deal with social change in general and with inequitable structures in particular. It provides individuals, communities, and organizations with the necessary skills, confidence, and countervailing power to deal effectively with social change in a world that distributes needs, resources, and power unequally. Empowerment privileges multiple voices and perspectives and truly facilitates equal sharing of knowledge and solution alternatives among the participants in the process.

SUMMARY

The dominant development paradigm has exacerbated gaps between the haves and have-nots and too often has resulted in worsened living conditions for people. Qualities and assumptions of modernization theory and practice that have contributed to this situation include: blaming the victim, social Darwinism, and sustaining conditions of dependency within and between societies. We argue that an ethical perspective on development must recognize and support the value of traditional cultures, consider all levels of society, involve people at the grassroots in all facets of the process, aim for a just and fair distribution of rewards, and prioritize basic needs as defined by those who experience them.

We introduce communitarian theory, which emphasizes preservation of community and emancipation from oppression at all levels. Liberation, feminist, environmentalist, and some Third World movements have made arguments consistent with communitarian theory. Hence it appears that communitarian theory offers potential as a general framework that could ground participatory and empowerment-oriented perspectives on communication and development.

We endorse a participation-as-end approach, assuming that participation is a basic right, not merely a means to a measurable development goal. The methodolgoy of participatory action research (PAR) is consistent with this assumption. The PAR aims to initiate collaborative social action and empower local knowledge. The methodology is experiential and allows participants to develop their own methods of consciousness-raising, followed by reflection, leading to participatory social action.

The external facilitator can only be helpful to the extent that he/she shares the goals of PAR, becomes immersed in the values of the community, and rejects an asymmetrical relationship. As the PAR process proceeds, the external facilitator role should become unnecessary. The PAR increasingly should lead to self-development initiatives that emerge from the people themselves.

A reconceptualization of development as empowerment is consistent with PAR and also suggests revisions in the role of the specialist in development support communication (DSC). A major goal of development as empowerment is to move the locus of control from outsiders and to the individuals and groups directly affected. Empowerment is the mechanism by which individuals, organizations, and communities gain control and mastery over social and economic conditions, over political processes, and over their own stories. Empowerment involves not merely increased influence over external forces (at multiple levels) but also over internal impediments to change.

The focus on unequal power dynamics has important implications for DSC. The goal is no longer information delivery and diffusion, but rather to work with individuals and groups at the grassroots so they may eventually have a voice in political, economic, and ideological processes in their societies. This involves: (*i*) understanding the importance of local organizations; (*ii*) recognizing that existing organizations are usually more effective than new ones, given strong and historic relational ties; and (*iii*) knowing how organizations may provide a context and process for critical reflection leading to social action. More specifically, the DSC professional may be of help in the following areas: (*i*) suggesting and facilitating activities that enhance experience and competence; (*ii*) enhancing group structure and capacity; (*iii*) removing social and environmental barriers; and (*iv*) enhancing environmental support and resources. In the end, the DSC professional's role should become redundant and he/she should withdraw, as should also be the case for the external facilitator in PAR.

NOTES

---

1. Another framework that uses consistent language and has also been applied to development communication is James Grunig's two-way symmetric model of public

relations, which assumes that the purpose of public relations is gaining mutual understanding via a process of two-way communication and feedback with contextually appropriate and balanced effects (Grunig and Hunt 1984).

2. The Internet has proven a useful tool in these efforts. The Environmental Law Alliance Worldwide uses the Internet to assist organizations in developing countries develop legal arguments and strategies to combat environmental hazards. For information, write to Environmental Law Alliance Worldwide, 1877 Garden, Eugene, OR 97403, USA.

3. We are tempted to replace "development support communication" with "empowerment support communication," as the term "development" carries negative baggage. However, as the term development as social change has remained in widespread use, we are comfortable with incorporating empowerment as an important objective within the development framework, as also noted in Chapter 1.

4. This organization was popular in the 1980s. However, we have retained this example in the revised edition of this book as it provides an example of best practice relating to participatory strategies for empowerment.

APPENDICES

APPENDICES

HISTORICAL OVERVIEW OF THIRD WORLD DEVELOPMENT/UNDERDEVELOPMENT*

I. Period of Great Development (3500BC to AD1700)

Ancient World Civilizations

North Africa and West Asia:
  Mesopotamia (3500BC to 2000BC);
  Egypt (3000BC to 2100BC)
Indian Subcontinent:
  Indus Valley (2700BC to 1700BC)
China:
  Shang (1500BC to 1000BC);
  Han (350BC to AD200);
  Ming (AD1368 to AD1644)
Sub-Saharan Africa:
  Axum (AD300 to AD1100);
  Ghana (AD700 to AD1200);
  Mali (AD1200 to AD1400);
  Songhai (AD1500 to AD1700);
  Zimbabwe (AD1200 to AD1500)
Central America:
  Mayan (AD500 to AD1500);
  Aztec (AD1325 to AD1525)
South America:
  Inca (AD1200 to AD1525)

*Prepared with the help of Dr. Joseph R. Ascroft, Iowa City, USA.

II. Period of Colonization: Emergence of the Third World (16th to 20th century)
(From a state of development to underdevelopment)

Period of Pillage and Rise of European Commerce (16th to 17th century)

European Expansion to the Americas:
Iberian settler migration to South and Central America;
Spanish Armada; English, French, North European settlers to North America.

European Expansion to Africa:
Portuguese slave traders to Angola;
French and English commercial traders to West African Coast;
Dutch to Cape of Good Hope.

European Expansion to Asia:
Portuguese to Malacca and coastal stations throughout the East;
Foundations of British and Dutch East India Companies;
English acquire Indian coastal towns;
Dutch take Malacca, dominate Eastern trade;
Spanish conquer Pacific Islands, notably the Philippines (AD 1570).

Period of Dominance of Merchant Capital (18th century)

Main period of slave trade:
From Africa to Americas;
Enforced labor through slavery and reduction to serfdom;
Enrichment of metropolitan Europe, especially its rulers.

Protectionism:
Iberian market closed to competing colonial produce;
British textiles protected from Indian cloth imports (AD1700);
Raw agricultural produce, precious metals, spices became colonial export staples.

Mercantilism:
Rise of merchant class;
Merchant marines, navy protection;
Colonies limited to trade only with motherland empires.

Britain and France vie for Global Dominance:
British Industrial Revolution and French Revolution;
British expansion into India and the plunder of Bengal.

Period of the Rise of Industrial Capital (19th century)

Britain defeats Napolean, gains worldwide naval supremacy:
British opium wars against China;
Chinese and Indian indentured labor to Africa and West Indies.

French conquest of Algeria and expansion to West Africa
European revolutions of mid-1800s:

European settlers to White Dominions in Africa, Asia, and Oceania.

Period of New Imperialism: Late 19th century

Scramble for Africa (and rest of Asia) by European powers (1880 to 1914);
Spanish–American War;
US acquisition of the Philippines and other Pacific territories.

III.   Period of Decolonization (19th to 20th century)
(Emancipation of underdeveloped colonies)

Rise of European liberalism and decolonization in the Americas (early 19th century);
Decolonization of Asia and most of Africa (1945–70).

HISTORICAL OVERVIEW OF DEVELOPMENT AND DEVELOPMENT
COMMUNICATION THEORIES SINCE WORLD WAR II*

I. Genesis of Organized Development Assistance (ODA)

Birth of Multilateral Development Assistance (1945):
International Monetary Fund (IMF), World Bank, the United Nations family
of specialized agencies.

Emergence of Bilateral Development Assistance (1949):
Truman's Point Four Program

II. Development of Emerging Third World (1950s)

Foster self-help by capital infusion and diffusion of modern innovations
mostly from the West;

Industrialization, urbanization, and westernization considered critical for
development;

Prescription of universal stages for industry-driven national growth (Rostow);

Emphasis on need for radical change in Third World social structure and
individual attitudes and behavior;

Subjugation of agriculture (large and small scale) to priorities of industrialization.

III. First Decade of Development (1960s)
(Period of great optimism)

Dominant Paradigm of Development

Economic growth through industrialization and urbanization
Capital-intensive technology
Centralized economic planning

*First edition version, prepared with the help of Dr. Joseph Ascroft, Iowa City, USA.

Underdevelopment in Third World is due to internal problems in a country:
Biased social structure;
Traditional attitudes and behavior that constrain development.

Dominance of the mass media and powerful media effects hypothesis

Belief in the bullet theory of communication effects: powerful, direct, and
uniform effects on people;
Mass media considered as magic multipliers of development benefits;
Mass media considered as agents and indices of modernization;
Potential of mass media to give rise to the Revolution of Rising Expectations;
Setting of standards for minimum criteria of media availability for develop-
ment: 10 newspapers, five radios, two televisions, and two cinema seats
per 100 people;
Importance attached to diffusion of modernizing (but mostly exogenous)
innovations.

IV.   Second Decade of Development (1970s)
   (Period of pessimism)

Disappointment with rate and nature of development;
Explication of the "Development of Underdevelopment" hypothesis:
   Focused on exploitation of the periphery (i.e., the Third World);
   Underdevelopment of the Third World seen as a consequence of develop-
      ment of Europe;
Critique of the Dominant Paradigm of Development:
   Neglect of social structural and political barriers to change;
   Exaggerated emphasis on the individual as locus of change;
   Victim-blame hypothesis;
Problems with the use of mass media for development:
   Potential to widen knowledge gaps between the information rich and the
      information poor;
   Could lead to Revolution of Rising Frustrations;
   Mass media not an independent variable in development but dependent
      on environmental factors;
Weaknesses of the diffusion of innovations model to help the disadvantaged
   due to:
   Communication effects bias;
   Pro-innovation bias;
   Pro-source bias;
   In-the-head variable bias;
   Pro-persuasion bias;
   Top-down flow bias of messages and decisions;

Authority-driven models rather than user-driven models;
Absence of a process orientation;
Widening of socio-economic and communication benefits gaps;
Gender gap increasingly evident.

V. Alternative Conceptions of Development (1970s)

Growth with Equity models: Reduce inequality and improve conditions of
the poorest of the poor;
Emphasis on active participation of the people in development activities;
Encouragement of self-determination and self-reliance of local communities;
freedom from external dependency;
Opening of the People's Republic of China to the world and the lessons
learnt from its development model;
Importance given to small, indigenous technology;
Emphasis on meeting basic needs of people: food, clean water, shelter, basic
education, security of livelihood;
Sustainable Environment Models first discussed;
UN Conference on Environment, Stockholm, 1972;
McNamara's (President, World Bank) New Directions Policy (1973):
Integrated rural development—all existing constraints to development must
be addressed simultaneously;
Percy Amendment to the United States Foreign Assistance Act (1973),
mandated that USAID projects to explicitly consider women;
Distinguished between relative poverty and absolute poverty: relative poverty
signifies that some countries/people are poorer than others while absolute
poverty means a life degraded by denial of basic human necessities;
Shifts in views on overpopulation as primary constraint. Population Con-
ference in Bucharest, 1974;
Proposed reorientation of development policy from trickle-down to equitable
distribution of economic benefits;
Proposed switch from economic targets to meeting basic needs;
Re-emergence of local culture and religion in development activities: renewed
interest in studying the positive role of local culture in social change;
Highlighted the role of folk media in development communication;
Growing awareness of gender inequities in development;
WID initiatives launched;
UN Decade for Women begun with 1975 conference in Mexico City;
New roles suggested for communication in development:
Communication in self-development efforts, i.e., user initiated activity at
the local level considered essential for successful development at the
village level;
Communication should be a catalyst for change rather than sole cause;

encouraged dialogue between users and experts. MacBridge Commission Report, *Many Voice, One World* discussed by UNESCO (later published, 1980);

Suggested communication strategies to narrow knowledge gaps between the information rich and information poor;

Reduce pro-literacy bias through tailored messages and formative evaluations;

Attempted the use of communication to conscientize the people to the harsh realities in their environment.

VI. Third Decade of Development (1980s)
(Lost Decade of Development)

Global recession in most industrialized countries;

Serious economic difficulties in developing countries: balance of payment problems, loan repayment difficulties, drastically lowered prices for exports;

Structural Adjustment Policy (SAP) adopted by lending agencies:

  A neo-liberal economic model employed;

  Role of the state curtailed;

  Increased reliance on the market;

  State expenditures in social services sectors significantly reduced;

Increase in poverty among the poor and marginalized; heavy pressure on the natural resource base among the poor and the marginalized;

Increased awareness of gender inequities and of global differences in women's priorities and analyses of inequities. Mid-Decade Conference, Copenhagen, 1980. End-of-Decade Conference, Nairobi, 1985.

VII. Decade of the 1990s and Beyond

Sustainable-environment perspective strengthened; Sensitivity to environmental degradation; Environment and Development Conference, Rio de Janeiro, 1992;

Human needs-oriented development proposed: concern for human rights, more humane values and respect for human life; Human Rights Conference, Vienna, 1993;

Discussions on global population policy. Population and Development Conference, Cairo, 1994;

Discussions on global social welfare policy. World summit on Social Development, Copenhagen, 1995;

Return to basic needs orientation;

Focus on participatory approaches in communication and development:

  Participatory Action Research;

  Strengthening of critical consciousness among people in a community;

  Empowerment strategies proposed;

Rise of postmodern, post-structuralist, postcolonial, and feminist scholarship:
  Challenges to logocentric and Western views and models;
  Questioning of universal truths and notions of objective social reality;
  Deconstruction of dominant ideology of power;
  Sensitivity to diversity in cultures, views, practices;
  Fourth World Conference on Women, Beijing, 1995;
People-centered development approaches stressed: self-reliant, participatory,
  local, and sustained;
Increased trends toward globalization in lifestyles, tastes, fashions, and mass
  mediated entertainment; Ascendancy of global markets and companies;
Rise of cyberspace, new information and communication technologies, and
  time–space compression;
Beijing+5 Women's Conference, New York, 2000.

REFERENCES AND SELECT BIBLIOGRAPHY

Abeysekeera, S. 1991. "Women in struggle: Part I." *Law and Society Trust: Fortnightly Review*, January (1). pp. 2–7.

Abraham, Francis. 1980. *Perspectives on Modernization: Toward a General Theory of Third World Development*. Washington, D.C.: University Press of America.

Abramovitz, M. 1956. "Resource and Output Trends in the United States since 1870." *American Economic Review*, 46. pp. 5–23.

Adams, M.E. 1982. *Agricultural Extension in Developing Countries*. London, UK: Longman.

Adams, W.M. 1995. "Green Development Theory?" In J. Crush (Ed.). *Power of Development*. London: Routledge. pp. 87–99.

Adelman, I. and **C.T. Morris.** 1973. *Economic Growth and Social Equity in Developing Countries*. Paolo Alto, CA: Stanford University Press.

Adhikari, A. February 24, 2000. "Satellite Mail—The Latest in Messaging." http://www.Hindustantimes.com/nonfram/250200/detECO03.htm.

Agrawal, Binod C. 1984. "Indianess of the Indian Cinema." In G. Wang and W. Dissanayake (Eds.). *Continuity and Change in Communication Systems*. New Jersey: Ablex. pp. 181–92.

Agrawal, B. 1998. "Cultural Influence of Indian Cinema on Indian Television." In S. Melkote, P. Shields, and B.C. Agrawal (Eds.). *International Satellite Broadcasting in South Asia*. New York: University Press of America. pp. 123–30.

Agricultural Support Program: Pochampad Project. 1974. Hyderabad, India: Command Area Development Department, Government of Andhra Pradesh.

Agunga, Robert. 1985. Unpublished Paper. Iowa City: University of Iowa.

Agunga, R.A. 1997, *Developing the Third World: A Communication Approach*. Commack, NY: Nova Science Publishers.

Ahmed, A.S., J. Amoak, and **K. Sakyi.** 1996. "Communication Campaign for the Muslim Population Health and Development Project in Ghana." Unpublished Paper.

Ahmed, L. 1992. *Women and gender in Islam.* New Haven, CT: Yale University Press.

Ajzen, I. and **M. Fishbein.** 1980. *Understanding attitudes and predicting social behavior.* Englewood Cliffs, NJ: Prentice-Hall.

Alamgir, Mohiuddin. 1988. "Poverty Alleviation through Participatory Development." *Development*, 2(3). pp. 97–102.

Alinsky, S.D. 1971. *Rules for Radicals.* New York, NY: Random House.

Allport, G. and **L.J. Postman.** 1947. *The Psychology of Rumor.* New York, NY: Holt.

Al-Qur'an. 1984. Translated by A. Ali. Princeton, NJ: Princeton University Press.

Althusser, L. 1971. *Lenin and Philosophy and Other Essays.* Translated by B. Brewster. London: New Left Review.

Alvares, C. 1992. "Science." In W. Sachs (Ed.). *Development Dictionary.* London: Zed Books. pp. 219–32.

Amoa, B.D. and **J.M. Assimeng.** 1993. *Report on Family Life/Welfare Activities in Religious Organizations in Ghana.* Accra, Ghana: UNFPA.

Anderson, B.R.O'G. (1983). *Imagined Communities: Reflections on the Origin and Spread of Nationalism.* London: Verso.

Andreason, A.R. 1995. *Marketing for Social Change.* San Francisco, CA: Jossey-Bass.

Appadurai, A. 1996. *Modernity at Large: Cultural Dimensions of Globalization.* Minneapolis: University of Minnesota Press.

Ariyaratne, A.T. 1987. "Beyond Development Communication: Case Study on Sarvodaya, Sri Lanka." In N. Jayaweera and S. Amunugama (Eds.). *Rethinking Development Communication.* Singapore: Asian Mass Communication Research and Information Center. pp. 239–51.

Arkes, Hadley. 1972. *Bureaucracy, Marshall Plan, and the National Interest.* Princeton, NJ: Princeton University Press.

Ascroft, Joseph 1971. "The Tetu Extension Pilot Project." *Strategies for Improving Rural Welfare.* Occasional Paper 4. Nairobi, Kenya: Institute for Development Studies, University of Nairobi.

———. Coordinator. 1973. "The Overall Evaluation of the Special Rural Development Program." Occasional Paper 8. Nairobi, Kenya: Institute for Develop-ment Studies, University of Nairobi.

———. 1974. "On the Art and Craft of Collecting Data in Developing Countries." Paper presented to the Workshop on Field Data Collection in Rural Areas of Africa and Middle East. Beirut, Lebanon.

———. 1976. "The Man Who Plays No Instrument: Toward a Guide for Integrating Rural Development." Paper presented at the ECA/PAID Sub-regional Workshop. Addis Ababa, Ethiopia.

———. 1985. "A Curriculum for Development Support Communication." Prepared for the Universities in Pakistan for a Development Communication Workshop held at the University of Punjab, Lahore, July 1–11, 1985.

Ascroft, J. and **R. Agunga.** 1994. "Diffusion Theory and Participatory Decision-Making." In S.A. White, K.S. Nair, and J. Ascroft (Eds.). *Participatory Communication: Working for Change and Development.* New Delhi, India: Sage. pp. 295–313.

Ascroft, Joseph and **Alan Brody.** 1982. "The Role of Support Communication in Knowledge Utilization: Theory and Practice." Paper presented at the conference on Knowledge Utilization: Theory and Practice. East–West Center, Honolulu, Hawaii.

Ascroft, Joseph and **Gary Gleason.** 1980. "Communication Support and Integrated Rural Development in Ghana." Paper presented at the 30th International Conference on Communication, Human Evolution and Development of International Communication Association. Acapulco, Mexico.

———. 1981. "Breaking Bottlenecks in Communication." *Ceres*, No. 80, 14(2). pp. 36–41.

Ascroft, Joseph and Sipho Masilela. 1989. "From Top-Down to Co-Equal Communication: Popular Participation in Development Decision-Making." Paper presented at the seminar on Participation: A Key Concept in Communication and Change. University of Poona, Pune, India.

Ascroft, Joseph and Sipho Masilela. 1994. "Participatory Decision-Making in Third World Development." In S.A. White, K.S. Nair, and J. Ascroft (Eds.). *Participatory Communication: Working for Change and Development*. New Delhi, India: Sage. pp. 259–94.

Ascroft, Joseph and Srinivas Melkote. 1983. "An Ethical Perspective on the Generation of Development Communication Research Useful to Policy Makers and Practitioners." Paper presented to the 33rd annual conference of the International Communication Association. Dallas, Texas, USA.

Ascroft, Joseph, Robert Agunga, Jan Gratama, and Sipho Masilela. 1987. "Communication in Support of Development: Lessons from Theory and Practice." Paper presented at the seminar on Communication and Change. The University of Hawaii and the East–West Center, Honolulu, Hawaii.

Ascroft, Joseph, Niels Roling, Joseph Kariuki, and Fred Chege. 1973. *Extension and the Forgotten Farmer*. Nairobi, Kenya: Institute for Development Studies, University of Nairobi.

Ateek, N.S. 1990. *Justice and Only Justice: A Palestinian Theology of Liberation*. Maryknoll, NY: Orbis Books.

Auerbach, J., C. Wypijewska, and K. Brodie. 1994. *AIDS and Behavior: An Integrated Approach*. Washington, D.C.: National Academy Press.

Bales, K. 1999. *Disposable People: New Slavery in the Global Economy*. Berkley, CA: University of California Press.

Bamberger, Michael. 1988. *The Role of Community Participation in Development Planning and Project Management*. EDI Policy Seminar Report, No. 13. Washington, D.C.: The World Bank.

Bandura, A. 1994. "Social Cognitive Theory and Exercise of Control Over HIV Infection." In R. DiClemente and J. Peterson (Eds.). *Preventing AIDS: Theories and Methods of Behavioral Interventions*. New York: Plenum. pp. 25–60.

Barkan, Joel, and McNulty 1979. "Small is Beautiful? The Organizational Conditions for Effective Small-Scale Self-Help Development Projects in Rural Kenya." University of Iowa: Center for Comparative Legislative Research.

Barr, D.F. 1998. "Integrated Rural Development through Telecommunications." In D. Richardson and L. Paisley (Eds.). *The First Mile of Connectivity*. Rome: FAO. pp. 152–67.

Barret, M. 1999. *Imagination in Theory: Essays on Writing and Culture*. Cambridge: Polity Press.

Barton, A. 1968. "Bringing Society Back In: Survey Research and Macromethodology." *American Behavioral Scientist*, 12. pp. 1–9.

Belbase, Subhadra. 1987. "Development Communication: A Nepali Experience." In N. Jayaweera and S. Amunugama (Eds.). *Rethinking Development Communication*. Singapore: Asian Mass Communication Research and Information Center. pp. 208–26.

Belbase, S. 1994. "Participatory Communication for Development: How Can We Achieve It?" In S.A. White, K.S. Nair, and J. Ascroft (Eds.) *Participatory Communication: Working for Change and Development.* New Delhi, India: Sage. pp. 446–61.

Bellah, Robert N. (Ed.). 1965. *Religion and Progress in Modern Asia.* New York: Free Press.

Beltran, Luis Ramiro S. 1974. "Rural Development and Social Communication: Relationships and Strategies." *Communication Strategies for Rural Development.* Ithaca, New York: Cornell University Press.

———. 1976. "Alien Premises, Objects, and Methods in Latin American Communication Research." *Communication and Development: Critical Perspectives.* Beverly Hills: Sage Publications. pp. 15–42.

Benor, Daniel and **James Harrison.** 1977. *Agricultural Extension: The Training and Visit System.* Washington, D.C.: World Bank.

Berger, Peter L. 1974. *Pyramids of Sacrifice.* New York: Basic Books.

Berlo, David K. 1960. *The Process of Communication: An Introduction to Theory and Practice.* San Francisco: Rinehart Press.

Bhaskaram, K. 1983. "An Evaluative Study of Training and Visit System in Andhra Pradesh." Paper presented to the conference on Management of Transfer of Farm Technology under the Training and Visit System. Hyderabad, India.

Bhawani, S. and **B. Gram.** 1994. "Poverty and Prostitution." International Conference on AIDS, 10(2): 322 (abstract no. PD0466), August 7–12.

Biegel, D. 1984. "Help Seeking and Receiving in Urban Ethnic Neighborhoods: Strategies for Empowerment." In J. Rappaport, C. Swift, and R. Hess (Eds.). *Studies in Empowerment.* New York: Haworth Press. pp. 119–44.

Blum, A. 1986. "Theory into Practice: A Case Study of Post-Graduate Agricultural Extension Training." In *Training for Agriculture and Rural Development.* Rome: FAO. pp. 105–16.

Blumer, J. and **E. Katz.** 1974. *The Uses of Mass Communication: Current Perspectives on Gratifications Research.* Beverly Hills, CA: Sage.

Boesak, A.A. 1987. *If this is Treason, I am Guilty.* Grand Rapids, MI: W.B. Eerdmans Pub. Co.

Boff, L. 1986. *Ecclesiogenesis: The Base Communities Reinvent the Church.* Translated by Robert M. Barr. Maryknoll, NY: Orbis Books.

Bookchin, M. 1982. *The Ecology of Freedom: The Emergency and Dissolution of Hierarchy.* Paolo Alto: Cheshire Books.

Bortei-Doku, E. 1978. "A Fresh Look at the Traditional Small-Scale Farmer." *The Ghana Farmer*, XVIII(1). Accra, Ghana: Ministry of Agriculture Review on Agricultural Development. pp. 4–6.

Boserup, E. 1970. *Woman's Role in Economic Development.* New York, NY: St. Martin's Press.

Bradfield, D.J. 1966. *Guide to Extension Training.* Rome: FAO of the United Nations.

Braidotti, R., E. Charkiewicz, S. Hausler, and **S. Wieringa.** 1994. *Women, the Environment and Sustainable Development.* London: Zed Books.

Brewer, A. 1980. *Marxist Theories of Imperialism: A Critical Survey.* London: Routledge & Kegan Paul.

Brookfield, Harold. 1975. *Interdependent Development.* Pittsburgh: University of Pittsburgh Press.

Brubaker, P.K. 1991. "Economic Justice for Whom? Women Enter the Dialogue." In M. Zweig (Ed.). *Religion and Economic Justice*. Philadelphia: Temple University Press. pp. 95–127.

Brundtland, Gro Harlem. 1989. "Sustainable Development: An Overview." *Development*, 2(3). pp. 13–14.

Brundtland, H. 1987. *Our Common Future*. Oxford: Oxford University Press for the World Commission on Environment and Development.

Buber, M. 1958. *I and Thou*. New York: Scribner.

Campbell, D. and **J. Stanley.** 1963. *Experimental and Quasi-Experimental Designs for Research*. Chicago: Rand-McNally.

Carey, J. 1989. *Communication as Culture: Essays on Media and Society*. Boston: Unwin Hyman.

Carillo, R. 1992. *Battered Dreams: Violence against Women as an Obstacle to Development*. New York: UNIFEM.

Casas, Bartolome de las. 1992. *A Short Account of the Destruction of the Indians, 1552*. London: Penguin.

Casey, Randall. 1975. "Folk Media in Development." *Instructional Technology Report*, No. 12 (September).

Castells, M. 1996. *The Information Age: Economy, Society and Culture. Vol I: The Rise of the Network Society*. Oxford, UK: Blackwell Publishers.

———. 1997. *The Information Age: Economy, Society and Culture. Vol II: The Power of Identity*. Oxford, UK: Blackwell Publishers.

———. 1998. *The Information Age: Economy, Society and Culture. Vol III: End of the Millennium*. Oxford, UK: Blackwell Publishers.

Catania, J., S. Kegeles, and **T. Coates.** 1990. "Psychosocial Predictors of People who Fail to Return for the HIV Test Results." *AIDS*, 4. pp. 262–82.

Ceres. 1977. FAO Review on Agriculture and Development, 10(4).

Chambers, Robert. 1983. *Rural Development: Putting the Last First*. New York: Longman.

Chander, Romesh. 1974. "Television Treatment of Folk Forms in Family Planning Communication." Paper presented to the Inter-Regional Seminar/Workshop on the Integrated Use of Folk Media and Mass Media in Family Planning Communication Programmes. New Delhi, October 7–16.

Chavis, D.M. and **A.W. Wandersman.** 1990. "Sense of Community in the Urban Environment: A Catalyst for Participation and Community Development." *American Journal of Community Psychology*, 18. pp. 55–82.

Chayanov, A.V. 1966. "Measure of Self-Exploitation of the Peasant Family Labor Force." In Daniel Thorner, B. Kerblay, and R.E.F. Smith (Eds.). *The Theory of Peasant Economy*. Illinois: American Economic Association.

Chenery, H., M.S. Ahluwalia, C.L.G. Bell. Duloy, and **R. Jolly.** 1974. *Redistribution with Growth*. Oxford: Oxford University Press.

Chiao, Chen and **M.T.K. Wei.** 1984. "The Chinese Revolutionary Opera: A Change of Theme." In G. Wang and W. Dissanayake (Eds.). *Continuity and Change in Communication Systems*. New Jersey: Ablex. pp. 81–94.

Childers, Erskine. 1976. "Taking Humans into Account." *Media Asia*. 3(2).

Chiranjit, H. 1974. "Radio Treatment of Folk Forms." Paper presented to the Inter-Regional Seminar/Workshop on the Integrated Use of Folk Media and Mass Media in Family Planning Communication Programmes. New Delhi, October 7–16.

Christians for Socialism. 1986. "Declaration of the 80." In W.D. Ferm (Ed.). *Third World Liberation Theologies: A Reader.* Maryknoll, NY: Orbis Books. pp. 12–14.

Chu, Godwin C. 1987. "Development Communication in the Year 2000." In N. Jayaweera and S. Amunugama (Eds.). *Rethinking Development Communication.* Singapore: Asian Mass Communication Research and Information Center. pp. 95–107.

Coleman, James S. 1958. "Relational Analysis: A Study of Social Organization with Survey Methods." *Human Organization,* 17. pp. 28–36.

Coleman, James S., E. Katz, and **H. Menzel.** 1957. "The Diffusion of an Innovation among Physicians." *Sociometry,* 20. pp. 253–70.

Colle, R.D. 1989. "Communicating Scientific Knowledge." In J.L. Compton (Ed.). *The Transformation of International Agricultural Research and Development.* Boulder, CO: Lynne Rienner. pp. 59–83.

Colletta, N.J., R.T. Ewing, Jr., and **T.A. Todd.** 1982. "Cultural Revitalization, Participatory Nonformal Education, and Village Development in Sri Lanka: The Sarvodaya Shramadana Movement." *Comparative Education Review,* 26(2). pp. 271–85.

Compton, J.L. 1989. "The Integration of Research and Extension." In J.L. Compton (Ed.). *The Transformation of International Agricultural Research and Development.* Boulder, CO: Lynne Rienner. pp. 113–36.

Cone, J.H. 1969. *Black Theology and Black Power.* New York: The Seabury Press.

Cook, G. 1985. *The Expectation of the Poor: Latin American Base Ecclesial Communities in Protestant Perspective.* Maryknoll, NY: Orbis Books.

———. 1994. "The Genesis and Practice of Protestant Base Communities in Latin America." In G. Cook (Ed.). *The New Face of the Church in Latin America: Between Tradition and Change.* Maryknoll, NY: Orbis. pp. 150–55.

Cooley, Charles H. 1962. *Social Organization.* Glencoe, Illinois: Free Press.

Coombs, P. and **M. Ahmed.** 1974. *Attacking Rural Poverty: How Non-Formal Education Can Help.* Washington, D.C.: World Bank.

Cornell Empowerment Group. 1989. "Empowerment and Family Support." *Networking Bulletin,* 1(2). pp. 1–23.

Cowen, M. and **R. Shenton.** 1995. "The Invention of Development." In J. Crush (Ed.). *Power of Development.* London: Routledge. pp. 27–43.

Cowley, G. 1989. "The Electronic Goddess: Computerizing Bali's Ancient Irrigation Rites," *Newsweek,* 113(10). p. 50.

Crishna, V., N. Baqai, B.R. Pandey, and **F. Rahman.** 1999. "Telecommunications Infrastructure: A Long Way to Go." *Economic and Political Weekly,* XXXIV (46 and 47). pp. 3309–16.

Crush, J. 1995. "Introduction: Imagining Development." In J. Crush (Ed.). *Power of Development.* London: Routledge. pp. 1–23.

Daniels, Walter M. 1951. *The Point Four Program.* New York: H.W. Wilson.

Dasgupta, Sugata. 1979. "Retooling of Social Work for the Eradication of Social Injustice." Keynote Address to Asian Regional Social Work Seminar. Melbourne, Australia.

———. 1982. "Towards a No Poverty Society." *Social Development Issues,* 6(2). pp. 4–14.

Davis, D. and **S.J. Baran.** 1981. *Mass Communication and Everyday Life: A Perspective on Theory and Effects.* California: Wadsworth Publishing.

Dawson, A. 1999. "The Origins and Character of the Base Ecclesial Community: A Brazilian Perspective." In C. Rowland (Ed.). *The Cambridge Companion to Liberation Theology.* Cambridge, UK: Cambridge University Press. pp. 109–28.

DeFleur, M. and **S. Ball-RoKeach.** 1975. *Theories of Mass Communication.* New York: David McKay.

de Groot, J. 1991. "Conceptions and Misconceptions: The Historical and Cultural Context of Discussion on Women and Development." In H. Afshar (Ed.). *Women, Development and Survival in the Third World.* London: Longman.

Denison, E. 1962. *The Source of Economic Growth in the United States and the Alternative before Us.* New York: Committee for Economic Development.

Dervin, B. and **R. Huesca.** 1997. "Reaching for the Communicating in Participatory Communication: A Meta-theoretical Analysis." *Journal of International Communication,* 46(2). pp. 46–74.

Deutsch, Karl. 1961. "Social Mobilization and Political Development." *American Political Science Review,* 55. pp. 463–515.

Dewey, J. 1933. *How We Think.* Boston: Heath.

Diaz-Bordenave, Juan. 1976. "Communication for Agricultural Innovations in Latin America." In E. Rogers (Ed.). *Communication and Development: Critical Perspectives.* Beverly Hills: Sage Publications. pp. 43–62.

———. 1977. *Communication and Rural Development.* Paris: USESCO.

———. 1980. "Participation in Communication Systems for Development." Unpublished Paper. Rio de Janeiro.

———. 1989. "Participative Communication as a Part of the Building of a Participative Society." Paper prepared for the seminar, Participation: A Key Concept in Communication for Change and Development. Pune, India.

Dissanayake, W. 1984. "A Buddhist Approach to Development: A Sri Lankan Endeavor." In G. Wang and W. Dissanayake (Eds.). *Continuity and Change in Communication Systems.* New Jersey: Ablex. pp. 39–52.

———. 1991. "Ethics, Development, and Communication: A Buddhist Approach." In F.L. Casmir (Ed.). *Communication in Development.* Norwood, NJ: Ablex. pp. 319–27.

Douglass III, Edward Fenner. 1971. "The Role of Mass Media in National Development: A Reformulation with Particular Reference to Sierra Leone." Ph.D. Dissertation. University of Illinois, Urbana-Champaign.

Due, J.M., N. Mollel, and **V. Malone.** 1987. "Does the T&V System Reach Female-headed Families? Some Evidence from Tanzania." *Agricultural Administration and Extension,* 26. pp. 209–71.

Dunn, P.D. 1978. *Appropriate Technology.* New York: Schocken Books.

Durkheim, Emile. 1933. *On the Division of Labor in Society.* New York: Macmillan.

Eapen, K.E. 1973. *The Media and Development: An Exploratory Survey in Indonesia and Zambia.* Leicester, England: Centre for Mass Communication Research, University of Leicester.

———. 1975. "Appropriate Structures and Organizations for Communication Agencies." In Mehra Masani (Ed.). *Communication and Rural Progress.* Mumbai: Leslie Sawhney Programme of Training in Democracy. pp. 35–40.

Edgar, T., M. Fitzpatrick, and **V. Freimuth** (Eds.). 1992. *AIDS: A Communication Perspective.* New Jersey: Lawrence Erlbaum Associates Inc.

Ehrlich, P. 1968. *The Population Bomb.* New York: Ballantine Books in association with the Sierra Club.

Eicher, C. and **L. Witt** (Eds.). 1964. *Agriculture in Economic Development.* New York: McGraw Hill.

Eisenstadt, S.N. 1964. "Social Change, Differentiation, and Evolution." *American Sociological Review*, 29 (June). pp. 375–86.

————. 1976. "The Changing Vision of Modernization and Development." In Wilbur Schramm and Daniel Lerner (Eds.). *Communication and Change: The Last Ten Years and the Next*. Honolulu: East–West Center, The University Press of Hawaii. pp. 31–44.

Ellis, M.H. 1990. *Toward a Jewish Theology of Liberation: The Uprising and the Future*. Maryknoll, NY: Orbis Books.

Ernberg, J. 1998. "Telecommunications for Sustainable Development." In D. Richardson and L. Paisley (Eds.). *The First Mile of Connectivity*. Rome: FAO. pp. 112–39.

Esack, F. 1997. *Qur'an, Liberation & Pluralism: An Islamic Perspective of Interreligious Solidarity against Oppression*. Oxford: Oneworld Publications.

Escobar, A. 1984–85. 'Discourse and Power in Development: Michael Foucault and the Relevance of his Work to the Third World." *Alternatives*, X. pp. 377–400.

————. 1992. "Imagining a Post-Development Era? Critical Thought, Development and Social Movements." *Social Text*, 10(2/3). pp. 20–56.

————. 1995a. "Imagining a Post-Development Era." In J. Crush (Ed.). *Power of Development*. London: Routledge. pp. 211–27.

————. 1995b. *Encountering Development: The Making and Unmaking of the Third World*. Princeton, NJ: Princeton University Press.

Esman, M. and **N. Uphoff.** 1984. *Local Organizations: Intermediaries in Rural Development*. Ithaca, NY: Cornell University Press.

Esteva, G. 1987. "Regenerating People's Space." *Alternatives*, XII. pp. 125–52.

————. 1992. "Development." In W. Sachs (Ed.). *Development Dictionary*. London: Zed Books. pp. 6–25.

Fair, J.E. 1989. "29 Years of Theory and Research on Media and Development: The Dominant Paradigm Impact." *Gazette*, 44. pp. 129–50.

Fair, J.E. and **H. Shah.** 1997. "Continuities and Discontinuities in Communication and Development Research since 1958." *Journal of International Communication*, 46(2). pp. 3–23.

Fals-Borda, O. 1991. "Some Basic Ingredients." In O. Fals-Borda and M.A. Rahman (Eds.). *Action and Knowledge: Breaking the Monopoly with Participatory Action-Research*. New York: Apex Press. pp. 3–12.

Farmers too Reap the Rewards of e-comm. February 28, 2000. http://www.indev.org.

FAO. 1977. "Review on Agriculture and Development." *Ceres*, 10(4).

————. 1988. *Effectiveness of Agricultural Extension Services in Reaching Rural Women in Africa*. Report of Workshop, Harare, Zimbabwe, Volume 2. Rome: FAO.

Fawcett, S.B., A. Paine-Andrews, V.T. Francisco, J.A. Schultz, K.P. Richter, R.K. Lewis, E.L. Williams, K.J. Harris, J.Y. Berkley, J.L. Fisher, and **C.M. Lopez.** 1995. "Using Empowerment Theory in Collaborative Partnerships for Community Health and Development." *American Journal of Community Psychology*, 23(5). pp. 677–97.

Fawcett, S.B., T. Seekins, P.L. Whang, C. Muiu, and **Y. Suarez de Balcazar.** 1984. "Creating and Using Social Technologies for Community Empowerment." In J. Rappaport, C. Swift, and R. Hess (Eds.). *Studies in Empowerment: Steps toward Understanding and Action*. New York, NY: The Haworth Press. pp. 145–72.

Fee, E. and **N. Krieger.** 1993. "Understanding AIDS: Historical Interpretations and the Limits of Biomedical Individualism." *American Journal of Public Health*, 83. pp. 1477–86.

Ferm, W.D. 1986a. *Third World Liberation Theologies: An Introductory Survey.* Maryknoll, NY: Orbis.

———. (Ed.). 1986b. *Third World Liberation Theologies: A Reader.* Maryknoll, NY: Orbis Books.

Fernandes, W. and **E.G. Thukral.** 1989. *Development, Displacement and Rehabilitation.* New Delhi: Indian Social Institute.

Firth, Raymond. 1964. "Capital, Saving and Credit in Peasant Societies." In Raymond Firth and B.S. Yamey (Eds.). *Capital, Saving and Credit in Peasant Societies.* Chicago: Aldine Publishing Company.

Firth, Raymond. 1965. *Primitive Polynesian Economy.* Second Edition. Hamden, Conn: Archon Books.

Fishbein, M. and **I. Ajzen.** 1975. *Belief, Attitude, Intention, and Behavior: An Introduction to Theory and Research.* Boston, MA: Addison-Wesley.

Fjes, Fred. 1976. "Communication and Development." Unpublished Paper. College of Communications, University of Illinois, Urbana-Champaign.

Foster, George M. 1962. *Traditional Cultures and the Impact of Technological Change.* New York: Harper.

Foucault, M. 1980. *Power/Knowledge.* New York: Pantheon Books.

Fox-Keller, Evelyn. 1985. *Reflections on Gender and Science.* New Haven: Yale University Press.

Frank, Andre G. 1969. *Latin America: Underdevelopment or Revolution.* New York: Monthly Review Press.

Freimuth, V. 1992. "Theoretical Foundations of AIDS: Media Campaigns." In T. Edgar, M. Fitzpatrick, and V. Freimuth (Eds.). *AIDS: A Communication Perspective.* New Jersey: Lawrence Erlbaum Associates Inc. pp. 91–110.

Freimuth, V.S., S.L. Hammond, T. Edgar, and **J.L. Monahan.** 1990. "Reaching those at Risk: A Content-analytic Study of AIDS PSAs." *Communication Research,* 17(6). pp. 775–91.

Freire, P. 1970. *Pedagogy of the Oppressed.* New York, NY: The Seabury Press.

———. 1973. *Education for critical consciousness.* New York, NY: The Seabury Press.

Frey, Frederick W. 1966. *The Mass Media and Rural Development in Turkey.* Cambridge: Massachusetts Institute of Technology, Center for International Studies, Rural Development Research Report 3.

———. 1973. "Communications and Development." In F. Frey, I. SolaPool, W. Schramm, N. Maccoby, and E. Parker (Eds.). *Handbook of Communication.* Chicago: Rand McNally College Publishing Company. pp. 337–461.

Friberg, M. and **B. Hettne.** 1985. "The Greening of the World—Towards a Non-Deterministic Model of Global Processes." *Development as Social Transformation.* London: Hodder and Stoughton. pp. 204–70.

Friesen, E. 1999. "Exploring the Links between Structuration Theory and Participatory Action Research." In T. Jacobson and J. Servaes (Eds.). *Theoretical Approaches to Participatory Communication.* Creskill, NJ: Hampton Press. pp. 281–308.

Frye, M. 1983. *The Politics of Reality: Essays in Feminist Theory.* New York: The Crossing Press.

Furtado, Celso. 1964. *Development and Underdevelopment.* Berkeley: University of California Press.

Gandhi, M. 1967. *The Mind of Mahatma Gandhi.* Edited by R.K. Prabhu and U.R. Rao. Ahmedabad, India: Navajivan Publishing House.

Gans, H. 1962. *The Urban Villagers*. New York: The Free Press.

Gaur, R.A. 1981. "Transfer of Technology: A Tool for Modernising Agriculture." *Management of Transfer of Farm Technology*. Hyderabad, India: National Institute of Rural Development. pp. 103–5.

Gaventa, J. 1980. *Power and Powerlessness: Quiescence and Rebellion in an Appalachian Valley*. Urbana, IL: University of Illinois Press.

Gersch, B. 1998. "Gender at the Crossroads: The Internet as Cultural Text." *Journal of Communication Inquiry*, 22(3). pp. 306–16.

Gill, H. and **S. Mohammed.** 1994. "Factors affecting Control of AIDS in Nigeria." International Conference on AIDS 10(2): 252 (abstract no. PC0371). August 7–12.

Gitlin, T. 1980. *The Whole World is Watching: Mass Media and the Making and Unmaking of the New Left*. Berkeley: University of California Press.

Golding, Peter. 1974. "Media Role in National Development: Critique of a Theoretical Orthodoxy." *Journal of Communication*. 24(3): pp. 39–53.

Goldthorpe, J.E. 1975. *The Sociology of the Third World*. Cambridge, UK: Cambridge University Press.

Good News Bible: Today's English Version. 1992. New York: American Bible Society.

Goswami, D. and **S.R. Melkote.** 1997. "Knowledge Gap in AIDS Communication." *Gazette*, 59(3). pp. 205–21.

Goulet, D. 1971. *The Cruel Choice: A New Concept in Theory of Development*. New York: Altheneum.

——. 1973. "Development—or Liberation." In C. Wilber (Ed.). *The Political Economy of Development and Underdevelopment*. New York: Random House.

Government of Ghana. June, 1996. *Project Agreement from the Government of the Republic of Ghana to United Nations Population Fund*. Accra, Ghana: Government of Ghana.

Government of India. 1981. *Agricultural Extension: The Training and Visit System—Operational Notes*. New Delhi: Ministry of Agriculture and Cooperation.

Gramsci, A. 1971. *Selection from the Prison Notebooks*. New York: Internationalist.

Gran, Guy. 1983. *Development by People: Citizen Construction of a Just World*. New York: Praeger.

Grant, James P. 1978. *Disparity Reduction Rates in Social Indicators*. Overseas Development Council, Monograph No. 11.

Grey, M. 1999. "Feminist Theology: A Critical Theology of Liberation." In C. Rowland (Ed.). *The Cambridge Companion to Liberation Theology*. Cambridge: Cambridge University Press. pp. 89–106.

Gross, S.O.P. 1990. "Religious Pluralism in Struggles for Justice." *New Blackfriars*, 71(841). pp. 377–86.

Grunig, J.E. and **T. Hunt.** 1984. *Managing Public Relations*. New York: Holt, Rinehart & Winston.

Gusfield, J.R. 1971. "Tradition and Modernity: Misplaced Polarities in the Study of Social Change." In J. Finkle and R. Gable (Eds.). *Political Development and Social Change*. New York: John Wiley. pp. 15–26.

Gutiérrez, G. 1973. *A Theology of Liberation: History, Politics and Salvation*. Siser Caridad Inda and John Eagleson (Eds.) and Trans. Maryknoll, NY: Orbis Books.

Hagen, Everett E. 1962. *On the Theory of Social Change*. Homewood, Illinois: Dorsey.

Halarnkar, S. 1998. "Harvest of Death." *India Today*. pp.48–54.

Hall, E.T. 1976. *Beyond Culture*. Garden City, NY: Anchor Press.

Halloran, James. 1981. "The Context of Mass Communication Research." In Emile McAnany, J. Schnitman, and N. James (Eds.). *Communication and Social Structure.* New York: Praeger. pp. 21–57.

Hamelink, C. 1983. *Cultural Autonomy in Global Communications.* New York: Longman.
——. 2001. "The Planning of Communication Technology: Alternatives for the Periphery?" In S. Melkote and S. Rao (Eds.). *Critical Issues in Communication.* New Delhi: Sage.

Haraway, D. 1991. *Simians, Cyborgs and Women: The Re-invention of Nature.* London: Free Association Books.

Harrison, Paul. 1979. *Inside the Third World.* New York: Penguin Books.

Havelock, R.G. 1971. *Planning for Innovation through Dissemination and Utilization of Knowledge.* In Juan Diaz-Bordenave, "Communication for Agricultural Innovations in Latin America." In E. Rogers (Ed.). *Communication and Development: Critical Per-spectives.* 1976. Beverly Hills: Sage.

Heath, C. 1992. "Structural Changes in Kenya's Broadcasting System: A Manifestation of Presidential Authoritarianism," *Gazette*, 37. pp. 37–51.

Hedebro, Goran. 1982. *Communication and Social Change in Developing Nations: A Critical View.* Ames: Iowa State University Press.

Heeks, R. 1999. "Information and Communication Technologies, Poverty and Development." *Development Informatics.* Working Paper Series, No. 5. Manchester, UK: Institute for Development Policy and Management.

Heine-Geldern, Robert. 1968. "Diffusion: I. Cultural Diffusion." In D.L. Sills (Ed.). *International Encyclopedia of the Social Sciences.* Vol. 4. New York: Macmillan. pp. 169–73.

Heise, L. 1992. *Fact Sheet on Gender Violence: A Statistics for Action Facts Sheet.* New York: IWTC/UNIFEM Resource Center.

Hellman, H. 1980. "Idealism, Aggression, Apology, and Criticism: The Four Traditions of Research on International Communication." Paper prepared for XII Congress of the IAMCR, Caracas.

Herskovits, Melville J. 1969. *Man and His Works.* New York: Knopf.

Hewitt, K. 1995. "Sustainable Disasters?" In J. Crush (Ed.). *Power of Development.* London: Routledge. pp. 115–28.

Hirschman, Albert O. 1958. *Strategy of Economic Development.* New Haven: Yale University Press.

Hobsbawm, E.J. 1968. *Industry and Empire: An Economic History of Britain since 1750.* London: Pantheon Books.

Honadle, G. 1999. *How Context Matters: Linking Environmental Policy to People and Place.* West Hartford, Connecticut: Kumarian Press.

Hoogvelt, A. 1982. *The Third World in Global Development.* London: Macmillan.

hooks, B. 1984. *Feminist theory: From margin to center.* Boston: South End Press.
——. 1989. *Talking Back: Thinking Feminist, Thinking Black.* Boston: South End Press.

Hornik, R.C. 1988. *Development Communication: Information, Agriculture and Nutrition in the Third World.* New York, NY: Longman.

Horowitz, Irving L. 1970. "Personality and Structural Dimensions in Comparative International Development." *Social Science Quarterly*, 51 (December). pp. 494–513.

Horton, D.E. 1991. "Social Scientists in International Agricultural Research: Ensuring Relevance and Contributing to the Knowledge Base." In W.F. Whyte (Ed.). *Participatory Action Research.* Newbury Park, CA: Sage. pp. 218–36.

Hoselitz, B.F. 1960. *Sociological Factors in Economic Development*. Glencoe: Free Press.

Hoskins, M. 1980. *Various Perspectives on Using Women's Organizations in Development Programming*. Washington, DC: USAID.

Hovland, C.I., A.A. Lumsdaine, and **F.D. Sheffield.** 1949. *Experiments in Mass Communication*. New York: Wiley.

Hovland, C.I., I.L. Janis, and **H.H. Kelley.** 1953. *Communication and Persuasion*. New Haven: Yale University Press.

Hoy, P. 1998. *Players and Issues in International Aid*. West Hartford, CT: Kumarian Press.

Hudson, H.E. 1984. *When Telephones Reach the Village: The Role of Telecommunications in Rural Development*. Norwood: Ablex.

Hudson, H.E. 1998. "Global Information Infrastructure: The Rural Challenge." In D. Richardson and L. Paisley (Eds.). *The First Mile of Connectivity*. Rome: FAO. pp. 270–86.

Hyden, G. 1980. *Beyond Ujamaa in Tanzania: Underdevelopment and an Uncaptured Peasantry*. Berkeley: University of California Press.

Illich, Ivan. 1969. *The Celebration of Awareness*. New York: Doubleday and Company.

India: A Reference Manual. 1982. New Delhi, India: Ministry of Information and Broadcasting, Government of India.

Inkeles, Alex. 1966. "The Modernization of Man." In M. Weiner (Ed.). *Modernization: The Dynamics of Growth*. New York: Basic Books. pp. 138–50.

———. 1969. "Making Men Modern: On the Causes and Consequences of Individual Change in Six Countries." *American Journal of Sociology*, 75 (September). pp. 208–25.

Inkeles, A. and **D.H. Smith.** 1974. *Becoming Modern: Individual Change in Six Developing Countries*. Cambridge: Harvard University Press.

Intensive Agricultural Extension in the Command Areas: The Training and Visit System. 1983. Hyderabad, India: Government of Andhra Pradesh, Department of Irrigation Utilization and Command Area Development.

Institute of Social Studies, The Hague. 1980. *Communication Research in Third World Realities*. The Hague: Institute of Social Studies.

International Network of Engaged Buddhists. http://www.bpf.org/ineb.html.

Isasi-Diaz, A.M. and **Y. Tarango.** 1988. *Hispanic Women, Prophetic Voice in the Church: Toward a Hispanic Women's Liberation Theology*. San Francisco: Harper & Row.

Isbister, J. 1991. *Promises not Kept: The Betrayal of Social Change in the Third World*. West Hartford, CT: Kumarian Press.

ITU (International Telecommunication Union). 1995. *World Telecommunication Development Report*. Geneva: ITU.

Jacobson, T.L. 1989. "Old and New Approaches to Participatory Communication for Development." Paper prepared for the seminar Participation: A Key Concept in Communication for Change and Development. Pune, India.

———. 1993. "A Pragmatist Account of Participatory Communication Research for National Development." *Communication Theory*, 3(3). pp. 214–30.

Jacobson, T.L. and **S. Kolluri.** 1999. "Participatory Communication as Communicative Action." In T. Jacobson and J. Servaes (Eds.). *Theoretical Approaches to Participatory Communication*. Creskill, NJ: Hampton Press. pp. 265–80.

Jacobson, T. and **J. Servaes** (Eds.). 1999. *Theoretical Approaches to Participatory Communication*. Creskill, NJ: Hampton Press.

Jaiswal, N.K. and **H.P.S. Arya.** 1981. "Transfer of Farm Technology in India: An Overview." *Management of Transfer of Farm Technology.* Hyderabad, India: National Institute of Rural Development. pp. 13–48.

James, S. 1994. "Facilitating Communication within Rural and Marginal Communities: A Model for Development Support." In S. White, K.S. Nair, and J. Ascroft (Eds.). *Participatory Communication: Working for Change and Development.* New Delhi: Sage. pp. 329–41.

Jaquette, J. and **K. Staudt.** 1985. "Women as 'At-Risk' Reproducers: Biology, Science and Population in U.S. Foreign Policy." In V. Shapiro (Ed.). *Women, Biology, and Public Policy.* Beverly Hills, CA: Sage. pp. 235–68.

Jayawardana, K. 1986. *Feminism and Nationalism in the Third World.* London: Zed Press.

Jayaweera, Neville. 1987. "Rethinking Development Communication: A Holistic View." In N. Jayaweera and S. Amunugama (Eds.). *Rethinking Development Communication.* Singapore: Asian Mass Communication Research and Information Center. pp. 76–94.

Jayaweera, N. and **S. Amunugama** (Eds.). 1987. *Rethinking Development Communication.* Singapore: Asian Mass Communication Research and Information Center.

Jesudasan, I. 1984. *A Gandhian Theology of Liberation.* New York: Maryknoll.

Jiggins, J. 1984. "Rhetoric and Reality: Where do Women in Agricultural Development Projects Stand Today?" *Agricultural Administration,* 15(2). pp. 157–75.

Johnston, B. and **J. Mellor.** 1961. "The Role of Agriculture in Economic Development." *American Economic Review,* (September). pp. 571–81.

Jones, E.E. and **R. Kohler.** 1958. "The Effects of Plausibility on the Learning of Controversial Statements." *Journal of Abnormal and Social Psychology,* 57. pp. 315–20.

Junic Report. 1980. "The Role of Information in Development: Development Support Communication." ACC/1980/11.

Jussawala, Meheroo. 1985. "International Telecommunication Policies." *Development,* 1. pp. 64–66.

Kabeer, N. 1994. *Reversed Realities: Gender Hierarchies in Development Thought.* London: Verso.

Kahl, Joseph A. 1968. *The Measurement of Modernism.* Austin, Texas: University of Texas Press.

Kantowski, D. 1980. *Sarvodaya: The Other Development.* New Delhi: Vikas Publishing House.

Kashima, Y. and **C. Gallois.** 1993. "The Theory of Reasoned Action and Problem-Focused Research." In D.J. Terry, C. Gallois, and M. McCamish (Eds.). *The Theory of Reasoned Action: Its Application to AIDS Preventive Behavior.* New York: Pergamon Press.

Kashima, Y., C. Gallois, and **M. McCamish.** 1992. "Predicting the Use of Condoms: Past Behaviors, Norms, and Sexual Partner." In T. Edgar, M. Fitzpatrick, and V. Freimuth (Eds.). *AIDS: A Communication Perspective.* New Jersey: Lawrence Erlbaum Associates Inc. pp. 21–46.

Katz, Elihu. 1957. "The Two-Step Flow of Communication." *Public Opinion Quarterly,* 21. pp. 61–78.

——. 1963. "The Diffusion of New Ideas and Practices." In Wilbur Schramm (Ed.). *The Science of Human Communication.* New York: Basic Books. pp. 77–93.

Katz, Elihu. 1968. "Diffusion: III. Interpersonal Influence." *International Encyclopedia of the Social Sciences.* Vol. 4. David L. Sills (Ed.). New York: Macmillan. pp. 178–84.

Katz, Elihu and **P. Lazarsfeld.** 1955. *Personal Influence.* New York: Free Press.

Kaye, G. 1990. "A Community Organizer's Perspective on Citizen Participation Research and the Research-Practitioner Partnership." *American Journal of Community Psychology,* 18(1). pp. 151–57.

Kellow, C.L. 1998. "Refugee Needs and Donor Agendas: Communication and Coordination of Services in Refugee Aid Programs." Unpublished Master's thesis. University of Oregon, Eugene, Oregon.

Kennedy, J.F. 1961. Special Message to the Congress, Washington, D.C.

Kerblay, B. 1971. "Chayanov and the Theory of Peasantry as a Specific Type of Economy." *Peasants and Peasant Society.* New York: Penguin Books.

Kerlinger, Fred N. 1973. *Foundation of Behavioral Research.* Second Edition. New York: Holt, Rinehart and Winston.

Khan, A.H. 1976. "The Comilla Experience in Bangladesh—My Lessons in Communication." In W. Schramm and D. Lerner (Eds.). *Communication and Change: The Last Ten Years and the Next.* Honolulu: The University Press at Hawaii. pp. 67–75.

Khan, A.W. 1987. "Role of Radio in Development Communication: A Country Cousin Syndromme." In K.E. Eapen (Ed.). *The Role of Radio in Growth and Development.* Bangalore: Bangalore University. pp. 29–36.

Kidd, Ross. 1984. "The Performing Arts and Development in India: Three Case Studies and a Comparative Analysis." In G. Wang and W. Dissanayake (Eds.). *Continuity and Change in Communication Systems.* New Jersey: Ablex. pp. 95–125.

Kidron, Michael and **Ronald Seagal.** 1995. *The State of the World Atlas, New Edition.* London: Penguin.

Kieffer, C. 1984. "Citizen Empowerment: A Developmental Perspective." In J. Rappaport, C. Swift, and R. Hess (Eds.). *Studies in Empowerment: Steps toward Understanding and Action.* New York, NY: The Haworth Press. pp. 9–36.

Kishore, D. 1968. "A Study of Effectiveness of Radio as a Mass Communication Medium in Dissemination of Agricultural Information." Ph.D. Dissertation. Indian Agricultural Research Institute, New Delhi, India.

Klapper, J.T. 1960. *The Effects of Mass Communication.* New York: Free Press.

Knitter, P.F. 1987. "Towards a Liberation Theology of Religion." In J. Hick and P.F. Knitter (Eds.). *The Myth of Christian Uniqueness.* Maryknoll, NY: CM Press. pp. 178–200.

Knott, K. 1998. *Hinduism: A Very Short Introduction.* Oxford: Oxford University Press.

Kothari, Rajni. 1984. "Communications for Alternative Development: Towards a Paradigm." *Development Dialogue.* pp. 1–2.

Kotler, P. 1984. "Social Marketing of Health Behavior." In L.W. Frederiksen, L.J. Solomon, and K.A. Brehony (Eds.). *Marketing Health Behavior.* New York: Plenum Press. pp. 23–39.

Kotler, P. and **G. Zaltman.** 1971. "Social Marketing: An Approach to Planned Social Change." *Journal of Marketing* (July). pp. 3–12.

Krippendorff, Sultana. 1979. "The Communication Approach to Development: A Critical Review." *Third World Mass Media: Issues, Theory and Research.* Williamsburg, Virginia: Studies in Third World Societies, College of William and Mary. pp. 71–82.

Krishnaswamy, M.V. 1974. "Film Treatment of Folk Forms." Paper presented to the Inter-Regional Seminar/Workshop on the Integrated Use of Folk Media and Mass Media in Family Planning Communication Programmes, New Delhi, October 7–16.

Kroeber, A.L. 1944. *Configurations of Culture Growth*. Berkeley: University of California Press.

Kronenburg, J. 1986. *Empowerment of the Poor: A Comparative Analysis of Two Development Endeavours in Kenya*. As Cited in Jan Servaes. 1989. "Participatory Communication Research within Social Movements." Paper prepared for the seminar Participation: A Key Concept in Communication for Change and Development, Pune, India.

Kumar, Kamlesh. 1981. "Technology Transfer in Indian Agriculture: Process and Problems." *Management of Transfer of Farm Technology*. Hyderabad, India: National Institute of Rural Development. pp. 106–16.

Lagos-Matus, Gustavo. 1963. *International Stratification and Underdeveloped Countries*. Chapel Hill: University of North Carolina Press.

Lasswell, H.D. 1935. *World Politics and Personal Insecurity*. Cited in D. Davis and S.J. Baran. *Mass Communication and Everyday Life*. California: Wadsworth Publishing.

———. 1948. "The Structure and Function of Communication in Society." In L. Bryson (Ed.). *The Communication of Ideas*. New York: Harper and Brothers.

———. 1951. "The Strategy of Soviet Propaganda." In W. Schramm (Ed.). *The Process and Effects of Mass Communication*. Urbana: University of Illinois Press.

Latouche, S. 1992. 'Standard of Living." In W. Sachs (Ed.). *Development Dictionary*: London: Zed Books. pp. 250–63.

Lazarsfeld, P. 1941. "Remarks on Administrative and Critical Communications Research." *Studies in Philosophy and Social Science*, 9. pp. 2–16.

Lazarsfeld, P., H. Berelson, and **H. Gaudet.** 1948. *The People's Choice*. New York: Columbia University Press.

Lenglet, Frans. 1980. "The Ivory Coast: Who Benefits from Education/Information in Rural Television?" In Emile G. McAnany (Ed.). *Communications in the Rural Third World*. New York: Praeger. pp. 49–70.

Lenin, V.I. 1939. *Imperialism: The Highest Stage of Capitalism*. New York: International Publishers.

Lent, John A. 1979. "Mass Communications in the Third World: Some Ethical Considerations." *Third World Mass Media: Issues, Theory and Research*. Williamsburg, Virginia: Studies in Third World Societies, College of William and Mary. pp. 1–16.

———. 1987. "Devcom: A View from the United States." In N. Jayaweera and S. Amunugama (Eds.). *Rethinking Development Communication*. Singapore: Asian Mass Communication Research and Information Center. pp. 20–41.

Lerner, Daniel. 1958. *The Passing of Traditional Society: Modernizing the Middle East*. New York: Free Press.

———. 1963. "Toward a Communication Theory of Modernization." In Lucien Pye (Ed.). *Communications and Political Development*. Princeton, NJ: Princeton University Press.

Lerner, M. 1991. "Jewish Liberation Theology and Emancipatory Politics." In M. Zweig (Ed.). *Religion and Economic Justice*. Philadelphia: Temple University Press. pp. 128–44.

Levine, J.M. and **G. Murphy.** 1958. "The Learning and Forgetting of Controversial Material." In E.E. Maccoby et al. (Eds.). *Readings in Social Psychology*. Third Edition. New York: Holt, Rinehart and Winston. pp. 94–101.

Levy, Marion Jr. 1966. *Modernization and the Structure of Society.* Princeton, NJ: Princeton University Press.

Lewis, M. 1992. *Green Delusions: An Environmentalist Critique of Radical Environmentalism.* Durham: Duke University Press.

Lewis, Oscar. 1961. 'The Culture of Poverty." In J.J. TePaska and S.N. Fisher (Eds.). *Explosive Forces in Latin America.* Columbus, Ohio: Ohio State University Press.

Linton, Ralph. 1936. *The Study of Man.* New York: Appleton–Century–Crofts.

Lionberger, Herbert F. 1960. *Adoption of New Ideas and Practices.* Ames: Iowa State University Press.

Liyanage, G. 1988. *Revolution under the Breadfruit Tree: The Story of Sarvodaya Shramadana Movement and its Founder Dr. A.T. Ariyaratne.* Nugegoda, Sri Lanka: Sinha Publishers.

Llyod, M. May 24, 2000. "Magic Box—A Lifeline to India's Poor Farmers." www.scmp.com/News/Comment/Article/FullText asp ArticleID-200005240 52040288.asp.

Lovelock, J. 1979. *Gaia: A New Look on Life on Earth.* Oxford, UK: Oxford University Press.

Lowery, Shearon and **Melvin L. DeFleur.** 1988. *Milestones in Mass Communication Research.* Second Edition. New York: Longman.

——. 1995. *Milestones in Mass Communication Research.* Third Edition. New York: Longman.

Lukes, S. 1974. *Power: A Radical View.* London, UK: Macmillan.

Luthra, R. 1988. "Communication in the Social Marketing of Contraceptives: A Case Study of the Bangladesh Project." Unpublished Ph.D. dissertation. University of Wisconsin, Madison.

——. 1991. "Contraceptive Social Marketing in the Third World: A Case of Multiple Transfer." *Gazette*, 47. pp. 159–76.

Macy, Joanna. 1983. *Dharma and Development: Religion as a Resource in the Sarvodaya Self-Help Movement.* West Hartford, CT: Kumarian Press.

Mahathera, D.N. August 4, 1998. "Introduction to Buddhism." http://www.buddhayana. nl/buddhism.html.

Maibach, E., G. Kreps, and **E. Bonaguro.** 1993. "Developing Strategic Communication Campaigns of HIV/AIDS Prevention." In S. Ratzan (Ed.). *AIDS: Effective Health Communication for the 90s.* Washington, D.C.: Taylor and Francis.

Maine, Henry. 1907. *Ancient Law.* London: John Murray Publishers.

Maitland Commission. 1984. *The Missing Link: Report of the Independent Commission for Worldwide Telecommunications Development.* Geneva: International Telecommunication Union.

Mamdani, M. 1972. *The Myth of Population Control.* New York: Monthly Review Press.

Mane, Vasant. 1974. "Identification of Flexible Folk Drama in Family Planning Communication." Paper presented to the Inter-Regional Seminar/Workshop on the Integrated Use of Folk Media and Mass Media in Family Planning Communication Programmes, New Delhi. October 7–16.

Manoff, R.K. 1985. *Social Marketing: A New Imperative for Public Health.* New York: Praeger.

March, K. and **R. Taggu.** 1986. *Women's Informal Association in Developing Countries.* Boulder, Co: Westview.

Masani, Mehra. 1975. "Introduction." *Communication and Rural Progress*. In Masani Mehra (Ed.). Mumbai: Leslie Sawhny Programme of Training in Democracy. pp. 1–6.

Masilela, S.T. 1994. "Communication Strategies for Community Participation in the non-Governmental Space of Development Efforts: The Case of Kibwezi, Kenya." Unpublished Ph.D. Dissertation. University of Iowa, Iowa City.

Mattis, Ann (Ed.). 1983. *A Society for International Development: Prospectus 1984*. Durham, North Carolina: Duke University Press.

Maududi, A.A. 1988. *Toward understanding the Qur'an*. Translated and Edited by Z.I. Ansari. Leicester: Islamic Foundation.

Mayo, J. and **J. Servaes.** 1994. *Approaches to Development Communication*. Paris/ New York: UNESCO/UNFPA.

Mayo, M. and **G. Craig.** 1995. "Community Participation and Empowerment." In M. Mayo and G. Craig (Eds.). *Community Empowerment: A Reader in Participation and Development*. London: Zed Books. pp. 1–11.

McAnany, Emile G. 1980a. "The Role of Information in Communicating with the Rural Poor: Some Reflections." In Emile G. MacAnany (Ed.). *Communications in the Rural Third World*. New York: Praeger. pp. 3–18.

———. 1980b. "Overview." In Emile G. McAnany (Ed.). *Communications in the Rural Third World*. New York: Praeger. pp. xi–xvi.

McClelland, David C. 1966. "The Impulse to Modernization." In M. Weiner (Ed.). *Modernization: The Dynamics of Growth*. New York: Basic Books. pp. 28–39.

———. 1967. *The Achieving Society*. New York: Free Press.

McQuail, D. 1983. *Mass Communication Theory*. Sage: London.

———. 1994. *Mass Communication Theory, Third Edition*. Sage: London.

McQuail, Denis and **Sven Windahl.** 1981. *Communication Models*. New York: Longman.

Mda, Z. 1993. *When People Play People: Development Communication through Theatre*. Johannesburg: Witwatersand University Press.

Meadows, D.H. 1972. *The Limits to Growth*. New York: Basic Books.

Meeker, J. 1987. "Misused Resources." *Resurgence*, 125 (December).

Mehta, A. and **S. Akthar.** 1999. "Promoting the Internet in South Asia." *Economic and Political Weekly*, XXXIV (46 and 47). pp. 3305–8.

Melkote, S. 1984. "The Biases in Extension Communication: Revealing the Comprehension Gap." Ph.D. Dissertation. University of Iowa, Iowa City.

———. 1987. "Biases in Development Support Communication: Revealing the Comprehension Gap." *Gazette*, 40. pp. 39–55.

———. 1989. "Effectiveness of Development Radio Programming among Poor Farmers." *Gazette*, 43. pp. 17–30.

———. 1991. *Communication for Development in the Third World: Theory and Practice*. New Delhi: Sage.

Melkote, S.R. and **K. Kandath.** 2001. "Barking Up the Wrong Tree? An Inward Look at the Discipline and Practice of Development Communication." In S. Melkote and S. Rao (Eds.). *Critical Issues in Communication*. New Delhi: Sage.

Melkote, S.R. and **A.H. Merriam.** 1998. "The Third World: Definitions and New Perspectives on Development." In A. Gonzalez and J. Norwine (Eds.). *The New Third World*. Second Edition. Boulder, Co: Westview Press. pp. 9–27.

Melkote, S.R. and **S. Muppidi.** 1999. "AIDS Communication: Role of Knowledge Factors on Perception of Risk." *Journal of Development Communication*, 10(1). pp. 16–26.

Melkote, S.R., S.R. Muppidi, and **D. Goswami.** 2000. "Social and Economic Factors in an Integrated Behavior and Societal Approach to Communications in HIV/AIDS." *Journal of Health Communication,* 5. pp. 1–11.

Mernissi, F. 1987. *Women and Islam: An Historical and Theological Enquiry.* Oxford, UK: Basil Blackwell.

Mesters, C. 1983. "The Use of the Bible in Christian Communities of the Common People." In N.K. Gottwald (Ed.). *The Bible and Liberation.* Maryknoll, NY: Orbis Books. pp. 119–33.

———. 1989. *Defenseless Flower.* London: CIIR.

Michal-Johnson, P. and **S. Bowen.** 1993. "The Place of Culture in HIV Education." In T. Edgar, M. Fitzpatrick, and V. Freimuth (Eds.). *AIDS: A Communication Perspective.* New Jersey: Lawrence Erlbaum Associates Inc. pp. 147–72.

Migdal, J. 1974. *Peasants, Politics and Revolution.* Princeton, NJ: Princeton University Press.

Milinkovic, Branko. 1999. "Languages Die of Globalization and Intolerance." *Junio,* 133.

Minh-ha, T.T. 1986–87. "Difference: A Special Third World Woman Issue." *Discourse,* 8. pp. 11–38.

Mitchell, T. 1995. "The Object of Development." In J. Crush (Ed.). *Power of Development.* London: Routledge. pp. 129–57.

Mody, B. 1991. *Designing Messages for Development Communication: An Audience Participation-based Approach.* New Delhi: Sage.

Moemeka, A.A. (Ed.). 1994. *Communicating for Development: A New Pan-Disciplinary Perspective.* Albany, NY: SUNY Press.

Mohanty, C.T. 1988. "Under Western Eyes: Feminist Scholarship and Colonial Discourses." *Feminist Review,* 30. pp. 61–88.

———. 1991a. "Introduction: Cartographies of Struggle: Third World Women and the Politics of Feminism." In C.T. Mohanty, A. Russo, and L. Torres (Eds.). *Third World Women and the Politics of Feminism.* Bloomington, IN: Indiana University Press. pp. 1–47.

———. 1991b. "Under Western Eyes: Feminist Scholarship and Colonial Discourses." In C.T. Mohanty, A. Russo, and L. Torres (Eds.). *Third World Women and the Politics of Feminism.* Bloomington, IN: Indiana University Press. pp. 51–80.

Morgan, James, K. Dickenson, J. Dickenson, J. Benus, and **G. Duncan.** 1974. *Five Thousand American Families: Patterns of Economic Progress.* Vol. 1, Ann Arbor: Survey Research Center, Institute for Social Research, University of Michigan.

Morris, Morris D. 1979. *Measuring the Condition of the World's Poor: The PQLI.* New York: Pergamon Press.

Morrison, J.F. 1993. "Communicating Healthcare through Forum Theater. *Gazette,* 52. pp. 109–21."

Moser, C. 1989. "Gender Planning in the Third World: Meeting Practical and Strategic Gender Needs." *World Development,* 17(11). pp. 1799–825.

Mowlana, Hamid and **Laurie Wilson.** 1988. *Communication Technology and Development.* Paris: UNESCO.

Myrdal, G. 1968. *Asian Drama,* London: Allen Lane.

Myrdal, Gunnar. 1970. *The Challenge of World Poverty.* New York: Vintage Books.

NACO. 1997–98. *Country Scenario 1997–98.* New Delhi: National AIDS Control Organization, Ministry of Health and Family Welfare, Government of India.

Nair, K.S. and S. White. 1987. "Participatory Message Development: A Conceptual Framework." *Media Development*. 34(3).

——.(Eds.). 1993. *Perspectives on Development Communication*. New Delhi: Sage.

Nandapurkar, G.G. and R.R. Rulkarni. 1983. "Training and Visit System: Some Observations and Suggestions." *Management of Transfer of Farm Technology under the Training and Visit System*. Hyderabad, India: National Institute of Rural Development.

Nandy, A. 1987. "Cultural Frames for Social Transformation: A Credo." *Alternatives*, XII. pp. 113–23.

——. 1992. "State." In W. Sachs (Ed.). *Development Dictionary*. London: Zed Books. pp. 264–74.

Narula, Uma and W.B. Pearce. 1986. *Development as Communication*. Carbondale. Illinois: Southern Illinois University Press.

Neurath, Paul. 1962. "Radio Farm Forum as a Tool of Change in Indian Villages." *Economic Development and Cultural Change*, 10. pp. 275–83.

——. 1976. "Types of Surveys." In Gerald Hursh-Cesar and Prodipto Roy (Eds.). *Third World Surveys*. New Delhi: Macmillan. pp. 91–140.

Nordenstreng, Kaarle. 1968. "Communication Research in the United States: A Critical Perspective." *Gazette*, 14.

Nordenstreng, K. and H.I. Schiller (Eds.). 1993. *Beyond National Sovereignty: International Communications in the 1990s*. Norwood, NJ: Ablex.

Noronha, Frederick. July 24, 2000. "Indian Duo Put Together a 'Dirt Cheap' Radio-Station-in-a-Briefcase." fred@goal.dot.net.in.

Nurske, Ragnar. 1953. *Problems of Capital Formation in Underdeveloped Countries*. Oxford, UK: Oxford University Press.

Nyerere, Julius. 1968. *Ujamaa: Essays in Socialism*. Dar es Salaam, Tanzania: Oxford University Press.

Obibuaku, L.O. 1983. *Agricultural Extension as a Strategy for Agricultural Transformation*. Nasukka: University of Nigeria Press.

Oshima, Harry T. 1976a. "Development and Mass Communication: A Re-examination." In W. Schramm and D. Lerner (Eds.). *Communication and Change*. Honolulu: University Press of Hawaii. pp. 17–30.

——. 1976b. "Old and New Strategies—An Economist's View." In W. Schramm D. and Lerner (Eds.). *Communication and Change*. Honolulu: University Press of Hawaii. pp. 53–56.

O'Sullivan, T., J. Hartley, D. Saunders, M. Montgomery, and J. Fiske. 1994. *Key Concepts in Communication and Cultural Studies, Second Edition*, London: Routledge.

Pace, Marie. 1993. "Awakening of All? A Feminist Appraisal of the Sarvodaya Shramadana Movement in Sri Lanka." Unpublished Master's Thesis. International Studies, University of Oregon.

Palda, K.S. 1966. "The Hypothesis of a Hierarchy of Effects: A Partial Evaluation." *Journal of Marketing Research*, 3. pp. 13–24.

Panos. 1998a. "The Internet and Poverty: Real Help or Real Hype?" Briefing No. 28, London: Panos. http://www.oneworld.org/panos/briefing/interpov.htm.

——. 1998b. *Information, Knowledge and Development*. London: Panos.

Parmar, Shyam. 1975. *Traditional Folk Media in India*. New Delhi: Geka Books.

Parpart, J.L. 1995. "Post-Modernism, Gender and Development." In J. Crush (Ed.). *Power of Development.* London: Routledge. pp. 253–65.

Parsons, Talcott. 1964a. *The Social System.* New York: Free Press.

——. 1964b. "Evolutionary Universals in Society." *American Sociological Review*, 29: 3 (June). pp. 339–57.

Patai, D. 1991. "U.S. Academics and Third World Women: Is Ethical Research Possible?" In S.B. Gluck and D. Patai (Eds.). *Women's Words: The Feminist Practice of Oral History.* New York: Routledge. pp. 137–53.

Perrett, Heli E. 1982. *Using Communication Support in Projects: The World Bank's Experience.* Washington, D.C.: The World Bank. Staff Working Paper Number 551.

Peterson, J. and **G. Marvin.** 1988. "Issues in the Prevention of AIDS among Black and Hispanic Men." *American Psychologist*, 43(11). pp. 871–77.

Piotrow, P.T., D.L. Kincaid, J.G. Rimon II, and **W. Rinehart.** 1997. *Health Communication: Lessons from Family Planning and Reproductive Health.* Westport, CT: Preager

Pletsch, C. 1981. "The Three Worlds, or the Division of Social Science Labor, circa 1950–1975." *Comparative Studies in Society and History*, 23. pp. 565–90.

Polsby, N.W. 1959. "The Sociology of Community Power: A Reassessment." *Social Forces*, 37. pp. 232–36.

Popkin, S. 1979. *The Rational Peasant.* Berkeley, California: University of California Press.

Portes, Alejandro. 1974. "Modernity and Development: A Critique." *Studies in Comparative International Development*, 9 (Spring). pp. 247–79.

——. 1976. "On the Sociology of National Development: Theories and Issues." *American Journal of Sociology*, 82(1). pp. 55–85.

Prochaska, J.O., C.C. DiClemente, and **J.C. Norcross.** 1992. "In Search of How People Change: Applications to Addictive Behaviors." *American Psychologist* 47(9): 1102–14.

Project Mass Communication. January 24, 2000. http://www.hindubusinessline.com.

Pye, L. 1963. *Communications and Political Development.* Princeton, NJ: Princeton University Press.

Queen, C.S. and **S.B. King** (Eds.). 1996. *Engaged Buddhism: Buddhist Liberation Movements in Asia.* Albany: State University of New York Press.

Quinn, S. 1993. "AIDS and the African American women: The triple burden of race, class, and gender." *Health Education Quarterly*, 20(3). pp. 305–20.

Rahim, Sayed A. 1976. "Diffusion Research—Past, Present and Future." In W. Schramm and D. Lerner (Eds.). *Communication and Change.* Honolulu: University Press of Hawaii. pp. 223–25.

Rahman, M.A. 1981. "Reflections." *Development*, 1. pp. 43–51.

——. 1991a. "The Theoretical Standpoint of PAR." In O. Fals-Borda and M.A. Rahman (Eds.). *Action and Knowledge: Breaking the Monopoly with Participatory Action-Research.* New York: Apex Press, pp. 13–23.

——. 1991b. "Glimpses of the 'Other Africa.'" In O. Fals-Borda and M.A. Rahman (Eds.). *Action and Knowledge: Breaking the Monopoly with Participatory Action-Research.* New York: Apex Press, pp. 84–108.

——. 1995. "Participatory Development: Toward Liberation or Co-optation?" In M. Mayo and G. Craig (Eds.). *Community Empowerment: A Reader in Participation and Development.* London: Zed Books, pp. 24–32.

Rai, C., K. Leslie, M. Dupar, and **N. Pyakuryal.** 1993. "Survey on Knowledge, Attitude and Practice regarding STDs/AIDS in Nuwakot, Nepal." Paper presented to the International Conference on AIDS, June 6–11.

Ranganath, H.K. 1975 "Traditional Media." *Instructional Technology Report.* No. 12 (September).

———. 1980. *Folk Media and Communication.* Bangalore, India: Chintana Prakashana Publishers.

Rao, Lakshmana. 1963. Communication and Development: A Study of Two Indian Villages. Doctoral Dissertation. University of Minnesota, St. Paul.

Rappaport, J. 1981. "In Praise of Paradox: A Social Policy of Empowerment over Prevention." *American Journal of Community Psychology,* 9(1). pp. 1–25.

Rappaport, J. 1984. "Studies in Empowerment: Introduction to the Issue." In J. Rappaport, C. Swift, and R. Hess (Eds.). *Studies in Empowerment: Steps toward Understanding and Action.* New York, NY: The Haworth Press. pp. 1–7.

———. 1987. "Terms of Empowerment/Exemplars of Prevention: Toward a Theory for Community Psychology." *American Journal of Community Psychology,* 15(2). pp. 121–44.

———. 1995. "Empowerment Meets Narrative: Listening to Stories and Creative Settings." *American Journal of Community Psychology,* 23(5). pp. 795–807.

Rappaport, J., C. Swift, and **R. Hess** (Eds.). 1984. *Studies in Empowerment: Steps Toward Understanding and Action.* New York, NY: Haworth.

Ratnapala, N. n.d. *Study Service in Sarvodaya.* Colombo: Sarvodaya Research Center, as cited in W. Dissanayake, "A Buddhist Approach to Development." 1984. In G. Wang and W. Dissanayake (Eds.). *Continuity and Change in Communications Systems.* New Jersey: Ablex.

Reddi, Usha V. 1987. "New Communication Technologies: What Sort of Development do They Bring in their Wake?" In N. Jayaweera and S. Amunugama (Eds.). *Rethinking Development Communication.* Singapore: Asian Mass Communication Research and Information Center. pp. 42–60.

Reddy, S.V. 1983. *Resource Utilization Pattern and Technological Gaps in the Adoption of Dry Land Agricultural Technology.* Hyderabad, India: Extension Education Institute, A.P. Agricultural University.

Reddy, S.V., B.V.S. Rao, and **S. Praveena.** 1983. "Intensive Agricultural Extension System (T&V System): A Critical Analysis." *Management of Transfer of Farm Technology under the Training and Visit System.* Hyderabad, India: National Institute of Rural Development.

Redfield, Robert. 1965. *Peasant Society and Culture.* Chicago: University of Chicago Press.

Reeves, G. 1993. *Communications and the "Third World."* New York: Routledge.

Reich, Robert B. 1982. "Ideologies of Survival." *The New Republic,* 3531 and 3532 (September). pp. 32–37.

Riano, P. (Ed.) 1994. *Women in Grassroots Communication: Furthering Social Change.* Thousand Oaks, CA: Sage.

Richardson, D. 1998a. "Rural Telecommunications Services and Stakeholder Participation: Bridging the Gap between Telecommunications Experts and Communication for Practitioners." In D. Richardon and L. Paisley (Eds.). *The First Mile of Connectivity.* Rome: FAO. pp. 14–35.

Richardson, D. 1998b. "The Internet and Rural Development." In D. Richardson and L. Paisley (Eds.). *The First Mile of Connectivity*. Rome: FAO. pp. 170–81.

Riley, J.W. and **M.W. Riley.** 1959. "Mass Communication and the Social System." In R.K. Merton, L. Broom, and L. Cottrell Jr. (Eds.). *Sociology Today*. New York: Basic Books.

Risseeuw, Carla. 1988. *The Fish don't Talk about the Water: Gender Transformation, Power and Resistance among Women in Sri Lanka*. Leiden, New York: E.J. Brill.

Robertson, Ian. 1977. *Sociology*. New York: Worth Publishers.

Rogers, Everett M. 1962. *Diffusion of Innovations*. New York: The Free Press.

———. 1965. "Mass Media Exposure and Modernization among Colombian Peasants." *Public Opinion Quarterly*, 29. pp. 614–25.

Rogers, Everett M. 1969. *Modernization among Peasants*. New York: Holt, Rinehart and Winston.

———. 1973. *Communication Strategies for Family Planning*. New York: Free Press.

———. 1975. "Network Analysis of the Diffusion of Family Planning Innovations over Time in Korean Villages: The Role of Mothers' Clubs." Paper presented at the Population Association of America, Seattle.

———. 1976a. "Where are we in Understanding the Diffusion of Innovations?" In W. Schramm and D. Lerner (Eds.). *Communication and Change*. Honolulu: University Press of Hawaii. pp. 204–22.

———. 1976b. "Communication and Development—The Passing of the Dominant Paradigm." In Everett M. Rogers (Ed.). *Communication and Development: Critical Perspectives*. Beverly Hills: Sage Publications. pp. 121–48.

———. 1976c. "The Passing of the Dominant Paradigm—Reflections on Diffusion Research." In W. Schramm and D. Lerner (Eds.). *Communication and Change*. Honolulu: University Press of Hawaii. pp. 49–52.

———. 1983. *Diffusion of Innovations*. Third Edition. New York: The Free Press.

———. 1986. *Communication Technology: The New Media in Society*. New York: Free Press.

———. 1987. "Communication and Development Today." Paper presented at the Seminar on Communication and Change: An Agenda for the New Age of Communication, Honolulu, July 20–August 1.

———. 1995. *Diffusion of Innovations*. Fourth Edition. New York: Free Press.

Rogers, Everett M. and **R. Adhikarya.** 1979. "Diffusion of Innovations: An Up-to-date Review and Commentary." In D. Nimmo (Ed.). *Communication Year Book 3*. New Jersey: International Communication Association, pp. 67–81.

Rogers, Everett M. and **D. Lawrence Kincaid.** 1981. *Communication Networks: Toward a New Paradigm for Research*. New York: The Free Press.

Rogers, Everett M. and **F.F. Shoemaker.** 1971. *Communication of Innovations: A Cross Cultural Approach*. New York: Free Press.

Roling, Niels G. 1973. "Problem Solving Research: A Strategy for Change." Paper presented at the International Seminar on Extension Education, Helsinki.

———. 1982. "Knowledge Utilisation: An Attempt to Relativate some Reified Realities." Paper presented to the Conference on Knowledge Utilisation: Theory and Methods at East West Center, Honolulu.

Roling, Niels G., Joseph Ascroft, and **Fred Wa Chege.** 1976. "The Diffusion of Innovations and the Issue of Equity in Rural Development." In Everett M. Rogers

(Ed.). *Communication and Development: Critical Perspectives*. Beverly Hills: Sage Publications. pp. 63–78.

Rose, Arnold M. 1970. "Sociological Factors affecting Economic Development in India." In Monte Palmer (Ed.). *The Human Factor in Political Development*. Waltham, Mass: Ginn and Company.

Rosenau, P.M. 1992. *Post-Modernism and the Social Sciences*. New Jersey: Princeton University Press.

Rosenstock, I., V. Stretcher and M. Becker. 1994. "The Health Belief Model and HIV Risk Behavior Change." In R. DiClemente and J. Peterson (Eds.). *Preventing AIDS: Theories and Methods of Behavioral Interventions*. New York: Plenum Press. pp. 5–24.

Rostow, W.W. 1960. *The Stages of Economic Growth: A Non-Communist Manifesto*. Cambridge, UK: Cambridge University Press.

Rothberg, D. 1993a. "The Crisis of Modernity and the Emergence of Socially Engaged Spirituality." *ReVision*, 15(3). pp. 105–14.

———. 1993b. "A Thai Perspective on Socially Engaged Buddhism: A Conversation with Sulak Sivaraksa." *ReVision*, 15(3). pp. 121–27.

Rozario, Santi. 1997. "Development and Rural Women in South Asia: The Limits of Empowerment and Conscientization." *Bulletin of Concerned Asian Scholars*, 30(1). pp. 45–53.

Rowlands, J. 1998. *Questioning Empowerment, Working with Women in Honduras*. London: Oxfam.

Ruigu, G.M. 1985. *Women Employment in Kenya*. University of Nairobi: Institute for Development Studies.

Ryan, Bryce and Neal Gross. 1943. "The Diffusion of Hybrid Seed Corn in Two Iowa Communities." *Rural Sociology*, 8. pp. 15–24.

Ryan, William. 1976. *Blaming the Victim*. New York: Vintage Books.

Sachs, W. 1992. "Environment." In W. Sachs (Ed.). *Development Dictionary*. London: Zed Books. pp. 26–37.

Said, E. 1978. *Orientalism*. New York: Pantheon.

Sainath. P. 1996. *Everybody Loves a Good Drought*. New Delhi: Penguin Books.

Salmon, C.T. 1989. "Campaigns for Social 'Improvement': An Overview of Values, Rationales, and Impacts." In C.T. Salmon (Ed.). *Information Campaigns: Balancing Social Values and Social Change*. Newbury Park, CA: Sage. pp. 19–53.

Samarajiwa, Rohan. 1987. "The Murky Beginnings of the Communication and Development Field: Voice of America and the Passing of Traditional Society." In N. Jayaweera and S. Amunugama (Eds.). *Rethinking Development Communication*. Singapore: Asian Mass Communication Research and Information Center. pp. 3–19.

Sandhu, A.S. 1970. "Characteristics, Listening Behaviour and Programme Preference of Radio Owning Farmers in Punjab." Ph.D. Dissertation. Indian Agricultural Research Institute, New Delhi.

Sarvodaya. "The Sarvodaya Shramadana Movement of Sri Lanka." http//:www.sarvodaya. org/index.html.

———. http://www.sarvodaya.org/Library/Pamphlets.pamphlet1/name.html.

———. http://www.sarvodaya.org/index.html.

———. "A Day in a Sarvodaya Shramadana Camp: Sharing and Meditation", http://www.sarvodaya.org/visualshramadanacamp/sharingandmeditation.html#top.

———. "Project 2000," http://www.sarvodaya.org/Project2000/index.html.

Sarvodaya. "The Mission of Sarvodaya USA," http://www.sarvodaya.org/SUSA/susa.html.

——. "Sarvodaya USA Partnership Projects," http://www.sarvodaya.org/partnerships/index.htm.

——. "Peace Meditation Programme," http://www.sarvodaya.org/PeaceInitiative/MeditationProgram.htm.

——. "Sarvodaya and the Elections in Sri Lanka," http://www.sarvodaya.org/Peace Initiative.

——. "The Gospel of Sarvodaya." http://nagpuronline.com/momgbook/chap45.html.

Schnaiberg, Allan. 1970. "Measuring Modernism: Theoretical and Empirical Explorations." *American Journal of Sociology*, 76 (December). pp. 399–425.

Schement, J.R., I.N. Gonzalez, P. Lum, and **R. Valencia.** 1984. "The International Flow of Television Programs." *Communication Research*, 11(2). pp. 163–82.

Schiller, Herbert. 1981. *Who Knows: Information in the Age of Fortune 500.* Norwood: Ablex.

——. 1986. "The Erosion of National Sovereignty." In Michael Traber (Ed.). *The Myth of Information Revolution, Social and Ethical Implications of Communication Technology.* London: Sage.

Schneider, B. 1992. "AIDS and Class, Gender, and Race Relations." In J. Huber and B. Schneider (Eds.). *The social context of AIDS.* Newbury Park, CA: Sage. pp. 19–46.

Schramm, Wilbur (Ed.). 1954. "How Communication Works." In *The Process and Effects of Mass Communication.* Urbana: The University of Illinois Press.

——. 1964. *Mass Media and National Development.* California: Stanford University Press.

——. 1971. "Communication in Family Planning." *Studies in Family Planning,* 7. pp. 1–43.

——. 1976. "End of an Old Paradigm?" In W. Schramm and D. Lerner (Eds.). *Communication and Change.* Honolulu: East–West Center, The University Press of Hawaii. pp. 45–48.

——. 1977. "Communication and Development—A Revaluation." *Communicator,* (April).

Schramm, Wilbur and **W.L. Ruggels.** 1967. "How Mass Media Systems Grow." In W. Schramm and D. Lerner (Eds.). *Communication and Change in Developing Countries.* Honolulu: East–West Center. pp. 57–75.

Schultz, T. 1963. *The Economic Value of Education.* New York: Columbia University Press.

Schultz, T.W. 1964. *Transforming Traditional Agriculture.* New Haven: Yale University Press.

Schumacher, E.F. 1973. *Small is Beautiful.* New York: Harper and Row.

Schumpeter, J. 1934. *The Theory of Economic Development.* Boston: Harvard University Press.

Scott, J. 1976. *The Moral Economy of the Peasant.* New Haven: Yale University Press.

Seager, J. 1997. *The State of Women in the World Atlas.* New Edition. London: Penguin.

Seers, Dudley. 1977a. "The New Meaning of Development." *International Development Review,* XIX(3). pp. 2–7.

——. 1977b. "The Meaning of Development." *International Development Review,* XIX(2). pp. 2–7.

Selltiz, Claire, Lawrence S. Wrightsman, and **Staurt W. Cook.** 1976. *Research Methods in Social Relations.* Third Edition. New York: Holt, Rinehart and Winston.

Sen, G. and C. Grown. 1987. *Development, Crises, and Alternative Visions*. New York: Monthly Review Press.

Seneviratne, Kalinga. 2000. "Villages get Wired on Air." http://www.EGroups.com/list/creative-radio.

Servaes, Jan. 1985. "Toward an Alternative Concept of Communication and Development." *Media Development*, 32.

———. 1989. "Participatory Communication Research within Social Movements." Paper prepared for the seminar Participation: A Key Concept in Communication for Change and Development. Pune, India.

———. 1999. *Communication for Development: One World, Multiple Cultures*. Creskill, NJ: Hamptom Press, Inc.

Servaes, J. and R. Arnst. 1999. "Principles of Participatory Communication Research: Its Strengths (!) and Weaknesses (?)." In T. Jacobsen and J. Servaes (Eds.). *Theoretical Approaches to Participatory Communication*. Creskill, NJ: Hampton Press. pp. 107–30.

Severin, Werner and James Tankard. 1987 [1979]. *Communication Theories*. New York: Hastings House.

Shannon, C. and W. Weaver. 1949. *The Mathematical Theory of Communication*. Urbana, Illinois: University of Illinois Press.

Shaull, R. 1971. Cited in Paulo Freire. 1973. *Education for Critical Consciousness*. New York, NY: The Seabury Press.

Shaw, D.L. and M.E. McCombs. 1974. *The Emergence of American Political Issues: The Agenda-Setting Function of the Press*. St. Paul, MN: West Publishing Company.

Shaw, Eugene. 1966. "An Intra-India Analysis of Selected Communication-Development Variables." Doctoral Dissertation. Stanford University.

Sherry, J.L. 1997. "Pro-Social Soap Operas for Development: A Review of Research and Theory." *Journal of International Communication*, 4(2). pp. 75–101.

Sheshadri, C.V. and V. Balaji. n.d. *Towards a New Science of Agriculture*. Madras, India: MCRC.

Shingi, Prakash M. and Bella Mody. 1976. "The Communication Effects Gap." In Everett M. Rogers (Ed.). *Communication and Development: Critical Perspectives*. Beverly Hills: Sage Publications. pp. 79–98.

Shiva, V. 1988. "Reductionist Science as an Epistemological Violence." In A. Nandy (Ed.). *Science, Hegemony and Violence: A Requiem for Modernity*. New Delhi: Oxford University Press.

———. 1992. "Resources." In W. Sachs (Ed.). *Development Dictionary*. London: Zed Books. pp. 206–18.

Shore, Larry. 1980. "Mass Media for Development: A Re-examination of Access, Exposure, and Impact." In Emile G. McAnany (Ed.). *Communications in the Rural Third World*. New York: Praeger Publishers. pp. 19–45.

Singer, Milton. 1966. "Modernizing Religious Beliefs." In Myron Weiner (Ed.). *Modernization: The Dynamics of Growth*. New York: Basic Books.

———. 1972. *When a Great Tradition Modernizes: An Anthropological Approach to Indian Civilization*. New York: Praeger.

Singh, Y.P. 1981. "Problems in Transfer of Agricultural Technology." In *Management of Transfer of Farm Technology*. India: National Institute of Rural Development. pp. 49–68.

Singhal, Arvind and Everett M. Rogers. 1988. "Television Soap Operas for Development in India." *Gazette*, 41(2). pp. 109–26.

Singhal, Arvind and **Everett M. Rogers.** 1989. *India's Information Revolution*. New Delhi, India: Sage.
——. 1999. *Entertainment-Education: A Communication Strategy for Social Change*. Mahwah, NJ: Lawrence, Erlbaum Associates/Publishers.
——. 2001. *India's Communication Revolution: From Bullock Carts to Cyber Marts*. New Delhi, India: Sage.
Singhal, Arvind, Everett M. Rogers, and **W.J. Brown.** 1993. "Harnessing the Potential of Entertainment-Education Telenovelas." *Gazette*, 51(1). pp. 1–18.
Singleton, Jr., R.A., B.C. Straits, and **M.M. Straits.** 1993. *Approaches to Social Research*. Second Edition. New York: Oxford University Press.
"Slum Kids Break Language Barriers, Get Web-Savvy." March 6, 2000 http://www.economictimes.com/today/07tech01.htm.
Smelser, Neil J. 1973. "Toward a General Theory of Modernization." In Amitai Etzioni (Ed.). *Social Change*. New York: Basic Books. pp. 268–84.
Smythe, Dallas. 1985. "Needs before Tools—The Illusions of Technology." *Media Development*, 4. pp. 8–17.
Snell, J. 1999. "The Looming Threat of AIDS and HIV in Latin America." *Lancet*, 354(9185). p. 1187.
Social Studies. Vol. 1. 1969. New Delhi. National Council of Educational Research and Training.
Solomon, B. 1976. *Black Empowerment: Social Work in Oppressed Communities*. New York: Columbia University Press.
Speer, P.W. and **J. Hughey** 1995. "Community Organizing: An Ecological Route to Empowerment and Power." *American Journal of Community Psychology*, 23(5). pp. 729–48.
Spivak, G.C. 1988. "Can the Subaltern Speak?" In L. Grossberg and C. Nelson (Eds.). *Marxism and the Interpretation of Culture*. Urbana: University of Illinois Press. pp. 271–316.
Srinivas, M.N. 1973. "Comments on Milton Singer's Industrial Leadership, the Hindu Ethic and the Spirit of Socialism." In Milton Singer (Ed.). *Entrepreneurship and Modernization of Occupational Cultures in South Asia*. Duke University: Program in Comparative Studies on South Asia, Monograph No. 12. pp. 279–86.
Staudt, K. 1985a. *Women, Foreign Assistance and Advocacy Administration*. New York: Praeger.
——. 1985b. *Agricultural Policy Implementation: A Case Study from Western Kenya*. West Hartford, CT: Kumarian Press.
——. 1991. *Managing Development: State, Society, and International Contexts*. Newbury Park: Sage.
Steeves, H.L. 1993. "Creating Imagined Communities: Development Communication and the Challenge of Feminism" *Journal of Communication*, 43(3). pp. 218–29.
——. 1996. "Sharing Information in Kenya: Communication and Information Policy Considerations and Consequences for Rural Women." *Gazette*, 56. pp. 157–81.
——. 1997. *Gender Violence and the Press: The St. Kizito Story*. Athens, OH: Ohio University Press. Monographs in International Studies.
——. 2000. "Gendered Agendas: Dialogue and Impasse in Creating Social Change." In K. Wilkins (Ed.). *Redeveloping Communication for Social Change: Theory, Practice and Power*. Boulder, CO: Rowman & Littlefield. pp. 7–25.
Steeves, H.L. and **R.A. Arbogast.** 1993. "Feminism and Communication in Development: Ideology, Law, Ethics, Practice." In B. Dervin and U. Hariharan (Eds.). *Progress in Communication Sciences*, XI. Norwood, NJ: Ablex. pp. 229–77.

Stevenson, R.L. 1994. *Global Communication in the 21st Century*. New York: Longman.
Stover, William J. 1984. *Information Technology in the Third World*. Boulder, Colorado: Westview Press.
Streeten, Paul. 1979. "Development Ideas in Historical Perspective." In K. Hill (Ed.). *Toward a New Strategy for Development*. New York: Pergamon Press. pp. 21–52.
Summary of World Religions. n.d. http://www.webstationone.com/fecha/religion.htm.
Sussman, G. and **J.A. Lent.** 1991. *Transnational Communications*. Newbury Park, CA: Sage.
Swift, C. 1984. "Empowerment: An Antidote to Folly." In J. Rappaport, C. Swift, and R. Hess (Eds.). *Studies in Empowerment: Steps toward Understanding and Action*. New York, NY: The Haworth Press. pp. xi–xv.
Talero, E. and **P. Gaudette.** 1996. *Harnessing Information for Development: A Proposal for a World Bank Group Strategy*. The World Bank: Telecommunications and Informatics Division. http://www.worldbank.org/html/fpd/harnessing.
Tarde, Gabriel. 1903. *The Laws of Imitation*. Translated by Elsie Clews Parsons. New York: Holt, Rinehart and Winston.
Tehranian, Majid. 1979. "Development Theory and Communications Policy: The Changing Paradigms." In Melvin J. Voigt and Gerhard J. Hanneman (Eds.). *Progress in Communication Sciences*. Vol. I. New Jersey: Ablex Publishing Corporation. pp. 119–66.
———. 1985. "Paradigms Lost: Development as Communication and Learning." *Media Development*, XXXII (4). pp. 5–8.
Tehranian, M. 1994. "Communication and Development." In D. Crowley and D. Mitchell (Eds.). *Communication Theory Today*. Stanford, CA: Stanford University Press. pp. 274–306.
Thomas, P. 1993. "Participatory Development Communication: Philosophical Premises." In S. White, K.S. Nair, and J. Ascroft (Eds.). *Participatory Communication: Working for Change and Development*. Thousand Oaks, CA: Sage. pp. 49–59.
Thorner, Daniel. 1966. "Chayanov's Concept of Peasant Economy." In Daniel Thorner, B. Kerblay, and R.E.F. Smith (Eds.). *The Theory of Peasant Economy*. Illinois: American Economic Association.
———. 1968. "Peasantry." In David L. Sills (Ed.). *International Encyclopedia of the Social Sciences*. Volume 2. New York: Macmillan and Free Press.
Tichenor, P.J., G. Donahue, and **C. Olien.** 1970. "Mass Media Flow and Differential Growth in Knowledge." *Public Opinion Quarterly*, 34. pp. 159–70.
Tilakaratna, S. 1991. "Stimulation of Self-Reliant Initiatives by Sensitized Agents: Some Lessons from Practice." In O. Fals-Borda and M.A. Rahman (Eds.). *Action and Knowledge: Breaking the Monopoly with Participatory Action-Research*. New York: Apex Press. pp. 135–45.
Tinker, I. (Ed.). 1990. *Persistent Inequalities*. Oxford: Oxford University Press.
Tipps, D.C. 1973. "Modernization Theory and the Comparative Study of Societies: A Critical Perspective." *Comparative Studies in Society and History*, 15. pp. 199–226.
Toennies, Ferdinand. 1957. *Community and Society*. East Lansing: Michigan State University Press.
Truman, H.S. 1949. "Inaugural Address, January 20, 1949." In *Documents on American Foreign Relations*. Princeton, NJ: Princeton University Press, 1967.
Tunstall, Jeremy. 1977. *The Media are American*. New York: Columbia University Press.

Turner, D. 1999. "Marxism, Liberation Theology and the Way of Negation." In C. Rowland, (Ed.). *The Cambridge Companion to Liberation Theology.* Cambridge, UK: Cambridge University Press. pp. 199–217.

Ullrich, O. 1992. "Technology." In W. Sachs (Ed.). *Development Dictionary.* London: Zed Books. pp. 275–87.

UNAIDS. 1999. *Sexual Behavioural Change for HIV: Where have Theories Taken Us?* Geneva: UNAIDS.

United Nations. 1995. *The World's Women 1995: Trends and Statistics.* New York: United Nations.

——. 1996. *The United Nations and the Advancement of Women, 1945–1996.* New York: United Nations.

——. http://www.un.org/members.

UNDP. 1992. *Human Development Report, 1992.* New York: Oxford University Press.

——. 1997. *Human Development Report, 1997.* New York: Oxford University Press.

——. 1998. *Human Development Report, 1998.* New York: Oxford University Press.

Uphoff, Norman and **M. Esman.** 1974. *Local Organization for Rural Development: Analysis of Asian Experience.* Ithaca, New York: Center for International Studies, Cornell University.

USAID. 1982. *Health Assistance.* Bureau for Program and Policy Coordination. Development Communication Archive, Center for American History, University of Texas, Austin.

——. February 17, 1984. *A.I.D. Policy Determination, Development Communication, Executive Summary.* Washington, D.C.: USAID.

Vallath, Chandrasekhar. 1989. "Weaknesses of Agricultural Extension: A Study of Extension Message Comprehension." Master's thesis. Bowling Green State University.

Van Hoosen, D. 1984. "The Barefoot Actors: Folk Drama and Development Communication in Asia." In G. Wang and W. Dissanayake (Eds.). *Continuity and Change in Communication Systems.* New Jersey: Ablex. pp. 127–37.

Van Soet, Jaap. 1978. *The Start of International Development Cooperation in the United Nations 1945–1952.* Assen, The Netherlands: Van Gorcum Press.

Veblen, T. 1966. *Imperial Germany and the Industrial Revolution.* Ann Arbor: University of Michigan.

Vilanilam, John. 1979. "The Meaning of Development." In John Lent and John Vilanilam (Eds.). *The Use of Development News.* Singapore: AMIC. pp. 2–19.

Vogeler, Ingolf and **A. De Souza.** 1980. *Dialectics of Third World Development.* New Jersey: Allanheld, Osmun and Co. Publishers.

Wallerstein, I. 1974. *The Modern World-System.* New York: Academic.

——. 1980. *The Modern World-System II.* New York: Academic.

Wall Street Journal. 1981. "Sudan Farmers Find that New Methods aren't Always Better." *Wall Street Journal,* LXII(32). November 27. p. 1, col. 4.

Wang, Georgette. 1984. "Television Puppetry in Taiwan—An Example of the Marriage between a Modern Medium and a Folk Medium." In G. Wang and W. Dissanayake (Eds.). *Continuity and Change in Communication Systems.* New Jersey: Ablex. pp. 169–80.

Wang, Georgette and **Wimal Dissanayake.** 1984a. "Culture, Development and Change: Some Explorative Observations." In G. Wang and W. Dissanayake (Eds.). *Continuity and Change in Communication Systems.* New Jersey: Ablex. pp. 3–20.

Wang, Georgette and **Wimal Dissanayake.** 1984b. "Indigenous Communication Systems and Development: A Reappraisal." In G. Wang and W. Dissanayake (Eds.). *Continuity and Change in Communication Systems.* New Jersey: Ablex. pp. 21–33.

Waters, M. 1995. *Globalization.* London: Routledge.

Weaver, James H. and **Kenneth Jameson.** 1978. *Economic Development: Competing Paradigms—Competing Parables.* Washington, D.C.: Development Studies Program, Agency for International Development.

Weber, M. *The Protestant Ethic and the Spirit of Capitalism.* New York: Charles Scribner and Sons.

———. 1964. *The Sociology of Religion.* Boston: Beacon Press.

Weiler, K. 1988. *Women Teaching for Change: Gender, Class and Power.* South Hadley, MA: Bergin and Garvey Publishers.

Weiner, Myron. 1966. "Introduction." In M. Weiner (Ed.). *Modernization: The Dynamics of Growth.* New York: Basic Books.

Westley, B.H. and **M. MacLean.** 1957. "A Conceptual Model for Communication Research." *Journalism Quarterly,* 34. pp. 31–38.

White, K. 1999. "The Importance of Sensitivity to Culture in Development Work." In T. Jacobson, and J. Servaes (Eds.). *Theoretical Approaches to Participatory Communication.* Creskill, NJ: Hampton Press. pp. 17–50.

White, S.A. 1994. "Introduction: The Concept of Participation." In S.A. White, K.S. Nair and J. Ascroft (Eds.). *Participatory Communication: Working for Change and Development.* New Delhi, India: Sage. pp. 15–32.

White, Shirley and **Pradeep Patel.** 1988. "Strategies for Message Development Using Participatory Video." Paper presented to Inculdevcom Division, International Communication Association. New Orleans.

White, S.A., K.S. Nair, and **J. Ascroft** (Eds.). 1994. *Participatory Communication: Working for Change and Development.* New Delhi: Sage.

Whitehead, A. 1990. "Food Crisis and Gender Conflict in the African Countryside." In H. Bernstein, B. Crow, M. MacKintosh, and C. Martin (Eds.). *The Food Question: Profits versus People?* London: Earthscan.

WHO. 1988. "London Declaration on AIDS Prevention." *AIDS Prevention and Control.* New York: Pergamon Press. pp. 122–24.

Whyte, W.F. 1991a. "Introduction." In W.F. Whyte (Ed.). *Participatory Action Research.* Newbury Park, CA: Sage. pp. 7–15.

———. 1991b. "Participatory Strategies in Agricultural Research and Development." In W.F. Whyte (Ed.). *Participatory Action Research.* Newbury Park, CA: Sage. pp. 169–78.

Wielenga, B. 1999. "Liberation Theology in Asia." In C. Rowland (Ed.). *The Cambridge Companion to Liberation Theology.* Cambridge, UK: Cambridge University Press. pp. 199–217.

Wilkins, K.G. 1997. "Gender, Power and Development." *Journal of International Communication,* 4(2). pp. 102–20.

———. 1999. "Development Discourse on Gender and Communication in Strategies for Social Change." *Journal of Communication,* 49(1). pp. 46–68.

Williams, E. 1964. *Capitalism and Slavery.* London: Russell Publishers.

Williams, Maurice. 1989. "Sustainable Development: A SID Perspective." *Development,* 2(3). pp. 7–9.

Williams, R. 1976. *Keywords: A Vocabulary of Culture and Society*. New York: Oxford University Press.

Williamson, A.H. 1991. "The Fogo Process: Development Support Communication in Canada and the Developing World." In F.L. Casmir (Ed.). *Communication in Development*. Norwood, NJ: Ablex. pp. 270–88.

Wimmer, R.G. and **J.R. Dominick.** 2000. *Mass Media Research*. Sixth Edition. Belmont, CA: Wadsworth.

Wolfensohn, James. March, 2000. (President World Bank) at the Second Global Knowledge Conference in Kuala Lumpur.

Wolff, T. 1987. "Community Psychology and Empowerment: An Activist's Insights." *American Journal of Community Psychology*, 15(2). pp. 151–67.

Woods, B. 1993. *Communication, Technology and the Development of People*. London: Routledge.

Woods, John L. 1982. "Making Rural Development Projects more Effective: A Systems Approach." Paper prepared for the conference on Knowledge Utilization: Theory and Methodology at East West Center, Honolulu, Hawaii.

World Bank. 1973. Annual Address by Robert S. McNamara, President, World Bank, to the Annual Meeting of the Board of Governors, Nairobi, Kenya, September 24–28.

World Bank. 1997. *Confronting AIDS: Public Priorities in a Global Epidemic*. New York: Oxford University Press.

——. 1998. *World Development Report*. Washington, D.C.: World Bank.

——. 1999. *World Development Report: Knowledge for Development*. New York: Oxford University Press.

Worthington, N. 1992. "Gender and Class in AIDS Education: An Analysis of the Aidscom Project in Africa." Unpublished Master's Thesis, University of Oregon, School of Journalism.

Young, I.M. 1994. "Punishment, Treatment, and Empowerment: Three Approaches to Policy for Pregnant Addicts." *Feminist Studies*, 20(1). pp. 33–57.

Young, K. 1993. *Planning Development with Women*. New York: St. Martin's Press.

Yount, Barbara. 1975. *IEC Newsletter*. No. 20. Honolulu: East West Communication Institute.

Zeitlin, Maurice. 1968. "The Social Determinants of Political Democracy in Chile." In J. Petras and M. Zeitlin (Eds.). *Latin America: Reform or Revolution*. Greenwich, Connecticut: Fawcett. pp. 220–34.

Zimmerman, M.A. 1990. "Taking Aim on Empowerment Research: On the Distinction between Individual and Psychological Conceptions." *American Journal of Community Psychology*, 18(1). pp. 169–77.

——. 1995. "Psychological Empowerment: Issues and Illustrations." *American Journal of Community Psychology*, 23(5). pp. 581–99.

Zimmerman, M.A. and **J.A. Rappaport.** 1988. "Citizen Participation, Perceived Control, and Psychological Empowerment." *American Journal of Community Psychology*, 16(5). pp. 725–50.

Zimmerman, M.E. 1990. "Deep Ecology and Ecofeminism: The Emerging Dialogue." In T. Diamond and G.F. Orenstein (Eds.). *Reweaving the World: The Emergence of Ecofeminism*. San Francisco: Sierra Club Books.

Zweig, M. 1991. "Economics and Liberation Theology." In M. Zweig (Ed.). *Religion and Economic Justice*. Philadelphia: Temple University Press. pp. 3–49.

INDEX

ABOUT THE AUTHORS

Srinivas R. Melkote has been a teacher in the field of journalism, communication, and media studies for almost 25 years. He has taught at universities in India and in the United Studies, and is currently a Professor at the Department of Telecommunications, Bowling Green State University. Professor Melkote has published extensively on issues such as satellite broadcasting, the role of communication media in development support and participatory communication, and the theory and practice of communication in the Third World. Among his previous publications is the widely used text *Communication for Development in the Third World* and his latest publication is *Critical Issues in Communication* (co-editor).

Professor Melkote's research interests include media effects, international communication, communication strategies for HIV and AIDS prevention, and the impact of satellite television in the developing world.

H. Leslie Steeves is Associate Professor and Director of Graduate Studies and Research at the University of Oregon. Prior to this, she was Assistant Professor, School of Journalism and Mass Communication, University of Iowa; Visiting Professor, School of Journalism, University of Nairobi, Kenya; and Visiting Professor, School of Communication Studies, University of Ghana, Ghana. Dr Steeves has been the recipient of two Fulbright grants for teaching and research in Africa. Her research focuses on to areas and their intersection: women's roles and representations in the media, and communication in developing countries, especially sub-Saharan Africa. Leslie Steeves has published several articles in reputed journals and is also the author of *Gender Violence and the Press: The St. Kizito Story*.